Malaysia's Socio-Economic Transformation

Malaysia's Socio-Economic Transformation

Ideas for the Next Decade

EDITED BY

SANCHITA BASU DAS
LEE POH ONN

LSEAS

INSTITUTE OF SOUTHEAST ASIAN STUDIES

Singapore

First published in Singapore in 2014 by
ISEAS Publishing
Institute of Southeast Asian Studies
30 Heng Mui Keng Terrace, Pasir Panjang
Singapore 119614

E-mail: publish@iseas.edu.sg • Website: bookshop.iseas.edu.sg

ISEAS Library Cataloguing-in-Publication Data

Malaysia's socio-economic transformation : ideas for the next decade / edited by Sanchita Basu Das and Lee Poh Onn.
1. Malaysia—Economic conditions.
2. Malaysia—Economic policy.
3. Malaysia—Social conditions.
4. Malaysia—Social policy.
5. Malaysia—Politics and government.
I. Basu Das, Sanchita.
II. Lee, Poh Onn.
HC445.5 M26 2014

ISBN 978-981-4459-69-3 (soft cover)
ISBN 978-981-4459-68-6 (E-book PDF)

Typeset by International Typesetters Pte Ltd
Printed in Singapore by Markono Print Media Pte Ltd

CONTENTS

II   POLITICS, DECENTRALIZATION AND ENVIRONMENT

FOREWORD

Since its independence in 1957, Malaysia had evolved from an agrarian economy into an industrial one envied by many other developing nations. In 1991, former Prime Minister Dr Mahathir Mohammed launched Vision 2020 as a roadmap for the country to achieve developed nation status. This vision called for a self-sufficient, democratic, economically just, mature, united, liberal and tolerant society by 2020, with US$6,000 in per capita income in 1980 prices. However, the Asian Crisis of 1998 significantly set this back, as Malaysia had to spend a number of years recovering from the crisis and regaining foreign investor confidence. The Global Financial Crisis of 2008 also negatively impacted on Malaysia's economic development and slowed its progress towards the achievement of Vision 2020.

Today, Malaysia is perceived by many as being stuck in a middle-income trap, facing challenges on many fronts. A disconnect appears to have developed between policy-making and the national economic reality. In addition, the challenges of globalization have meant that Malaysia has to significantly increase its productivity, especially in the services sector in order to stay relevant. The shortage of skills necessary for a move towards a knowledge-based economy compounds the problem, the infrastructure has expanded significantly but only in certain parts of the country, with many other areas left with little development.

Since assuming office in April 2009, Prime Minister Najib Tun Razak has shown his determination to stay on course to achieve the goals of Vision 2020. In June 2010, he unveiled the 10th Malaysian Plan

(2011–15) to chart Malaysia's development from a middle- to a high-income nation. In dollar terms, Malaysia will need to achieve an income level of US$15,000 per capita by 2020. More importantly, its economy will need to be restructured to one which is driven by productivity, innovation, and a focused specialization on selected economic sectors.

Malaysia is also working intensively on bilateral and regional trade agreements. In addition to the commitment to be a member of the ASEAN Economic Community, Malaysia has signed or is negotiating thirteen bilateral FTAs. It is a member of ASEAN+1 FTAs and is negotiating its way to be a part of the ASEAN-led Regional Comprehensive Economic Partnership (RCEP) and the US-led Tran-Pacific Partnership (TPP) Agreement. One important rationale for Malaysia to be part of these FTAs is its intention to undertake difficult domestic reforms, which currently face serious domestic opposition. This bodes well for its objective to be a self-sufficient industrialized nation by 2020.

Given this background, this book enumerates some important lessons from the past and tries to indicate where Malaysia may go wrong, and where it can do better in order to achieve its aspirations. The authors, with varied backgrounds, are recognized experts in their areas of research. The various chapters will help key stakeholders and interested members of the public understand the current state of affairs, as well as future challenges to the Malaysian economy. We hope the many recommendations found here will be of great assistance to policy-makers.

Tan Chin Tiong
Director
Institute of Southeast Asian Studies, Singapore

PREFACE

The Malaysian economy has seen many notable developments since its independence in 1957 from the British rule. Initially a commodity exporter of rubber and tin, it has undergone several structural changes and is now a diversified economy with 75 per cent of its gross domestic product (GDP) coming from the manufacturing and services sectors. The economy has emerged as a modern, high middle income nation with strong economic fundamentals. Indeed, these economic achievements have been well supported by visionary leadership and proper policies. The developmental journey has spanned 2 Malaya Plans, 9 Malaysia Plans, 3 Outline Perspective Plans as well as a National Mission before coming to this juncture today.

During the Sixth Malaysia Plan in 1991, Vision 2020 or *Wawasan 2020* was introduced by the then Malaysian Prime Minister, Dr Mahathir bin Mohamad. The vision called for a self-sufficient, democratic, economically just, mature, liberal and tolerant society, and united Malaysian nation which would achieve US$6,000 per capita income in 1980 prices by 2020. The essence of this transformation has been again outlined in the Tenth Malaysia Plan (2011–15) which was unveiled by Prime Minister Mr Najib Razak in June 2010. In this plan, a clearer perspective has been laid out on how Malaysia can transform itself from a developing country status to a developed country status.

But there remain many pressing challenges which need to be addressed if the country were to implement the Plan and to achieve a high-income status, transforming itself into a developed economy by 2020. In the past decade, the economic landscape, with increasing globalization and emergence of China, India and Brazil, has changed significantly. Hence, Malaysia can no longer depend on a low-cost structure economy to remain competitive internationally. In addition, Malaysia also faces internal challenges to drive economic growth to a higher level, while having to implement a prudent fiscal policy. The nation is confronted with the challenge of providing a conducive investment environment as well as developing high quality human capital, which is critical to enable the shift to a higher level of value added and productivity.

In light of this, a "stock-take" by academics, policy-makers, and the private sector to capture the past, and more importantly, apply lessons from the past to deal with challenges remaining before 2020 would be timely. It would also be appropriate to examine what Malaysia needs in the next decade to climb the economic ladder and achieve the status of a developed country, as stated in the Tenth Malaysia Plan.

In order to discuss and address these issues, the Regional Economic Studies at the Institute of Southeast Asian Studies (ISEAS), along with the Konrad Adenauer Stiftung (KAS), organized a workshop at ISEAS, Singapore on 28–29 September 2011.

The workshop gathered experts from the Asia-Pacific region, who gave their authoritative thinking. The workshop had Professor K.S. Jomo, then Assistant Secretary-General for Economic Development, United Nations Department of Economic and Social Affairs, New York, as the keynote speaker, who gave an account of Malaysia's economic development in the past and its prospects for the future. Thereafter, the sessions examined different socio-economic issues in Malaysia that could aid or hinder the country from achieving its 2020 goals, as stated in the Malaysia Plans.

The vigorous discussions during the workshop constitute the chapters in this volume. It begins with an introduction and brings out the key challenges discussed during the sessions. The chapter concludes with the recommendations made in the discussions. The introductory part is followed by chapters on economic, political, environmental and social issues by distinguished writers from academics, international organizations and the private sector. The book also contains short commentaries, especially commissioned to provide a greater insight into the dynamics of economic development in Malaysia.

The book, with contributions from specialists intimately familiar with their topics, will be useful to academics, analysts, students and policy-makers.

Sanchita Basu Das and Lee Poh Onn
Editors

ACKNOWLEDGMENTS

We would like to thank the chapter writers for their contributions, especially their excellent work in revising their draft chapters to meet the guidelines of the overall book project. We would also like to thank the writers who shared their knowledge with us in the form of short commentaries.

We were assisted by Thanut Tritasavit, Hnin Wint Nyunt Hman and Karthi Nair at critical junctures of the workshop and for editorial assistance. We thank them all. We would also like to thank Mrs Y.L. Lee, Head of Administration, for her kind assistance in overseeing the administrative and financial issues. Many thanks to experts of the Malaysia Study Group — Dr Johan Saravanamuttu, Dr Ooi Kee Beng, Dr Lee Hock Guan and Dr Francis Hutchinson — for their valuable advice.

We would like to thank the current and the previous ISEAS Directors, Ambassador Tan Chin Tiong and Ambassador K. Kesavapany respectively, for their support during the two-day workshop and to see the book project through to completion. We are grateful to Dr Wilhelm Hofmeister, Director, Regional Program "Political Dialogue with Asia", Konrad Adenauer Stiftung, Singapore, for his interest in the region and for supporting our workshop.

Our sincere thanks to staff of the ISEAS Publications Unit, especially its previous Head, Mrs Triena Ong, for their professionalism in getting this book published.

Sanchita Basu Das and Lee Poh Onn
Editors

THE CONTRIBUTORS

Rokiah Alavi is a Professor at the Department of Economics, International Islamic University Malaysia.

Sanchita Basu Das is a Fellow and Lead Researcher for Economic Affairs at the ASEAN Studies Centre, Institute of Southeast Asian Studies (ISEAS), Singapore.

Theresa W. Devasahayam is a Fellow at the Institute of Southeast Asian Studies (ISEAS), Singapore.

G. Naidu is an Industry Expert at the East Coast Economic Region Development Council (ECERDC).

G. Sivalingam is a Visiting Senior Research Fellow at the Institute of Southeast Asian Studies (ISEAS), Singapore.

Francis E. Hutchinson is a Fellow and Coordinator of the Regional Economic Studies Programme of the Institute of Southeast Asian Studies (ISEAS), Singapore.

Jomo Kwame Sundaram has been Assistant Director General at the Food and Agriculture Organization since August 2012.

Cassey Lee is a Senior Fellow at the Institute of Southeast Asian Studies (ISEAS), Singapore.

Lee Hock Guan is a Senior Fellow at the Regional Social and Cultural Studies Programme of the Institute of Southeast Asian Studies (ISEAS), Singapore.

Hwok-Aun Lee is a Senior Lecturer at the Department of Development Studies, Faculty of Economics and Administration, University of Malaya, Malaysia.

Lee Poh Onn is a Senior Fellow at the Regional Economics Studies Programme of the Institute of Southeast Asian Studies (ISEAS), Singapore.

Loke Wai Heng is an Assistant Professor in the Division of Economics at the University of Nottingham, Ningbo China.

Jayant Menon is a Lead Economist at the Office of Regional Economic Integration, Asian Development Bank (ADB), Manila.

Ooi Kee Beng is the Deputy Director of the Institute of Southeast Asian Studies, Singapore.

Phang Siew Nooi is a Professor and a Senior University Research Advisor at Sunway University, Malaysia.

Ragayah Haji Mat Zin is a Principal Research Fellow at the Institute of Malaysia and International Studies (IKMAS), Universiti Kebangsaan Malaysia.

Rajah Rasiah is Professor and Acting Dean of the Faculty of Economics and Administration, University of Malaya.

Rusaslina Idrus is an Associate Fellow at the Institute of Southeast Asian Studies (ISEAS), Singapore, and a Senior Lecturer at University Malaya, Malaysia.

Johan Saravanamuttu is a Visiting Senior Research Fellow at the Institute of Southeast Asian Studies, Singapore.

Sharbanom Abu Bakar is Director of Government Programs in IBM Malaysia Sdn Bhd.

Sri Ranjini Mei Hua is a Knowledge Broker at the UNDP Global Centre for Public Service Excellence.

Tan Teck Hong is Associate Professor in Sunway University Business School, Malaysia.

Teh Chi-Chang was Director of Research for Social Advancement Bhd (REFSA), Malaysia at the time of writing. He is presently an independent analyst and Petaling Jaya City Councillor.

Tham Siew Yean is a Professor and Principal Research Fellow at the Institute of Malaysian and International Studies (IKMAS), Universiti Kebangsaan Malaysia.

Wee Chong Hui is a Lecturer at the Faculty of Business Management in the Universiti Teknologi MARA, Sarawak, Malaysia.

Bridget Welsh is an Associate Professor in Political Science at Singapore Management University.

1

THE ECONOMY OF MALAYSIA
Present, Problems, Prospects

Sanchita Basu Das and Lee Poh Onn

Introduction

The economic development of Malaysia since 1957, by all accounts, has been a spectacular trajectory of restructuring and of rapid economic growth, punctuated only by the Asian Financial Crisis in 1997, and by the economic crisis in 2008. Malaysia has also been able to graduate from a predominantly agricultural base to that of a manufacturing and services base through prudent economic management, balancing economic efficiency considerations with that of the redistribution of the economic pie. In recent years, however, the government has come to realize that the traditional approach of restructuring and diversifying the economy may not be sufficient to propel Malaysia to the level of other high-income nations. Furthermore, the historical engines of agriculture and manufacturing that have been driving Malaysia's economic growth has been losing its momentum over the past decade. Part of the slowing momentum is largely due to the fall in private investments: from 25 per cent of GDP throughout the 1990s to about 10 per cent in the past decade.

The Tenth Malaysian Plan (2011–15) succinctly outlines what needs to be undertaken for Malaysia:

> [the] challenge is to move from an economy that competes on cost and natural resources, to an economy that is driven by productivity, innovation and that is able to nurture, attract and retain talent, companies and capital. In order to move into the league of high income economies, Malaysia will also need to move from a strategy of diversification of the economic base, which successfully elevated the nation to a middle-income economy, to a strategy which focuses on specialisation in a few selected economic sectors and geographies where Malaysia has a relative competitive advantage.[1]

Can Malaysia transform its economy up to the level of other high income countries? How has Malaysia landed in its present dilemma of the middle income trap? What are some of the challenges that need to be overcome that will move the country to join the ranks of a high-income and developed country? What are some of the suggested policies that can bring Malaysia to the next stage of development?

A number of recent works have been undertaken on the Malaysian economy. Notably, three recent publications, dealing with a mix of issues confronting Malaysia's economic development all have one aim: to examine the economic challenges facing the country in order to reach the status of a high-income country, and to escape from the current trap of being a middle-income economy.

The publication edited by Hal Hill, Tham Siew Yean and Ragayah Haji Mat Zin (2012) examines the various economic, political and developmental challenges facing Malaysia in its aim to graduate from a middle-income to high-income economy.[2] In this volume, microeconomic, macroeconomic and distributional factors have been analysed to be crucial to Malaysia's transformation to become a developed nation.

Another publication edited by Rajah Rasiah (2011) on the *Malaysian Economy: Unfolding Growth and Social Change* systematically and collectively examines development from a sectoral perspective, filling the gaps in macroeconomic and microeconomic developments with a historical anchor. Notably, the publication by the Institute of Strategic and International Studies (ISIS) Malaysia (2011), on *Malaysia:*

Policies and Issues in Economic Development involves a thematic approach which includes economic analysis balanced with historical, socio-economic and institutional approaches in looking at Malaysia's economic development process.[3]

The present volume builds on the works published in these publications but it adopts a different approach in that it is a stocktake by individuals from the academia, international organizations, and the private sector to understand the past; to discuss and analyse the reasons behind Malaysia's successes in graduating from a low-income to middle-income economy; and to critically analyse the challenges and obstacles that Malaysia needs to overcome in order to become a developed country by 2020.

The various chapters are broken down into thematic approaches which focus on economic issues; political, decentralization, and environmental issues; and social issues confronting Malaysia's development. In doing so, this book hopes to provide a multi-disciplinary approach to understand and analyse Malaysia's economic development and the challenges confronting the country. Short commentaries are also interspersed between some of the chapters. These provide a quick and sharp analyses of certain issues that are also pertinent to Malaysia's transformation process.

The Present Malaysian Economy

After a feeble growth rate of 1.6 per cent during 2008–09, the US$306 billion Malaysian economy bounced back and showed many signs of improvement. In real terms, the economy grew at a rate of 5.6 per cent during 2010–12, at par with an average growth rate of 5.7 per cent for its neighbours[4] in Southeast Asia (see Figure 1.1). It was the third largest economy in the region by purchasing power parity (PPP), and its per capita at US$15,568 (in terms of PPP) put it in the middle income bracket among the world economies (see Figures 1.2*a* and 1.2*b*). The economy also exhibited a modest inflation rate of 2.5 per cent during the period, with low interest rates at 3.0 per cent by end of 2011. Externally, the country's exports were growing by 20 per cent in U.S. dollar terms (see Figure 1.3) during 2010–11, despite uncertainty in the U.S. and the EU economies. These feel good factors have also been reflected in the stock market as

FIGURE 1.1
Average GDP Growth Rate in Southeast Asia, 2010–12

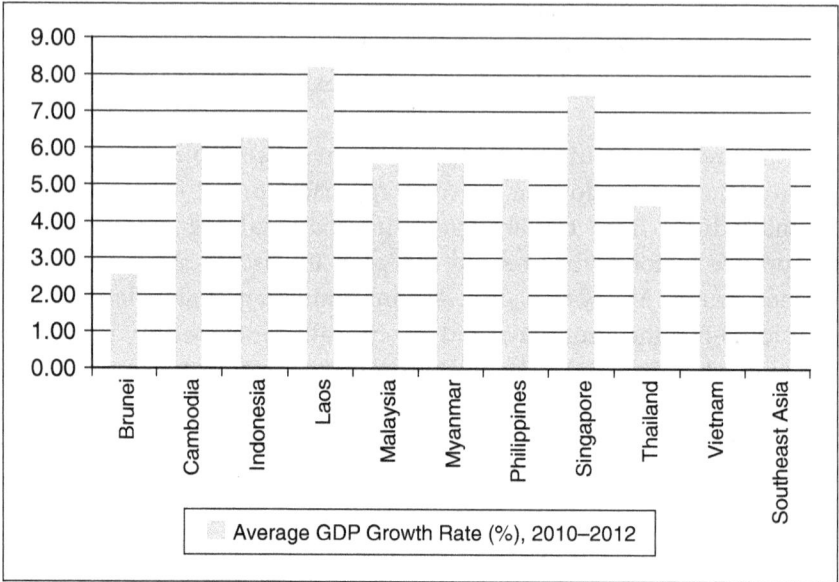

Source: World Economic Outlook Database, IMF, April 2012.

FIGURE 1.2a
GDP (based on PPP) of Southeast Asian Nations, 2011

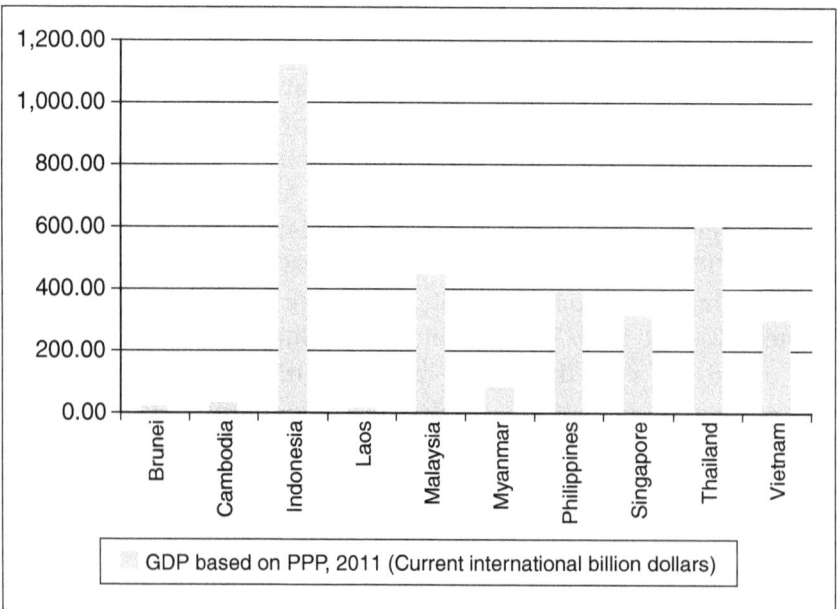

Source: World Economic Outlook Database, IMF, April 2012.

FIGURE 1.2*b*
Per Capita GDP (based on PPP) of Southeast Asian Nations, 2011

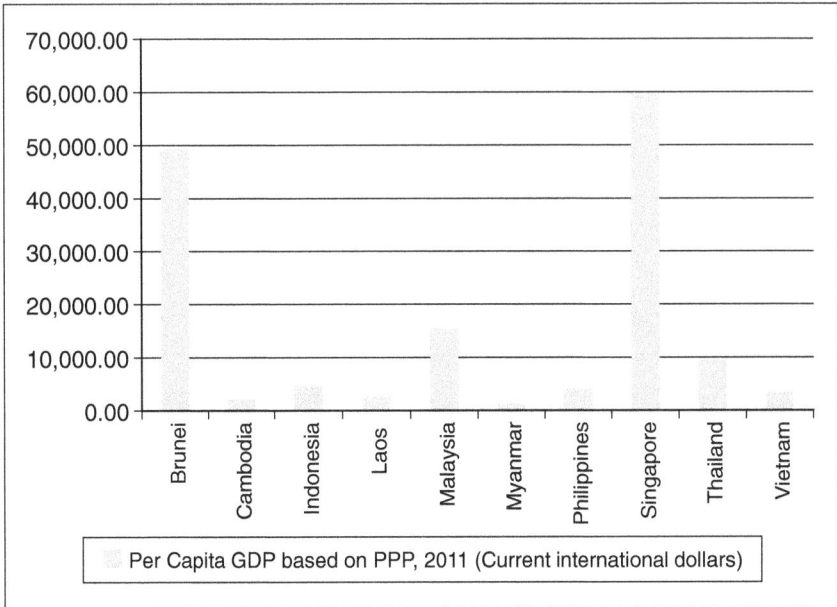

Per Capita GDP based on PPP, 2011 (Current international dollars)

Source: World Economic Outlook Database, IMF, April 2012.

FIGURE 1.3
Trend in Malaysia's Merchandise Trade, 2001–11

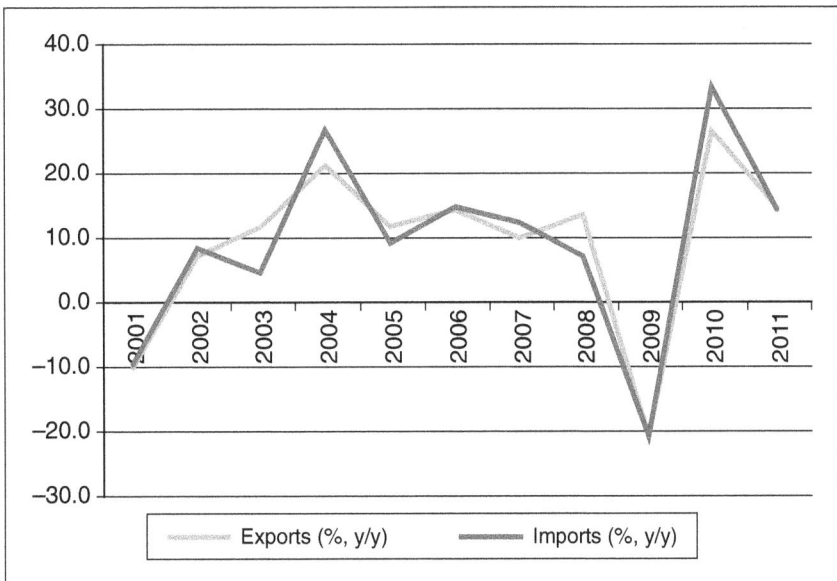

Exports (%, y/y)   Imports (%, y/y)

Source: WTO Trade Database, authors' calculation.

FIGURE 1.4
Monthly Kuala Lumpur Composite Index (KLCI), 2009–12

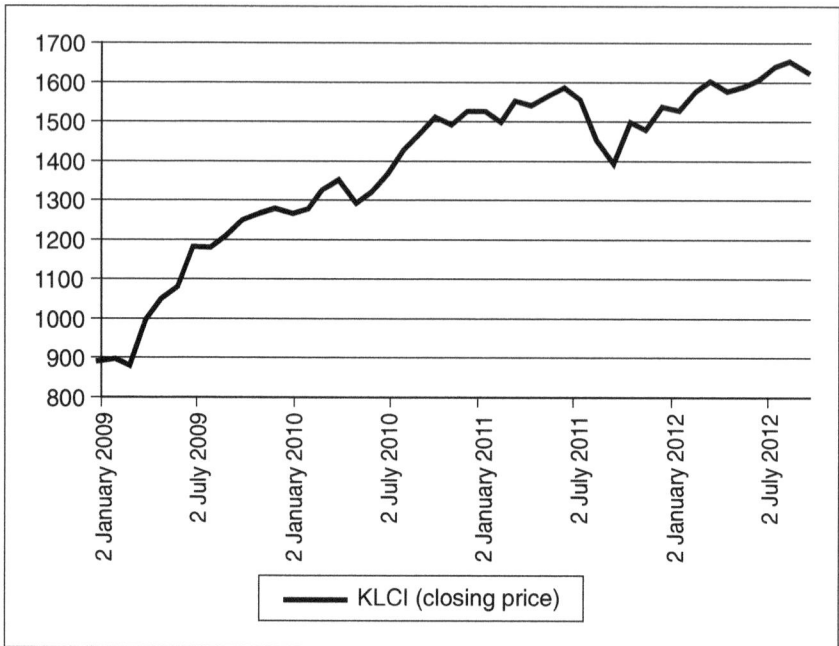

Source: Yahoo Finance.

the Kuala Lumpur Composite Index (KLCI) has jumped 83 per cent (in absolute terms) since early 2009 (see Figure 1.4). The Malaysian economy was also ranked tenth in the World Competitiveness Scoreboard in 2010. This was a significant improvement from a ranking of 18th in 2009.

Despite these positives, the Malaysian economy is said to be a classic case of the "middle-income trap". After rising rapidly at 7.0 per cent from 1991–2000, the economy grew by only 4.6 per cent from 2001–10, far short of the 6.7 per cent average growth rate targeted for the decade (8MP target: 7.5 per cent and 9MP target: 6.0 per cent). Investment rate went down by 10–15 per cent compared to the same period in the 1990s. The 1997–98 Asian Financial Crisis caused a dent in Malaysia's growth story. The economy suffered from a lack of creativity and innovation needed for technological transformation and economic development as concluded in the New Economic Model (NEM) report.[5]

In general, the middle income trap represents a stage where a country is stuck at a relatively comfortable level of per-capita income (World Bank: US$1,006–US$12,275) but cannot seem to take the next big step to become a developed nation. It is relatively simple to get into the middle income level. With low levels of income in the country, it can make the transition by taking advantage of the cheap labour available and make the economy competitive in labour-intensive manufacturing. The real challenge comes when a country has to leap into the ranks of advanced economies. This is because, as income increases, so does cost, which means that a country like Malaysia has to move up the value chain of production and export more technologically advanced products. In addition, the country needs to innovate and use capital and labour more productively. This calls for a highly educated workforce and more investment in research and development (R&D). Hence, the middle-income trap is a development problem for Malaysia.

Things have become further complicated with the presence of big Asian neighbours, China and India, who can squeeze labour costs both in low and high value-added jobs. Moreover, Malaysia's policy of lifting the poor ethnic Malays (Bumiputera) to a higher level of income by introducing quotas and preferential treatment in education, jobs, housing etc. since the 1970s has become a barrier in itself.[6]

Aiming to be a developed nation within thirty years from 1990, the then Malaysian Prime Minister Mahathir bin Mohamad announced Vision 2020 or *Wawasan 2020*. The vision called for a self-sufficient, democratic, economically just, mature, liberal and tolerant society, and a united Malaysian nation which would achieve US$6,000 per capita income in 1980 prices by 2020. Vision 2020 became a part of the Sixth Malaysian Plan in 1991 and remained an important vision for the subsequent five-year development plans. As Malaysia continued to struggle with its vision for a developed economy, Prime Minister Najib Razak in 2010 felt it necessary to undertake bold economic reforms.

The Government Transformation Programme (GTP) was introduced in 2010 to address seven key areas concerning the people of the country. These are — reducing crime, fighting corruption, improving student outcomes, raising living standards of low income households, improving rural basic infrastructure, improving urban public transport and addressing the issue of cost of living. The programme was planned to be implemented until 2012 as a foundation for the transformation of Malaysia. The objective was to improve the lives of all Malaysians regardless of race, religion and social status.

In the same year, Malaysia unveiled the New Economic Model (NEM), which was expected to improve competition, double per capita income in 2020 and start abolishing ethnic preferential treatment for Malays (e.g., in education, public sector jobs and housing). The overall objectives, policy framework, and specific strategies of the NEM were integrated into the Tenth Malaysian Plan (10MP) and the Economic Transformation Programme (ETP). In the Tenth Malaysian Plan (10MP) 2011–15, the focus was on higher education, recruitment and large brain drain from Malaysia. The main macroeconomic objectives were to sustain 6.0 per cent average annual GDP growth rate during the 10MP. This was on the back of stronger domestic demand, increased private investment, and improved productivity. Gross national income (GNI) per capita was targeted to increase to around US$17,700 by 2020.

The Economic Transformation Programme (ETP) was launched in September 2010. It focused on the key growth areas known as twelve National Key Economic Areas (NKEAs) — oil, gas and energy; palm oil; financial services; tourism; business services; electronic and electrical; wholesale and retail; education; healthcare; communications content and infrastructure; agriculture and greater Kuala Lumpur/Klang Valley. ETP suggests ways for Malaysia to come out of the trap between middle and high-income economy and tend to help Malaysia to achieve the targets set under Vision 2020. All these show the sense of urgency to shift Malaysia to a high income gear.

Given this background, the chapter is organized as follows. The next section briefly discusses Malaysia's economic journey since 1970. Despite being one of the Newly Industrialized Economies (NIE) in the 1990s, Malaysia was hit hard by the 1997–98 Asian Financial Crisis and since then it is struggling to come out of its lackluster performance. Section 3 throws light on some of the important issues that have become a drag for the Malaysian economy. The last section argues that given its current state, it is difficult for Malaysia to achieve a developed country status by 2020. The chapter concludes by giving some policy recommendations.

The Economy of Malaysia

1970–2000

The economy of Malaysia has always been hailed as a model of export-led growth. Foreign Direct Investment (FDI) has played an important part in its transformation from a largely agrarian economy to a manufacturing-based one. In 1970, the primary sector was dominated by plantation agriculture and tin mining. But soon the government realized the need for diversification and in its New Economic Policy (NEP)[7] of 1971, the stance moved to stimulate manufacturing growth by attracting FDI.

The NEP was launched through the Second Malaysia Plan in 1971 with the two objectives of alleviating poverty and restructuring the economy. At the same time, the Malaysian government implemented policies to favour bumiputera (including affirmative action in public education) to create opportunities, and to defuse inter-ethnic tensions following the extended violence against Chinese Malaysians in 1969. The policy also aimed to increase capital ownership among the Malays ethnic groups comparable to other races, especially Chinese.

This was followed by the New Development Policy[8] (NDP) in 1990, which avoided a blanket measure to redistribute wealth and employment and emphasized assistance only to "Bumiputera with potential, commitment and good track records" (Malaysian Government 1991).[9] The NDP was part of a larger plan, known as Vision 2020, aimed to turn Malaysia into a fully industrialized country and to quadruple its per capita income by the year 2020. This required the country to rise up the technological "ladder" from low- to high-tech types of industrial production, with a corresponding increase in the intensity of capital investment.

With all these measures in place, the Malaysian economy grew at an unprecedented rate of 8.0 per cent during 1971–80, 6.1 per cent during 1981–90 and 9.3 per cent during 1991–97. The per capita income, at current prices, grew from US$1,812 in 1980 to

TABLE 1.1
Structural Change in GDP
(% share)

Year	Agriculture	Industry	Services
1970	29	27	43
1980	23	41	36
1990	15	42	43
2000	9	48	43
2010	11	44	45

Source: *The World Bank, World Development Indicators Online, October 2012,* available at <http://data.worldbank.org/country/Malaysia> (accessed 17 October 2012).

US$4,029 in 2000. The country invested heavily in infrastructure and the volume of manufactured exports, notably electronic goods and electronic components increased rapidly. The economy also underwent a complete transformation with significant changes in GDP composition (see Table 1.1). In the 1970s, the agricultural sector contributed 29 per cent to GDP, while manufacturing contributed 27 per cent, and services 43 per cent in the same year. By 1980, manufacturing had increased from a 27 per cent to 41 per cent share of GDP. In tandem, the incidence of poverty fell from 52.4 per cent in 1970 to 16.5 per cent in 1990 and further reduced to 5.7 per cent in 2005. In line with policy objectives, the proportion of Bumiputeras in the administrative and managerial job category increased from 22.4 per cent in 1970 to 36.6 per cent in 2000.

In between, in 1997–98, Malaysia became a major victim of the Asian Financial Crisis (AFC). With heavy outflow of foreign capital, the Malaysian ringgit against one U.S. dollar fell from RM2.42 to RM4.88 by January 1998. To counter the crisis the International Monetary Fund (IMF) recommended austerity changes to fiscal and monetary policies. While some countries (Thailand, South Korea, and Indonesia) reluctantly adopted these, the Malaysian government made the ringgit non-convertible externally and pegged the ringgit at RM3.80 to the U.S. dollar. Despite international criticism, these actions stabilized the domestic situation, restoring net growth at 8.9 per cent in 2000.

2001–10

In 2001, the National Vision Policy (NVP) was launched, which incorporated the critical thrust of the previous development policies. Thus, poverty eradication, restructuring of society and balanced development remained as key strategies until the year 2010. In addition, focus was given to developing local skills and raising productivity in order to increase national competitiveness.

During 2001–10, although GDP went up by 5.0 per cent, private investment remained relatively small compared to public investment (see Table 1.2). This reflected the fact that Malaysia's economic growth was led by the public sector, despite its strategy to increase the role of private sector in the economy.

Through all these years, manufacturing sector remained the main sector for the economy and it dominated the share of overall gross exports. Malaysia continued to work as an open economy with trade to GDP ratio at 152 per cent in 2010 and its external sector enjoyed a surplus balance after the 1997–98 crisis (see Figure 1.5).

In 2010, Malaysia unveiled the New Economic Model (NEM), which intended to more than double the per capita income in Malaysia by 2020. The programme aimed to shift affirmative action from being ethnically-based to being need-based and hence becoming more competitive as well as market and investor friendly. This was again reflected in the Tenth Malaysia Plan (10MP: 2011–15), where the private sector was expected to take the lead.

TABLE 1.2
Resource Balance 2000–10
(% of GDP)

Sector	2000	2005	2010
Public Saving	17.6	16.5	13.9
Public Investment	13.9	11.7	10.5
Private Saving	22.5	20.6	21.2
Private Investment	15.9	9.0	11.2
Total Saving	40.1	37.1	35.1
Total Investment	29.8	20.7	21.7
Balance in Total	10.3	16.4	13.4

Source: Malaysia, 2006, 9MP and 2011, 10MP.

FIGURE 1.5
Malaysia's Merchandise Trade, 1980–2010

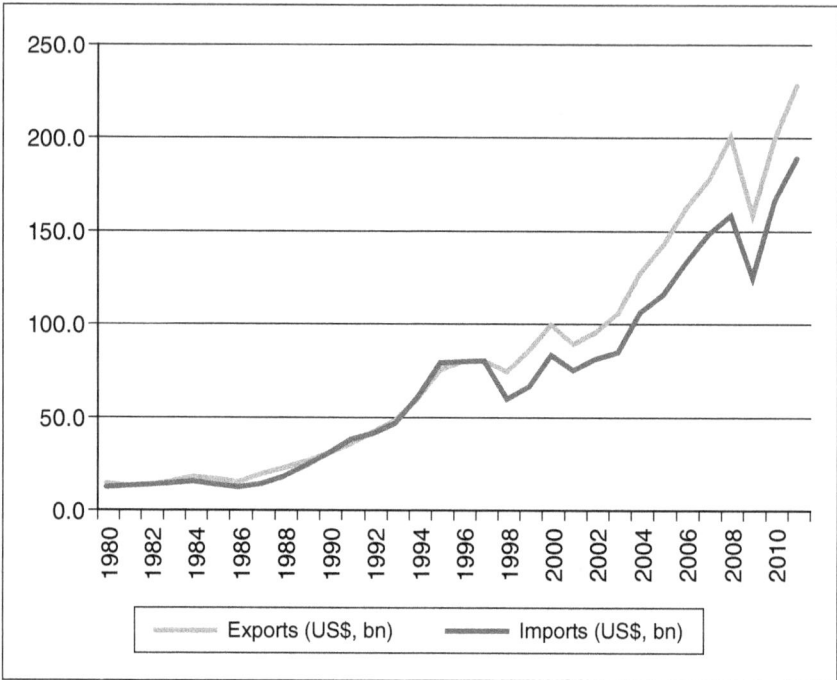

Source: WTO Trade Database.

Malaysia's Key Ailments

Despite Malaysia's achievements in terms of economic growth, per capita income and poverty eradication, the country has been unable to come out of its lackluster performance post the 1997–98 crisis and move to a "higher-income" bracket (see Figure 1.6). Why has it been so difficult?

Pre-mature De-industrialization: Malaysia has undergone considerable structural change since 1970s. From being predominantly mining and agriculture-based economy in the 1970s and 1980s, it moved to become a manufacturing driven economy by late 1980s and foreign capital was injected to promote export manufacturing. Manufacturing expanded strongly until 2000, when it began to cool off due to a lack of human capital and policy support to stimulate firms' participation

FIGURE 1.6
Malaysia's GDP Growth Rate, 1980–2010

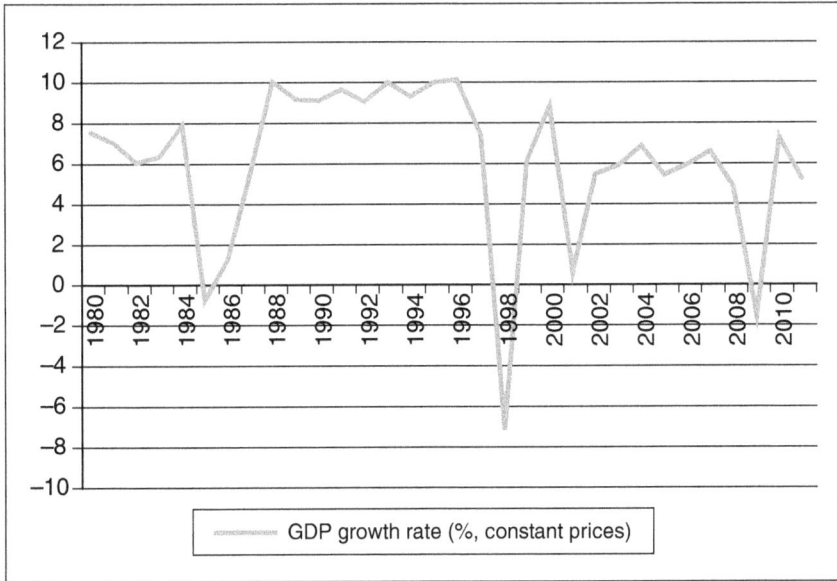

Source: World Economic Outlook Database, IMF, April 2012.

in higher value added activities. Since then, services have become the most important sector, which in the 1990s mainly focused on infrastructure development. The government concentrated on expanding the knowledge infrastructure and gave attention especially to finance, insurance, real estate, business services, trade, accommodation, and restaurants. But the country was not yet ready for a service-based economy as it was challenged by lack of education and cheap and unskilled labour.

The government has recognized that the lack of human capital and innovative capacity have restricted the country's progress. Keeping this in mind, ETP has been introduced as a new initiative in 2010, but this has no linkages to the actual structure of the national economy. Rajah Rasiah in Chapter 3 states that the disconnect between policy-making and the national economic reality is mainly due to over reliance on outside experts to suggest policies, whose understanding of the ground realities of the national economy remain shallow.

Services Sector: While Malaysia's services sector has grown to be the largest in terms of its contribution to GDP and employment, its labour productivity and share in total exports are lower than that of the manufacturing sector. Thus, although the government has targeted the services sector as a new engine of growth, it continues to behave like a supporting sector for manufacturing and domestic consumers. Things got more complicated with the changing nature of the services sector — the consumers and producers are no longer required to be in the same geographical location. Moreover, Malaysia's services sector is confronted with increased competition. This is due to the country's foreign policy to pursue bilateral and regional trade agreements in order to improve market access.

One should note that the services sector is labour intensive and when it is coupled with unskilled labour, productivity suffers. Thus, according to Tham Siew Yen and Loke Wai Heng in Chapter 4, the challenge lies in the rise in efficiency and productivity of the sector, which is again linked to Malaysia's shortage of skilled workers. Despite the country's early effort to promote the sector (the Multimedia Super Corridor was established in 1996), the shortage of skills have restrained the export of information and technology services.

Migrant workers have also made a significant contribution to the Malaysian economy, and have been critical to Malaysia's economic growth in the last two decades. Theresa Devasahayam in Chapter 17 highlights that migrant workers make up around 16 per cent of Malaysia's total labour force. However the employment of migrant labour has led to a complexity of issues. While the Malaysian government has acknowledged that migrant labour is important for the economy, it has also had to carefully and strategically regulate the import of labour, and stem its over reliance on this source of labour. Migrant workers have also at times been blamed for worsening security in the country.

Productivity: In recent years, Malaysia has slipped in meeting its growth targets (see Table 1.5). The gap between the growth accounting targets and actual performance for both the 8MP and 9MP suggests that of the three sources of growth, the targets for Total Factor Productivity (TFP) have been the most difficult to achieve. Malaysia's labour productivity growth has lagged behind several other Asian countries, and its annual average change post-1997 has been lower in the period 1998–2007 (see Tables 1.3 and 1.4).

TABLE 1.3
Malaysia's Productivity Growth Compared to Selected Asian Countries

	Pre-Crisis: 1987–97	Post-Crisis: 1998–2007
China	4.5	9.2
India	3.5	4.4
Asian NIEs	4.8	3.4
Malaysia	5.5	2.9
Thailand	5.2	3.1
Indonesia	3.1	3.0
Singapore	4.5	2.4
Philippines	–0.7	2.3

Source: Tenth Malaysia Plan.

TABLE 1.4
**Sources of Growth for Malaysia's Labour Productivity,
Annual Average Change**

	1987–97	1998–2007
Labour Productivity	5.5	2.9
Contribution of:		
Capital	3.4	1.0
Education	0.3	0.3
Land	0.0	–0.1
Total Factor Productivity	1.7	1.6

Source: Tenth Malaysia Plan.

TABLE 1.5
Growth Targets and Actual Performance

	8MP (2001–05)		9MP (2006–10)		10MP (2011–15)
	Target	Achieved	Target	Achieved	Target
GDP Growth (%)	7.5	4.7	6.0	4.2	6.0
Contribution of Capital	N.A.	1.8	2.0	1.4	2.3
Contribution of Labour	N.A.	1.5	1.8	1.3	1.4
Contribution of TFP	N.A.	1.4	2.2	1.5	2.3

Sources: Eighth, Ninth and Tenth Malaysia Plans.

According to Cassey Lee in Chapter 5, TFP's contribution to growth after increasing from 1.1 per cent (1996–2000) to 1.4 per cent (2001–05), stagnated at 1.5 per cent in the five years to 2010.

For the 10MP, the growth strategy is targeted at the private sector (microeconomic reforms to enhance the dynamism of the private sector, promotion of innovation, rationalization of government activities and SME development), and the private sector investment is expected to go up by 12.8 per cent during 2011–15. This is a significant challenge given that private investment only grew at a rate of 2 per cent in the 2006–10 period. Moreover, with the global economic slowdown and the sovereign debt crisis in Europe, it would be more difficult to raise the private investment, especially the FDI.

Private Investment: FDI played a critical role in this transformation, and domestic investment was also robust at around 40 per cent of GDP, up until the Asian Financial Crisis (AFC). Since then, both the domestic and foreign private investment in Malaysia remained weak, with Malaysia finally turning a net exporter of capital since 2005. Jayant Menon argues that (Chapter 6) Malaysia's investment malaise can be attributed to two inter-related factors: (a) distortions introduced by the New Economic Policy (NEP) and its reincarnates, and (b) the widespread presence and overbearing influence of government-linked corporations (GLCs) that deter new investment. While the impact of both factors may have been masked before the AFC, it is no longer the case in the current competitive environment.

Fixing the problem requires addressing the distortions of the NEP and curtailing the influence of the GLCs. Although there have been a few recent moves to dilute the NEP, some of these measures have already been reversed. Similarly, while there has been an active programme of divestment from GLCs, there have also been GLC acquisitions in new sectors, making it more of a diversification than a divestment programme.

Infrastructure: The development of infrastructure is crucial to a country's economic development. G. Naidu in Chapter 7 provides a detailed discussion of investment and infrastructural modernization in Malaysia by categorizing development into the pre-privatization phase from 1966 to 1990 and the private-participation phase from 1991 onwards.

Starting from the Sixth Malaysia Plan (1991–2000), the private sector started to participate in infrastructure development but public sector spending did not decrease as a result of the private sector. Public sector investment between 1991 and 2010 was RM166.5 billion compared to RM60 billion during the 1966–90 period. Nevertheless private sector investment supplemented public sector investment, boosting total investment in infrastructure.

The road network in Malaysia increased eightfold between 1965 to 2010, from 15,000 km to 135,000 km. There has also been the development of the urban railway sector in the 1990s in Kuala Lumpur. Likewise, the development of port facilities, telecommunications, and electricity infrastructure has risen manifold and generally kept pace with economic growth.

Nevertheless, challenges still remain, the government has to address the growing needs of the external sector as Malaysia continues to become increasingly globalized. There is also a need for the state to ensure that the provision of infrastructure continues for the poorer and less developed parts of Malaysia, and that these less developed regions are not inadvertently overlooked. Another important aspect would be the need to promote efficiency and to continue to remove regulatory oversight.

Malaysian Politics: As Ooi Kee Beng in Chapter 11 points out, major ills became evident with the success of the opposition parties in the general elections of 2008. Power had become centralized in the hands of UMNO. This was apparent in the steady abolition of local elections, which became complete in 1976 when the Local Government Act was passed in 1976. While the NEP sought to push Malays into the fields where they were under-represented, no outflow of Malays from areas where they were over-represented took place. Where the civil service in general was concerned, as was the case with the military, the paramilitary, the police and even the judiciary, the NEP ambition "to reduce and eventually eliminate the identification of race with economic function" was ignored.

To be sure, many Malay leaders did not see the NEP as a temporary affirmative action programme aimed at dissipating socio-economically defined racial divisions, but as the concrete formulation of the indeterminate "special privileges" expressed in Article 153 of the Constitution. UMNO's wish for permanent power could therefore ride steadily on the back of the wish for permanent special rights for the Malays.

Federal System: Francis E. Hutchinson in Chapter 12 states that the Malaysian state is one of the world's most centralized federations. The centre receives almost 90 per cent of all government revenue and performs duties beyond fiscal, monetary, and trade policy measures. The federal government is also responsible for most types of infrastructure, science and technology policy, and all levels of education. However, this overlooks the fact that Malaysia has thirteen state governments that are responsible for particular jurisdictions. They are important providers of goods and services, and can play a role in creating an enabling environment for business.

The chapter further stipulates that an excessive concentration of responsibilities may not always be an optimal condition. Public finance literature holds that an appropriate attribution of responsibilities and revenue sources between levels of government can enhance welfare. For example, while some services benefit from economies of scale and are best provided nationally, others require detailed knowledge of local conditions and should be supplied locally. Despite this, Malaysia has continued to centralize responsibilities at the national level. Its policy frameworks such as the 10MP, NEM, and ETP have the potential to further undercut the effective functioning of state governments. If this continues, it will stifle the vital role that state governments can play in creating an enabling environment for business and leveraging local-level knowledge to foster economic growth.

Environment: As Wee Chong Hui argues in Chapter 13, Malaysia struggles with conflicting demands on the finite environment. Urgent attention is required on the conservation of forest resources and gene pools, sufficient supplies of energy and clean water, and the prevention of water and air pollution. As Malaysia continues to grow, transport and communication infrastructure, industries, township and residential projects will compete for its forested land, which will adversely affect water catchment for human and industrial needs. The increasing commercial and household demands for energy are a strain on resources, and, together with growing industries and human settlements, degrade water and air resources for a long-term liveable quality of life.

Education System: Hwok-Aun Lee writes that in the past (Chapter 14), partly due to government's higher budgetary allocation to education,[10] there were considerable quantitative gains in primary and secondary levels of education. More recently, the nation witnessed rapid expansion in tertiary education. Despite this, Malaysia has witnessed a decay in the quality of education. This has been demonstrated by a lack of basic skills, critical thinking, English proficiency and racial integration among students and graduates.

It was also observed that the quality of institutions has fallen short or even regressed and most of the time the fundamental problem lay in a systemic decline in the calibre of educators and a demoralization of the teaching profession. While national examination results continued to be decked with stellar performances, other trends, such as a strong preference for vernacular schools over national ones, suggest loss of confidence in the national schooling system.

The new administration has, once again, made education a priority, but the proposed policies refrain from systemic reforms and only rely on marginal measures and small-scale programmes. They do not look to promote excellence or to prevent the "brain drain" of highly qualified citizens to other countries for work.

In terms of the provision of higher education, financing higher education has also become an important issue. In Lee Hock Guan's Chapter 15, he discusses the funding of higher education in Malaysia in some detail and points to the importance placed by the Malaysian government in prioritizing higher education as a proportion of the total education expenditure. Increasing privatization has helped to ease government higher education spending, such that increasingly, students and parents are responsible for the costs.

The growth and pattern of financing higher education has been shaped by Malaysian politics and the political system prevailing in the country, where the government has intervened in the equity and access aspects of higher education to ensure that enrolment would reflect the country's racial breakdown. These mandated racial quota policies has affected the equity and access to and thus the financing of higher education. In addition, shifting the responsibility to financing education to students and parents would make it increasingly difficult for lower-income students to attend higher education. This is an important consideration which the state has to take into account if inequity is to be reduced in the years ahead.

Income Inequality: In Chapter 16, Ragayah Haji Mat Zin observed that inequality, as measured by the Gini ratio was rising prior to 1976. But it was reduced by about 16.6 per cent by the end of the

NEP 1971–90. Income inequality has fluctuated in the last twenty years and currently remains at the same level as in 1990. Income disparities between urban and rural areas remain high. Explanations for the persistent high inequality include trade and globalization, labour market policies, constraints on the process of internal migration, formation of clusters and agglomeration effects, and state-government-party collusion. The high inequality in Malaysia can hinder the process of absolute poverty eradication and jeopardize economic growth.

Again, the strategies for accomplishing a 6 per cent growth under the 10MP tend to be inequality widening (driving growth by urban agglomerations, cluster- and corridor-based economic activities, and focusing on the National Key Economic Areas (NKEAs)). While the plan provides for various programmes to assist the bottom 40 per cent of households, the strategies are not that much different from what have been recommended in the earlier plans. Hence, the outcomes are not expected to be really transformational. Further, liberalization of selected sectors in the economy and low economic growth outlook in global economy would also tend to enhance inequality.

Growth and Liveability: The structural change in Malaysia from being agriculture dependent to industry driven has led to rapid industrialization and to the concentration of economic activities in a few urban areas. This led to the services sector development in the existing urban areas, compounding the concentration of population further. From 1980 to 2010, the urbanization rate increased from 34.2 per cent to 71 per cent (Department of Statistics 2010). The problems associated with rapid urbanization include transportation and traffic woes, lack of housing resources among the low income group, and social crime. In Tan Teck Hong's and Phang Siew Nooi's chapter (18), it is estimated that over 75 per cent of the nation's population will be urban by 2020, up from 71 per cent in 2010. This will be the fundamental obstacle in securing a better quality of life in the long term.

In order to cope with the problem, the Malaysian government has implemented various measures in relation to issues of environment, politics, governance, and the ethnic composition of the population. The chapter notes that the urban management will increasingly take on an integrated approach, and will be much aligned to the Government Transformation Programme (GTP) of 2010. Moreover, as cities are the powerhouses of economic growth, their sustainability lies within the ways to address the challenges in the urban areas. The government and economic transformation programmes exemplify this concept. Some of the outstanding issues of the transformation programme that are relevant to deal with greater urbanization are reducing crime, improving urban transport, and improving housing affordability. Another significant area is good governance (accountability, transparency, equity, etc.).

Malaysia by 2020

Looking at the above, one can conclude that although Malaysia has successfully achieved its upper middle income country status, its path to graduating to a high income country remains highly uncertain. Moreover, the on-going global economic problems and slowdown in key export markets, makes the annual growth target of 6 per cent, under the 10MP, unlikely to be achieved. Achieving the targeted growth rate during 2011–15 also requires the private investment to grow by more than 12 per cent annually. This is very ambitious, after a 2 per cent annual growth rate achieved during the Ninth Malaysia Plan (Menon, Chapter 6).

Policy Recommendations[11]

- To promote the manufacturing sector, Malaysia must invest in technology. Despite policy efforts, the lack of human capital and poorly led R&D organizations have denied the country the knowledge synergies essential to stimulate firms' upgrading to high value-added activities. Similarly, for the services sector, efforts are needed to improve the human capital resources so as to increase labour productivity and enhance its linkages with the manufacturing sector. In the longer term, enhancing export competitiveness in both manufacturing and services sector will require increasing domestic competition, reducing regulatory burden, understanding the free trade agreements as well as knowing the regulatory requirements of the targeted country of export.
- The Malaysian government needs to undertake significant fiscal reforms. This includes broadening the tax revenue base via Goods and Services Tax (GST) and reducing the size of public sector.

The government should not attempt to compensate any decline in private investments by undertaking public investments either directly or indirectly (via GLCs). These reforms should be accompanied by actions to improve economic and regulatory governance aimed at reducing arbitrary decisions in development spending and regulatory matters. They should also aim at bringing about more transparent and non-discriminatory procurement and regulatory systems. These are essential to deal with problems such as lack of FDI, inefficient infrastructure services, lack of human capital and brain drain.

- There is increasing recognition that the slump in Malaysia's private investment is rooted in the distortions resulting from the workings and implementation of the NEP and its reincarnates. It is believed that GLCs have crowded out private investment in a wide range of sectors. Hence, it is more important to address the GLC problem for the revival of investment, before turning into the NEP. However, it remains to be seen if the plans announced for government divestment in some of these GLCs will progress in a way that removes all barriers that have prevented or discouraged new firms from entering what have been traditional strongholds. Whether divestment proceeds will be channelled back into government involvement in different sectors, as has been happening lately, is another concern.

- Malaysia is on its way to be a part of an ASEAN Economic Community (AEC) by 2015. But implementing the AEC Blueprint at the national economic level is not easy. The country faces resistance from affected parties, monopolists and lobbyists apprehensive of increased competition and transparency in the economy (Rokiah Alavi, Chapter 10). Moreover, in Malaysia, there are some sectors and domestic regulations that are considered sensitive and strategic for national economic development. This is slowing down the progress of liberalization in Malaysia. Nevertheless, meeting the goals under AEC Blueprint is very crucial as this will not only be important for raising the country's competitiveness *vis-à-vis* other nations in the region but also to attain its own goals of Vision 2020. This will require strong motivation, political will and leadership.

- Malaysia needs to empower its state governments. The most effective means of revitalizing initiative at the state level is to increase incentives for performance. At present, rankings of investor inflows to each state are published yearly, but current fiscal arrangements mean this has no impact on centre-state transfers. Thus, state governments have no direct incentive to engage in their investor liaison roles.

- The potential for innovation and policy transfer can be encouraged and systematized by more regular incorporation of state-level development plans into the federal government's Malaysia Plans. Many state-level plans have been financed exclusively by state governments, drawing on extensive local level knowledge and social capital. Yet, it is a frequent refrain from state government officials that their planning processes are by-passed by federal planning machinery. These plans, accompanied by transparent key performance indicators, would greatly enrich plans at both the state and national levels.

- In environmental conservation, Malaysia should intensify efforts for international cooperation on technology sharing, support in environmental management and collective responsibility. Carbon trading better captures environmental costs worldwide. Malaysia has one of the remaining tropical rainforests with a large gene pool and contribution as carbon sink. The burden of custody should not lie on Malaysia alone.

- Malaysia must work hard on reversing the decay in education, beginning with the public schools. This will entail difficult decisions to be made, in terms of the allocation of education funds, specifically to avail more for teacher's salaries and benefits. The relatively heavy spending in tertiary education, alongside persistent national under-achievement in secondary school enrolment and completion, warrant an examination of the distribution of spending between education levels. Another important area concerns the extent to which Malaysia's highly staffed public sector and administrative positions consume resources that could otherwise be directly committed to educational work.

- Raising the quality of teaching professionals is one element in a set of necessary changes. The increasing weight attached to performance auditing warrants reconsideration, taking cognizance of the need to balance policies that extract effort and meet targets against those that give space for capable teachers, academicians, and students to thrive. Without political will and bold leadership, these necessary transformations will fail to materialize and academic mediocrity will persist.

- In order to reduce the income inequality, Malaysia must implement its plan of NEM efficiently. It has been more than a year since the NEM was introduced, but the ordinary public has yet to feel the changes. The government must have more political will to ensure that ordinary *rakyat* benefit from the programmes. Moreover, big cases of corruption still hog the limelight and these need to be tackled more seriously.
- Malaysia should look to increase labour mobility and raise labour market competition. Sharing information on job availabilities to reduce the costs of job search, as well as further easing of the regulations for setting up new businesses, would result in competitive labour markets that will make the firms more efficient and more conducive to better compensation practices. Regulations in hiring and firing workers should be reviewed. In addition, the government should intensify its efforts to encourage greater automation and mechanization of labour-intensive industries in order to reduce the dependence on foreign unskilled labour. Employers must provide continuous training for workers and the latter must be willing to be retrained and become multi-skilled in order to increase productivity.
- To raise its labour standards, Malaysia must set a minimum wage. Currently, workers are paid below their productivity. Workers would be motivated to be more productive with a higher incentive. The government has set up the National Wage Consultative Council to look into this matter. At the same time, employers must also provide workers with training and new skills while paying workers the appropriate incentives.
- The pressure of urbanization has made it necessary for urban planners to manage the cities efficiently. As mentioned in Chapter 18, a lot of politics in Malaysia is entrenched in the system, but urban planners have to enhance their abilities to cope with emerging issues of politics, finance, equity, corruption, and public awareness. Hence, capacity building is necessary for urban officials.

- Another critical factor for the success in urban management hinges upon the commitment of the public to sustain government strategies and initiatives. Every individual should be encouraged to take responsibility for their urban environment and governance of their city. This encompasses the NGO, the private sector, and some international agencies.

NOTES

1. Tenth Malaysia Plan, 2011–2015 (Malaysia: Economic Planning Unit, 2010).
2. Hall Hill, Tham Siew Yean, Ragayah Haji Mat Zin, eds., *Malaysia's Development Challenges: Graduating from the Middle* (London and New York: Routledge, 2012).
3. Institute of Strategic and International Studies (ISIS) Malaysia, *Malaysia: Policies and Issues in Economic Development* (Kuala Lumpur: Institute of Strategic and International Studies (ISIS) Malaysia, 2011).
4. Brunei, Cambodia, Indonesia, Laos, Myanmar, Philippines, Thailand, Singapore and Vietnam
5. Shankaran Nambiar, *East Asia Forum*, 27 December 2011.
6. The Bumiputera policy, enjoyed by an ethnic majority (Malays constitute around 50 per cent of the total population) and held up by the powerful Malay elite and the governing Malay majority party (UMNO), is difficult to reverse.
7. NEP was an ambitious socio-economic restructuring affirmative action programme launched by the Malaysian government in 1971 under the then Prime Minister Tun Abdul Razak. The NEP ended in 1990, and was succeeded by the National Development Policy in 1991.
8 The NDP replaced the NEP in 1990 but continued to pursue most of NEP policies.
9. Malaysian Government, *The Second Outline Perspective Plan, 1991–2000* (Kuala Lumpur: Government Printer, 1991).
10. Malaysia public expenditure of tertiary education is 92.7 per cent, the highest among Southeast Asian countries.
11. This section is derived from the subsequent chapters in the book.

REFERENCES

Hill, Hall, Tham Siew Yean, Ragayah Haji Mat Zin, eds. *Malaysia's Development Challenges: Graduating from the Middle*. London and New York: Routledge, 2012.

Institute of Strategic and International Studies (ISIS) Malaysia. *Malaysia: Policies and Issues in Economic Development*. Kuala Lumpur: Institute of Strategic and International Studies (ISIS) Malaysia, 2011.

Malaysian Government. *The Second Outline Perspective Plan, 1991–2000*. Kuala Lumpur: Government Printer, 1991.

Rajah, R., ed. *Malaysia Economy: Unfolding Growth and Social Change*. Kuala Lumpur: Oxford University Press, 2011.

Shankaran Nambiar. *East Asia Forum*. 27 December 2011.

Tenth Malaysia Plan: 2011–2015. Malaysia: Economic Planning Unit, 2010.

2

MALAYSIA'S ECONOMIC DEVELOPMENT AND TRANSFORMATION
Looking Back, Looking Forward

Jomo Kwame Sundaram

The Malaysian economy and society has changed significantly for the better over the last half-century. The current challenges that the economy is facing can be better understood and dealt with if seen against the background of its past. This chapter will therefore analyse Malaysia's economic development and transformation over a long term historical perspective, and look at what has happened to the Malaysian economy, as well as at how it has changed over time.

The transformation of Malaysian society has been noteworthy. Malaysian society has become increasingly urbanized over the decades, as indicated by Table 2.1. In 1957, over 90 per cent of Malaya's population lived in rural areas. By 2010, only about 37 per cent of the Malaysian population lived in the countryside.

In terms of structural change or sectoral transformation, manufacturing and services contributed more than 80 per cent of total output of the economy in 2009 (see Table 2.2); both sectors only contributed about

TABLE 2.1
Population by Location, 1957–2010
(%)

	1957*	1970	1980	1990	2000	2010
Rural	91.0	71.2	62.5	45.3	38.1	36.6
Urban	19.0	28.8	37.5	54.7	61.9	63.4

Note: * Peninsular Malaysia.
Source: Official Malaysia Plan documents.

TABLE 2.2
Output by Sector, 1970–2009
(%)

	1970	2000	2009
Agriculture	29.0	8.7	7.7
Mining	13.7	6.3	7.7
Manufacturing	13.9	33.4	26.6
Construction	3.8	3.3	3.3
Services	36.2	52.4	57.6

half of total output in 1970. Malaysia has seen a dramatic transformation of its economy in terms of the rapid growth of manufacturing and services as agriculture continued to expand, as well as the shift of its population from rural to urban areas over the past half century.

This is, of course, very much reflected by employment patterns. Table 2.3 shows that the transformation has been very significant, especially in terms of the share of services (Khong with Jomo 2010).

The official poverty rate has also fallen, although there is some debate on its measurement. Nevertheless, these figures suggest significant improvements in general living standards in Malaysia, not only in urban areas, but also in the countryside, as indicated in Table 2.4 and Figure 2.1.

Unlike many other developing countries, official Malaysian data suggest not only a decline of poverty, but also a decline in inequality — of overall inequality, not just of inter-ethnic disparities. Most other countries in the West, the former Soviet Union, China and most

TABLE 2.3
Employment by Sector, 1970–2009
(%)

	1970	1980	1990	2000	2009
Agriculture and Forestry	53.5	39.7	26.0	20.0	12.0
Mining and Quarrying	2.6	1.7	0.5	0.5	0.4
Manufacturing	8.7	15.7	19.9	23.9	27.6
Construction	2.7	5.6	6.3	7.4	6.6
Services	32.5	37.4	47.3	48.2	53.4

Source: Official Malaysia Plan documents.

TABLE 2.4
Poverty, 1970–2009

	1970	1990	1999	2009
Total	49.3	16.5	7.5	3.8
Rural	58.6	21.1	12.4	–
Urban	24.6	7.1	3.4	–
Poorest	–	3.9	1.4	0.7

Source: Official Malaysia Plan documents.

FIGURE 2.1
Poverty Rates and Gini Coefficients, 1970–2007

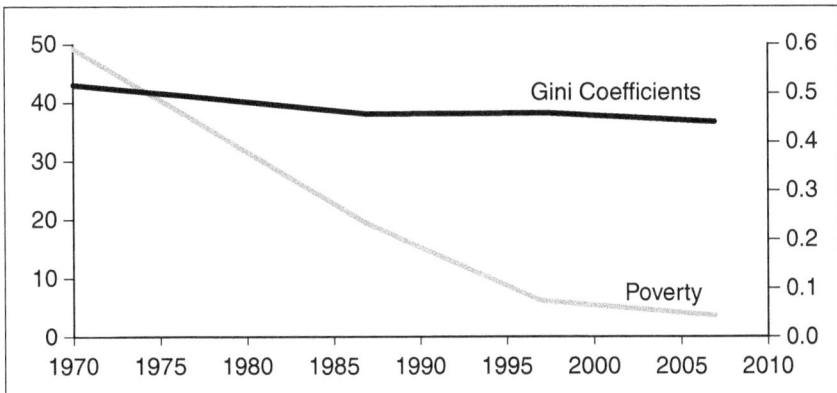

Source: Official Malaysia Plan documents; NEAC (2010*a*).

developing countries have experienced rising inequality over the same period. Only Northern Europe and Northeast Asia (Korea and Japan) have maintained low inequality, while some countries in South America have seen recent declines in inequality in the last decade after decades of rising inequality.

The share of wage earning Malaysians among those working has significantly increased from slightly over half to over three-quarters of the labour force, as shown in Table 2.5.

There has been a very significant reduction in inter-ethnic income disparities over the last four decades, especially during the 1970s and 1980s. In 1970, at the time of the introduction of the New Economic Policy (NEP), the ratio of the average incomes of ethnic Chinese to ethnic Malays was 2.29, but declined greatly to 1.31 in 2009; other similar inter-ethnic disparities have significantly fallen as well, as shown by Table 2.6.

TABLE 2.5
Employment Status, 1957–2005

	1957	1980	2005
Employer	}35.0	3.8	3.4
Own account worker		27.0	16.6
Employee	56.7	58.3	75.7
Unpaid family worker	8.3	11.0	4.5

Source: Khong with Jomo (2010).

TABLE 2.6
Inter-Ethnic Average Income Ratios, 1970–2009

	1970	2009
Chinese/Malay	2.29	1.31
Chinese/Indian	1.30	1.25
Indian/Malay	1.78	1.04
Urban/Rural	2.14	1.85

Source: Official Malaysia Plan documents.

There are different measures of inter-ethnic disparities, and Table 2.7 provides evidence of similar trends during 1970–87.

Average gross household incomes have significantly increased for all ethnic groups, including the bottom 40 per cent of the population, as Table 2.7 shows. The increase in average incomes has been greatest for the top fifth of households. Table 2.8 also suggests some decrease in overall income disparities, but this conclusion is disputed by other measures.

Inter-ethnic occupational disparities have greatly declined in most occupations, as indicated in Table 2.9. One exception is agriculture, where the share of Bumiputeras is greater than ever. The proportion of ethnic Indians in agriculture, even on plantations, has also declined greatly.

TABLE 2.7
Inter-Ethnic Household Income Ratios, 1970–87

	1970	1973	1976	1979	1984	1987
Chinese/Malay	2.29	2.21	2.28	1.91	1.76	1.65
Chinese/Indian	1.30	1.31	1.46	1.24	1.37	1.31
Indian/Malay	1.77	1.69	1.56	1.54	1.28	1.25
Urban/Rural	2.14	2.12	2.12	1.77	1.87	1.72

Source: Official Malaysia Plan documents.

TABLE 2.8
Mean Gross Household Incomes by Income Grouping, 1970–2009

	Top 20%	Middle 40%	Bottom 40%
1970	3,111	914	322
1979	4,781	1,411	512
1984	5,610	1,058	663
1989	5,263	1,831	750
1999	7,786	2,738	1,074
2009	9,987	3,631	1,440

Source: Official Malaysia Plan documents.

TABLE 2.9
Occupations by Ethnicity, 1970–2005
(%)

	1970			2005		
	Bumiputera	Chinese	Indians	Bumiputera	Chinese	Indians
Managers	24.1	62.9	7.8	41.9	50.0	7.5
Professionals	47.0	39.5	10.8	58.6	31.8	9.0
Technicians	–	–	–	64.7	26.1	8.5
Clerical	35.4	45.9	17.2	59.6	32.5	7.4
Services	44.3	39.6	14.6	59.6	33.6	5.7
Sales	26.7	61.7	11.1	–	–	–
Agriculture	72.0	17.3	9.7	84.4	11.3	2.7
Crafts and Trades	–	–	–	52.6	40.5	5.9
Production	34.2	55.9	9.6	66.5	17.4	15.2
Elementary	–	–	–	70.0	16.2	12.2
Total	51.8	36.6	10.6	62.6	28.2	8.2

Source: Khong with Jomo (2010) from official Malaysia Plan documents.

Employment statistics also suggest dramatic changes since Malayan independence in 1957 (see Table 2.10). Tables 2.11 and 2.12 summarize employment status in 1980 and 2007 respectively, pointing to a major increase in wage employment among Malays and other Bumiputeras as well as Chinese, with a corresponding decline of unpaid family workers as well as own account workers, i.e., the self-employed.

TABLE 2.10
Peninsular Malaysia: Employment Status by Ethnicity, 1957
(%)

	Malays	Chinese	Indians	Others	Total
Employer and own account worker	48.9 (66.1)	28.3 (28.8)	9.8 (4.1)	14.5 (1.1)	35.0
Unpaid family worker	14.1 (80.0)	4.2 (17.8)	0.5 (0.9)	4.1 (1.3)	8.3
Employee	37.0 (31.0)	67.6 (42.5)	89.6 (22.9)	81.4 (3.7)	56.7
In employment	(47.3)	(35.7)	(14.5)	(2.6)	

Source: Khong with Jomo (2010).

TABLE 2.11
Peninsular Malaysia: Employment Status by Ethnicity, 1980
(%)

	Malays	Chinese	Indians	Others	Total
Employer	2.6 (35.5)	5.8 (51.5)	4.6 (12.3)	4.1 (0.7)	4.0
Own account worker	32.9 (64.5)	24.7 (31.5)	8.3 (3.2)	32.1 (0.8)	27.4
Unpaid family worker	9.2 (67.9)	5.4 (26.2)	3.3 (4.9)	10.1 (1.0)	7.3
Employee	55.2 (48.3)	64.1 (36.5)	83.8 (14.6)	53.8 (0.6)	61.4
In employment	(53.6)	(35.0)	(10.7)	(0.7)	

Source: Khong with Jomo (2010).

TABLE 2.12
Peninsular Malaysia: Employment Status by Ethnicity, 2007
(%)

	Bumiputera	Chinese	Indians	Others	Total
Employer	2.5 (44.9)	8.4 (49.6)	3.0 (5.3)	0.6 (0.1)	3.9
Own account worker	21.7 (74.8)	18.5 (20.7)	10.7 (3.6)	22.9 (0.8)	20.3
Unpaid family worker	5.3 (68.7)	6.4 (26.9)	3.0 (3.9)	3.7 (0.5)	5.4
Employee	70.5 (69.7)	66.7 (21.4)	83.3 (8.1)	72.8 (0.8)	70.5
In employment	(69.7)	(22.7)	(6.9)	(0.7)	

Source: Khong with Jomo (2010).

The main bone of contention in Malaysian political economy discourse is over the question of share ownership. There was a very significant increase in the Bumiputera ownership share from the time of the May 1969 riots until the early 1980s. The Bumiputera proportion of share ownership has, however, risen only modestly since then, from above 18 per cent to about 23 per cent. The share of foreigners went down very dramatically in the 1970s, but has gone up equally dramatically to over 40 per cent recently.

One interesting trend after the early 1980s has been the rise in the share of individual Bumiputera wealth, as reflected in Table 2.13. During the 1970s, Bumiputera wealth was largely held through state owned enterprises; since then, however, there has been a large increase in individual Bumiputera wealth ownership. There is now a class of Bumiputera wealth owners or capitalists, but it is unclear to what extent they are entrepreneurial.

Malaysian economic performance has been very susceptible to changes in the global economy, as indicated in Figure 2.2. But Malaysian economic vulnerability has changed over time. Earlier, vulnerability to commodity prices was very important, but more recently, variations in demand for manufactured outputs have been more significant. Especially since the 1990s, the Malaysian economy has become more vulnerable to movements on the capital account, as during the 1997–98 crisis.

TABLE 2.13
Bumiputera Ownership of Share Capital, 1970–2006
(%)

	1970	1985	1990	2000	2006
Total	2.4	19.1	19.3	18.9	19.4
Individuals	1.6	11.7	14.2	14.2	15.1
Institutions	} 0.8	} 7.4	} 5.1	3.0	2.6
Trust agencies				1.7	1.7

Source: Official Malaysia Plan documents.

FIGURE 2.2
Malaysian Growth Cycles, 1970–2008

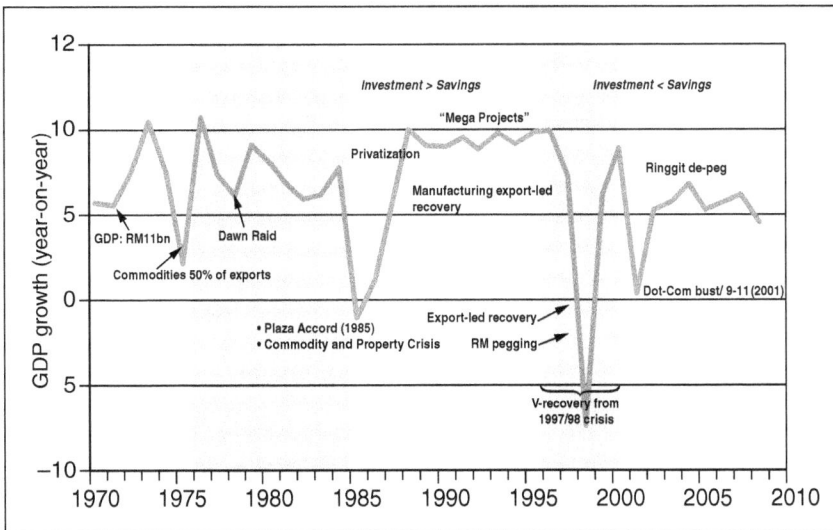

Note: During 2001–07, the fiscal deficit averaged 4.3 per cent, doubling the total public debt.
Source: NEAC (2010*a*).

Malaysian economic growth performance was reasonably strong for about a decade before the 1997–98 East Asian crisis. But it has never really recovered since that crisis. Since 1998, Malaysian economic growth has averaged over 5 per cent. But on a per capita basis, this came down to over 3 per cent. Growth in the decade-and-a-half since the 1997–98 crisis has been just over half the per capita average of over 6 per cent in the decade before that crisis.

Very importantly, private investment has gone down very dramatically since the 1997–98 crisis, as can be seen in Figures 2.3 and 2.4.

Most attribute this to a collapse of foreign direct investment. Looking at the lighter shade line, foreign direct investment was never really all that high, and has remained more or less at the same level since the mid-1990s, i.e. before and after the 1997–98 crisis (see Figure 2.5).

FIGURE 2.3
Asian Growth Before and After the 1997–98 Crisis

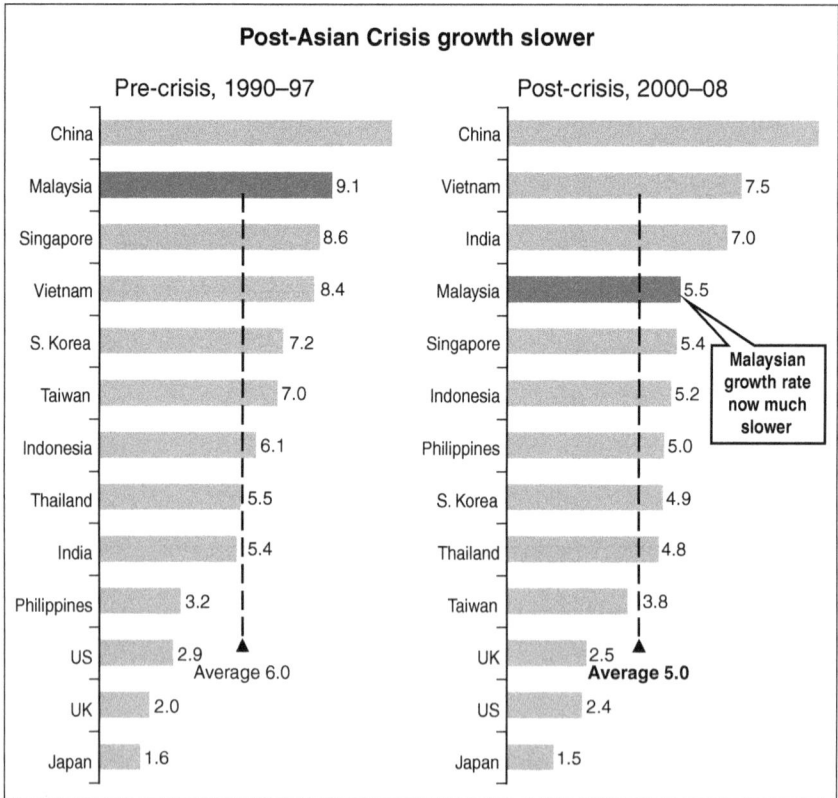

Source: NEAC (2010*a*).

FIGURE 2.4
Spending Before and After the 1997–98 Crisis

Pre- and post-Asian crisis spending growth rates (%)

Private consumption   Govt spending   Investment down

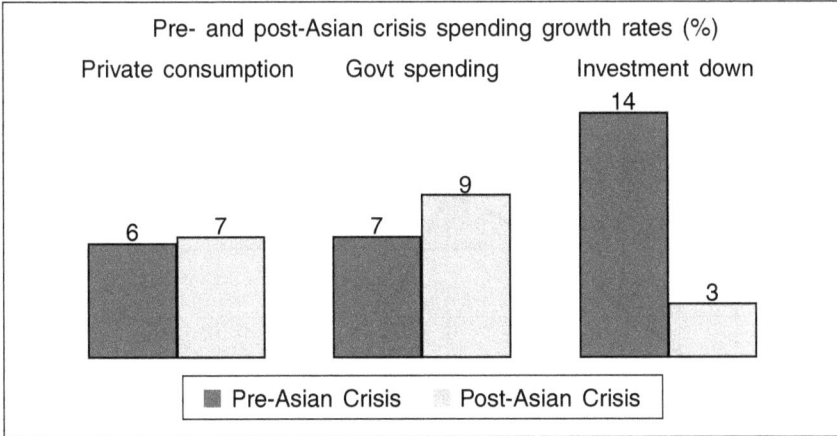

- Pre-Asian Crisis   Post-Asian Crisis

Source: NEAC (2010a).

FIGURE 2.5
Investments Before and After the 1997–98 Crisis, 1987–2007

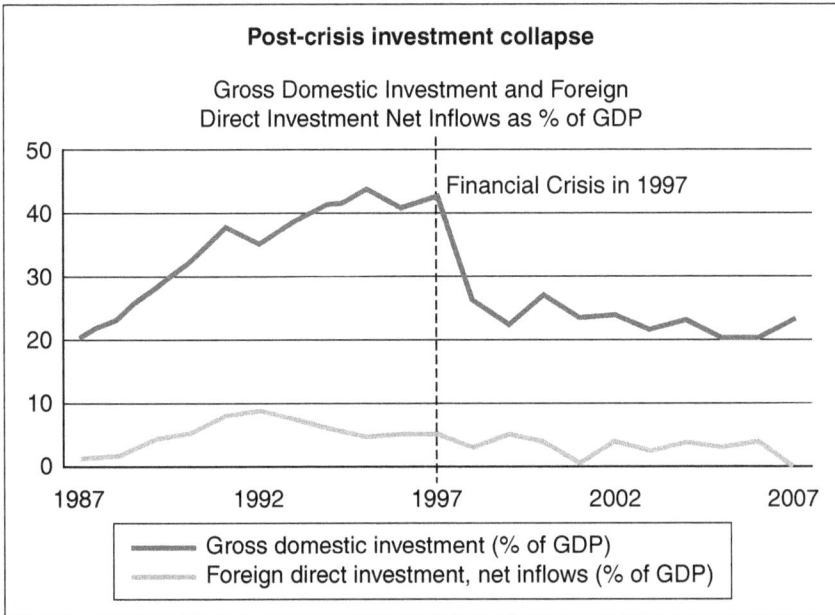

Post-crisis investment collapse

Gross Domestic Investment and Foreign
Direct Investment Net Inflows as % of GDP

Financial Crisis in 1997

——— Gross domestic investment (% of GDP)
········ Foreign direct investment, net inflows (% of GDP)

Source: NEAC (2010a).

FIGURE 2.6
Private and Public Cumulative Aggregate Growth Rate (CAGR) Before
and After the 1997–98 Crisis, 1991–2006

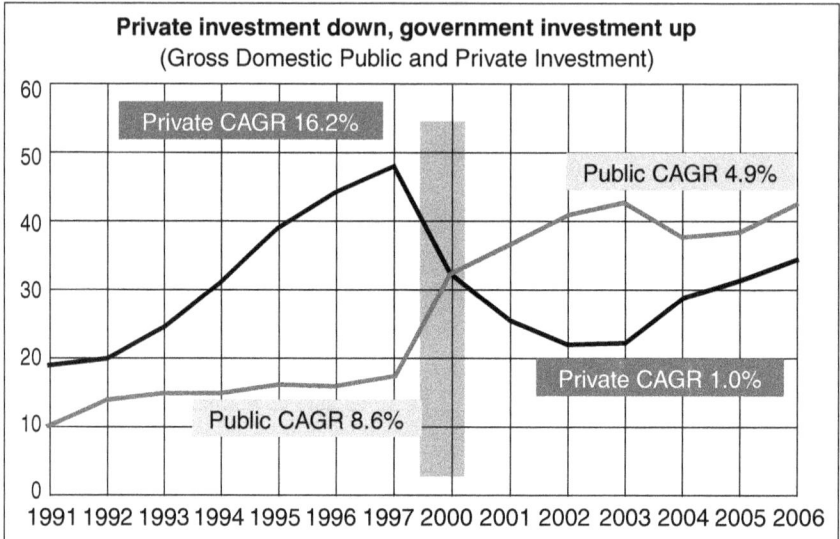

Private investment down, government investment up
(Gross Domestic Public and Private Investment)

Private CAGR 16.2%

Public CAGR 4.9%

Private CAGR 1.0%

Public CAGR 8.6%

1991 1992 1993 1994 1995 1996 1997 2000 2001 2002 2003 2004 2005 2006

Source: NEAC (2010*a*).

Clearly, domestic investor confidence fell significantly after the 1997–98 crisis. Many are under the illusion that foreign investment leads, and domestic investment follows. On the contrary, in general, domestic investment leads and foreign investment follows. This is an important reversal of the orthodoxy that must be recognized.

The collapse in private investment has been partially compensated for by increased government spending. But this increased government spending has actually been compromised by its nature. Government spending has gone up, both government consumption as well as investment. Higher Malaysian government expenditure has been made possible by a constant fiscal deficit since 1998, which has been propping up economic growth (see Figure 2.7). So, the modest 5+ per cent post-crisis growth rate — in contrast to the 8+ per cent earlier — has been largely due to greater government spending.

A temporary increase in government spending during a downturn is desirable from a counter-cyclical point of view, but its stance has not been consistently counter-cyclical. Of course, deficit funded development

FIGURE 2.7
Expenditure, Consumption, Investment Before and After the 1997–98 Crisis

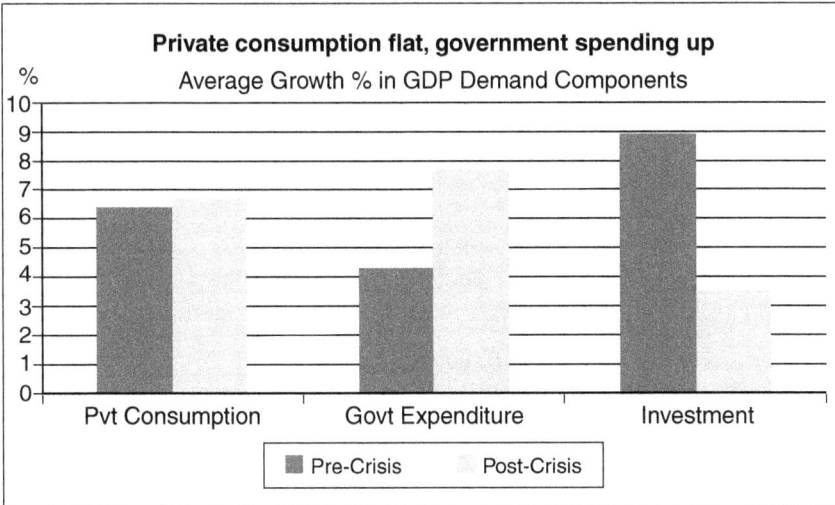

Source: NEAC (2010*a*).

FIGURE 2.8
Consumption as the Engine of Growth Before and After the 1997–98 Crisis

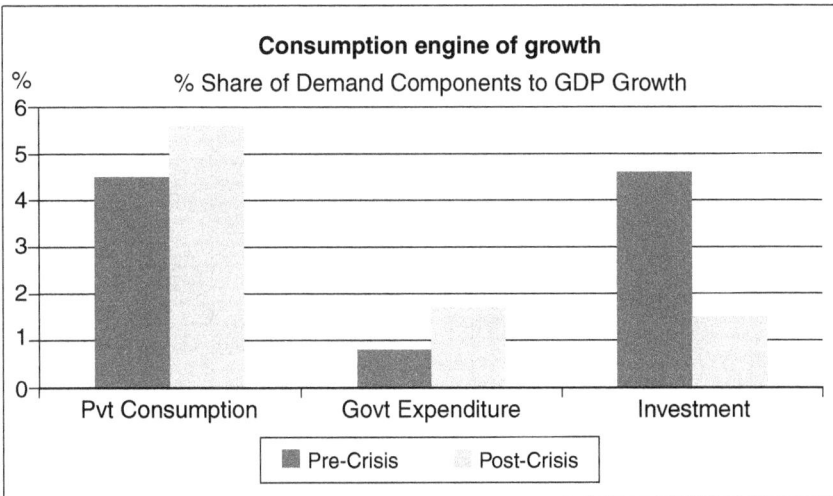

Source: NEAC (2010*a*).

expenditure can also be defended, but much of the increased expenditure has been for consumption, especially government consumption, rather than for investment, let alone productive investment. This consistent support for growth for almost a decade-and-a-half has been possible only because of revenue streams associated with oil wealth.

There has been little progress on education, including university education (see Figure 2.10). Technical and vocational education is also

FIGURE 2.9
Lack of University/Tertiary Graduates

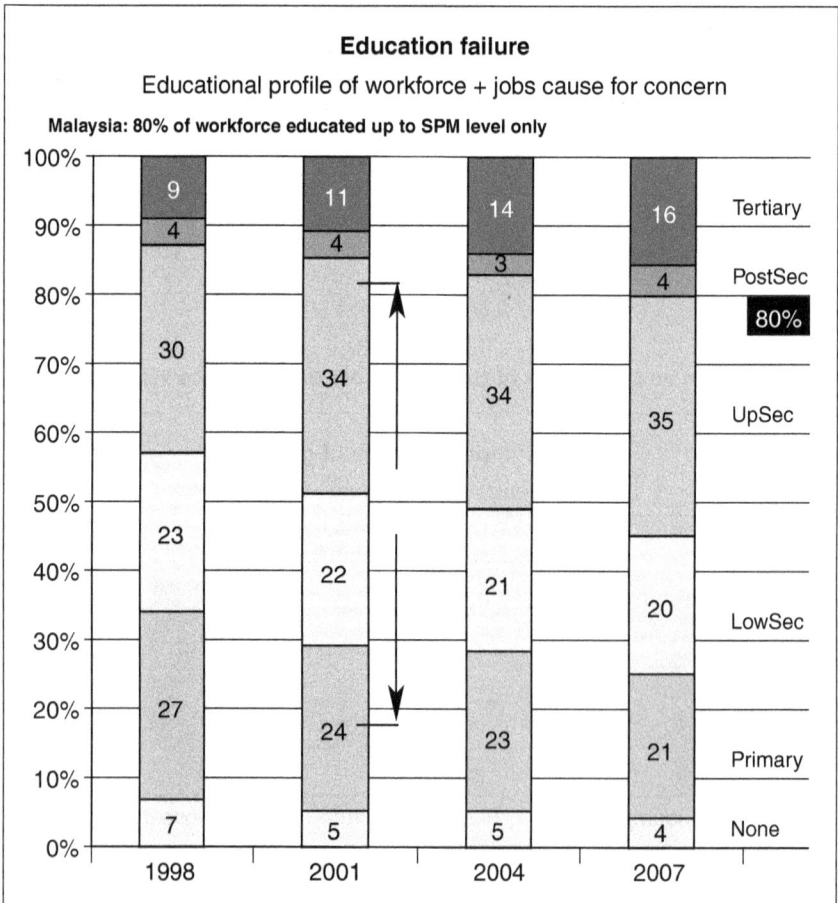

Source: NEAC (2010*a*).

FIGURE 2.10
Arts versus Technical and Science Graduates, 2002–07

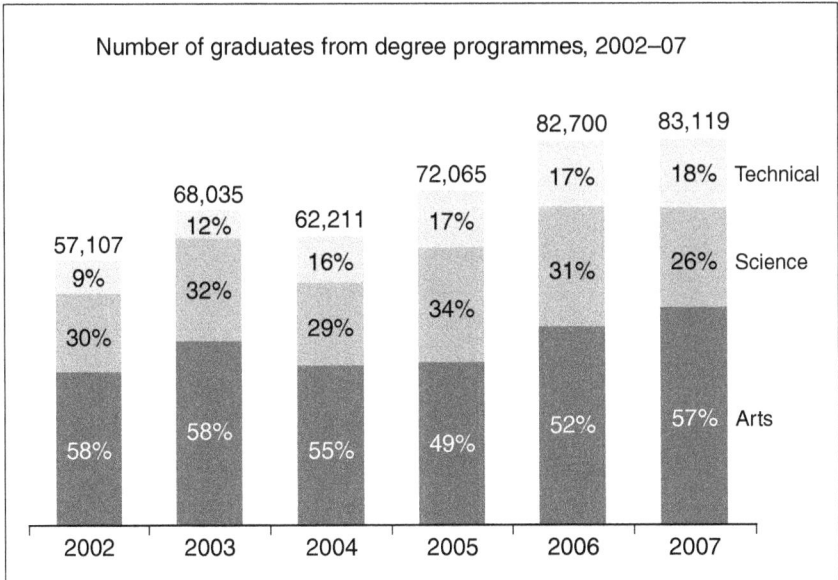

Number of graduates from degree programmes, 2002–07

				82,700	83,119
			72,065	17%	18% Technical
	68,035	62,211	17%		
57,107	12%	16%		31%	26% Science
9%	32%		34%		
30%		29%			
	58%			52%	57% Arts
58%		55%	49%		
2002	2003	2004	2005	2006	2007

Source: NEAC (2010*a*).

FIGURE 2.11
Lack of Technical and Vocational Graduates, 1999–2001

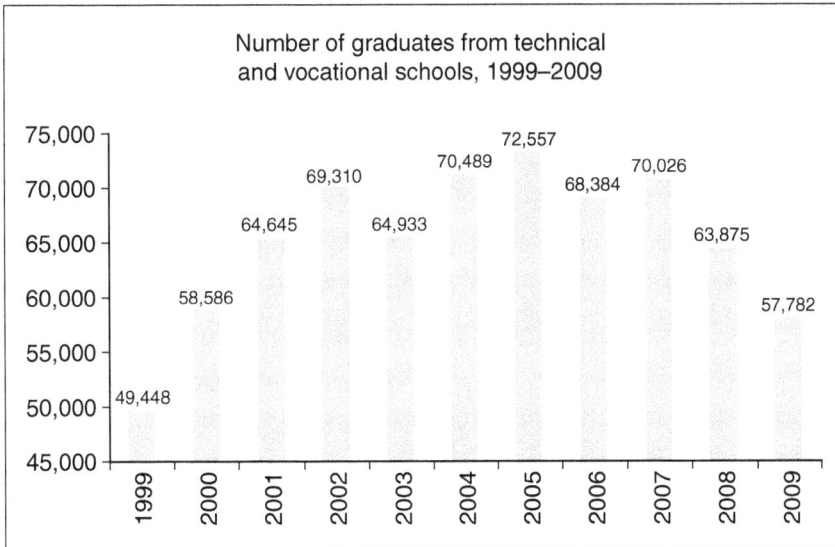

Number of graduates from technical
and vocational schools, 1999–2009

							72,557			
					70,489			70,026		
75,000			69,310					68,384		
70,000		64,645		64,933					63,875	
65,000										57,782
60,000	58,586									
55,000										
50,000	49,448									
45,000	1999	2000	2001	2002	2003	2004	2005	2006	2007	2008	2009

Source: NEAC (2010*a*).

FIGURE 2.12
Skilled Management and Professional, Semi-Skilled and Unskilled Jobs

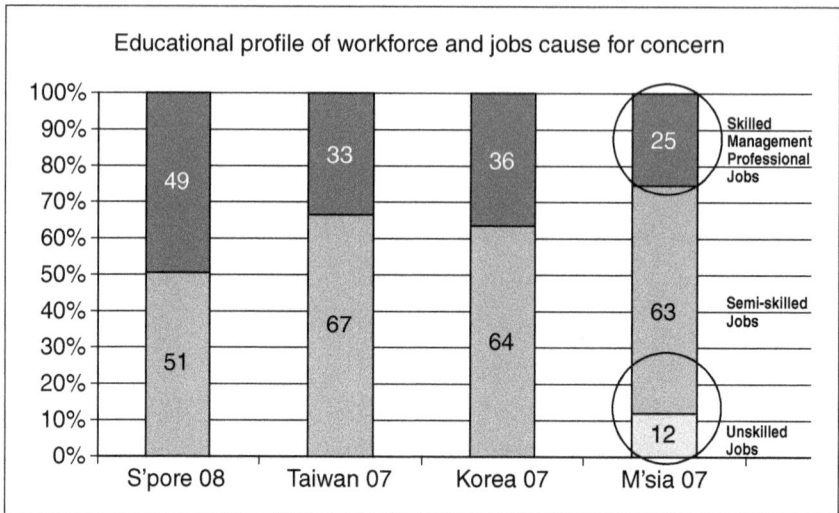

Educational profile of workforce and jobs cause for concern

	S'pore 08	Taiwan 07	Korea 07	M'sia 07	
Skilled Management Professional Jobs	49	33	36	25	
Semi-skilled Jobs	51	67	64	63	
Unskilled Jobs				12	

Note: Only 25% of Malaysian jobs are in the higher skill bracket.
Source: NEAC (2010a).

very much wanting. As a consequence, work skills are lacking. There is obviously a need to upgrade skills in many industries as indicated by Figures 2.9 to 2.13.

Interestingly, in the post-1997–98 crisis period, there has been an exodus of skilled expatriates, as shown in Figure 2.14. There was a period during the early and mid-1990s when there were many expatriates coming into the country. But this has been reversed in the more recent period, especially post-2005.

Infrastructure support provided for the sciences has been dismal. There have been some impressive successes in Malaysia in the past, for example, with the Rubber Research Institute of Malaysia (RRIM) and the Palm Oil Research Institute of Malaysia (PORIM), but this has not been sustained. As a consequence, there have been modest infrastructure improvements to support science education, research and development.

R&D investments have also been very modest, with most from state owned enterprises such as Petronas and Proton.

FIGURE 2.13

Need to Upgrade Skills: Low Level of Skills in Most Industries

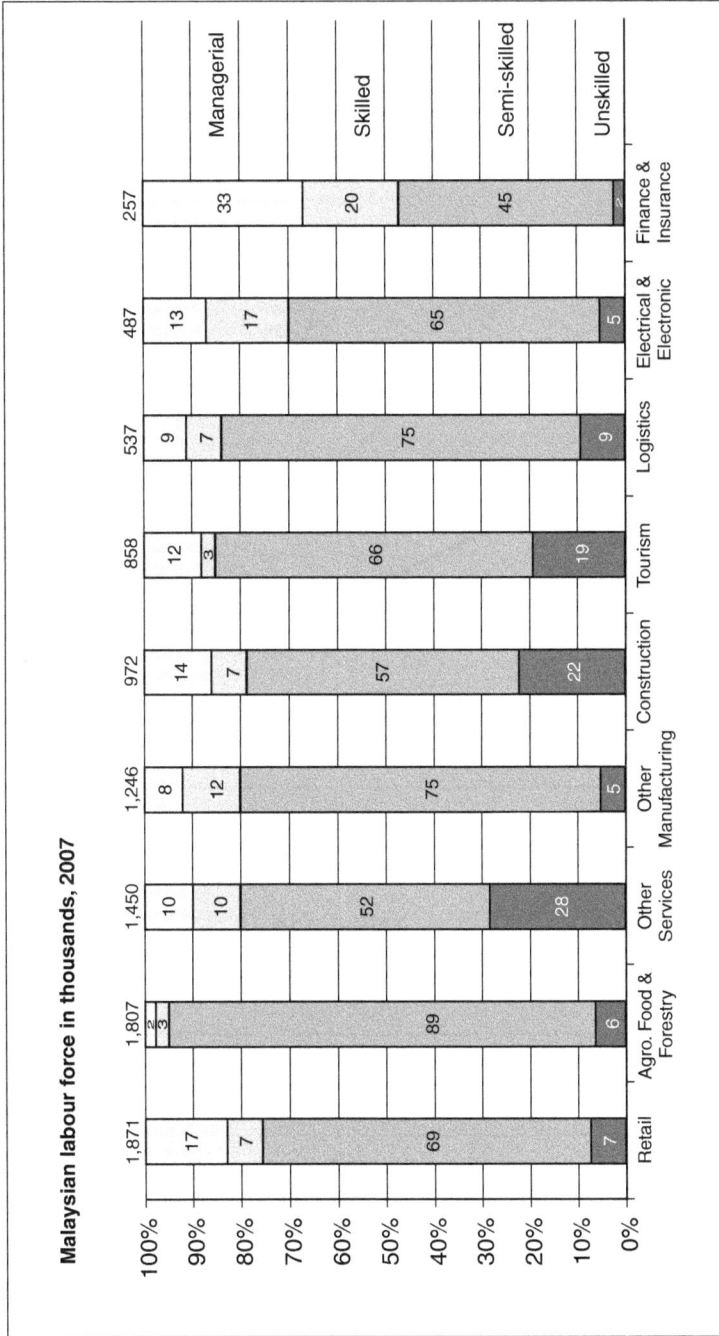

Source: NEAC (2010a).

FIGURE 2.14
Departure of Skilled Expatriates

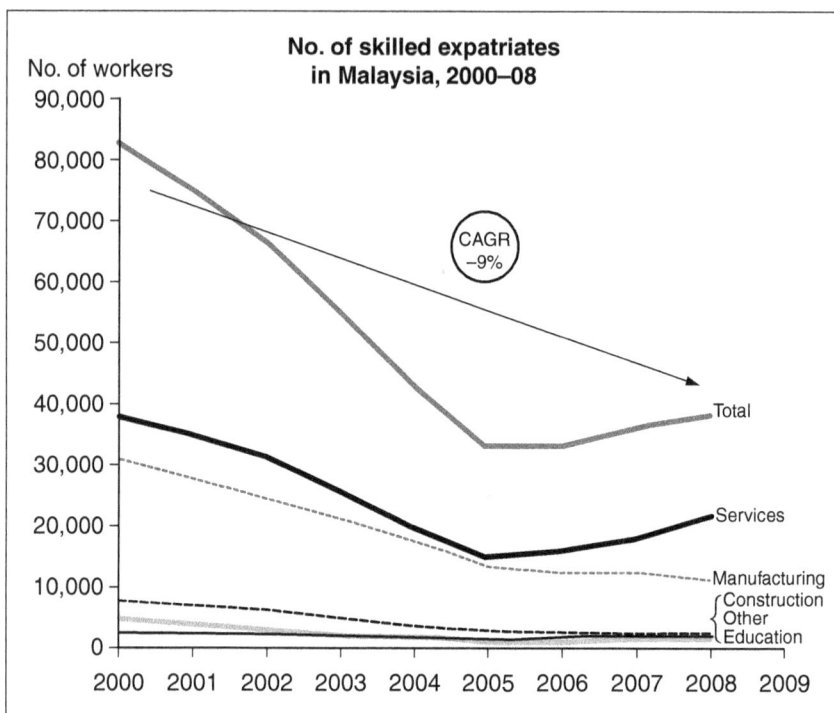

No. of workers

No. of skilled expatriates in Malaysia, 2000–08

CAGR –9%

Total

Services

Manufacturing
Construction
Other
Education

Source: NEAC (2010a).

TABLE 2.14
Infrastructure for the Sciences
(%)

Country Scientific Infrastructure Ranking (Ranking out of 55 countries)

Ranking	1997	2008
China	28	6
Indonesia	35	25
Malaysia	**24**	**28**
India	29	29

Source: NEAC (2010a).

FIGURE 2.15
R&D Investments, 1997, 2007

Expenditure on R&D (% of GDP)

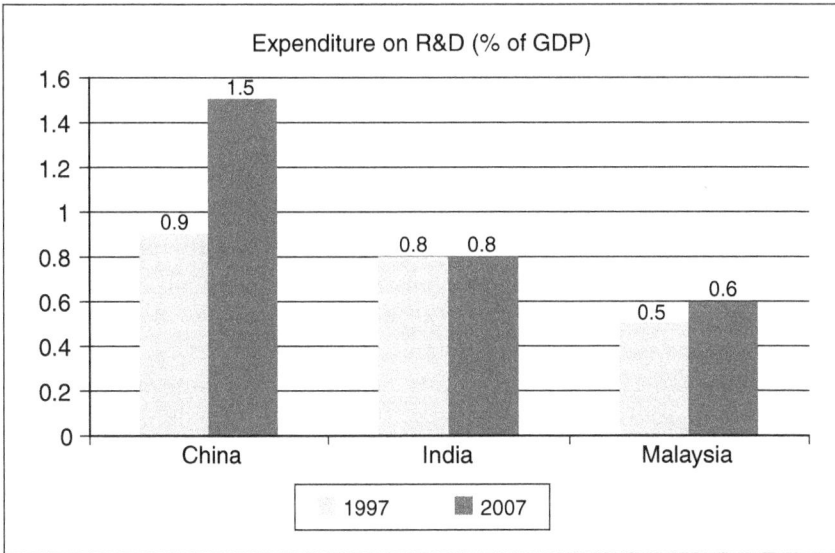

Source: NEAC (2010*a*).

The sources of growth suggest that per capita growth has actually been highest when it was least expected. During the early years of the NEP in the 1970s, per capita growth was actually very high for a variety of reasons; this went on into the first half of the 1980s. Much of this has been sustained by fiscal means. Deficits have, however, not been characteristic of the earlier period. Part of this was because of the advent of oil revenues from the mid-1970s which has given much more fiscal space to the authorities. But a variety of factors, including the change of tax structure after 1984, which was justified in terms of attracting more private investment, have also constrained fiscal space. As a consequence, the government authorities have not been able to do as much as they were able to in the past.

Why was high growth experienced in the so-called MIT economies — Malaysia, Indonesia, and Thailand — after the mid-1980s? The major factor was because of deliberately depreciated exchange rates. Indonesia depreciated its exchange rate thrice in the mid-1980s, from

1984 to 1987. Thailand had a major depreciation in 1985 while the Malaysian ringgit depreciated slightly against the US dollar during 1984–87, from RM2.4 to RM2.7 against the U.S. dollar. But the strength of the yen grew in the period of the "high yen" (endaka) from 1985 to 1995. Thus, the modest depreciation of the ringgit against the U.S. dollar meant a much greater depreciation against the yen. And it was not just against the yen, but also the Korean won, the new Taiwan dollar, the Singapore dollar, the Deutschemark and so on.

Malaysia was able to attract investment, not only from Japan, but also from the first generation East Asian newly industrialized economies. Although not all that successful operationally, SIJORI (the Singapore-Johor-Riau Triangle) was a very important means for the transfer of activities, particularly manufacturing activities and, to a lesser extent, 'lower-level' service activities, from Singapore into its Southeast Asian periphery, particularly into Malaysia, especially Johor.

Why are there serious problems in sustaining growth in Malaysia? One big problem in Malaysia has been its weak industrialist class. It is partly a "chicken and egg" issue, but one consequence of this is that finance has become very dominant. This is true throughout the region, and is not a peculiarly Malaysian phenomenon. The consequences in Malaysia have been quite important, especially in causing the 1997–98 financial crisis (Jomo 1998, 2001).

Another important factor is that recovery efforts, including the counter-cyclical measures in Malaysia, have often been "perverted" by giving "jobs to the boys" with political connections. Government contracts and privatization projects have often been suspected of going to those politically well-connected, rather than on the basis of demonstrated capacities and capabilities. This is partly the reason why government investments have not been as effective in contributing to sustained growth. Government investments can "crowd in", rather than 'crowd out' private investments, though this is not inevitable, but instead has to be well-managed to make sure that is the outcome.

There is now a popular middle income country "cul-de-sac" argument arguing that there is a limit to how much manufacturing growth can sustain rising incomes, summarized in Figure 2.16. Malaysia's high point in manufacturing growth was probably achieved just before the 1997–98 Asian crisis. Ever since then, manufacturing growth has been less impressive or significant for the Malaysian economy and Malaysian economic growth.

FIGURE 2.16
Manufacturing Ceiling?

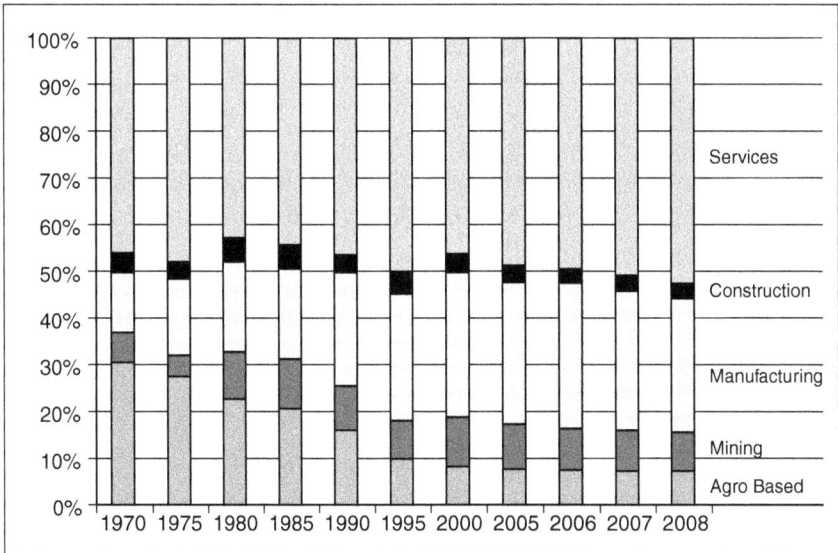

Source: NEAC (2010a).

Another popular argument put forward, especially for Malaysia, is that redistribution has been the problem. But redistribution during the 1970s was associated with high economic growth. So, it is difficult to sustain the argument that redistribution has been subverting growth. It is more useful to look at what redistribution measures have taken place to understand how they may have subverted growth, rather than just accepting the blanket argument that redistribution is bad for growth.

Looking at the post-war European economies, and the social market economy in Germany, the welfare state and redistribution were actually very important for growth. For example, the success of Finland in recent years in education policy and redistribution have been very important for sustaining growth efforts. Care has to be exercised to not 'throw the baby out with the bath water' when it comes to redistribution, and to recognize that wasteful political patronage, which is ostensibly ethnic, may have undermined growth.

As a consequence of this, the rentiers rule. There is a tendency to use the term "rent-seeking" essentially as a polite semi-academic surrogate term for "corruption". The popular use of term "rent-seeking" to refer to corruption is normative and problematic. For example, responding to investment incentives is rent-seeking because it is undertaken to capture rents offered by the state to invest in a particular area. Or consider what Michael Porter means by securing "competitive advantage". The point is to capture a niche (monopoly) position within the economy or industry which allows for profits to be "maximized" by capturing associated rents. In other words, profit maximization, in and of itself (since there is only a notional "normal profit rate"), is precisely about capturing rents of some kind or other, including the so-called producer surplus.

Rent-seeking is not necessarily debilitating and wasteful, but rather, is the basis for profit maximization in any situation other than textbook perfect competition. In Korea and many other economies, rent-seeking ensures that investors and entrepreneurs responded to incentives given to develop and transform economies much faster than they would otherwise have transformed by themselves. In this sense, there was nothing necessarily debilitating or wasteful unless not well conceived or structured.

What is the problem then? The problem may be more usefully associated with clientelism. Clientelism is undoubtedly a problem in many societies which, in Malaysia, takes a particular ethnic and political hue. In other societies, it takes on other hues.

A quick comparison reveals how Southeast and Northeast Asia have developed differently. At the outset, Southeast Asia's development has been inferior to that of Northeast Asia's. If you look at growth rates before the Asian crisis, Southeast Asia was averaging about 6 per cent while Northeast Asia was averaging about 8 per cent. A two per cent difference extended over about a quarter of a century is very significant for the economic development rates in the two East Asian regions. Another difference is that Southeast Asia's population was growing at a much faster rate than Northeast Asia's. As a consequence, the 2 per cent gap became almost 3 per cent on a per capita basis.

Another important factor, of course, is that Southeast Asia began on a more unequal footing. Northeast Asia had post-war land reforms, which enabled them to become more stakeholder economies. Southeast Asia has also been much more reliant than Northeast Asia on foreign direct investment. In Northeast Asia, before the end of the last century, FDI accounted for less than 2 per cent of gross domestic capital formation. In Southeast Asia, FDI has generally averaged more than the developing country average of about 5 to 6 per cent. In Malaysia, it was long in the double digits. Of course, in Singapore, FDI has been much higher, partly for political and strategic reasons. Privileging FDI in Malaysia has become quite problematic as high levels of FDI have basically meant limited manufacturing capabilities and capacities, with domestic industrialization becoming more reliant on foreign capital, markets, technology and management, and hence, less sustainable.

Also, there has been less policy space for reasons mentioned earlier. Malaysia has a weak industrialist class. In the absence of a strong industrial class, it has been financial interests — financial rentiers, as Keynes put it — who have become more dominant in influencing policy.

Going back to the "middle-income trap" hypothesis, it is a Latin American fable as Latin America achieved much higher incomes than Southeast Asia much earlier. However, they have not been able to make much progress in recent decades. For two to three decades, they were told that their problem was that their economies were not sufficiently liberalized or globalized. So, in the last three decades, Latin American countries have opened their economies, and not only in terms of trade. Their capital accounts have been opened, and foreign investment has been encouraged.

In spite of these measures, there has not been significant progress in Latin America compared to East Asia since the 1980s. In fact, much of the limited industrial capacities developed in the earlier period were considered "bad" and have actually been lost in the process. In the aftermath of the most recent crisis since 2007–08, there is now a two-track recovery in which rich countries are becoming more protectionist, and developing countries can no longer rely on export-oriented growth, but have limited domestic markets which they cannot easily turn back to. It is not easy to switch policies at will, e.g., WTO trade commitments cannot be reversed. Capacities have already been developed in many developing economies for export orientation, but many parts of the world, including Southeast Asia, are now being told to rely less on export-led growth.

There is little strong empirical basis for the claim that productivity trends have not kept up with wage trends; productivity itself has not been the issue. In many developing countries, the subsistence wage is the prevailing wage rate floor in the Arthur Lewis sense. In industrial economies, workers were able to capture part of their productivity gains in the form of higher wages or remuneration, at least until recently. But in developing countries, with mass unemployment, there is less pressure to push up wages due to weak unions, etc. So, for example, China has recently seen significant real wage increases, not only due to deliberate government policy, including the renminbi or yuan appreciation of recent years, but also because labour supplies have been exhausted and skill requirements are going up as China moves rapidly into higher value-added production.

Likewise, Malaysia and Thailand have seen an increase in wage rates after full employment was achieved in the 1990s. Productivity and wage rates are not directly related, as suggested by conventional economic theory. (Malaysia is not considered a high-cost destination for investment. In fact, in the last decade, Kuala Lumpur came to be considered a lower cost investment location than Bangkok.)

One big problem in Southeast Asia generally (Singapore is an important exception) is the lack of explicit industrial policy. Where it exists in the region, industrial policy has been weak or compromised. There have been efforts at formulating industrial policy, e.g., in Malaysia, but they have not been sustained or well implemented. As a consequence, a strong industrial capitalist class is absent.

One important measure to break out of the "middle income trap" would be the formulation and implementation of effective and sustained industrial policy. Industrial policy — or more accurately, investment and technology policy — is not only relevant to the manufacturing sector. Industrial policy, for example, could be used to develop high-end services as well. But all these are not going to emerge spontaneously. They would need to be deliberately developed through a variety of interventions — not just one-shot interventions, but rather, well-designed, coherent and sustained interventions. But such sustained interventions are often associated with protracted, dirigiste government rule. In Malaysia, protracted rule has certainly been present: the ruling coalition has ruled since independence. But unfortunately, there has not been a corresponding sustainability of policy priorities or implementation.

In conclusion, this chapter has presented an alternative view of the challenges Malaysia is facing. The Malaysian economy and society have achieved significant progress in past decades. Many popular bogeys, often mentioned in the discourse on Malaysia, need to be re-examined. There is a critical need to re-examine the claim that it is stuck in a "middle-income country trap" — as suggested in the last decade by the World Bank for Latin America and elsewhere. Instead, one has to look at what underlies the economic and social phenomena associated with the alleged "middle-income country trap" problem from a historical and policy perspective.

REFERENCES

Ghani, Ejaz, Homi Kharas, Aaron Flaaen, and Saurabh Mishra. *How to Avoid Middle Income Traps?* World Bank, Washington, D.C., 2009.

Jomo K.S. *Malaysian Eclipse*. London: Zed Books, 2001.

———. *M Way: Mahathir's Economic Legacy*. Kuala Lumpur: Forum, 2004.

Jomo K.S., ed. *Privatizing Malaysia: Rents, Rhetoric, Realities*. Boulder: Westview Press, 1995.

———. *Tigers in Trouble*. Hongkong: University of Hongkong Press, 1998.

———. *After The Storm: Crisis, Recovery and Sustaining Development in East Asia*. Singapore: Singapore University Press, 2004.

———. *Malaysian Industrial Policy*. Singapore: Singapore University Press, and Honolulu: University of Hawaii Press, 2007.

Jomo K.S. and Wee Chong Hui. *Malaysia@50 Disparities, Policies, Development*. Singapore: World Scientific Publishing, 2014.

Khan, Mushtaq, and Jomo K.S., eds. *Rents, Rent-Seeking and Economic Development: Theory and the Asian Evidence*. Cambridge: Cambridge University Press, 2000.

Khong How Ling with Jomo K.S. *Labour Market Segmentation in Malaysian Services*. Singapore: National University of Singapore Press, 2010.

Malaysia. *The Second Malaysia Plan, 1971–1975*. Kuala Lumpur: Economic Planning Unit, 1971.

———. *Mid-Term Review of the Second Malaysia Plan, 1971–1975*. Kuala Lumpur: Economic Planning Unit, 1973.

————. *The Third Malaysia Plan, 1976–1980*. Kuala Lumpur: Economic Planning Unit, 1976.

————. *Mid-Term Review of the Third Malaysia Plan, 1976–1980*. Kuala Lumpur: Economic Planning Unit, 1979.

————. *The Fourth Malaysia Plan, 1981–1985*. Kuala Lumpur: Economic Planning Unit, 1981.

————. *Mid-Term Review of the Fourth Malaysia Plan, 1981–1985*. Kuala Lumpur: Economic Planning Unit, 1984.

————. *The Fifth Malaysia Plan, 1986–1990*. Kuala Lumpur: Economic Planning Unit, 1986.

————. *Mid-Term Review of the Fifth Malaysia Plan, 1986–1990*. Kuala Lumpur: Economic Planning Unit, 1989.

————. *The Sixth Malaysia Plan, 1991–1995*. Kuala Lumpur: Economic Planning Unit, 1991*a*.

————. *The Second Outline Perspective Plan, 1991–2000*. Kuala Lumpur: Economic Planning Unit, 1991*b*.

————. *Mid-Term Review of the Sixth Malaysia Plan, 1991–1995*. Kuala Lumpur: Economic Planning Unit, 1994.

————. *The Seventh Malaysia Plan, 1996–2000*. Kuala Lumpur: Economic Planning Unit, 1996.

————. *Mid-Term Review of the Seventh Malaysia Plan, 1996–2000*. Kuala Lumpur: Economic Planning Unit, 1999.

————. *The Third Outline Perspective Plan, 2001–2010*. Putrajaya: Economic Planning Unit, 2001*a*.

————. *The Eighth Malaysia Plan, 2001–2005*. Putrajaya: Economic Planning Unit, 2001*b*.

————. *Mid-Term Review of the Eighth Malaysia Plan, 2001–2005*. Putrajaya: Economic Planning Unit, 2003.

————. *The Ninth Malaysia Plan, 2006–2010*. Putrajaya: Economic Planning Unit, 2006.

————. *Mid-Term Review of the Ninth Malaysia Plan, 2006–2010*. Putrajaya: Economic Planning Unit, 2008.

————. *The Tenth Malaysia Plan, 2011–2015*. Putrajaya: Economic Planning Unit, 2010.

Malaysia, Bank Negara Malaysia. *Annual Report*, various issues. Kuala Lumpur: Bank Negara Malaysia, various years.

————. *Monthly Statistical Bulletin*, various issues. Kuala Lumpur: Bank Negara Malaysia, various years.

Malaysia, Department of Statistics. *Labour Force Survey Report*, various issues. Kuala Lumpur: Department of Statistics, various years.

————. *Labour and Manpower Report*, various issues. Kuala Lumpur: Department of Statistics, various years.

Malaysia, Ministry of Finance. *Economic Report*, various issues. Kuala Lumpur: Ministry of Finance, various years.

NEAC. *New Economic Model for Malaysia: Part I.* Kuala Lumpur: Putrajaya, National Economic Advisory Council, 2010*a*.

————. *New Economic Model for Malaysia: Part II: Market Friendly and Transparent Affirmative Action.* Processed. Kuala Lumpur: Putrajaya, National Economic Advisory Council, 2010*b*.

Wong Sook Ching and Jomo K.S. with Chin Kok Fay. *Malaysian "Bail-Outs"? Capital Controls, Restructuring and Recovery in Malaysia.* Singapore: Singapore University Press, 2005.

World Bank. *Malaysia: Structural Change and Stabilization.* Washington, D.C.: World Bank, 1983.

PART I

Economic Issues

3

MALAYSIA'S ROUTE TO MIDDLE INCOME STATUS

Rajah Rasiah

Introduction

By the time the World Bank started to classify countries by per capita incomes into low, middle and high income countries in the 1980s, Malaysia was already a middle income country. The World Bank used Gross National Income (GNI) per capita of US$1,006–3,975 and US$3,976–12,275 in 2010 to classify countries into lower and upper middle incomes, respectively (World Bank 2011a). Based on the 1985 World Bank classification, Malaysia was already a middle income country with a per capita income of US$2,161 (US$2,027 in current prices) (World Bank 2011b). With a per capita income of US$5,264 in 1985 prices (US$8,519 in current prices), Malaysia managed to remain an upper middle income country. This chapter attempts to explain how Malaysia became an upper middle income country.

Natural resources (minerals, forest products, and agriculture) and industrialization have been the prime routes taken by developing countries to reach middle income status. Major oil exporters such as the North African, Middle Eastern, and Venezuelan economies have relied almost exclusively on oil exports to record middle incomes. Oil has only been one of the exports that drove income growth in Brazil, Malaysia, and Mexico. The only developing countries to graduate into developed high income economies, i.e., Korea, Singapore, and Taiwan, used manufacturing as the prime path to rapid Gross Domestic Product (GDP) growth. Malaysia was no different from most developing countries as its economy was driven by plantation agriculture and tin mining during the British administration until the New Economic Policy (NEP) was launched. The Malaysian government recognized that the supply of natural resources would not be infinite[1] and that dependence on agriculture alone could be catastrophic if the terms of trade are affected by the fallacy of composition problem.[2] Hence, the approach the government took was to diversify primary exports and to stimulate manufacturing growth by attracting foreign direct investment (FDI) (Malaysia 1971).

At the time the NEP was introduced, ethnic identification of the economy in Malaysia was sharp as the Bumiputeras populated mainly in the rural areas, the Chinese concentrated in urban business and mining, and the Indians confined to plantation agriculture and urban occupations as labourers. Coming after the bloodshed on 13 May 1969 that had threatened to erupt into an ethnic crisis, the NEP was crafted with the twin goals of alleviating poverty and restructuring the economy to remove ethnic identification. Launched through the Second Malaysia Plan in 1971, the NEP targeted growth and ethnicity as the basis of economic restructuring. The emphasis on each of the broad economic sectors was different with the foreign driven export manufacturing sector, which was largely shielded from ethnic restructuring. Government forays into the economy also evolved periodically, with the focus shifting from the poverty alleviation prong to the creation of a Bumiputera bourgeoisie since the promulgation of the Permodalan Nasional Berhad (PNB) in 1978 (Rasiah 1997).

Economic restructuring also saw government-driven acquisitions of large estate companies from the late 1960s, as Bumiputera nominee companies expanded to replace foreign ownership in agriculture (Saham 1980; Jomo 1986). Except for the crisis years of 1973–75 (high inflation caused by soaring oil prices) and 1985–86 (collapse in GDP growth caused by a sharp fall in oil prices, a rise in debt service as the yen appreciated, and a cyclical downturn in the electronics industry), both rising commodity prices and growth in manufactured exports have helped Malaysia sustain GDP growth rates of at least 6 per cent per annum. The fastest annual GDP growth rates exceeding 8 per cent per annum were achieved over the period 1988–93 when a massive inflow of FDI from Japan, Korea, Singapore, and Taiwan and a devaluation of the Ringgit in 1996 helped expand the manufacturing sector sharply.[3] The government also retracted its pro-national capital policies adopted over the period 1981–95, to renew tax incentives to foreign export-oriented manufacturing firms, which were introduced through the Industrial Master Plan of 1996 (Malaysia 1996).

This chapter seeks to provide evidence to argue that Malaysia has been facing premature deindustrialization since the turn of the millennium. The rest of the chapter is organized as follows: the second section provides a theoretical guide explaining why the Malaysian government focused so much on supporting manufacturing growth; the third section examines the significance of Malaysia's manufacturing sector in comparison with the main market economies of Southeast Asia; the fourth section analyses the growth, trade, and productivity trends in the manufacturing sector; and the final section presents the conclusions and policy implications.

Theoretical Considerations

Since governments' focus in terms of economic development is largely on driving growth to generate employment, alleviate poverty, and raise standards of living, the theoretical issues to consider here are the drivers of economic growth and poverty alleviation, rather than the elevation of the middle income status. Malaysia's efforts to stimulate economic development in the 1960s and 1970s very much emphasized these issues (Malaysia 1971).

Neoclassical economists call for governments to confine their roles to following market signals (relative prices) to provide the infrastructure and security for the development of economic sectors based on factor endowments. While Friedman (1968) and Lucas (1972) have arguably defined the broad neoclassical functioning of economies, Bhagwati (1988) and Krueger (1980) drew the positive implications of removing protection and allowing markets to function for economies to grow. Neoclassical arguments received a boost when the World Bank, in 1993, called for the emulation of the liberal approach used by the Southeast Asian high performing economies, arguing that the interventionist path of the Northeast Asian high performing economies was neither desirable nor possible because of a changing global environment. This study has since been criticized for its misleading use of evidence and biased conclusions (Fishlow et al. 1994; Rasiah and Ishak 2001). The Malaysian experience shows that liberalization has generally worked only in circumstances of unclear and ethnic-based interventions without a regulatory framework to meet performance standards (Rasiah 1995).

Focus on the manufacturing sector as the engine of growth began with the argument over its association with increasing returns that propel not only its own expansion, but also that of other sectors (Young 1928; Kaldor 1957). The primary sectors of agriculture and mining are generally considered the early drivers of economic growth, gradually providing the support for manufacturing and services to evolve (Kaldor 1967). It is considered that as manufacturing evolves, it synergizes the whole economy through its increasing returns activities (Reinert 2007). Although Rowthorn and Wells (1987) made the observation that at some point services will take over as the leading component of GDP, they maintained that positive deindustrialization is associated with continuously rising productivity gains in the manufacturing sector despite its relative decrease in GDP share.

A parallel argument, focused on raising agricultural productivity, was articulated by Lewis (1954). Lewis (1954) and Myrdal (1957) advanced the "two-sector surplus labour" model, modified later by Fei and Ranis (1964) and Jorgenson (1967), to explain how differences in returns drive movement of surplus labour from agriculture to manufacturing. This process of self-sustaining growth is assumed to continue until all surplus agricultural labour is absorbed by the expanding industrial sector (Lewis 1954).

In contrast, Kuznets (1965, 1966), Chenery (1979) and Syrquin (1988) argued that a set of interrelated demographic changes in the economic structure are necessary to affect a transition from a traditional economic system to a modern one. With the shift from agricultural to industrial production, these include the steady accumulation of physical and human capital, the change in consumer demands from emphasis on food and basic necessities to diverse manufactured goods and services, and from rural development to urbanization.

Against the aforementioned arguments, the dependency school[4] called for a delinking from the capitalist system because of its so-called imperialistic exploitation, which causes the underdevelopment of developing countries (Baran 1962; Frank 1966; Amin 1976). The underdevelopment thesis, explained by capitalist exploitation, became popular following the failure of several developing countries to generate significant levels of GDP growth despite increasing exports of agricultural commodities (Singer 1950; Prebisch 1950). This came to be known as the Singer-Prebisch hypothesis and was predicated on the following terms of trade between agricultural and manufactured products. Sarker and Singer (1991) subsequently found that developing countries had substantially diversified exports to include light manufacturing and yet continued to face falling terms of trade. The fallacy of composition, or the Singer-Sarker thesis, was avoided by some countries by focusing on raising value added through technical change and diversification (Rasiah, Osman and Alavi 2000).

Although the share of agriculture in developed economies has fallen with long term growth owing to structural change towards other activities (Kuznets 1966; Chenery and Syrquin 1975; Maddison 1989), governments have continuously earmarked the sector to alleviate poverty and ensure sufficient supply of essential staples through technological upgrading. Also, as with the positive deindustrialization articulated by Rowthorn and Wells (1987), a productive focus on agriculture would simply require that agricultural productivity rises despite a relative fall in its contribution to GDP. Even China has experienced sustained growth in agricultural productivity over the period 1980 until 2010, despite the gradual fall in the sector's contribution to GDP (Rasiah, Kong and Zhang 2011).

Hence, we analyse in the remaining sections the drivers of per capita income growth by focusing on government efforts to stimulate GDP growth in Malaysia. Since the primary sectors drove early growth in Malaysia, followed by manufacturing, the initial focus in the chapter will be on agriculture and manufacturing, before moving on to examine the services sector. The contribution of mining and quarry has been important, but has emerged more as a complimentary sector cushioning GDP growth, especially during times of crisis.

Economic Growth and Structural Change

Malaysia has undergone considerable structural change since independence, which has helped raise the country's per capita income in trends over the period 1960–2010. Four major developments are important in explaining the sustained increase in per capita income. First, the government targeted agriculture to alleviate poverty, to eliminate division of the economy along ethnic lines, and to encourage Bumiputera equity participation in the corporate sector. Second, manufacturing was identified and promoted as the chief engine of economic growth. Third, foreign capital was successfully stimulated to promote export manufacturing. Fourth, mineral resources — tin until 1980 and petroleum and gas thereafter — played an important role in boosting national GDP, especially bailing out the country during crises.

Despite their gigantic contribution to the national economy in the nineteenth and twentieth centuries (Jomo 1986), tin and rubber had declined in importance since 1980, following the collapse of Malaysian Mining Corporation (Maminco) in 1980 and a sharp fall in commodity prices in the early 1980s (Jomo 1990a, 1990b). Agricultural value added grew much more over the period 2000–09 than in 1990–2000, because of efforts taken to reduce burgeoning food imports (see Table 3.1). Also, assisted by the opening of new wells off Terengganu and the second oil crisis of 1979, petroleum and gas became the main mineral exports from 1980.

TABLE 3.1
Sectoral GDP Growth, Malaysia, 1990–2009

	1990–94	1995–99	2000–04	2005–09
Agriculture	0.4	0.7	3.3	2.8
Mining	2.7	3.0	3.2	−1.3
Manufacturing	11.7	5.9	4.5	0.2
Electricity, gas, and water	14.9	4.8	5.4	2.8
Construction	13.0	−1.7	1.6	4.2
Trade	12.8	3.8	4.2	7.7
Transport and communication	11.4	5.7	5.6	5.9
Finance[a]	16.0	9.6	5.9	8.1
Public administration	5.7	4.5	5.8	6.9
Others[b]	10.6	4.9	4.1	4.9
GDP	9.4	3.8	4.6	3.8

Notes:
[a] – refers to finance, insurance, real estate, and business services;
[b] – refers to community, social and personal services, producers of private non-profit services and domestic services of households including owner-occupied dwellings.
Source: Asian Development Bank (2010).

Manufacturing overtook agriculture to become the leading propeller of GDP among the primary and secondary sectors in 1988 (Rasiah 2011). The swiftest growth in manufacturing was achieved over the period 1971–94. However, average annual manufacturing growth fell from 11.7 per cent in 1990–94 to 5.9 per cent in 1995–99 and 4.8 per cent in 2000–05 (see Table 3.1). The contribution of manufacturing, which had risen from 24.6 per cent in 1990 to 30.9 per cent in 2000, fell gradually to 30.1 per cent in 2007 (see Table 3.2). Unless institutional change helps upgrade the manufacturing sector, it is expected to contract further.

The services sector recorded the biggest expansion as its share in GDP grew from 31.6 per cent in 1990 to 46.0 per cent in 2009 (see Table 3.2). The government's efforts to target the services sector were initially sporadic and confined to infrastructure development (including health and education), transport and telecommunications, trade promotion, and banking and finance. Government administration has been growing strongly since 1971. However, because the inter-sectoral dynamics of structural change has not evolved sufficiently well, the expansion in services is unlikely to produce the synergies required to transform its role to a dynamic one. Apart from investment forays into infrastructure, telecommunications, and banking services development abroad, the services sector is not a major foreign exchange earner. The emphasis on research and development (R&D), human capital upgrading, and upgrading of logistics coordination must be raised to connect with the primary and secondary sectors are critical to achieve

TABLE 3.2
Structure of GDP, Malaysia, 1970–2009
(%)

	1970	1975	1980	1985	1990	1995	2000	2005	2009
Agriculture	29.0	27.7	22.9	20.8	15.2	12.9	8.6	8.4	9.5
Mining	13.7	4.6	10.1	10.5	11.8	6.2	10.6	14.4	12.9
Manufacturing	13.9	16.4	19.6	19.7	24.2	26.4	30.9	29.6	26.6
Construction	3.5	3.8	4.6	4.8	3.5	4.5	3.4	2.7	2.6
Utilities	0.3	2.5	2.7	0.7	2.8	3.1	2.5	2.4	2.4
Services	39.6	45.0	40.1	43.5	42.5	46.9	44.0	42.5	46.0
GDP	100	100	100	100	100	100	100	100	100

Source: Malaysia (1971–2011).

this. Nevertheless, the services sector has performed remarkably well as
a complementary sector in boosting the growth of the other sectors.

From its 60 per cent contribution in 1957, agriculture remained
the main employment generator in Malaysia until around 1990 when
services took over as the lead job creator (see Table 3.3). Manufacturing
overtook agriculture around 1995 to become the next biggest employment
generator in Malaysia, but its overall contribution has started to fall
from its peak in 2000.

Rapid inter-sectoral structural change also took place with exports.
Agriculture still accounted for 57 per cent of Malaysian exports in
1970, but its share in total exports fell dramatically to its trough of
3.7 per cent in 2000, before rising again to 2.8 per cent in 2008 (see
Table 3.4). Manufactured exports made the biggest expansion, rising
from 11.1 per cent of the total in 1970 to reach its peak of 90.1 per
cent in 2000, before falling to 76.2 per cent in 2008. Following soaring
oil prices, mineral exports rose from 21.4 per cent in 1970 to 30.0 per
cent in 1980. However, tin exports plummeted after their peak in 1980
(Jomo 1990b; Thoburn 2011).

Although a number of sectors have been important in driving GDP
growth in Malaysia, we focus on the sectors of agriculture, manufacturing,
and services as they have arguably been the most important since
the 1980s. In particular, the diversification of agricultural exports and
expansion in manufacturing has been central to sustaining long term
growth in the country. Since the exhaustion of tin by 1980, petroleum
has played a complimentary role in cushioning the country's trade
balance sheet, especially during times of high prices.

Agriculture

Agriculture contributed to almost 40 per cent of GDP and 60 per cent
of the labour force of Malaysia in 1957, with the sector divided into two
sub-sectors: the more advanced sector, comprising estate-type agriculture,
mining, and commercial enterprises in the rural areas; and the less
advanced peasant sector dominated by smallholdings producing rubber,
copra, rice, and coastal fishing. For most of the 1960s, the advanced
sub-sector was owned and managed mainly by foreign capital. Some
estates were owned by Chinese and Indians who also largely worked
in the tin mines and rubber estates, respectively, whilst the backward
sector was dominated by Malay subsistence farmers (Fisk 1963).

TABLE 3.3
Sectoral Employment Structure, Malaysia, 1970–2009

Sector	1970	1975	1980	1985	1990	1995	2000	2005	2009
Agriculture	53.5	49.3	39.7	35.7	26.0	19.0	16.0	12.9	12.0
Mining and Quarrying	2.6	2.2	1.7	1.1	0.6	0.5	0.5	0.4	0.4
Manufacturing	8.7	10.1	15.7	15.1	19.9	25.7	27.1	28.7	28.8
Construction	2.7	2.9	5.6	6.9	6.3	8.9	9.2	7.0	6.6
Services*	20.5	22.5	23.6	26.2	34.5	35.1	37.2	51.0	52.6
Employment ('000)	3,340	3,928	4,817	5,625	6,686	8,024	8,547	10,895	11,609

Note: * – includes gas, water and electricity.
Source: Malaysia (1971–2011); adapted from Osman, Pazim and Rasiah (2011).

TABLE 3.4
Sectoral Export Structure, Malaysia, 1970–2008
(%)

	1970	1975	1980	1985	1990	1995	2000	2005	2008
Agriculture	57.0	49.8	39.9	30.2	19.1	9.3	3.7	7.1	9.6
Mining	21.4	18.6	30.0	29.6	15.9	5.0	6.1	9.3	13.7
Manufacturing	11.1	20.9	21.8	32.7	58.8	84.2	90.1	81.6	76.2
Others*	10.5	10.6	8.3	7.4	6.2	1.4	0.1	2.0	0.5
Total (MYR Billion)	5.6	10.2	30.7	42.5	88.7	204.0	427.0	552.1	624.5

Note: * – includes unclassified agricultural, mining and manufactured goods and services.
Source: Malaysia (1971–2011).

Rural development programmes targeted at poverty alleviation dominated agriculture in the 1960s. The Rural Industry and Smallholders Development Authority (RISDA), Federal Land Development Authority (FELDA), Federal Land Consolidation and Rehabilitation Authority (FELCRA), State Economic Development Corporations (SEDCs), State Land Development Board (SLDB) and State Agricultural Development Corporation (SADC) started sometime in the 1960s, to target poverty alleviation through agricultural development and settlement. Of these, FELDA has been the biggest land development and settlement agency in the country.[5] The government agricultural development programmes aimed at increasing the incomes of farmers — mostly Bumiputeras — were enhanced by in-situ Integrated Agricultural Development Projects (IADPs) (Osman, Pazim and Rasiah 2011).

Figure 3.1 shows the breakdown of the main agricultural policy thrusts since the 1950s. This was the period when the economy depended heavily on the primary sectors, and its productivity created surpluses for exports to support the rest of the economy, including manufacturing. A significant source of government revenue came from direct and indirect taxation of primary products, which helped finance infrastructure development and maintenance. The second and third phases in the 1960s and 1970s targeted rural development, following government efforts to achieve the goals of NEP.

Since the Fifth Malaysia Plan (Malaysia 1986), the government has initiated longer term agricultural policies as a guideline for the future growth and development of the agricultural sector (see Table 3.5). The First National Agricultural Policy (NAP1) of 1984–91 was drafted to plug the gaps left behind by the NEP, to eradicate poverty and sluggish performance of the agricultural sector. The underlying objective was "maximizing income from agriculture through the efficient utilization of the country's resources" (Malaysia 1984, p. 4), which was to be achieved through raising farm productivity, expanding production of traditional export crops, development and promotion of potential export crops, development and expanding production of food and agricultural-industrial crops, and achievement of at least 80 per cent self-sufficiency in domestic food production through the opening up of new land schemes, expansion of in-situ development projects, provision of physical infrastructure, provision of support services and incentives and increased cooperation between public and private operators.

TABLE 3.5
Agricultural Development Expenditure, Malaysia, 1991–2009
(RM million)

Programme	5MP 1986–90	6MP 1991–95	7MP 1996–2000	8MP 2001–05	9MP 2006–10
New Land Development	2,117.5	1,184.0	475.9	–	–
Regional Development	657.1	930.5	807.0	1,059.9	1,754.9
In-situ Land Development[1]	2,669.3	3,019.6	2,941.9	1,629.7	2,613.7
Forestry	120.8	156.4	143.8	199.6	251.5
Fishery	264.4	370.0	465.3	663.8	798.8
Livestock	130.9	191.4	176.3	202.8	519.8
Support Services[2]	1,011.8	1,282.5	354.3	1,305.8	2,558.0
Irrigation and Drainage	77.2	844.6	1,929.9	780.0	1,458.1
Other Programmes	239.3	236.2	844.9	366.3	606.5
TOTAL	7,325.0	8,215.2	8,139.3	6,207.9	11,435.0
Agriculture as % of total	11.8	7.0	3.7	4.6	5.7

Notes:
[1] Includes IADPs, replanting scheme and land consolidation and rehabilitation programmes;
[2] Includes agricultural credit, R&D (excluding those under IRPAs), marketing and other services.
Source: Malaysia Plans (various issues).

Government expenditure allocated for the agricultural sector represented a sizeable component of the total budget, especially during the earlier periods. Table 3.5 shows federal government development expenditure devoted to agriculture from 1986 to 2010. Agricultural expenditure accounted for 11.8 per cent in the Fifth Malaysia Plan, going down to 3.7 per cent in the Seventh Malaysia Plan, before rising to 5.7 per cent in the Ninth Malaysia Plan. In nominal prices, the allocation in the Ninth Malaysia Plan (MYR11.4 billion) almost doubled over the Eighth Malaysia Plan (RM6.2 billion).

The third phase, between the 1980s and 1990s, was targeted at integrating agriculture into the macroeconomy through export-oriented industrialization and the First National Agricultural Policy (NAP1) (see Figure 3.1). Over this period, the incidence of poverty declined further but income inequality increased. Concerns over food security, agricultural productivity, and sustainability also rose in this period. Malaysian agriculture entered the third phase in 1998 with New Agriculture. Under pressure to improve economic efficiency, the government promoted the application of biotechnology to strengthen

FIGURE 3.1
Agricultural Policies, Malaysia, 1950–2010

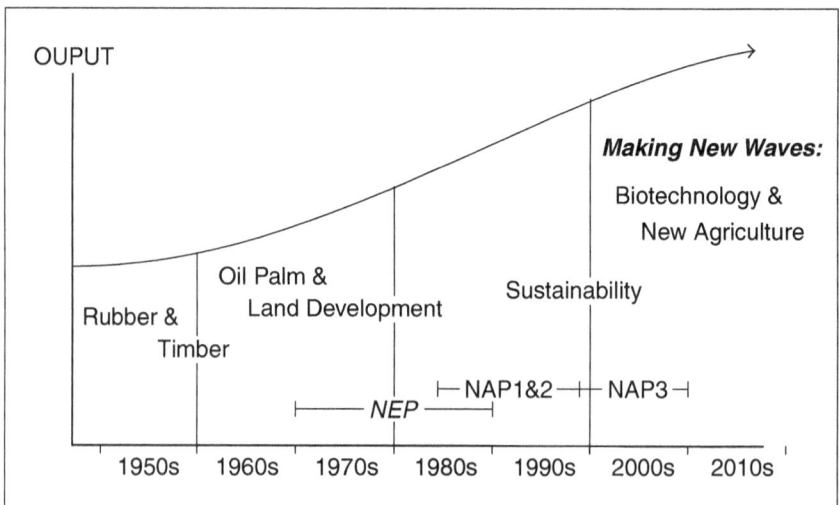

Source: Osman, Pazim and Rasiah (2011), p. 65; adapted and expanded from Timmer (1988).

market linkages and competitiveness, and introduced instruments to integrate rural-urban sectors. Osman, Pazim, and Rasiah (2011) consider the third phase as the nurturing for the launching of the fourth phase around 2003, where agriculture was expected to be modernized enough to be integrated horizontally with industry. According to Timmer (1988), the link between agriculture and industry would be horizontal in this mature phase. While some might claim that this maturity will be achieved with Vision 2020, the evidence is not very convincing. Agricultural output has risen, but the rise has been slow and industry has been stagnant since 2000.

The allocation of new land for development ceased after the Seventh Malaysia Plan, owing to its exhaustion. In the earlier plan periods, big allocations went to land development, but in the latter plan periods there was a shift in policy toward support services, which included agricultural credits, R&D, marketing, and extension services. Hence, the expenditure allocated for irrigation and flood mitigation has increased many folds since the Fifth Malaysia Plan. Irrigation and drainage has been a very important physical infrastructure input for crop cultivation, especially for rice.

The Second National Agricultural Policy (NAP2), 1992–2010, sought to achieve balanced development between agriculture and the other sectors of the economy, wider participation by the Bumiputeras in modern and commercial agriculture, agribusiness and agricultural trade, and address sustainable development. NAP2 was replaced by the NAP3 (1998–2010), as the government sought to ameliorate burgeoning food imports (Malaysia 1999, p. 11), enhance food security, increase the productivity and competitiveness of the sector, deepen linkages with other sectors, create new sources of growth for the sector, and promote sustainable development. The NAP3 used two major strategic approaches to achieve these goals — agro-forestry and product-based agro-business.

Export earnings of primary commodities, including minerals, declined over the period 1970–2000 because of falling prices and competition from other exporters, such as Indonesia, Thailand, and Vietnam (see Table 3.6). Agricultural exports have faced volatile prices because of unstable world demand and supply. Rubber's contribution to agricultural exports fell from 53.3 per cent in 1970 to 13.4 per cent in 2008, whereas

TABLE 3.6
Composition of Exports, Malaysia, 1970–2008

	1970	1975	1980	1985	1990	1995	2000	2005	2008
Palm Oil	9.4	25.6	20.4	31.1	26.0	50.9	63.3	49.8	78.1
Rubber	53.3	39.3	37.5	22.6	17.7	22.0	16.6	14.9	13.4
Sawn logs	18.8	13.8	21.2	21.8	23.6	12.1	16.0	6.4	3.3
Others	18.5	21.3	20.8	24.5	32.6	15.0	4.1	28.9	5.2
Total (MYR Billion)	3.2	5.1	12.3	12.9	16.9	19.1	15.6	38.9	60.3

Source: Malaysia, Economic Report (various issues).

that of palm oil rose from 9.4 per cent in 1970 to 78.1 per cent in 2008. The contribution, to total exports, of other agricultural commodities such as coconuts, cocoa, and vegetables fluctuated considerably in this period, reaching high percentages in 1970–90 and 2005, and contracting to less than 10 per cent in 2000 and 2008. Nevertheless, it can be seen that nominal exports of agricultural goods rose sharply in 2005 and 2008, owing to a combination of both rising commodity prices and government promotion of exports through agri-business.

The government tried to transform both the image and the orientation of agriculture towards stimulating higher value-added activities by renaming the Ministry of Agriculture to Ministry of Agriculture and Agro-based Industry (MAABI). The focus has since shifted to the sale and processing of agricultural products to final markets and, within that transformation, to its orientation towards a demand driven sector, including the promotion of sustainable green agriculture. World Bank consultants played an important role by convincing the government to encourage private entrepreneurs to penetrate global value chains linking producers to consumers (World Bank 2007, p. 8). Wong (2007, p. 1) identified two further reasons for this transformation, i.e., agro-food supply chain management (driven by supermarkets), and advancements and application of bio-informatics in linking production with markets.[6]

The agricultural sector in Malaysia specializes in the production of two major types of commodities — agro-industrial and food products. Crude palm oil (CPO) led in the first group, with production rising from 2.6 million tonnes in 1980 to 10.8 million tonnes in 2000, and

15.0 million tonnes in 2005 with a projected expansion of 19.6 million tonnes in 2010 (see Table 3.6). Palm kernel oil came second, with production rising from 1.2 million tonnes in 1985 to 1.9 million tonnes in 2005. The production of pineapples and flowers also increased significantly to 14,000 tonnes and 126.4 million stalks, respectively, in 2005. Production of rubber began to rise from 1.1 million tonnes in 2005, to a forecasted amount of 1.3 million tonnes in 2010, owing to a steep rise in prices. The production of other commodities, such as sawn logs, cocoa, pepper and tobacco, also declined. Agro food has enjoyed a rise in production owing to a steep rise in domestic demand, which include paddy, fruits, vegetables, fisheries and most livestock. Cocoa, coconuts, and eggs were the only exceptions.

Rising incomes drove the expansion of supermarkets in the domestic retail sales of agricultural products.[7] These were new opportunities opened for farmers to diversify into high-value crops, and thus capture some of the value-added being generated by the increasingly sophisticated supply chains and international networks. They also increasingly connected farmers and other stakeholders more directly to changing consumer preference and demand. Wong noted that, "From a policy and institutional standpoint, most government interventions and programmes in Malaysia are invariably overtly 'production-centric' so much so that the farming/production subsystem is not well linked or integrated (and often 'out-of-sync') with the post-harvest subsystem" (Wong 2007, p. 6). According to him, whether this is a boom or not, farmers and stakeholders at different levels of the supply chain depend as much on public policies as on their own ability to be proactive, adaptable, and cooperative.

Productivity levels of estates were higher than those of smallholders, but the gap has narrowed considerably due to government efforts. The productivity of smallholdings was close to 60–80 per cent of estates by 2009 (Osman, Pazim and Rasiah 2011). However, oil palm smallholders produced only around 25 per cent of fresh fruit bunches per hectare per year of what estate output was, in 2009.[8] Irrigated farms also produced double the yield of non-irrigated farms in paddy cultivation.

In the spirit of re-inventing the agricultural sector, it is very pertinent that special emphasis be made to increase farm productivity for all commodities through: (i) enhancement of R&D in plant breeding; (ii) enhancing the adoption of hybrid seeds among farmers; (iii) re-organization of small-sized farms, especially the padi subsector,

TABLE 3.7
Production of Agricultural Commodities, Malaysia, 1980–2010
('000 tonnes)

Commodities	1980	1985	1990	1995	2000	2005	2010[1]
Agro-industrial							
Rubber	1,530.0	1,470	1,291.0	1,106	928	1,124	1,293
Crude Palm Oil	2,575.9	4,123	6,094.6	7,814	10,842	14,961	19,561
Palm Kernel Oil	222.3	1,212	1,844.7	2,396	1,384	1,868	2,570
Sawlogs[2]	27,916	30,956	40,099.0	32,200	23,074	21,334	19,475
Cocoa	36.5	100	247.0	152	70	28	57
Pepper	31.6	19	31.0	17	24.0	19.1	30.0
Pineapples	185.3	153	168.3	178	265.7	407.6	1,106.0
Tobacco	n.a.	9	10.2	10	7.4	14.0	12.0
Flowers[3]	n.a.	n.a.	56.5	113	120.4	126.4	147.3
Food							
Paddy	2,040.2	1,953	2,016.3	2,159	2,141	2,400	3,202
Fruits	n.a.	852	1,530.8	2,191	993.0	1,587	2,555.7
Vegetables	n.a.	184	693.9	793.8	404.0	771	1,133.3
Coconuts[4]	787.5	1,826	1,257.0	1,136.0	475.7	602	660.0
Fisheries	743.7	626	1,003.6	1,306.2	1,454	1,575	2,071
Marine	n.a	575	951.3	1,181.2	1,286	1,325	1,409
Aquaculture	n.a	51	52.3	125.0	168	250	662

Livestock	17.2	17	12.8	15.6	17.5	28.5	45.0
Beef	0.8	0.6	0.8	1.1	0.9	1.5	2.3
Mutton	135.9	164	385.9	647.0	159.8	209.0	241.0
Pork	125.6	251	227.9	305.0	714.3	980.1	1,295.0
Poultry	2,535	3,395	5,505.0	7,750	399.0	443.0	600.0
Eggs[4]	8.3	24	28.9	33.8	29.5	41.1	68.4
Milk[5]							

Notes:
[1] Forecast;
[2] thousand cubic metres;
[3] million stalks;
[4] million units (referred to as copra in 1980 and measured in '000 tonnes);
[5] million litres.

Source: Malaysia (1996, 2001, 2006).

into larger plots through cooperative efforts or the adoption of the Seberang Perak Felcra-model; and (iv) effective application of the Green Revolution (GR) technology and the latest advancement in biotechnology in farming activities.

The amount of land used for the cultivation of various crops indicates the degree of importance of the crop to the Malaysian economy. The total area under the cultivation of major crops amounted to 6.9 million hectares in 2010 (see Table 3.8). As expected, oil palm is the leading crop, occupying 4.6 million hectares (63.4 per cent) of total cultivated land areas (2005) followed by rubber at 1.2 million hectares (20.6 per cent) and paddy at 0.5 million hectares (7.1 per cent). As agricultural development takes its momentum, more lands are required. As shown in Table 3.11, land use for agriculture has increased by 46 per cent within 25 years, that is, from 4.4 million hectares in 1980 to 6.4 million hectares in 2005, and expected to increase further to 6.9 million hectares in 2010.

TABLE 3.8
Agricultural Land Use by Major Crops, Malaysia, 1980–2010
('000 hectares)

Crop	1980	1985	1990	1995	2000	2005	2010[1]
Oil Palm	1,023	1,482	2,029	2,479	3,377	4,049	4,555
Rubber	2,005	1,949	1,823	1,696	1,431	1,250	1,179
Paddy[2]	735	649	683	666	478	452	450
Fruits[3]	105	119	177	244	304	330	375
Coconuts	349	334	314	284	159	180	180
Cocoa	124	303.9	419.8	275	76	33	45
Vegetables	12.8	14.6	31.5	36.3	40	64	86
Tobacco	12.5	16.2	10.2	10.5	15	11	7
Pepper	12.7	5.2	11.5	8.6	13	13	14
TOTAL[4]	4,380	4,952	5,489	5,712	5,893	6,383	6,891

Notes:
[1] Forecast by the Ministry of Agriculture and Agro-Based Industry;
[2] Based on padi parcel;
[3] For 1980, fruits were categorized as orchards (includes bananas, watermelon and pineapple);
[4] Excludes other crops like tea, coffee and herbs as well as aquaculture.
Source: Malaysia (1996, 2001, 2006); reproduced from Osman, Pazim and Rasiah (2011).

Manufacturing

The biggest driver of income growth in Malaysia since the 1980s is manufacturing. Table 3.9 shows average annual growth in value added experienced by the manufacturing industries in Malaysia. Foreign capital has been the prime driver of manufactured exports, as large waves of foreign capital relocated textile and garment, and electric-electronics assembly, and processing plants in Malaysia in the early 1970s. Further waves of foreign capital, with significant inflows from Japan and the Asian Newly Industrialized Economies, helped to further expand export manufacturing.

Although the expansion of manufacturing began from 1971, it was only when the government introduced the Industrial Master Plan (IMP) in 1986 (Malaysia 1986) and the Second Industrial Master Plan (IMP2) in 1996, that the government showed efforts to build meso-organizations to support industrial structural change. The first plan targeted incentives to attract foreign capital and to stimulate training, while the second continued this with the addition of incentives and grants for clustering and R&D activities (Malaysia 1996). Serious shortages in human capital and the failure of the meso-organizations to stimulate knowledge-based activities, such as designing and R&D, undermined the capacity of IMP2 to stimulate industrial deepening (Rasiah 1999).

However, manufacturing growth has slowed down considerably since the turn of the millennium. The government introduced the Third Industrial Master Plan (IMP3) in 2006, which attempted to continue its focus on clustering, with additional support for services. However, the IMP3 neither carried the IMP2 elements of clustering nor addressed the latter's weakness of not comprehending complimentary activities effectively, becoming a weaker instrument than its predecessor (Rasiah 2011). Value added for manufacturing only grew by 0.2 per cent annually, on average, in the period 2005–08 (see Table 3.9). The fastest growing industries in 2005–08 were beverages and footwear, and the resource-based industries of petroleum, coal, and metals. The textile and garment industries faced the biggest contraction in 2000–08, recording an annual average reduction in growth of –11.5 per cent in 2000–05, and –5.1 per cent in 2005–08. The electronics industry, which is Malaysia's largest manufacturing industry, recorded an annual average growth rate of 0.5 per cent in 2000–05 and a reduction of –2.2 per cent in 2005–08.

TABLE 3.9
Manufacturing Value Added Growth, Malaysia, 1979–2008

	1979–85	1985–90	1990–95	1995–2000	2000–05	2005–08
Food	5.5	6.6	12.2	10.7	3.0	8.9
Beverages	-0.3	2.4	-3.0	5.5	20.0	52.6
Tobacco			15.2	-13.7	4.4	1.5
Textiles and garments	4.7	12.8	17.1	6.8	-11.5	-5.1
Footwear (except rubber)	n.a.	n.a.	10.2	7.3	-2.7	14.3
Wood	-4.5	13.1	16.4	3.8	-0.3	-6.8
Furniture and fixtures	n.a.	n.a.	35.8	19.3	2.6	-9.6
Printing, publishing and allied	n.a.	n.a.	17.9	5.1	4.5	1.7
Paper	n.a.	n.a.	20.3	15.0	-3.3	-4.9
Leather	n.a.	n.a.	29.4	-2.4	2.9	-34.9
Rubber	4.2	25.0	13.6	7.6	-1.6	-27.3
Chemical	2.8	7.9	12.5	12.0	12.3	2.8
Petroleum and coal	n.a.	n.a.	25.3	37.4	11.1	17.2
Non-metallic mineral	3.6	7.4	16.7	4.4	1.3	31.2
Basic metal	9.8	5.0	8.7	10.2	4.4	7.6
Fabricated metal			23.9	9.9	1.7	12.6
Machinery	9.0	6.6	26.0	25.3	-16.5	3.8
Electrical machinery	8.0	16.4	26.8	12.1	0.5	-2.2
Transport equipment	9.0	15.0	17.6	6.5	4.6	3.2
Miscellaneous	n.a.	n.a.	21.7	13.9	0.0	-31.5
Manufacturing	8.5	10.2	11.6	5.8	4.9	0.2

Source: Computed from Malaysia (1986, 1991, 1996, 2001, 2007, 2010).

Whereas the contraction of the textiles industry appears as an unavoidable result of the termination of the Multi-Fibre Agreement (MFA) and rising competition from China, India, Vietnam, and the Least Developed Countries (LDCs),[9] the contraction and slowdown in other manufacturing industries are a consequence of slow upgrading.

Interviews show that the picture in early 2009 has worsened, as declining demand in the developed economies, arising out of the banking crisis, has forced down exports from Malaysia.

Trade Performance

This sub-section examines the trade performance of manufacturing. The indices examined are the trade balance, share of imports in domestic demand, export intensity of output, and the shares of manufacturing in overall exports.

The trade balance (TB) index denotes the relative significance of exports against imports and the estimations are shown in Table 3.10. The TB index varies between −1 and 1 with negative balances denoting that imports exceed exports. It can be seen that food and beverage and wood, petroleum, and coal products have enjoyed the highest trade balances over the period 1990–2005 (see Table 3.4). The data shows that the TB improved for most industries over the period 1990–2000 and started to worsen over the period 2000–05. However, other than food and other industries, the remaining industries recorded improvements in their trade balance in 2005–08. The withdrawal of MFA quotas, in 2004, suggests that textiles and garments are likely to face further contraction. The machinery industry enjoyed improvements over the period 1990–2000, with its TB recording a positive index in 2000 and 2008, suggesting that the strategic instruments used to promote the industry following the launch of the Third Industrial Master Plan of 2006 have not been materialized.

The transport equipment industry has enjoyed strong protection, since the promulgation of the heavy Industries Corporation of Malaysia (HICOM) in 1980 and subsequent launching of Proton (Alavi 1996). The government has also approved further domestic automobile manufacturers in Perodua, Naza Motors, Modenas and Inakom. However, the trade balance account of the transport equipment industry has shown little improvement (see Table 3.4). The export value of automotive products from Malaysia rose from US$121 million in 1990, to only US$369 million in 2000 and US$1,154 million in 2008. The commensurate export figures for Indonesia rose from US$22 million in 1990, to US$369 million in 2000 and US$2,783 million in 2008, while those of Thailand rose from US$108 million in 1990, to US$2,417 million in 2000 and US$16,227 million in 2008 (WTO 2009, Table 11.60). Clearly, exports from Thailand and Indonesia have grown significantly faster than exports from Malaysia over the period 1990–2008.

TABLE 3.10
Manufacturing Trade Balance, Malaysia, 1979–2008

Industry	1979	1985	1990	1995	2000	2005	2008
Food and beverage	-0.171	-0.327	0.594	0.641	0.520	0.594	0.159
Textiles and garments	-0.058	0.106	0.082	0.122	0.271	0.082	0.302
Wood	0.913	0.874	0.660	0.491	0.417	0.660	0.854
Chemicals	-0.710	-0.721	-0.635	-0.428	-0.176	-0.635	0.174
Petroleum and coal	n.a.	n.a.	0.512	0.382	0.379	0.512	0.052
Rubber and plastics	0.470	0.113	0.218	0.177	0.106	0.218	0.734
Non-metallic mineral	-0.335	-0.518	-0.464	-0.420	-0.156	-0.464	0.155
Basic metal	0.570	0.252	-0.492	-0.517	-0.393	-0.492	-0.393
Machinery (inc electrical)	-0.069	-0.071	-0.093	-0.019	0.104	-0.093	0.087
Transport equipment	-0.652	-0.624	-0.598	-0.502	-0.518	-0.598	-0.407
Professional and scientific	-0.477	-0.451	-0.385	-0.279	-0.150	-0.385	-0.322
Others	n.a.	n.a.	0.357	0.024	0.223	0.357	0.288

Note: Formula used: (Export-Import)/(Export+Import).
Source: Malaysia (1983–91, 2010); Asian Development Bank (2008).

The results suggest that domestic capabilities seem to have developed more in resource-based industries enjoying natural endowments in the country. However, given that these industries are dependent on finite non-renewable resources, the government will have to gradually reduce overdependence on these industries. A sustained long term strategy of industrial deepening cannot be built on these industries.

Machinery (mainly electric-electronics products) has dominated manufactured exports from Malaysia over the period 1990–2008 (see Table 3.11). Petroleum and coal products enjoyed the next highest share of exports. However, whereas the share of machinery and petroleum products showed an increased over the 2000–05 and a fall subsequently in 2005–08, machinery recorded the opposite, falling in 2005 before rising in 2005–08. Whereas the relative contraction in exports in the 1990s was a consequence of massive expansion in electric and electronics exports, the fall after 2000 was caused by the termination of the MFA and increased exports from China and least developed countries such as Cambodia (Rasiah 2009a).[10]

TABLE 3.11
Composition of Manufacturing Export, Malaysia, 1979–2008

	1979	1985	1990	1995	2000	2005	2008
Food and beverage	0.123	0.127	0.101	0.088	0.044	0.059	0.038
Textiles and garments	0.072	0.100	0.049	0.036	0.027	0.019	0.021
Wood	0.043	0.028	0.122	0.070	0.041	0.035	0.021
Chemicals	0.034	0.033	0.014	0.021	0.030	0.041	0.088
Petroleum and coal	n.a.	n.a.	0.193	0.073	0.098	0.141	0.067
Rubber and plastics	0.016	0.009	0.064	0.054	0.039	0.053	0.027
Non-metallic mineral	0.010	0.011	0.022	0.016	0.014	0.016	0.011
Basic metal	0.307	0.140	0.033	0.029	0.025	0.031	0.017
Machinery (inc electrical)	0.321	0.497	0.341	0.533	0.624	0.541	0.597
Transport equipment	0.033	0.043	0.025	0.029	0.008	0.010	0.020
Professional and scientific	n.a.	n.a.	0.014	0.016	0.020	0.023	0.018
Others	n.a.	n.a.	0.023	0.035	0.030	0.031	0.075

Note: Formula used: Export of the industry divided by total manufactured exports; NA – not available.
Source: Malaysia (1983–90); computed from Asian Development Bank (2008).

Petroleum and coal, beverages, tobacco, and chemicals were the only manufacturing industries to record improvements in labour productivity over the period 2000–05 (see Table 3.12). The productivity

TABLE 3.12
Average Annual Manufacturing Labour Productivity Growth, Malaysia, 1979–2008

	1979–85	1985–90	1990–95	1995–2000	2000–05	2005–08
Food	2.4	2.4	7.5	56.7	−29.8	1.4
Beverages	2.3	3.4	−4.6	3.4	13.1	42.1
Tobacco			−8.0	−4.4	11.5	17.2
Textiles and garments	3.2	0.7	12.5	6.9	−8.8	−2.5
Footwear (except rubber)	n.a.	n.a.	−7.7	−11.2	−1.2	5.9
Wood	−5.7	2.1	5.9	6.6	−1.0	−3.8
Furniture and fixtures	n.a.	n.a.	10.9	8.3	−2.7	−5.5
Printing, publishing and allied	n.a.	n.a.	8.1	4.7	−2.3	−3.4
Paper and paper products	n.a.	n.a.	8.5	6.4	−5.4	−4.4
Leather	n.a.	n.a.	19.1	2.1	2.2	−1.9
Rubber	5.5	7.6	8.5	7.9	−3.8	−1.8
Chemicals	0.1	1.3	5.0	3.2	6.9	−5.2
Petroleum and coal	n.a.	n.a.	10.0	19.9	23.9	−5.6
Non-metallic mineral	−2.0	14.8	7.4	−1.7	−1.1	−8.5
Basic metal	7.2	−5.4	−1.6	9.7	1.4	8.2
Metal			6.4	10.9	−4.9	1.6
Machinery (except electrical)	9.6	−7.6	6.3	29.7	−17.0	−3.4
Electric-electronics	5.9	3.9	12.4	7.9	1.4	0.3
Transport equipment	4.6	8.6	2.6	4.2	−7.8	−1.9
Others	n.a.	n.a.	14.9	10.5	−1.7	12.3
Manufacturing	2.8	8.4	8.4	11.1	−1.4	2.7

Note: Value added computed using 2000 prices; NA – not available.
Source: Computed from Malaysia (1981, 1986, 1991, 1996, 2001, 2007, 2010).

of food products, non-electrical machinery, textiles, and transport equipment shrank considerably in this period. Labour productivity of the electric-electronics industry grew at an annual average of 12.4 per cent in 1990–95, but fell to 7.9 per cent in 1995–2000, and a mere 1.4 per annum in 2000–05. The strong technological synergies offered by multinational corporations in the late 1980s and early 1990s appear to have been undermined by a lack of effective rooting policies for local firms to upgrade to the technology frontier.

There is evidence of an expansion of local suppliers that benefited from dynamic corporate changes, especially in American multinationals.[11] The number of electronics firms in Malaysia engaged in designing and R&D activities only constituted 1.0 per cent of the total in 2007 (Rasiah 2010, p. 310). As the firms failed to evolve technological capabilities to designing and R&D activities in the face of rapid expansion in China and Vietnam, the supplier base began to contract from the late 1990s (Grunsven 2006; Rasiah 2010). The lack of engineers and scientists in particular, has been a glaring problem that has slowed down productivity growth in the industry. For example, Malaysia only had 729 researchers per million people, when there were 7,059 in Singapore and 6,028 in Korea in 2007 (UNESCAP 2009, p. 97).

The declining trend in manufacturing labour productivity growth, with the key export-oriented industries and inward-oriented industry of transport equipment recording either a sharply declining or negative growth rates over the period 2000–08, is a consequence of falling competitiveness arising from slow upgrading. Beverages and tobacco enjoyed the highest productivity growth in 2005–08. Whereas the share of electronics exports from Singapore and Thailand in global exports rose from 7.6 per cent and 1.9 per cent, respectively, in 2000, to 2.0 per cent and 8.1 per cent, respectively, in 2006, the commensurate shares from Malaysia fell from 5.4 per cent in 2000, to 4.7 per cent in 2006 (Rasiah 2009*b*).

Massive inflows of foreign capital into the manufacturing sector also helped reduce the pressure on the government to create jobs (Ariff 1991; Rasiah 1995, 1999). The focus of industrial policy has since shifted towards industrial deepening, as the government attempted to take advantage of low unemployment levels which reached 2.7 per cent in 1995. The Action Plan for industrial Technology Development (APITD) of 1990 helped provide the groundwork for the opening of the Human Resource Development Fund (HRDF), Malaysian Technology

Development Corporation (MTDC), the Malaysia Industry Government High Technology (MIGHT), the cluster-based Second Industrial Master (IMP2) plan, the Multimedia Super Corridor (MSC), and the Multimedia Development Corporation (MDeC) in the 1990s to support technological deepening.[12] The Malaysian Institute of Microelectronics Systems (MIMOS) was also corporatized in the 1990s. Unfortunately, a combination of poor coordination and the lack of performance standards reduced the effectiveness of these instruments to stimulate value addition in the manufacturing sector. Hence, firms approached the government to import foreign labour to sustain their operations, which aggravated further the situation by reducing the pressure to upgrade. The government focus on unskilled labour, over the 1980s and the 1990s, undermined firm-level initiatives to upgrade. These developments led a number of authors to warn that the Malaysian industrialization project may have stalled (Rasiah 1999; Best and Rasiah 2003; Henderson and Phillips 2007).[13]

Services

Despite its complimentary role in the early stages of economic development, no discussion about Malaysia's path to upper middle income status will be complete without an account of the role of the services sector. Not only has the development of roads and railways, transport and telecommunications, education and health, and trade and finance been important to facilitate the evolution of a market economy, Malaysian service operators have also expanded activities abroad, since the 1990s, to earn foreign exchange. Attempts to modernize and internationalize services began in the 1990s, when the government realized that growth in manufacturing was cooling off and pressures were put to liberalize services. In addition, the government's role in managing macro-micro coordination to insulate the primary (particularly agriculture) and manufacturing industries from external shocks has also been critical in ensuring rapid growth.

The government's early focus on services was to develop infrastructure through the development of roads, railways, irrigation, and drainage to support the other sectors. The focus then included education, health, and military in the 1970s, with the proliferation of the NEP objectives of poverty alleviation and ethnic restructuring. The 1960s and 1970s were primarily driven by revenue obtained from exports of rubber and tin expended into these sectors.

The construction of modern highways and bridges dominated the 1980s, which led to technology transfer from foreign firms and the emergence of United Engineering Malaysia (UEM). This firm has subsequently successfully continued highway construction in Malaysia and in a few foreign countries (including India). The expansion of manufacturing in particular led to severe congestion in the 1990s, which was eased through the construction of roads, railways (commuter trains). In addition to meeting the target of reducing congestion and lowering delivery times in manufacturing and agriculture, it also stimulated considerable expansion in construction and services.

As labour shortages intensified and wages rose, the government expanded incentives and grants to attract firms into providing education and training, designing, and R&D services starting in the 1990s for the achievement of APITD's goals. The Multimedia Super Corridor (MSC) and the opening of MDeC in the second half of the 1990s, in the Kelang Valley, was driven at providing the IT infrastructure to stimulate firms' participation in information and communication services. The city of Cyberjaya was developed specifically for this purpose. Malaysia's proficiency in IT services led to Malaysian companies successfully attracting contracts to build IT infrastructure abroad (e.g., in India and Laos). The Knowledge Infrastructure report and strategic plans for improving services through the National Key Results Areas (NKRA) and the Ministerial Key Performance indicators (MKPI) were introduced in 2010 to raise the service delivery system of government (Malaysia 2011). Although these initiatives did attract firms and expand value added, a lack of regulation and coordination on the quality of education and training, and massive imports of unskilled labour from abroad cooled off much of the efforts (Rasiah 1999).

Government services constituted a significant proportion of overall services during the period of 1970–90, when considerable attention was given to poverty alleviation and ethnic restructuring (see Table 3.13). Government services began to fall in significance as wholesale and retail trade, accommodation and restaurants, and finance, insurance, real estate and business services expanded. In addition to offering incomes directly by hiring, government services also included targeting the poor by subsidies during times of crisis (e.g., part of the fiscal stimulus of 2008–09 were distributed to the poor) and through interest free loans to the poor (e.g., through the administration of the Amanah Ikhtiar Malaysia (AIM) programme) (Ragayah 2011).

TABLE 3.13
Contribution to Value Added in Services, Malaysia, 1970–2009
(%)

	1970	1975	1980	1985	1990	1995	2000	2005	2009
Utilities	3.1	4.7	3.6	3.8	4.5	4.9	7.3	6.0	5.2
Trade, accommodation and restaurant	10.1	13.7	14.3	14.6	16.4	18.1	27.4	26.7	27.5
Transport, storage and communication	31.7	28.4	30.2	27.8	26.0	26.9	15.2	14.3	13.8
Finance, insurance, real estate and business	23.8	18.8	20.7	20.6	22.9	24.2	23.2	28.5	29.8
Other private	5.7	6.1	5.7	5.2	4.9	4.9	14.1	11.3	10.5
Government	25.7	28.3	25.6	28.0	25.3	21.0	12.8	13.2	13.2
Total	100.0	100.0	100.0	100.0	100.0	100.0	100.0	100.0	100.0

Source: Compiled from Malaysia, *Economic Report*, various issues.

Stock markets were promoted in 1985 and became an important reservoir for attracting finance for private sector investment in particular. Although excessive deregulation has been part of the cause of stock market crashes when destabilized by external shocks (e.g., Asian Financial crisis of 1997–98) (Jomo 1998; Rasiah 1998), the Central Bank has often intervened prudently to limit losses. Capital controls that helped insulate the country from bearish runs, in both the stock market and the currency market, were instrumental in the recovery from late 1998 (Rasiah 2000). Following the financial crisis of 1997–98, the government decided to increase the size of national banks by forcing a number of them to merge. The directive was to strengthen the capacity of the banks against liberalization trends, as well as for Bank Negara to coordinate its activities better. In addition, the opening up and acquisition of banks in Cambodia and Indonesia led to some reversal in net foreign currency receipts. The finance, insurance, real estate, and business subsectors have since grown strongly to become the leading contributor to GDP among the services sectors over the period 2005–09 (see Table 3.13).

Conclusions and Policy Implications

Malaysia was already a middle income country when the World Bank introduced classifications to differentiate countries by incomes, in the 1980s. Nevertheless, Malaysia has continued to experience a rise in per capita income since the introduction of such a classification, moving into the upper middle income category when the classification was further stratified. Investment into the primary sectors of agriculture and mining dominated early expansion in GDP until the late 1980s, when their role was overtaken by manufacturing in 1988. Manufacturing expanded strongly until 2000, when it began to cool off due to a lack of human capital and embedding support to stimulate firms' participation in high value added activities. Since 2000, the electronics and palm oil related industries in particular, have remained important export earners. Services have since become the most important sector, especially in finance, insurance, real estate, business services, trade, accommodation, and restaurants. The government's focus on services has, since the 1990s, moved from a focus on infrastructure development to expand the knowledge infrastructure.

The government has recognized that the lack of human capital and innovative capacity have restricted the country's progress. However, this realization came sixteen years after these weaknesses were highlighted (Rasiah 1999) and reflects government's obsessive reliance on consultants who vacillated between telling the government that relative prices of the country supported resource-based industries in low value added activities should be maintained (World Bank 1993, 1995) and coordinating the preparation of policy blueprints that contradicted from the outset (e.g. the second industrial master plan of 1996 and the Economic Transformation Plan (ETP) of 2010) without efforts to reinvigorate existing meso organizations such as universities and R&D labs. In fact, the ETP is a new initiative prepared without linkages to the actual structure of the national economy. Unless the government realizes that it must appoint capable Malaysians and have them reform the meso organizations created to stimulate knowledge accumulation, rather than simply rely on experts whose understanding of the national economy is shallow, it will be difficult to orient these organizations towards technological deepening similar to that of Korea, Singapore, and Taiwan. There must also be a clear institutional framework, to impose performance standards on any governance institution (including incentives and grants), introduced to stimulate a structural shift of the national economy to higher value added activities.

Hence, while Malaysia has successfully advanced into an upper middle income country, its efforts to become a high income country appear uncertain. Policy framework must target sectors that require restructuring for technological upgrading, so that their value added will grow fast enough to drive per capita income in the country higher to a developed country's level. With growth of the primary and secondary sectors slowing down, services have become the most important sector since the turn of the millennium. However, for the sector to become a dynamic driver of GDP growth, efforts must be taken to transform its focus into knowledge-based activities, such as designing and R&D services, to support structural change in Malaysia into higher value added activities. Economies have become developed through the advancement of technology either in specific sectors or in the whole economy. Despite policy efforts, the lack of human capital and poorly led R&D organizations have denied the country the knowledge synergies essential to stimulate firms' upgrading to high value added activities. Hence, unless focused technological upgrading policies are implemented and carefully monitored, Malaysia's graduation into a high income country will remain an elusive goal.

NOTES

1. The Dutch disease is the phenomenon referred to when countries are over-dependent on natural resources to the extent of facing underdevelopment as those resources become exhausted.
2. Sarker and Singer (1991) had showed how the fallacy of composition problem leads to falling terms of trade involving agricultural and light manufactured exports from developing economies.
4. FDI inflows to Southeast Asia rose sharply following the Plaza Accord of 1985 that saw their currencies appreciate sharply against the US dollar and the withdrawal of the Generalized System of Preferences from Korea, Singapore and Taiwan in February 1988 (see Rasiah 1988, 1995).
4. There are variations of this model, such as the "dependency model" based on neo-Marxist thinking of capitalist system exploitation, and the "dualistic-development model" based on the notion of dualism between rich and poor groups/regions (see Rasiah 1995a). Some versions of these models enjoy support from anti-globalization analysts (see Lewellen 1995; Anderson et al. 2000; Gray 2000).

5. For example, in the period 1971–80, 866,058 hectares were developed through these programmes, of which FELDA developed 373,705 hectares (43.2 per cent), FELCRA 50,710 hectares (5.8 per cent), RISDA 31,463 hectares (3.6 per cent), other state agencies combined 290,133 hectares (33.5 per cent) and private sector 120,047 hectares (13.9 per cent) (Malaysia 1981, p. 300; cited from Osman, Pazim and Rasiah 2011).

6. The role of supermarkets in transforming global value chains in agriculture is extensively discussed by Dolan and Humphrey (2000) and Rasiah (2004).

7. In the small and fast growing countries of Asia (Taiwan, Korea, Hong Kong, Thailand, Malaysia and the Philippines), their average share of supermarkets in national food retail accounts for around 50–60 per cent (Reardon and Timmer 2005, cited in Wong 2007).

8. The production level of palm oil in Table 3.7 refers to the average (only some 30 per cent of total cultivated area in oil palm belongs to the smallholding sector).

9. Particularly from Cambodia (Rasiah 2009a).

10. A number of Malaysian firms have even relocated manufacturing in Cambodia to access developed markets (see Rasiah 2009a).

11. American multinationals initiated such efforts for their own self expansion (Rasiah 1988, 1994; Narayanan and Lai 2000).

12. Malaysia, Action Plan for Industrial Technology Development, Kuala Lumpur: Ministry of Science, Technology and Environment, 1991; Malaysia, Second Industrial Master Plan 1991–96 (Kuala Lumpur: Ministry of International Trade and Industry, 1991).

13. Rasiah (2011) offered conclusive evidence to show that the manufacturing sector have been facing negative deindustrialization since 2000.

REFERENCES

Alavi, R. *Industrialization in Malaysia: Import Substitution and Infant Industry Protection*. London: Routledge, 1996.

Amin, S. *Unequal Development*. New York: Monthly Review Press, 1976.

Anderson, S., J. Cavanagh, T. Lee. *Field Guide to the Global Economy*. New York: The New Press in conjunction with the Institute for Policy Studies, 2000.

Ariff, K.A.M. *The Malaysian Economy: Pacific Connections*. Kuala Lumpur: Oxford University Press, 1991.

Asian Development Bank. *Asian Development Outlook*. Manila: Asian Development Bank, 2008.

———. *Asian Development Outlook*. Manila: Asian Development Bank, 2010.

Baran, P. *The Political Economy of Growth*. New York: Monthly Review Press, 1962.

Best, M. and Rasiah, R. *Malaysian Electronics at the Crossroads*. Vienna: United Nations Industrial Development Organization, 2003.

Bhagwati, J. *Protectionism*. Cambridge: MIT Press, 1988.

Chenery, H.B. *Structural Change and Development Policy*. Baltimore: John Hopkins University Press, 1979.

Chenery, H. and M. Syrquin. *Patterns of Development 1950–1970*. London: Oxford University Press, 1975.

Dolan, C. and J. Humphrey. "Governance and Trade in Fresh Vegetables: The Impact of UK Supermarkets on the African Horticulture Industry". *Journal of Development Studies*, vol. 37, no. 2 (2000): 147–76.

Fei, J. and G. Ranis. *Development of the Labour Surplus Economy: Theory and Policy*. Irwin: Homewood III, 1964.

Fishlow, A., C. Gwin, S. Haggard, D. Rodrik, and R. Wade. *Miracle or Design: Lessons from the East Asian Experience*. Washington, D.C.: Overseas Development Council, 1994.

Fisk, E.K. "Features of the Rural Economy". In *The Political Economy of Independent Malaya*, edited by T.H. Silcock and E.K. Fisk. Singapore: Eastern University Press, 1963.

Frank, A.G. "The Development of Underdevelopment". *Monthly Review*, vol. 18, no. 4 (1966): 4–17.

Friedman, M. "The Role of Monetary Policy". *American Economic Review*, vol. 58, no. 1 (1968): 1–17.

Gray, J. *False Dawn: The Delusions of Global Capitalism*. New York: The New Press, 2000.

Grunsven, V.L. "New Industries in Southeast Asia's Late Industrialization: Evolution versus Creation — The Automation Industry in Penang (Malaysia) considered". Papers in Evolutionary Economic Geography (PEEG) 0611, Utrecht University, Section of Economic Geography, 2006.

Henderson, J. and P. Phillips. "Unintended Consequences: Social Policy, State Institutions and the 'Stalling' of the Malaysian Industrialization Project". *Economy and Society*, vol. 36, no. 1 (2007): 78–102.

Jomo, K.S. *A Question of Class: Capital, the State and Uneven Development in Malaya*. Singapore: Oxford University Press, 1986.

———. *Undermining Tin*. Kuala Lumpur: Forum Press, 1990a.

———. *Growth and Structural Change in Malaysia*. Basingstoke: Macmillan, 1990b.

———. "Malaysian Debacle: Whose Fault?". *Cambridge Journal of Economics*, vol. 22, no. 6 (1998): 707–22.

Jorgenson, D.W. "Surplus Agricultural Labour and the Development of a Dual Economy". *Oxford Economic Papers*, vol. 19, no. 3 (1967): 288–312.

Kaldor, N. "A Model of Economic Growth". *Economic Journal* 67 (1957): 83–100.

———. *Strategic Factors in Economic Growth*. Ithaca: Cornell University Press, 1967.

Krueger, A. "Trade Policy as an Input to Development". *American Economic Review*, vol. 70, no. 2 (1980): 288–92.

Kuznets, S. *Modern Economic Growth: Rate, Structure and Spread*. New Haven: Yale University Press, 1966.

Lewellen, T.C. *Dependency and Development: An Introduction to the Third World*. Westport: Bergin and Garvey, 1995.

Lewis, A. "Economic Development with Limited Supplies of Labour". *Manchester School of Economic and Social Studies*, vol. 22, no. 2 (1954): 139–91.

Lucas, R. "Expectations and the Neutrality of Money". *Journal of Economic Theory*, vol. 4, no. 2 (1972): 103–24.

Maddison, A. *The World Economy in the 20th Century*. Paris: Organization for Economic Cooperation and Development, 1989.

Malaysia. *Second Malaysia Plan 1971–1976*. Kuala Lumpur: Government Printers, 1971.

———. *Fourth Malaysia Plan 1981–1985*. Kuala Lumpur: Government Printers, 1981.

———. *External Trade Statistics*. Kuala Lumpur: Ministry of International Trade and Industry, 1983–90.

———. *National Agricultural Policy 1984–1991*. Kuala Lumpur: Ministry of Agriculture, 1984.

———. *Fifth Malaysia Plan 1986–1990*. Kuala Lumpur: Government Printers, 1986.

———. *Action Plan for Industrial Technology Development*. Kuala Lumpur: Ministry of Science, Technology and Environment, 1991.

———. *Second Industrial Master Plan*. Kuala Lumpur: Ministry of International Trade and Industry, 1996.

———. *Eighth Malaysia Plan 2001–2005*. Putra Jaya: Government Printers, 2001*a*.

———. *Industrial Surveys*. Kuala Lumpur: Department of Statistics, 2001*b*.

———. *Third Industrial Master Plan*. Putrajaya: Ministry of International Trade and Industry, 2006.

———. *Industrial Surveys*. Putrajaya: Department of Statistics, 2007.

———. *Industrial Surveys*. Putrajaya: Department of Statistics, 2010.

———. *The Economic Transformation Plan*. Putrajaya: Prime Minister's Department, 2011.

———. *Economic Report*, various issues. Kuala Lumpur: Finance Ministry, 1971–2011.

Myrdal, G. *Economic Theory and Underdeveloped Regions*. London: Duckworth, 1957.

Narayanan, S. and Y.W. Lai. "Technological Maturity and Development Without Research: The Challenge for Malaysian Manufacturing". *Development and Change*, vol. 31, no. 2 (2000): 435–58.

Osman, R.H., O. Pazim, and R. Rasiah. "Development of Agriculture". In *Malaysian Economy: Unfolding Growth and Social Change*, edited by R. Rasiah. Kuala Lumpur: Oxford University Press, 2011.

Prebisch, R. *The Economic Development of Latin America and Its Principal Problems*. New York: United Nations, 1950.

Ragayah. R. "Poverty and Income Distribution". In *Malaysian Economy: Unfolding Growth and Social Change*, edited by R. Rasiah. Kuala Lumpur: Oxford University Press, 2011.

Rasiah, R. "The Semiconductor Industry in Penang: Implications for the New International Division of Labour Theories". *Journal of Contemporary Asia*, vol. 18, no. 1 (1988*a*): 24–46.

————. "Flexible Production Systems and Local Machine Tool Subcontracting: Electronics Component Multinationals in Malaysia". *Cambridge Journal of Economics*, vol. 18, no. 3 (1988*b*): 279–98.

————. "Flexible Production Systems and Local Machine Tool Subcontracting: Electronics Component Transnationals in Malaysia". *Cambridge Journal of Economics* 18, no. 3 (1994): 279–98.

————. *Foreign Capital and Industrialization in Malaysia*. Basingstoke: Macmillan, 1995.

————. "Class, Ethnicity and Economic Development in Malaysia". In *Political Economy of Southeast Asia*, edited by G. Rodan, R. Robison and K. Hewisen. Sydney: Oxford University Press, 1997.

————. "The Malaysian Financial Crisis: Capital Expansion, Cronyism and Contraction". *Journal of the Asia Pacific Economy* 3, no. 3 (1998): 358–78.

————. "Malaysia's National Innovation System". In *Technology, Competitiveness and the State*, edited by K.S. Jomo and G. Felker. London: Routledge, 1999.

————. "International Portfolio Equity Flows and the Malaysian Financial Crisis". *Journal of Contemporary Asia* 30, no. 3 (2000): 369–401.

————. *Foreign Firms, Technological Capabilities and Economic Performance: Evidence from Africa, Asia and Latin America*. Cheltenham: Edward Elgar, 2004.

————. "Garment Manufacturing in Cambodia and Laos". *Journal of Asia Pacific Economy*, vol. 14, no. 2 (2009*a*): 150–61.

————. "Growth and Slowdown in the Electronics Industry in Southeast Asia". *Journal of Asia Pacific Economy*, vol. 14, no. 2 (2009*b*): 123–37.

————. "Are Electronics Firms Catching Up in the Technology Ladder". *Journal of Asia Pacific Economy*, vol. 15, no. 3 (2010): 301–19.

————. "Is Malaysia Facing Negative Deindustrialization?". *Pacific Affairs*, 2011.

Rasiah, R., M. Zhang, and X.X. Kong. "Can China's Miraculous Growth Continue?". *Journal of Contemporary Asia* 43, no. 2 (2013): 295–313.

Rasiah, R., R.H. Osman, and R. Alavi. "Changing Dimensions of Malaysian Trade". *International Journal of Business and Society*, vol. 1, no. 1 (2000): 1–29.

Rasiah, R. and R. Ishak. "Market, Government and Malaysia's New Economic Policy". *Cambridge Journal of Economics* 25, no. 1 (2001): 57–78.

Reardon and Timmer. "Transformation of markets for agricultural output in developing countries since 1950: How has thinking changed?" In *Handbook of agricultural economics* (Vol. 3A), edited by R. Evenson and P. Pingail. Amsterdam: North Holland Press, 2005.

Reinert, E. *How the Rich Countries Got Rich .... And Why Poor Countries Stay Poor*. London: Constable, 2007.

Rowthorn, R. and A. Wells. *Deindustrialization and Foreign Trade*. Cambridge: Cambridge University Press, 1987.

Saham, J. *British Investment in Malaysia 1963–1971*. Kuala Lumpur: Oxford University Press, 1980.

Sarker, P. and Singer H. "Manufactured exports of developing countries and their terms of trade since 1965". *World Development* 19, no. 4 (1991): 333–40.

Singer, H. "The Distribution of Gains between Investing and Borrowing Countries". *American Economic Review*, vol. 40, no. 2 (1950): 473–85.

Syrquin, M. "Patterns of Structural Change". In *Handbook of Development Economics*, edited by H. Chenery and T.N. Srinivasan. Amsterdam: North-Holland, 1988.

Thoburn, J. "From Tin to Petroleum". In *Malaysian Economy: Unfolding Growth and Social Change*, edited by R. Rasiah. Kuala Lumpur: Oxford University Press, 2011.

Timmer, C.P. "The Agricultural Transformation". In *Handbook of Development Economics*, volume one, edited by H. Chenery and T.N. Srinivasan. Amsterdam: North Holland, 1988.

UNESCAP. *Statistical Yearbook for Asia and the Pacific*. Bangkok: United Nations Economic and Social Commission for Asia and the Pacific, 2009.

Wong, L. "Development of Malaysia's Agricultural Sector: Agriculture as an Engine of Growth?". Paper presented at the ISEAS Conference on the Malaysian Economy: Development and Challenges. Singapore, 25–26 January 2007.

World Bank. *The East Asian Miracle*. New York: Oxford University Press, 1993.

———. *World Development Report*. Washington, D.C.: World Bank, 1995.

———. *World Development Indicators*. Washington, D.C.: World Bank Institute, 2007.

————. "World Development Indicators", 2011a. Available at <http://databank. worldbank.org/ddp/home.do?Step=2&id=4&hActiveDimensionId=WDI_ Series> (accessed 13 September 2011).

————. "Middle-income Developing Country", 2011b. Available at <http:// www.britannica.com/EBchecked/topic/381337/middle-income-developing-country> (accessed 13 September 2011).

WTO. *International Trade Statistics*. Geneva: World Trade Organization, 2009.

Young, A. "Increasing Returns and Economic Progress". *The Economic Journal*, vol. 38 (1928): 527–42.

4

HARNESSING SERVICES FOR DEVELOPMENT IN MALAYSIA

Tham Siew Yean and Loke Wai Heng

Introduction

In general, increasing per capita income is associated with an increasing share of services in the Gross Domestic Product (GDP) of a country. Developed countries are therefore generally characterized with a relatively higher share of services in their GDP and total employment, compared with developing countries. There is, however, considerable debate on the contribution of services to growth in terms of both theory and empirical evidence. While part of the controversy is due to the ongoing debate on the growth of services and its impact on labour productivity (Maroto-Sanchez and Cuadrado-Roura 2011), part of the controversy is also due to the rapidly changing nature of services.

Traditionally, services are viewed as non-storable and non-tradable due to its proximity burden where they are used as mere inputs in the production of goods and for personal consumption within the confines of the domestic economy. These services are therefore associated with relatively low-skilled jobs and low productivity. In contrast, the twin revolutions in information and communication technology and what is commonly referred to as the 3Ts — technology, transportability, and tradability (Mishra et al. 2011), has transformed the nature of services in several significant ways such as increasing its storability, reducing its proximity burden and increasing its tradability across borders, including digital trading.

Services are therefore no longer used as a mere input for the production and trade in goods alone. Instead, services are exported as "final exports" for direct consumption as well. More importantly, services as in the case of goods, are also becoming fragmented in its production as a single service activity is increasingly unbundled and produced separately in different geographic locations.

Empirically, United Nations Conference on Trade and Development (UNCTAD 2004, p. 20) found services exports to be a significant factor in the growth performances of developed countries in the 1990s. But the services exports and GDP growth nexus is weaker in developing countries. There is also increasing evidence that some service activities have contributed to an increase in labour productivity which is comparable to, or even higher than those corresponding to manufacturing, in a sample of 16 European countries (Maroto-Sanchez and Cuadrado-Roura 2011).

In the case of Malaysia, there is increasing emphasis on the service sector as a new engine of growth as growth in the manufacturing sector has faltered since the Asian Financial Crisis (AFC). This is seen in the recent Plan documents of the country. For example, in the New Economic Model that was launched in 2010 (NEAC 2010), harnessing services is one of the strategies proposed for enabling Malaysia to shift to a high income economy, with education services, logistic services, tourism, and distributive services highlighted as "economic sweet spots" (NEAC 2010). Similarly in the Tenth Malaysia Plan (Malaysia 2010), twelve national key economic areas (NKEAs) were targeted for facilitating the necessary growth over the Plan period from 2010–15. Seven of the NKEAs are in the service sector, namely financial services, wholesale and retail, tourism, information and communication technology (ICT), education, business services, and private healthcare.

While the Plan documents highlight specific subsectors within the services sector for promotion and development, there is no comprehensive review of the performance of this sector and its relationship with manufacturing. In view of this, the objectives of the chapter are: (i) to characterize the nature of the services sector in Malaysia, and (ii) to identify the challenges facing the future development of this sector. There are four main sections in this chapter. The salient features of this sector are summarized in Section 2. This is followed by an analysis of the challenges facing its future development (Section 3). The conclusion in Section 4 summarizes the key findings of this chapter.

Salient Features of the Services Sector in Malaysia

Profile of Services

The services sector, in terms of its contribution to real GDP, has been the largest sector in the Malaysian economy for the period shown in Figure 4.1. Its share has grown steadily over time, as in the case

FIGURE 4.1
Services Share in Malaysia's GDP

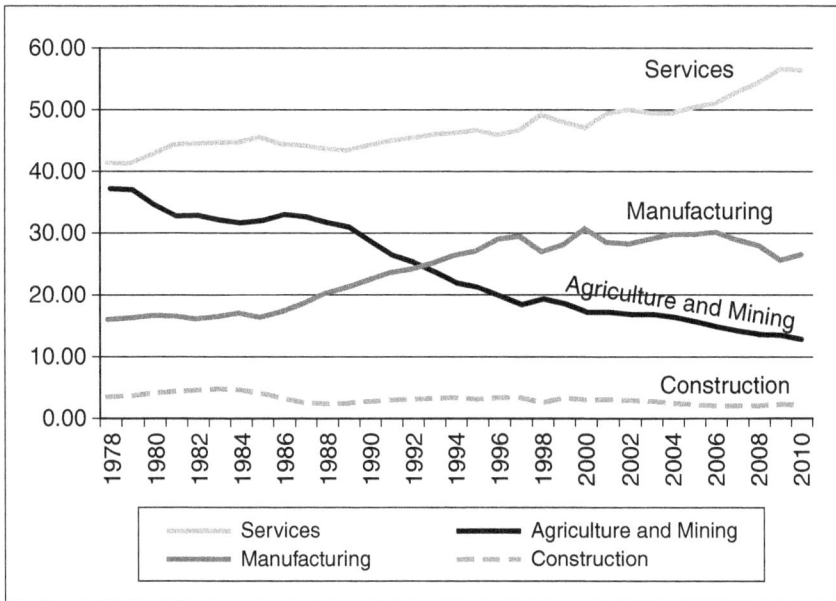

Note: All figures are in 2000 constant prices.
Source: *Malaysia's Economic Report*, various years.

of manufacturing. By 2007, its share has grown to be more than 50 per cent of the country's GDP. Its share in total employment in the country has also grown to be more than 50 per cent by 1990 (see Figure 4.2). However in terms of its labour productivity, Figure 4.3 shows that this was less than the labour productivity for the overall economy from 1985 to 2008. This is due to the higher labour productivity in manufacturing (Aldaba and Pasadilla 2011). But there are some service subsectors such as utilities, transport and finance where the growth in labour productivity is higher than that of manufacturing (Tham and Loke 2012).

It is important to note that the services sector is heterogeneous and that its structure has changed over time as shown in Figure 4.4. The share of government services in the service sector has fallen significantly

FIGURE 4.2
Services Share in Employment
(%)

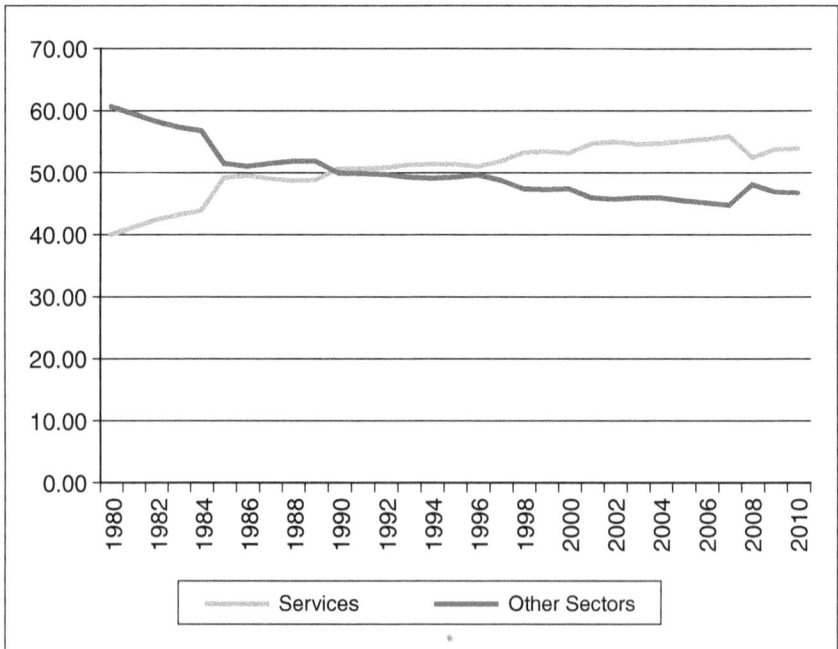

Source: *Malaysia's Economic Report*, various years.

FIGURE 4.3
Services Labour Productivity

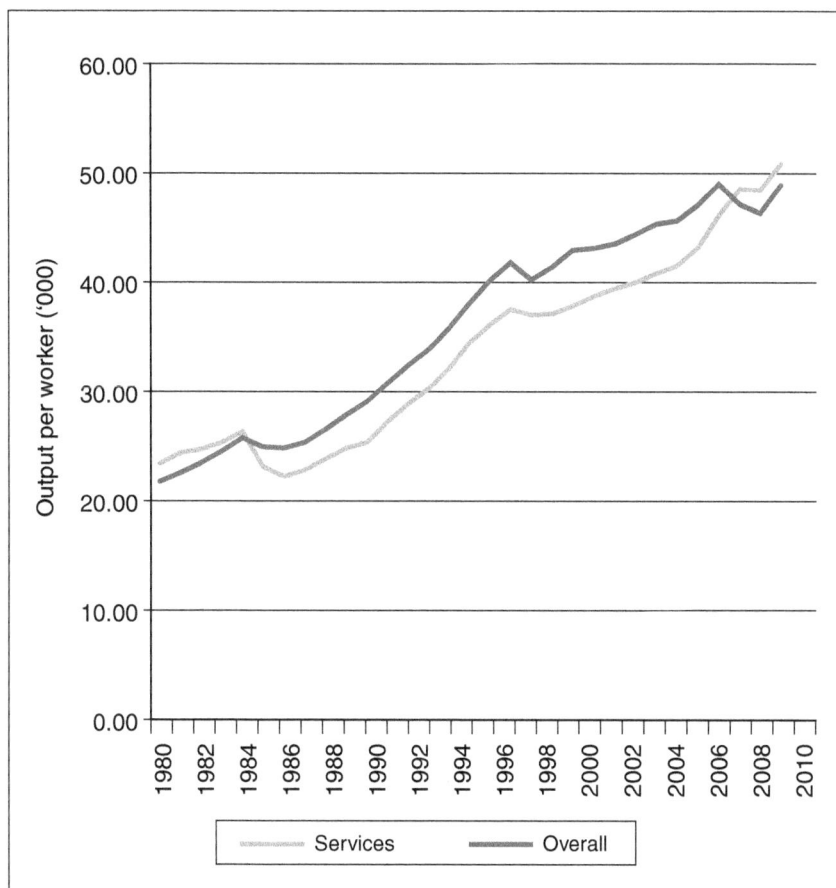

Note: Labour productivity is defined as output per worker.
Source: Authors' calculations based on data from *Malaysia's Economic Report*, various years.

since 1995 and it is now the smallest subsector within services. In contrast, the share of finance, insurance, real estate and business services has grown to be the largest subsector within services, followed by wholesale and retail, hotels, and restaurants. Transport, storage, and communication has been the second smallest subsector since 1995.

FIGURE 4.4
Services Subsector Share
(%)

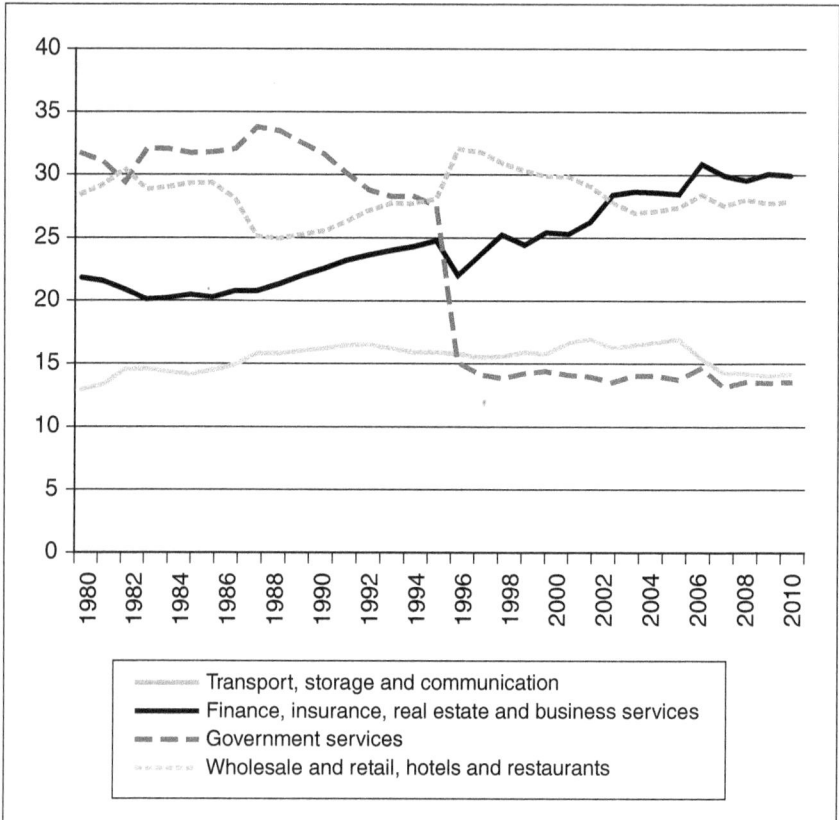

Source: *Economic Report*, various years.

Service Sector Linkages: Within Sector and with Other Sectors

Analysis of the multiplier effects reveals some interesting points about the services sector in Malaysia. First, in terms of its potential multiplier effects to the whole economy when the sector expands, the service sector is the second most important sector in the economy, after the manufacturing sector. Further analysis shows that if the sector experiences a RM1 increase in demand in each of its twenty-nine subsectors, the whole economy is expected to expand by RM54.58, with the services sector itself receiving the largest impact of RM44.44 (see Table 4.1). Second, an expansion of the services sector is expected to bring about a significant impact on the manufacturing sector. If there is a RM1 increase in demand in each twenty-nine subsectors, the manufacturing sector is expected to grow by RM5.89.

The strong multiplier effects of the service sector, particularly on the sector itself and with the manufacturing sector are due to the relative strong linkages of the sector with the economy, through both backward (sourcing inputs from other sectors) and forward (supplying services as inputs to other sectors) linkages.

As shown in Table 4.2, reading column-down, the services sector has a strong backward linkage with its own industries. An index of 7.05 suggests that the services sector has an above average dependency, seven times the overall economy's average, on the sector itself for input requirements. Among the other sectors, the services sector is found to depend most on the manufacturing sector as input source, although the degree of dependency, with an index of 0.93, is slightly below the overall industry average. The services sector also has the least dependence on the agriculture, fishery and forestry sector as shown by the backward linkage index of only 0.04.

Reading row-right from the same table indicates the extent of forward linkages of the services sector with other sectors. The services sector, apart from having the strongest link with its own sector, is found to have the strongest forward linkage with the manufacturing sector with an index of 2.02, indicating two times the overall economy's average. This also suggests that the manufacturing sector depends on the services sector as a source of inputs more than the service sector's dependence on the manufacturing sector.

A closer examination on linkages of the services subsectors with the overall economy is reported in Table 4.3. Five services subsectors are found to have both strong backward and forward linkages with the economy. They are water transport, air transport, other transport services, banks, and amusement and recreational services. Subsectors that are found to have strong backward linkages only are: restaurants; port and airport operation services; highway, bridge and tunnel operation services; financial institution; public administration; and health services. Subsectors that have strong forward linkages only are wholesale and retail trade; land transport; communication; real estate; and professional services.

Table 4.1

Impact of an Increased Demand in One Sector on Other Sectors and the Whole Economy, 2005

A RM1 increase in demand in every subsector within each main sector:

Impact on:	Services	Agriculture, Fishery and Forestry	Mining and Quarrying	Manufacturing	Construction	Utilities
Services (92–120)	44.44	1.44	0.76	12.74	1.17	0.31
Agriculture, Fishery and Forestry (1–12)	0.28	14.05	0.06	7.53	0.10	0.02
Mining and Quarrying (13–16)	1.11	0.20	4.21	3.05	0.26	0.21
Manufacturing (17–85)	5.89	3.40	1.24	108.44	2.17	0.69
Construction (88–91)	1.85	0.03	0.49	0.77	4.10	0.19
Utilities (86–87)	1.03	0.22	0.06	1.91	0.08	2.44
Total Impact	54.58	19.34	6.83	134.44	7.88	3.87

Source: Computed based on the 2005 *Input-Output Table Malaysia*, published by the Department of Statistics.

TABLE 4.2
Malaysia's Sectoral Linkages: Backward and Forward, 2005

	Services	Agriculture, Fishery and Forestry	Mining and Quarrying	Manufacturing	Construction	Utilities
Services (92–120)	7.05	0.23	0.12	2.02	0.19	0.05
Agriculture, Fishery and Forestry (1–12)	0.04	2.23	0.01	1.19	0.02	0.00
Mining and Quarrying (13–16)	0.18	0.03	0.67	0.48	0.04	0.03
Manufacturing (17–85)	0.93	0.54	0.20	17.20	0.34	0.11
Construction (88–91)	0.29	0.00	0.08	0.12	0.65	0.03
Utilities (86–87)	0.16	0.04	0.01	0.30	0.01	0.39

Source: Computed based on the 2005 *Input-Output Table Malaysia*, published by the Department of Statistics.

TABLE 4.3
Services Subsector Linkages with the Overall Economy, 2005

	BW	FW
Wholesale and retail trade	0.79	3.94
Accommodation	0.98	0.76
Restaurants	1.20	0.84
Land transport	0.83	1.17
Water transport	1.35	1.55
Air transport	1.52	1.42
Other transport services	1.19	1.44
Port and airport operation services	1.05	0.63
Highway, bridge and tunnel operation services	1.32	0.64
Communication	0.98	1.85
Banks	1.07	4.21
Financial institutions	1.03	0.75
Insurance	0.95	0.67
Other financial institutions	0.95	0.70
Real estate	0.86	1.46
Ownership of dwellings	0.85	0.54
Rental and leasing	0.91	0.62
Computer services	0.91	0.98
Research and development	0.66	0.61
Professional	0.79	1.07
Business services	0.66	0.78
Public administration	1.09	0.83
Education	0.80	0.57
Health	1.04	0.71
Defence and public order	0.92	0.56
Other public administration	0.97	0.53
Private non-profit institutions	0.88	0.70
Amusement and recreational services	1.24	1.05
Other private services	1.08	0.60

Note: We follow Rasmussen's method (1956), using the Leontief inverse matrix to compute both BW and FW linkages.
Source: Computed based on the *2005 Input-Output Table Malaysia*, published by the Department of Statistics.

Trade in Services

Malaysia is ranked globally as 16th and 20th respectively in the Asia-Pacific region, in terms of the export and import of commercial services in 2009 (UNESCAP 2011). Its share in world export and import of commercial services is 1.1 per cent each, respectively. Services exports and imports as a percentage of total exports and imports in the country grew intermittently from 12.3 per cent and 16.8 per cent, respectively, in 2000, to 14 per cent and 16.3 per cent, respectively, in 2010.

The trade balance in services has been in deficit since independence due largely to the country's production and export structure in goods, where a large portion of its manufactured goods and exports is contributed by multinational corporation (MNC) production. These MNCs, in turn, have a preference to utilize transportation from their own home countries resulting in outflows of freight and insurance as well as the repatriation of profits and transfers (WTO 2005). However, since 2007, there has been a small surplus registered in the balance of services account, as shown in Figure 4.5.

Travel services have contributed greatly toward the improvement in the balance of services. In particular, health tourism is gaining grounds, with Malaysia's share in the global medical tourism market, estimated at 0.27 per cent in 2006 (Choy 2010). The number of foreign patients from medical tourism has grown from 102,946 in 2003 to 341,288 in 2007, while revenues have grown from RM58.9 million to RM253.8 million for the same period (Ang 2009). The buoyant growth is boosted by the availability of accredited private hospitals, medical experts in the country, as well as competitive advantages in terms of cost, language and cultural diversity. These same competitive advantages have also facilitated the growth in education service exports, especially private higher education, with the inflow of international students growing to 86,923 in 2010, available at <http://www.mohe.gov.my> (accessed 1 July 2011).

The relatively strong growth in the export of travel services has led to increasing positive net trade in travel services over time, except for 2003 when the decline in export revenue from travel services is attributed to the negative impact from the outbreak of Severe Acute Respiratory Syndrome (SARS) and geopolitical uncertainties on tourist arrivals in the country. In contrast, transportation and other services registered negative trade balance throughout the period shown in Figure 4.5. This is supported by the RCA (revealed comparative

FIGURE 4.5
Services Trade Balance, 1999–2010
(RM million)

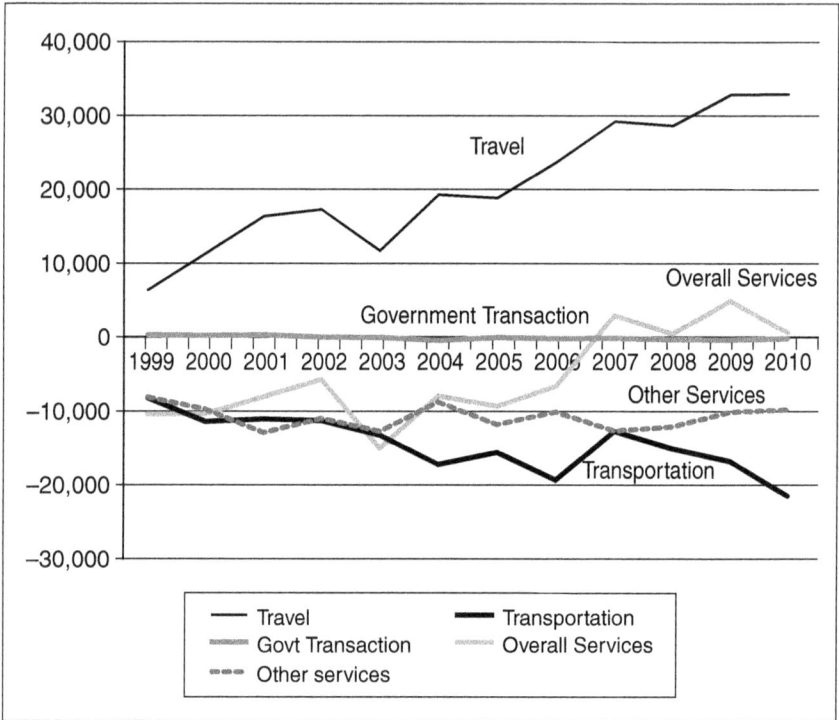

Source: *Balance of Payments in Malaysia's Economic Report*, various years.

advantage) calculated for selected services based on available data (see Table 4.4). Transport services show a RCA of less than one, as in the case of insurance and financial services for the whole period. In the case of computer, communication and other services, the RCA indicated a steady decline from 1999 to 2009.

Several factors have contributed to the relatively strong trade performance in the travel subsector. First, the natural endowment of the country has provided the natural resources for attracting tourists, especially those in search of sun and surf. Second, its proximity to Singapore, which is also the largest destination source for tourist arrivals in the country, has attracted a large number of Singaporean tourists as well as Malaysians working or residing in Singapore due to its low

TABLE 4.4
RCA for Selected Services, 1999–2009

	1999	2000	2001	2002	2003	2004	2005	2006	2007	2008	2009
Computer, Communication and other services	1.21	1.07	0.77	0.78	0.81	0.75	0.78	0.74	0.64	0.61	0.62
Insurance and Financial Services	0.39	0.36	0.42	0.20	0.35	0.32	0.25	0.21	0.18	0.19	0.20
Transport Services	0.85	0.82	0.78	0.81	0.87	0.78	0.86	0.80	1.02	0.91	0.73
Travel	0.95	1.15	1.55	1.62	1.51	1.68	1.63	1.80	1.82	1.95	2.11

Source: Authors' calculations based on BOP data from *World Development Indicators (WDI) 2009*.

cost advantage and family ties with Malaysia. Third, the development of low-cost carriers such as Air Asia in Malaysia and other countries in the region has also reduced the cost of travelling, making travel more affordable and accessible to both domestic as well as foreign travellers. Fourth, the relatively high growth in the region, especially before the Asian Financial Crisis in 1997, has created a growing middle class with effective demand for travel. The Revealed Comparative Advantage (RCA) for services as shown in Table 4.4 confirms the steady improvement in the trade competitiveness of this sector as its RCA has grown steadily from 1999 to 2009.

It should be noted that the Balance of Payments (BOP) data does not capture completely the full extent of services exports as domestic expenditures involved in Mode 2 exports are not always reflected in the cross border financial transactions made through the banking system that is used in the BOP (Mahani et al. 2011). Similarly, financial services in the BOP do not completely capture the export of some financial instruments and bonds, which is to the disadvantage of Malaysia as the country is promoting and launching large amounts of Islamic bonds. More importantly, of the four modes of supply is services,[1] commercial presence or mode 3 is not captured in BOP data (Lim and Saner 2011).

Data on inflows and outflows of direct investment from the Central Bank provides some indication of services trade in the form of mode 3. In terms of inflows, foreign equity ownership has been capped at 30 per cent in services subsectors since the implementation of the New Economic Policy (NEP) in 1970. However, data on mode 3 imports after the Asian Financial Crisis (AFC) indicate an increase in the share of services from 15 per cent to 37 per cent, comparing the two periods shown in Table 4.5. This is in line with the current policy focus on the promotion of Islamic finance in order to achieve the country's goal of being a global hub for Islamic finance. Consequently, an increasing number of banking licences with 100 per cent foreign equity have been given for Islamic banks over time, leading to a net inflow in the financial sector for the period 1999–2009 (Mahani et al. 2011). On 22 April 2009, foreign equity constraints on twenty-seven service subsectors were removed, followed a week later by the relaxation of foreign equity ownership in financial services. In June 2009, the government announced that the FIC guidelines would be deregulated and that limitations on foreign equity would be decided by the regulator for the respective industry. The progressive liberalization of equity constraints in the service sector indicates the current policy emphasis to increasingly open up the service sector to foreign investors.

Data on outflows or exports of capital from Malaysia also show that the share of services exports have increased over time from 49 per cent to 70 per cent (see Table 4.5). Further disaggregation by subsectors indicate it is also highly concentrated in financial sector (see Table 4.6), with the government-linked companies (GLCs) leading in the outflows as reported in *Central Bank Annual Report 2009*. This is due

TABLE 4.5
Share of Cumulative Net FDI Flows and
Direct Investment Abroad (DIA) in Services, 1990–2009
(% of total)

Sectors	1990–99 (% of total)	2000–09 (% of total)
Services: Net inflows	15	37
Servies: Net outflows or DIA	49	70

Source: Central Bank Annual Report 2009.

TABLE 4.6
DIA by Sectors, 2003–10
(as % of total in the economy)

Sector	Year							
	2003	2004	2005	2006	2007	2008	2009	2010
Electricity, Gas & Water Supply	2.28	0.32	2.80	2.42	1.82			
*Electricity, Gas, Steam and Air Conditioning Supply						5.51	1.68	3.35
*Water Supply, Sewage, Waste Management and Remediation activities						0.24	0.32	0.15
Construction	−0.21	0.60	−0.37	0.03	16.15	1.53	3.41	−0.57
Whole Sale & Retail Trade; Repair	−4.47	−0.10	−0.31	2.66	0.44	−1.83	−4.45	1.43
Hotel & Restaurant	−0.03	0.00	0.02	1.23	0.86	0.03	0.02	6.71
Transport, Storage & Communications	0.75	−18.45	0.87	10.27	1.50			
*Transportation & Storage						1.27	0.88	0.06
*Information and Communication						8.61	16.62	3.51
Financial Intermediation	48.88	34.28	49.09	81.22	24.81	38.24	24.37	44.11
Others	−3.55	−1.28	−0.33	0.64	8.02	0.93	7.32	2.59

Note: * Categories change from 2008 onwards.
Source: Department of Statistics.

to the mandate for GLCs to establish a regional presence, especially in the banking sector. The two leading GLCs in the banking sector, namely Maybank and CIMB reportedly had 342 and 212 branches abroad in 2009, including representative offices and offshore banking units (Mahani et al. 2011).

In terms of mode 4 trade or the movement of natural persons, data on Malaysians working overseas is generally sparse. There is an estimated number of 350,000 Malaysians working in Singapore, with 150,000 commuting from Johor Bahru and the rest residing in Singapore (Mahani et al. 2011).

Inflows of foreign workers are mainly concentrated in the manufacturing sector from 1999 to 2009 (see Figure 4.6). Share of these workers in services sector has grown from 8.9 per cent to 10.6 per

FIGURE 4.6
Share of Foreign Workers, by Sectors, 1999–2009

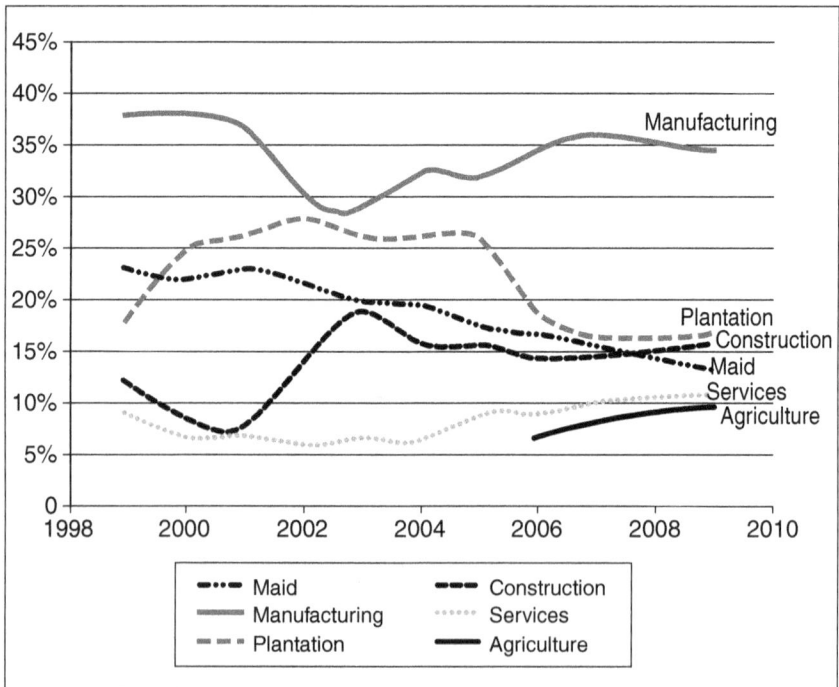

Source: Ministry of Home Affairs.

cent over the period shown. The total presence of foreign workers is much more than this when maids working in the country are included. In total, the number of foreign workers in these two service sectors has increased more than threefold from 130,902 to 454,994 over the stated period. However, the percentage of foreign workers in these two sectors have fallen from 32 per cent in 1999 to 24 per cent in 2009 due mainly to a fall in the share of maids. Excess demand in Malaysia and a positive wage differential between Malaysia and source countries have contributed to the strong growth for foreign workers in the country.

Indonesians form the largest group of foreign workers in the country, due to both geographical and cultural proximity, a common religion in Islam, as well as similarity in language (see Figure 4.7).

FIGURE 4.7
Share of Foreign Workers, by Source Countries, 1999–2009

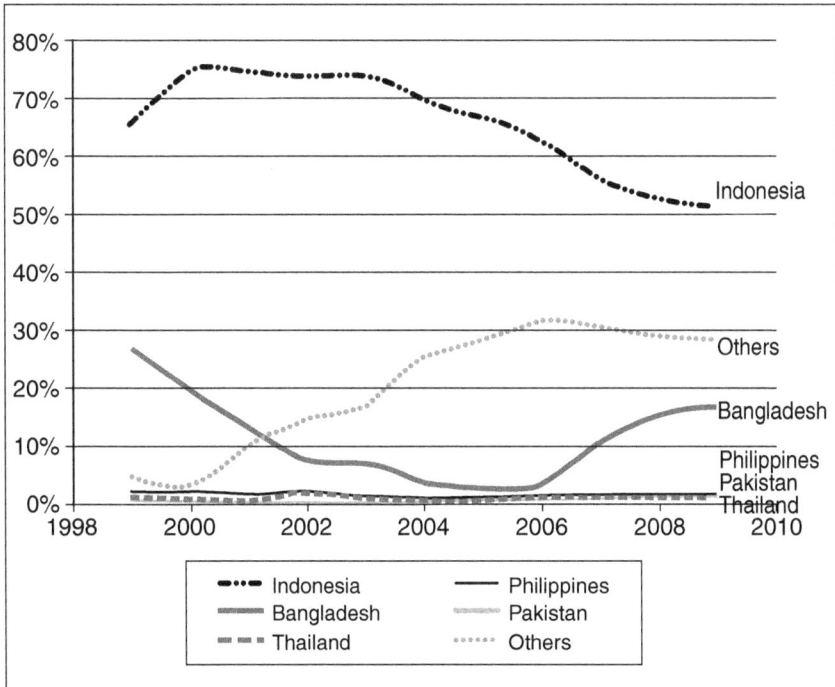

Source: Ministry of Home Affairs.

In contrast, inflows of expatriates working in Malaysia has fallen progressively over time from over 80,000 in 2000 to around 45,000 in 2008 (NEAC 2010).

Challenges in Developing Services Sector

In harnessing services for development, the profile of trade in services shows that most of the production of services is directed inwards towards the domestic economy, rather than outwards as shown by the relatively low export competitiveness of this sector, with the exception of travel services. The primary role of services is to service the manufacturing sector and domestic consumers. The challenge in the short and medium terms is to raise the efficiency and productivity of the service sector so as to strengthen its linkages with the manufacturing sector and the competitiveness of manufactured exports. The longer term challenge is to enhance the export competitiveness of services exports and increase its share in total exports as well as GDP of the country.

The greatest challenge in raising productivity in the services sector is human capital. Malaysia's shortage of skilled workers is exacerbated by a mismatch between the supply and demand for human capital. Graduate unemployment therefore coexists with job vacancies in the economy. It was reported in the NEAC (2010) that about a quarter of the graduates from local public universities remained unemployed six months after completing their studies. The shortage of skills have also restrained the export of information and technology services, despite Malaysia's early foray into this sector with the establishment of the Multimedia Super Corridor in 1996.

Workers for producing services that are needed to upgrade the economy and the services sector are essentially knowledge workers. This is especially important to avoid the drop in overall productivity of the country when it shifts resources, especially labour resources from manufacturing to services. It is only the knowledge-intensive services that will serve to increase overall productivity and growth in the economy, while shifting to unskilled and labour-intensive services can lead to a converse effect. Hence, the main challenge is to improve the quality and quantity of the labour force so as to provide the necessary human capital for developing the services sector.

Malaysia's current approach toward improving market access for its service providers is to engage in trade agreements, especially at the bilateral and regional level, given the current state of development in the Doha Round. Malaysia has currently concluded five bilaterals with Japan, Pakistan, New Zealand, Chile and India. It also has a regional agreement with the Association of Southeast Asian Nations (ASEAN) and it is also a member of five other ASEAN extra-regional agreements, namely with China, Japan, Korea, Australia and New Zealand and India. It is also currently negotiating bilaterally with Turkey, the European Union, Australia and also another regional agreement under the TransPacific Partnership Agreement (TPP). While these agreements seek to increase market access for Malaysian service providers, these providers will still have to compete with domestic providers and other providers from the region in the case of region wide agreements, as well as contend with domestic regulations. Hence, domestic providers have to first enhance their domestic competitiveness before they can compete at a regional or bilateral level. For that purpose, domestic regulations that hinder domestic providers have to be removed or streamlined (Tham and Loke 2012; Aldaba and Pasadilla 2011). After improving their domestic competitiveness, exporters have to understand the ratified trade agreements in order to utilize them. More importantly, exporters also have to understand the domestic regulations of the destination country of their exports as they will still have to fulfil these requirements.

Conclusion

Malaysia's service sector has grown to become the largest sector in the country in terms of its contribution to GDP and employment. However, its labour productivity and multiplier effect is second to that of manufacturing sector. Moreover, its exports are also relatively small, in terms of its contribution to total exports and GDP. Thus, although the government has targeted the services sector as a new source of growth for the country, the sector is still basically a supporting sector for manufacturing at this point in time.

In the short and medium term, improving the human capital resources needed to provide knowledge workers for upgrading services will increase labour productivity in this sector and enhance its linkages with the manufacturing sector as well as the competitiveness of the manufacturing sector itself. In the longer term, enhancing export competitiveness will require increasing domestic competition, reducing regulatory burden, understanding the free trade agreements that have been ratified as well as knowing the regulatory requirements of the targeted country of export interest.

NOTE

1. These are cross-border supply (mode 1), consumption abroad (mode 2), commercial presence (mode 3), and presence of natural persons (mode 4).

REFERENCES

Aldaba, R.M. and G. Pasadilla. *The ASEAN Services Sector and the Growth Rebalancing Model*. Discusssion Paper Series No. 2011-01. Manila: Philippine Institute for Development Studies (PIDS), 2011.
Ang, Elaine. "Malaysian Medical Tourism Growing". *The Star*, 14 February 2009.
Choy, L.B. "Heathcare Travel: Government's Role". Paper presented at the *Healthcare Tourism Congress*, Kuala Lumpur, 12–13 April 2010.
Department of Statistics (DOS). *Input-Output Table 2005*. Kuala Lumpur: DOS, 2010.
Lim, Aik Hoe and Raymond Saner. "Rethinking Trade in Education Services: A Wake-Up Call for Trade Negotiators". *Journal of World Trade*, vol. 45, no. 5 (2011): 993–1036.
Mahani, Z.A., S.Y. Tham and W.H. Loke. *Exploring Niches for Exporting: The Case of Malaysia*. Chapter 5 in *Exporting Services: A Developing Country's Perspective*, edited by A.G. Goswami, A. Mattoo, and S. Saez. Washington, D.C.: The World Bank, 2011.
Malaysia. *Economic Reports*, various issues. Putrajaya: Ministry of Finance, various years.
———. *Tenth Malaysia Plan 2011–15*. Putrajaya: Economic Planning Unit, 2010.
Maroto-Sanchez, A. and J. Cuadrado-Roura. *Analyzing the Role of Service Sector on Productivity Growth across European Regions*. Serie Documentas De Trabajo April 2011. Available at <http://ww.iaes.es/publicaciones/DT_04_11_ing.pdf> (accessed 5 September 2011).
Ministry of Higher Education. *Statistics*. Available at <http://www.mohe.gov.my> (accessed 1 July 2011).
Mishra, S., S. Lundstrom, and R. Anand. "Sophistication in Services Exports and Economic Growth". Available at <http://www.worldbank.org/economicpremise> (accessed 5 September 2011).

National Economic Advisory Council (NEAC). *New Economic Model for Malaysia*. Kuala Lumpur: Percetakan Nasional Malaysia Bhd, 2010.

Tham Siew Yean and Loke Wai Heng. "Services Liberalization: The Need for Complementary Policies". In *Malaysia's Development Challenges: Graduating from the Middle*, edited by Hal Hill, S.Y. Tham, and H.M.Z. Ragayah. London: Routledge, 2012.

United Nations Conference on Trade and Development (UNCTAD). *Exports of Services and Economic Growth in Developing Countries*. UNCTAD/DITC/ TNCD/MISC/2003/6. 3 June 2004. Geneva: UNCTAD, 2004.

United Nations Economic and Social Commission for Asia and the Pacific (UNESCAP). *Asia Pacific Trade and Investment Report 2011*. New York: UNESCAP, 2011.

WTO. *Trade Policy Review: Malaysia*. WT/TPR/156. Geneva: WTO, 2005.

Commentary 1

Malaysian Success Story:
The Development of Low Cost Carriers, Focusing on Air Asia

Tham Siew Yean

The development of services is vital for transforming Malaysia as it provides both backbone and other producer services that can contribute towards enhancing the competitiveness of other sectors in the country. However, some services face regulatory structures that may impede its effectiveness in playing this role. Some sectors are also controlled by government-linked companies that were formerly "legacy" monopolies. The continued protection of these companies usually reinforces the inefficiencies in these sectors. Thus, deregulation, liberalization and the injection of competition through private entrepreneurship is necessary for improving the performance of these sectors. This can in turn have spillover effects on other sectors. In this box story, the development of a low cost carrier (LCC), namely Air Asia, is used to illustrate the positive impact of deregulation, liberalization and private entrepreneurship on air travel and tourism in the country.

As in all developing economies, Malaysia Airlines, the national carrier operated as a monopoly until 2001 when the government approved the establishment of Air Asia as a LCC based in Malaysia. Since market access or airline routes are controlled by the government and bilateral air service agreements, Air Asia's entry essentially required the government to provide entry to domestic routes or short haul markets for the new entrant, which constituted a major step in deregulation in the typically highly regulated airline market. This had an immediate impact on prices since budget airlines operate on the basis of costs cutting measures through a reduction in the range of services that are normally offered by full service airlines (FSA) (Button undated). In turn, these lower prices did not just attract existing passengers away from the incumbent carrier but it also created new demand as it made it possible for "now everyone to fly" as in the tagline of the new airline. Indeed, substitution is imperfect as the government continued to protect the national carrier because civil servants are directed to use the FSA for their official duties. Further, some business travellers also preferred full services to "no-frill" services that characterizes the LCC. Unexpected flight delays that initially plagued the new carrier also deterred some business travellers from using the LCC. On the other hand, new demand was facilitated by external factors, namely, the rise of the middle income groups in Southeast Asia, China and India due to the robust growth experienced in these countries before the emergence of the Asian Financial Crisis (AFC) in 1998. Likewise, the emergence of the middle income group in Malaysia also supported new demand for affordable air travel. The first mover advantage of Air Asia bore fruit as by 2007, the number of passengers using Air Asia had reached 5.1 million (Tham 2010).

Nonetheless, competing on the basis of low cost alone is not sustainable without constant product innovation and differentiation as the airline industry is highly competitive and it is plagued with sunk costs as scheduled flights have to be offered even when the load factor is low. Thus, private entrepreneurship that is governed by the need to stay profitable tends to be more responsive to these innovative pressures and challenges. This can be illustrated by Air Asia's venture beyond domestic shores to regional routes with its inaugural flight to Bangkok in 2006 and later into long-haul flights with the establishment of Air Asia X in 2007 and its first long-haul flight in 2009. As in the case of other LCCs, cost cutting strategies used for long-haul included the use of a simple aircraft fleet and a route network based on low cost airports. Similarly, a complementary product such as the "limited service" hotel chain was also started in 2007, first in Malaysia and later overseas. The idea and business model behind this hotel chain is akin to the LCC model as the hotel provides basic fare with charges for each additional service that is needed by the customer. Continuous business innovation therefore contributed to the increase in the number of passengers travelling by Air Asia which increased to 14.3 million in 2009, 16 million in 2010 and to 18 million in 2011. The airline also won Skytrak World's best low cost airline award in 2007, 2009, 2010 and 2011.

But, the competitive environment in the airline industry generally means that any 'successful' strategy is immediately "mimicked" by the competitors in the industry, thereby eroding the first mover advantage of Air Asia. Within the country, MAS itself established as a wholly owned subsidiary, a community airline to complement its air routes and to compete with Air Asia by flying to destinations that are not financially viable for the mother airline. MAS further adopted the zero fare strategy commonly used by LCCs by offering "free seats" or seats that charge only surcharges such as fuel, insurance, airport tax and administration fee for all domestic seats in 2008 (Tham 2010). Tiger Airways of Singapore and Jetstar of Australia were also established respectively in 2005 and 2003. In 2011, Singapore announced a new LCC that is targeted at the medium and long haul market in an attempt to recover some of the loss in market share by its national carrier.

Air Asia's success, however, cannot be completely attributed to business acumen alone due to the peculiarities of the airline industry that depend on the liberalization of airline routes and capital-intensive complementary developments such as airports. For example, the liberalization of the lucrative Kuala Lumpur-Singapore air route to three budget carriers, including Air Asia, enabled the LCC to tap on this market. Similarly, further liberalization under ASEAN Open Skies will be advantageous for Air Asia as it is the biggest LCC in Southeast Asia by fleet size with a strategic presence in Thailand, Indonesia and Vietnam. Infrastructure provision through the establishment of the first LCC terminal, located at about 20 kilometres from the Kuala Lumpur International Airport (KLIA) at a cost of RM108 million, provided the facilities needed to grow the LCC in Malaysia. Nevertheless, the rapid growth of Air Asia and low cost travel has outstripped the capacity of the existing terminal and a new LCCT is under construction and expected to be completed in 2012. This is also expected to contribute to the future growth of Air Asia and other LCCs.

Despite Air Asia's sterling success, LCCs will be operating in an increasingly difficult environment due to rising fuel costs, a weak external environment as both the USA and EU continue to struggle from the aftermath of the global financial crisis in 2008/09, and continued uncertainty over the sustainability of China's growth as well as the entry of even more competitors in both the short, medium, and long-haul markets. The rampant failure of numerous LCCs in Europe and the USA testify to the precarious nature of this business. Within Malaysia, the equity swap deal between Air Asia's and MAS's respective parent companies would have created the necessary condition for network rationalization. However, this deal was subsequently scrapped due pressures from MAS's Employees' Union who feared that MAS may have adopted the cost cutting model of LCCs with Air Asia sitting on the MAS Board under the share swap deal (*The Star*, 3 May 2012). Although it was reported that both airlines will still continue to cooperate on several areas to save costs, the future of Air Asia will have to lean more heavily on its own innovations rather than collaborative measures between the two airlines.

REFERENCES

Button, Kenneth. Undated. "Low Cost Airlines: A Failed Business Model?". Available at <http://ww.garsonline.de/Downloads/.../Ken_Button_GARS_2009.pdf> (accessed 19 April 2012).

Tham Siew Yean. "ASEAN Open Skies and the Implications for Airport Development Strategy in Malaysia". In *Trade Facilitation and Regional Cooperation in Asia*, edited by D.H. Brooks and S.F. Stone. Cheltenham: Edward Elgar and ADBI, 2010.

The Star, 3 May 2012. Biz Page 1. "Its Official, Swap Deal Off".

5

PRODUCTIVITY LED GROWTH

Cassey Lee

"Productivity isn't everything, but in the long run it is almost everything."

— Paul Krugman

Introduction

Sustained economic growth is commonly associated with higher living standards. It is for this reason that the preoccupation with economic growth is an ancient one which continues until today. Within the economics literature proper, theories of economic growth dates back to as far as Adam Smith's *Wealth of Nations*, published in 1776. More than two centuries later, growth theories continue to interest scholars and policy-makers albeit such theories have undergone significant changes, due partly to economic structure and development. The classical theories of Smith, Malthus and Ricardo, forged during the nascent stage of industrial revolution, were premised upon specialization, rapid population growth and diminishing returns. The post-World War II saw the formulation of growth theories by Harrod, Domar, Swan and Solow, which were primarily driven by capital accumulation within the Keynesian mode. The most recent vintages by Lucas and Romer in the 1980s broaden the scope of such theories to include human capital and technological innovation, factors that would imply increasing returns and the promise of sustained growth.

Today, the cumulative theoretical and empirical literature is vast and substantial. Its influence on academics, officials from aid agencies and policy-makers has been substantial. Malaysia is no exception in this regard. For example, in the Sixth Malaysia Plan (1986–90), there is explicit mention of achieving higher growth through improvements in total factor productivity (p. 19). Malaysia's growth record since the country's independence in 1957 is quite enviable. However, the country's growth rate in recent years, especially since the Asian Financial Crisis, has been relatively sluggish. This has led to concerns on whether Malaysia is currently facing the problem of the middle-income trap.

The objective of this chapter is to critically examine Malaysia's economic growth for the past two decades as well as discuss some of the policy options that might be useful for sustainable growth in the future. Section 2 of the chapter provides a brief summary of Malaysia's economic growth and economic structure during the period 1990–2010. Section 3 analyses the sources of growth of the Malaysian economy. Section 4 discusses some of the challenges and policy options for sustainable growth in the future. Section 5 concludes.

Growth and Structural Change

The Malaysian economy grew an average growth rate of about 5.8 per cent during the period 1990–2010 (see Table 5.1). How does this performance compare with previous periods? This is slightly lower than the 6.0 per cent achieved during 1980–90 and considerably lower than the 8.3 per cent registered during 1970–80. The country's growth performances in the past two decades were punctuated by two contractions, the first due to the Asian Financial Crisis (AFC) in 1997/98 and more recently the Global Financial Crisis (GFC) in 2008/09. Economic growth in the pre-AFC period (1990–97) at 9.2 per cent was considerably higher than in the 5.3 per cent registered in post-AFC (and pre-GFC) period (1998–2010).

TABLE 5.1
Real GDP Growth Rate

Period	Growth Rate* (%)
1970–80	8.3
1980–90	6.0
1990–95	9.5
1995–2000	4.8
2000–05	4.5
2005–10	4.4
1990–2010	5.8
1990–97	9.2
1998	−7.4
1999–2008	5.3
2009	−1.7
2010	7.2

Note: * Compound average growth rate.
Source: Compiled using data from Department of Statistics.

TABLE 5.2
Structure of the Malaysian Economy, 1990–2010
(GDP Composition, %)

	1990	1995	1997	2000	2005	2010
Agriculture	15.2	12.9	11.9	8.8	8.0	7.3
Mining and quarrying	11.8	6.2	6.7	10.9	9.5	7.2
Manufacturing	24.2	26.4	35.7	32.6	30.7	27.7
Construction	3.9	6.2	4.8	4.0	3.3	3.3
Services	46.4	50.5	44.9	48.3	51.2	57.4
Less: Undistributed FISIM	5.2	5.6	8.2	6.4	3.9	4.1
Plus: Import duties	3.6	3.4	4.1	1.7	1.3	1.3
GDP at purchasers' prices	100.0	100.0	100.0	100.0	100.0	100.0

Source: Compiled using data from Department of Statistics.

In terms of economic structure, the services sector has become increasingly more important compared to the manufacturing sector in the period under review. The Gross Domestic Product (GDP) share of the manufacturing sector today (27.7 per cent in 2010) is only slightly higher than that achieved two decades ago (24.2 per cent in 1995). The decline in the GDP share of the manufacturing sector is particularly evident in the post-AFC period. In 1997, the manufacturing sector's share of GDP stood at 35.7 per cent in 1997. The decline in the manufacturing sector's share in GDP has been accompanied by an increase in services sector's share of GDP — which increased by 11 per cent from 46.4 per cent in 1990 to 57.4 per cent in 2010.

Sources of Growth

The sources of economic growth are usually analysed using the growth accounting method and macroeconomic data. This has the main approach adopted and reported in official reports. In addition, studies using micro data such as plant or firm-level data shed additional insights on the sources of growth. The section reviews the evidence from both types of studies.

Macro Data Evidence

The standard way to investigate the sources of growth has been the growth accounting method. A basic exposition of this method begins by assuming that the aggregate production function takes the following form:

$$Y_t = A_t K_t^{(1/3)} L_t^{(2/3)}$$

where Y_t is GDP, A_t the stock of ideas, K_t capital stock and L_t labour. Restating this in terms of growth, economic growth (g_{Yt}) can be decomposed into three sources, namely growth rates of total factor productivity (TFP), capital and labour:[1]

$$g_{Yt} = g_{At} + \frac{1}{3} g_{Kt} + \frac{2}{3} g_{Lt}$$

In the following discussions, we examine what is known about the sources of growth in the past two decades in terms of the growth accounting method.

Growth accounting data from the five-year plans indicates that the factors driving Malaysia's economic growth for the past two decades have changed over time (see Table 5.3). In the decade from 1990–2000, growth were driven primarily by the accumulation of physical capital. In contrast, the contribution of capital accumulation to growth has declined significantly to just 1.4 per cent during the 2006–10 period. This is due to a consistent decline in the contribution of capital accumulation to growth since 1990. The contribution of labour has remained relatively unchanged at around 1.3 per cent–1.5 per cent in the past fifteen years. TFP's contribution to growth increased from 1.1 per cent during 1996–2000 to 1.4 per cent during 2001–05. However, TFP has stagnated at 1.5 per cent in the past five years from 2006–10.

A sectoral analysis of the composition and changes in real net capital stock in Malaysia provides further insights into the decline in capital accumulation. The services sector account for some 70 per cent of total net capital stock (see Table 5.4). The decline in capital accumulation within the services sector has been very significant (see Table 5.5). Even though the increase in the rate of capital accumulation in the mining sector in recent years (2005/06–10) have been substantial, this appears to be insufficient to off-set the decline experienced by the services sector.

TABLE 5.3
Growth Accounting for Malaysia, 1990–2010
(Percentage contribution)

	6MP 1990–95	7MP 1996–2000	8MP 2001–05	9MP 2006–10
GDP Growth	9.5	4.8	4.7	4.2
Contribution of Capital	4.7	2.2	1.8	1.4
Contribution of Labour	2.3	1.5	1.5	1.3
Contribution of TFP	2.5	1.1	1.4	1.5

Sources: Eighth, Ninth and Tenth Malaysia Plans.

TABLE 5.4
Sectoral Distribution of Real Net Capital Stock in Malaysia, 1990–2009
(%)

	1990	1995	2000	2005	2009
Agriculture	5.27	3.58	2.39	2.32	2.07
Mining and Quarrying	9.75	8.23	8.20	11.04	17.57
Construction	1.97	1.34	0.98	0.95	0.85
Manufacturing	12.94	15.56	14.91	16.48	15.83
Services	70.08	71.30	73.52	69.21	63.68
Total	100.00	100.00	100.00	100.00	100.00

Source: Compiled using data from Department of Statistics.

TABLE 5.5
Growth in Real Net Capital Stock in Malaysia, 1990–2009
(%, compound average growth rate)

	1990–95	1995–2000	2000–05	2005–09
Agriculture	1.77	−0.03	0.02	1.59
Mining and quarrying	6.30	4.55	9.25	14.08
Construction	1.78	−1.68	2.32	1.64
Manufacturing	14.11	3.72	5.01	3.14
Services	10.35	5.26	1.70	2.25
Total	9.97	4.61	2.94	3.96

Source: Compiled using data from Department of Statistics.

Table 5.6 provides a summary of growth accounting performance by sectors. The contribution of capital accumulation to growth is clearly larger than from TFP across the different sectors. The gap is particularly large in the manufacturing sector where the TFP contribution to growth (0.78 per cent) is only half of that from capital accumulation (1.56 per cent) during the 2006–10 period. This capital accumulation-TFP gap is also observed in most of the services subsectors with the

TABLE 5.6
Sectoral Growth Accounting for Malaysia, 2001–10
(Percentage contribution)

	8MP	9MP
	2001–05	2006–10
Agriculture		
GDP growth	3.19	2.59
Contribution of capital	0.41	1.09
Contribution of labour	1.05	0.48
Contribution of TFP	1.73	1.03
Mining		
GDP growth	2.32	−0.82
Contribution of capital	0.44	0.06
Contribution of labour	0.39	0.24
Contribution of TFP	1.9	−1.12
Manufacturing		
GDP growth	4.75	2.55
Contribution of capital	1.99	1.56
Contribution of labour	1.69	0.21
Contribution of TFP	1.08	0.78
Services	2001–10	
GDP growth	1.6	
Contribution of capital	0.57	
Contribution of labour	0.58	
Contribution of TFP	0.44	

Source: Malaysia Productivity Corporation, *Productivity Report 2010/11*.

exception of finance (see Table 5.7). In addition, Table 5.7 also suggested that capital accumulation and TFP growth rates in some of the services sector during the 2006–10 period were higher than those achieved by the mining and manufacturing. However, almost all services subsectors experienced a significant contraction in TFP in year 2009 (Malaysia Productivity Corporation 2011).

The TFP has also been decomposed by using a number of proxies representing factors related to human capital and technological change

TABLE 5.7
Growth Accounting for Services Subsectors, 2001–10
(Percentage contribution)

| | 8MP | 9MP |
	2001–05	2006–10
Utilities		
GDP growth	5.42	3.94
Contribution of capital	1.74	1.93
Contribution of labour	2.48	0.56
Contribution of TFP	1.20	1.44
Transport		
GDP growth	5.72	6.32
Contribution of capital	0.84	2.81
Contribution of labour	3.94	1.05
Contribution of TFP	0.94	2.45
Wholesale and retail		
GDP growth	5.10	7.68
Contribution of capital	1.70	3.45
Contribution of labour	2.46	1.11
Contribution of TFP	0.94	3.12
Finance		
GDP Growth	6.05	8.13
Contribution of capital	1.03	3.86
Contribution of labour	4.07	1.24
Contribution of TFP	0.96	3.03

Source: Malaysia Productivity Corporation, *Productivity Report 2010/11*.

(see Table 5.8). Of these factors, demand intensity and human capital are the most important. The contribution of technical progress to TFP is relatively small by comparison. These results suggest that economic growth is not strongly driven by innovation. Due to the difficulties in constructing appropriate variables and factors as well as potential endogeneity problems (e.g., the interactions between human capital and technical progress), such results should be interpreted as tentative rather than conclusive.

TABLE 5.8
Components of TFP in Malaysia, 2001–10
(Percentage contribution)

	Description/Proxies	8MP 2001–05	9MP 2006–10
TFP		1.39	1.65
Economic restructuring	Share of employment in higher value-added activities	0.36	0.15
Human capital	Enrolment in higher education	0.34	0.45
Capital structure	Total investment approved	0.32	0.29
Demand intensity	Capacity utilization	0.20	0.56
Technical progress	Process innovation, organizational innovation	0.17	0.20

Source: Malaysia Productivity Corporation, *Productivity Report 2010/11*.

Micro Data Evidence

Micro-level studies using plant-level or firm-level data provides additional insights into growth and productivity performances in Malaysia. Aside from avoiding problems associated with data aggregation (at macro-level), such studies can study firm-level characteristics that influence productivity performance. There are a number of studies that contain analysis of firm-level productivity performance in Malaysia. These include the following:

- Knowledge Content in Economic Sectors in Malaysia (MyKE) — based on the knowledge economy surveys conducted by Economic Planning Unit;
- Productivity and Investment Climate Surveys (PICS) — conducted by the World Bank; and
- National Surveys of Innovation (NSI) — conducted by MASTIC.

Table 5.9 provides a summary of these studies. Of these studies, only studies and reports using PICS and NSI have examined TFP at the firm level.

TABLE 5.9
Summary of Firm-Level Studies/Reports

Study	Period	Sample Size	
MyKE Study I (2004)	2002	Manufacturing:	1,118
		Services:	380
MyKE Study II (2009)	2007	Agriculture:	99
		Manufacturing:	1,140
		Services:	957
		Construction:	237
PICS I (2005)	1999–2001	Manufacturing:	1,151
		Services:	249
PICS II (2009)	2004–06	Manufacturing:	1,115
		Services:	303
NSI I	1997–99	Manufacturing:	1,004
NSI II	2000–01	Manufacturing:	749
NSI III	2002–04	Manufacturing:	485

Source: Compiled by the author.

The low level of TFP growth in manufacturing is confirmed in PICS II, which reported that the average level of TFP among Malaysia's manufacturing firms "only increased slightly at 0.6 percent from 2004 to 2005 and remained unchanged from 2005 to 2006" (World Bank 2009, p. 42). In both PICS I and PICS II, manufacturing TFP is found to be positively correlated to size (albeit inverse-U), exporting and Foreign Direct Investment (FDI). Research and Development (R&D) is found to be positively related to TFP in the PICS II. In addition, a proxy for human capital, as a percentage of employees with a college degree, is also positively correlated to TFP.

Using data from the NSI, Lee (2011) provides further evidence that firm-level productivity (measured by TFP and labour productivity) is driven by capital intensity and human capital. Larger firms and those with foreign ownership are more likely to export. The study found that the relationship between productivity and export is weak — suggesting that, productivity improvements *per se* does not necessarily enhance exports. Given the evidence on the self-selection of firms with high productivity to export in other studies, the above results may imply that current productivity levels may be too low to induce export (that is, after controlling for foreign ownership and firm size). Innovation, however, is related to export. This is of importance given the recent World Bank (2009) findings that Malaysia's innovation capabilities might have deteriorated. Trade liberalization is also found to be positively related to export of non-innovating firms.

Challenges and Policy Options

Achievements and Targets

There is no doubt that the growth performance of the Malaysian economy has been below the expectations of policy-makers in recent years. Both growth targets for the Eighth and the Ninth Malaysia Plans were not met (see Table 5.10). An examination of the gap between the growth accounting targets and actual performance for both the 8MP and 9MP suggests that of the three sources of growth, the targets for TFP have been the most difficult to achieve.

For the Tenth Malaysia Plan (10MP), the growth target at 6 per cent is not overly ambitious given that the average annual growth rate between 1999 and 2008 (between the AFC and GFC) is 5.3 per cent per annum. In terms of sources of growth, the key drivers are both capital accumulation and TFP, with each contributing 38.3 per cent of the growth

TABLE 5.10
Growth Targets and Performance, 1990–2010
(Percentage contribution)

	Target	Achieved	Target	Achieved	Target
	8MP	8MP	9MP	9MP	10MP
	2001–05	2001–05	2006–10	2006–10	2011–15
GDP growth	7.5	4.7	6.0	4.2	6.0
Contribution of capital	n.a.	1.8	2.0	1.4	2.3
Contribution of labour	n.a.	1.5	1.8	1.3	1.4
Contribution of TFP	n.a.	1.4	2.2	1.5	2.3

Note: n.a. – not available.
Source: Eighth, Ninth and Tenth Malaysia Plans.

in GDP over the plan period. The real challenge will be to achieve the 2.3 per cent growth in TFP. The TFP growth rates in Malaysia have not exceeded 1.5 per cent since the Asian Financial Crisis.

Whether the targets for the 10MP can be met will require an analysis of the proposed development strategies and policies stated in the Plan. Such an analysis can be undertaken by drawing from what is known about the current economy as well as findings from the research literature.

Growth Strategies in the Tenth Malaysia Plan

From a growth accounting perspective, the key drivers of growth in the Tenth Malaysia Plan (10MP) are capital accumulation and productivity growth (TFP). What programmes and activities are proposed to achieve these? Chapter 3 of the 10MP report provides a list of key activities and programmes that form details of the growth strategy for the next five years. They are summarized as follows.

(a) Microeconomic reforms to enhance the dynamism of the private sector:

- Improvements in business climate via reducing the cost of doing business (e.g., World Bank's Doing Business Report);
- Liberalization of the services sector through the relaxation of foreign equity restrictions and employment of foreign workers in selected services subsectors;
- Removal of subsidies and price controls that distort resource allocation;
- Implementation and enforcement competition law to promote competition in the domestic markets; and
- Improvements in the delivery of government services to businesses.

(b) Promotion of innovation:

- Improvements in the national innovation system via human capital development;
- Investments in innovation-related infrastructure (e.g., broad-band);
- Incentives for knowledge transfer in FDI; and
- Greater support for innovation activities (e.g., incubators).

(c) **Rationalization of government activities:**

- Privatization of more projects under improved processes;
- Strategic targeting of new projects via a Facilitation Fund aimed at improving project viability (land cost and infrastructure);
- Rationalization of government and government-linked company (GLC) activities in the economy;
- Regulatory reforms to enhance regulatory regimes in a number of sectors.

(d) **Small and medium enterprise (SME) development:**

- Reduction in regulatory burdens faced by SMEs;
- Capacity building via training programmes;
- Creation of entrepreneurial culture via enhancing entrepreneurship in university curricula;
- Assistance of SMEs in quality certification and branding;
- Improvements in financing access via venture capital, private equity, guarantees and preferential loans.

The list of activities and programmes suggest that the overall growth strategy is one targeted at the private sector. In terms of capital accumulation, private sector investment is targeted to increase by 12.8 per cent over the 10MP period (2011–15). This is a significant challenge given that private investment only grew at a rate of 2 per cent in the 2006–10 period. The post-GFC recovery in private investment is promising (7 per cent in 2010) but fragile given the unfavourable external economic environment in the near future. The global economic slowdown following the GFC and more recently, the sovereign debt crisis, will certainly imply that it would be difficult to achieve the target for private investment particularly when much of this is expected to be driven by FDI.

In the case of productivity growth, the dominance of services sector implies that significant progress needs to be made in this sector. Based on productivity growth estimates by Malaysia Productivity Corporation (MPC), services subsectors with high productivity growth levels (exceeding 5 per cent p.a.) in the past five years include distributive trade, financial services and telecommunications. The impact of ownership liberalization in these subsectors on productivity can be substantial but there is some uncertainty about this given that no specifics were given in terms of the subsectors involved as well as the quantum of liberalization. It is difficult to assess how innovation-related initiatives will impact the services sector. Investments in ICT-related can potentially bring about significant impact on productivity growth in services but the listed strategies appear to focus more on manufacturing activities. Much will also depend on how GLCs will be restructured given their heavy involvement in the services sector.

In the manufacturing sector, productivity growth is likely to be high in subsectors with heavy presence of multinational corporations (MNCs). These include in many of the export-oriented industries such as electrical and electronics (Shahrazat 2010). The focus on FDI-related technology transfer is justified given the productivity differentials between foreign and domestically-owned firms in the sector as well as the low degree of spillovers from the former to the latter. The focus on SMEs is also likely to impact productivity growth positively but there is great uncertainty in terms of its quantum given the relatively lower share of SMEs in total output in the manufacturing sector.

The focus on human capital development and entrepreneurship in the 10MP is crucial for productivity growth and innovation. However, this is a difficult area to manage given the relative decline in research capabilities and the brain drain problem in recent years. The extent and impact of university and curricula reforms is uncertain. Recent exercises in further liberalization of the private education sector could provide the needed impetus in this area.

Beyond the Tenth Malaysia Plan

The Tenth Malaysia Plan covers the period 2011–15. The annual growth target of 6 per cent is unlikely to be achieved given the adverse external conditions for 2011 which may stretch up to 2013. Thus, there is a need to go beyond the 6 per cent growth or Vision 2020 rhetoric in policy proclamations. A more meaningful approach when considering the period up to 2020 may be to consider some of the reforms that need to be carried out.

Unless significant fiscal reforms are implemented, the government will not be able to undertake counter-cyclical policies. These should include broadening the tax revenue base via Goods and Services Tax (GST) and reducing the size of public sector. Even if such reforms are carried out after 2015, the government should not attempt to compensate any decline in private investments by undertaking public investments either directly or indirectly (via GLCs). In fact, the government should reduce the role of GLCs in the private sector.

Such reforms should also be accompanied by actions to improve economic and regulatory governance aimed at reducing arbitrary decisions in development spending and regulatory matters. These reforms should aim at bringing about more transparent and non-discriminatory procurement and regulatory systems. These are essential to deal with problems such as lack of FDI, inefficient infrastructure services, lack of human capital and brain drain.

The above reforms, if carried out, are likely to positively enhance the innovation capabilities in Malaysia. In addition, as human capital is the key factor in innovation-driven growth, further and more targeted liberalization of the private education sector together with immigration policies favouring skilled migrants is likely to bring about a more innovative private sector.

Conclusions

The key growth strategy in the Tenth Malaysia Plan is that of a private sector-driven growth through capital accumulation and productivity gains. The task at hand is a challenging one given the lethargic levels of private investment (domestic and FDI). Improvements in the institutional and business environment are likely to be helpful. Productivity improvements will play an equally important role.

The proposed microeconomic reforms can potentially increase productivity levels in the economy. What is less certain is how such reforms will impact the services sector which is today the dominant sector in the economy. In the manufacturing sector, FDI will play an important role given the higher productivity levels of MNCs and positive links between exporting and productivity. It is difficult to ascertain whether the proposed specific incentives and microeconomic reforms will be sufficient to attract high levels of FDI inflows in the next five years. This will also depend on whether efforts to deepen the country's human capital and entrepreneurship will be effective.

A significant feature of the Tenth Malaysia Plan is the set of reforms in the government machinery. These include streamlining and reduction of regulations. The state bureaucracy is still large in Malaysia. The presence of GLCs in the Malaysian economy is still substantial. Beyond the Tenth Malaysia Plan, further reforms aimed at improving the state of economic and regulatory governance is crucial. The benefits from such reform are likely to be very broad. More targeted policies in the private education and skilled migration are also important for an innovation-driven economy.

NOTE

1. This formulation follows the standard assumption that capital and labour account for one-third and two-third of total income.

REFERENCES

Lee, Cassey. "Trade, Productivity and Innovation". *Journal of Asian Economics*, no. 22 (2011): 284–94.

Malaysia Productivity Corporation. *Productivity Report 2010/11*. Petaling Jaya, Selangor: MPC, 2011.

Shahrazat, Haj Ahmad. "A Quantitative Study on the Productivity of the Manufacturing Industry in Malaysia". Ph.D. thesis, Graduate School of Social System Studies, University of Kitakyushu, 2010.

Syverson, Chad. "What Determines Productivity?". *Journal of Economic Literature*, vol. 49, no. 2 (2011): 326–65.

World Bank. "Malaysia: Productivity and Investment Climate Assessment Update". Report No. 49137-MY (2009).

6

MALAYSIA'S INVESTMENT MALAISE
What Happened and Can It be Fixed?[1]

Jayant Menon

"Unfortunately, the protection and privileges accorded by the NEP may weaken the Malays further by lulling the next generation into complacency, thinking that the NEP's affirmative action will always be there for them to fall back upon. I have spoken about this danger many times, likening the NEP to crutches which, when used too long, would result in atrophy of the muscles. The NEP can make the users so dependent that their inherent capability regresses."

— Tun Mahathir Mohamad (2011)
Former Prime Minister of Malaysia

Introduction

It was not long ago that the Malaysian development story was hailed as a model of foreign direct investment (FDI)-driven, export-led industrialization worthy of emulation by aspirants in the developing world. The transformation from a largely agrarian economy in the 1950s and 1960s to a manufacturing-based one was rapid and spectacular, with the share of agriculture in gross domestic product (GDP) falling from 30 per cent in 1970 to 8 per cent today, and that of industry increasing from 27 per cent to 55 per cent over the same period. Per capita income almost doubled each decade to reach more than US$8,000 per year in 2012. These economic achievements are reflected in dramatic improvements in social conditions. Extreme poverty has almost been eliminated, despite persistently high inequality, and access to all kinds of social services has improved dramatically. FDI played a critical role in this transformation. Domestic investment was also robust at around 40 per cent of GDP at the onset of the Asian Financial Crisis (AFC). Yet, although the slump in economic growth during the AFC was quickly reversed in the ensuing V-shaped recovery, private investment — both foreign and domestic — never really recovered.

These days, references to Malaysia in the development economics literature tend to highlight it as a classic case of the "middle income trap". No longer able to compete in the labour-intensive manufacturing activities that drove its transformation, due to factor price adjustments, it also finds itself unable to move up the value chain to more sophisticated activities within manufacturing and services in order to graduate to developed country status. The revival of domestic and foreign private investment must play a key role in raising productivity levels in order to break out of the middle income trap. The need to revive private investment is recognized in all government strategic and planning documents, particularly the Tenth Malaysia Plan (TMP), and also the New Economic Model (NEM) and Economic Transformation Programme (ETP).

The purpose of this chapter is to critically examine the factors underlying the decline in private domestic and foreign investment in Malaysia, with a view to identifying policy changes that could reverse this trend. The remainder of the chapter is divided into five parts. The next section examines the trends in domestic investment, both private and public, in the pre- and post-AFC periods. Section 3 focuses on foreign investment, both in terms of inflows and outflows, also for the pre- and post-AFC periods. This is followed by discussions on possible reasons underlying the performance of private investment, focusing on the period after the AFC. Policy changes required to improve the investment climate is the subject of Section 5. The final section concludes.

Domestic Investment (pre- and post-AFC)

In the five years leading up to the AFC (1993–97), total investment (public and private) averaged a robust 41.3 per cent of GDP (see Figure 6.1), peaking at 43.6 per cent in 1995. Investment rates were so high that there was even some concern that Malaysia had been over-investing (ADB 2012). There were a slew of mega-projects that underpinned the robust investment numbers. However, investment levels fell sharply to an annual average of 22.1 per cent of GDP in the period following the AFC (1998–2011). The onset of the global financial crisis (GFC) pushed investment below 15 per cent of GDP in 2009, the lowest level in recent history. Although preliminary estimates for 2011 suggest a recovery to the period average of about 22 per cent, there has been a clear trend of decline from 2001 onward.

FIGURE 6.1
Malaysia Gross Capital Formation, 1993–2011
(% of GDP)

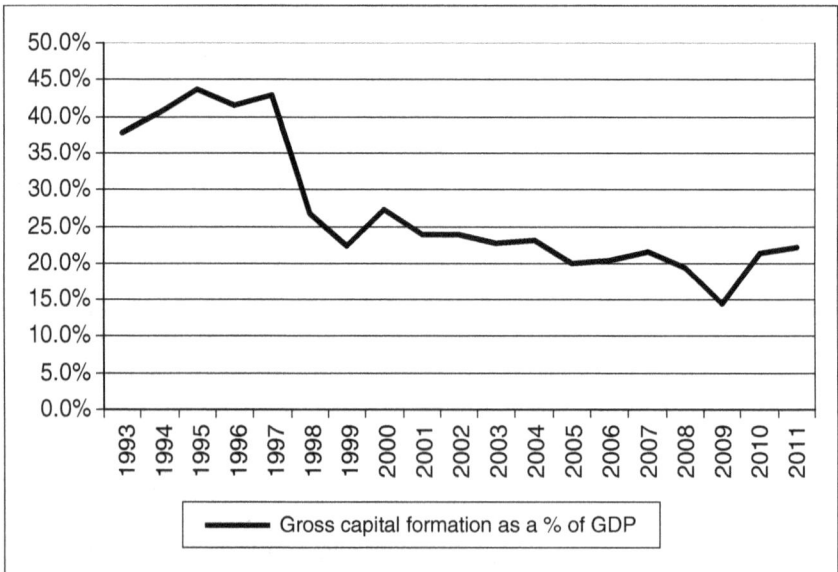

Note: GDP = gross domestic product.
Sources: Bank Negara Malaysia Annual Report (various years) and Bank Negara Malaysia Q1 2012 Bulletin.

Even these dismal figures mask the much more disturbing decline in private investment. While private investment accounted for more than 70 per cent of total investment in the boom years leading up to the AFC (1993–97), its share had fallen to about half of this ratio (or less) in the years following the AFC. For ten out of the fourteen years since 1998, private investment has been about equal to or less than public investment. In 2002–03, when private investment as a share of GDP slumped to about 8 per cent (see Figure 6.2), its share was only about half that of public investment. In other words, if not for the increase in public investment following the AFC, the overall investment picture in Malaysia would have been even more dismal. Unlike private investment, public investment as a share of GDP has remained relatively stable over the past two decades, averaging about 11.5 per cent. Underlying this stable but robust share of public investment over

FIGURE 6.2
Malaysia Gross Fixed Capital Formation (Public and Private), 1993–2011
(% of GDP)

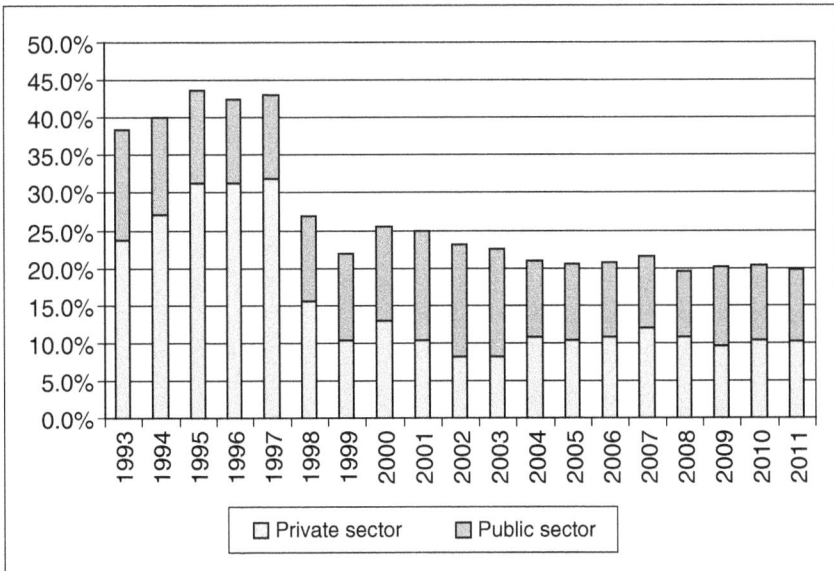

Note: GDP = gross domestic product.
Sources: Bank Negara Malaysia Annual Report (various years) and Bank Negara Malaysia Q1 2012 Bulletin.

the years has been the gradual encroachment of the public sector into activities that would usually be associated with private firms. This is an issue that will be discussed in Section 4, in order to look at whether private investment may have been crowded out by public investment.

Foreign Inward and Outward Investment (pre- and post-AFC)

Foreign Inward Investment

Inflows of FDI have been the engine of manufactured export expansion in Malaysia. FDI flows to Malaysia grew remarkably in the two decades leading up to the AFC,[2] particularly in the decade from the mid-1980s. From the mid-1980s up until the onset of the AFC, FDI flows to Malaysia had been increasing at a faster rate than flows to all other Association of Southeast Asian Nation (ASEAN) countries. Between 1987 and 1991, FDI inflows increased by more than ten-fold to reach US$4 billion. This amount doubled again by the mid-1990s, when Malaysia accounted for one-fourth of total inflows to ASEAN, second only to Singapore.

From 1991 up until the AFC, the volume of FDI flowing to Malaysia remained higher than in any other ASEAN country, with the exception of Singapore. In the wake of the AFC, FDI to Malaysia fell from US$7.2 billion in 1996 to US$2.7 billion in 1998 (see Figure 6.3). During the same period, FDI as a percentage of GDP and gross fixed capital formation fell from 7.0 per cent to 3.6 per cent, and from 16.6 per cent to 13.6 per cent, respectively (see Figures 6.4 and 6.5).

This sharp contraction in FDI was common among all of the original ASEAN members. The depleted FDI inflows that were triggered by the AFC continued well into the recovery and up until about 2001. In 2001, FDI flows to Malaysia fell to US$554 million, the lowest level since 1987. The persistence of contracting FDI is attributable to the global slowdown in FDI flows, which declined by more than half from US$134 billion in 2000 to US$63 billion in 2003. Total inflows during the four years from 2001 to 2004 were 24 per cent lower than the comparable figure for the preceding four years (1998–2000) (Athukorala and Wagle 2011).

But the experience in Malaysia was different. FDI did not recover like it did in the other crisis-affected countries. After having been

FIGURE 6.3
Inward FDI at Current Prices and Exchange Rates, 1990–2010 for
Malaysia, Philippines, and Thailand
(US$ million)

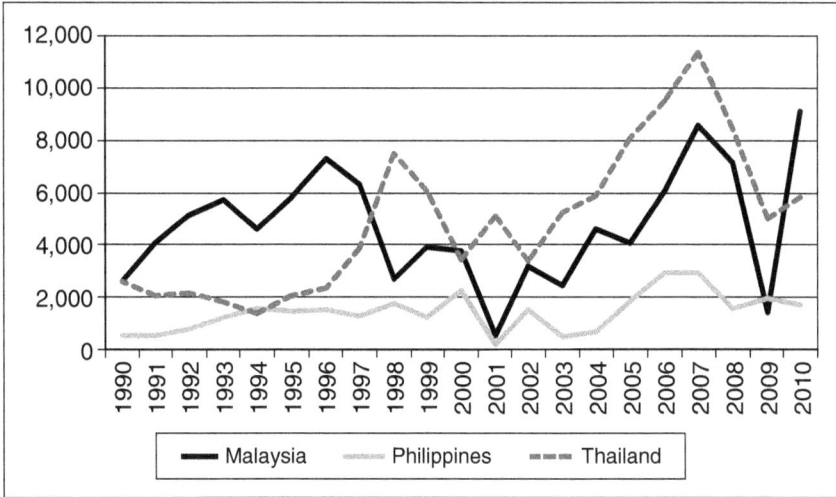

Note: FDI = foreign direct investment.
Sources: UNCTAD, UNCTADstat.

FIGURE 6.4
Inward FDI, 1990–2010 for Malaysia, Philippines, and Thailand
(% of GDP)

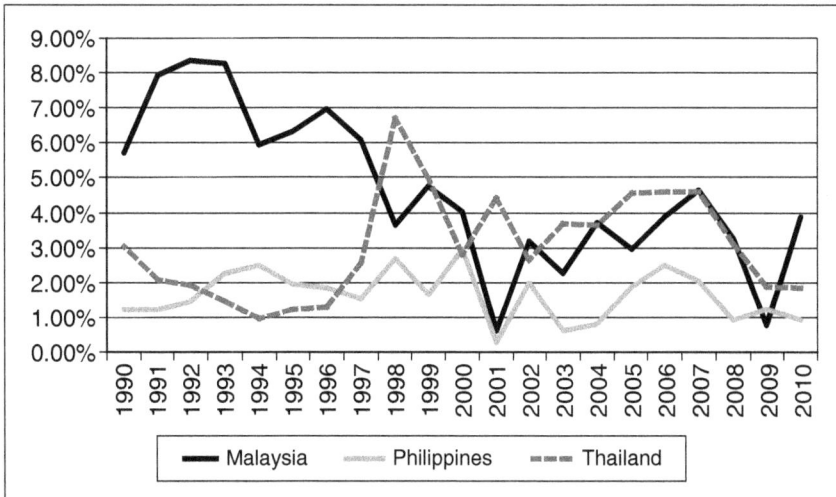

Note: FDI = foreign direct investment.
Sources: UNCTAD, UNCTADstat.

FIGURE 6.5
Inward FDI as Percentage of Gross Fixed Capital Formation, 1990–2009
for Malaysia, Philippines, and Thailand

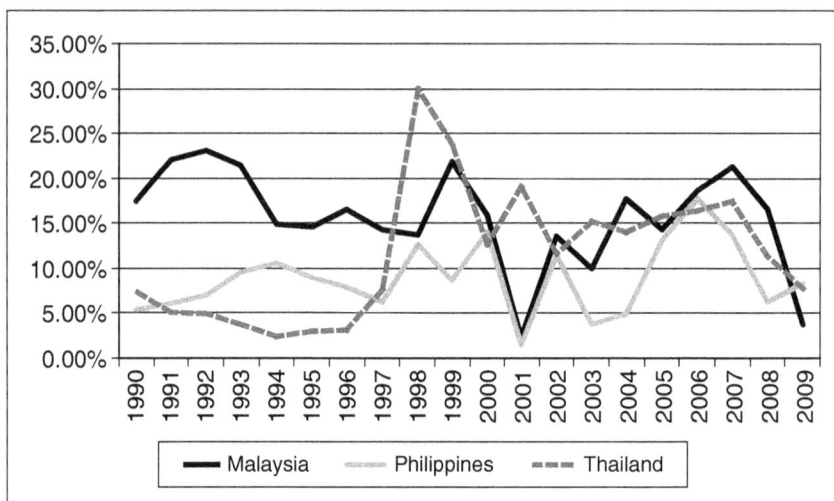

Note: FDI = foreign direct investment.
Sources: UNCTAD, UNCTADstat.

the second largest recipient of FDI in ASEAN after Singapore prior to the AFC, Malaysia was overtaken by Thailand in 2000, Indonesia and Vietnam in 2008, and the Philippines in 2009. There was mild recovery in 2005–07, when FDI inflows to Malaysia rose slightly above the amount flowing to Indonesia, although this period corresponded with some unusual sectoral shifts in the composition of the inflows. During this period, FDI flows to agriculture averaged US$671 million annually, second only to the People's Republic of China (PRC) in terms of volume. As a share of gross fixed capital formation, it was the highest among all ASEAN countries at 21.9 per cent, beating even the predominantly agrarian, new member countries that have historically recorded high shares (UNCTAD 2009). In 2007, inflows to this sector were attributed mainly to the merger (and subsequent restructuring) of PPB Oil Palms with the Singapore-based Wilmar International. The total value of this merger and acquisition (M&A) was roughly US$1.1 billion. In 2009, FDI flows slumped again to US$1.4 billion, the least among the ASEAN-5 countries, and less than a third of the FDI flows to Indonesia or Thailand.[3]

Following this slump, there appears to have been a recent uptick in FDI flows to Malaysia in 2010 and 2011. After rebounding in 2010 to US$9.1 billion, preliminary estimates suggest that FDI may have grown a further 12.3 per cent in 2011 to reach US$10.2 billion. Almost all of these inflows went to the services sector, mainly real estate.[4] The composition of the inflows tends to support the view that a significant share of the recent increase is attributable to the rapid development of the Iskandar Region of Johor state, especially Johor Baharu and its surrounding towns. Almost all of the capital inflows to this region were from Singapore. It is estimated that the region received almost MYR70 billion (US$24 billion) in investments through December 2010, of which about 40 per cent was in the form of FDI (Bhaskaran 2011). Almost all of these investments were in the non-tradable goods sector, and it is unclear if this trend can continue for much longer amid limited absorptive capacity.

There is also the environmentally controversial investment in the north of Kuantan by an Australian mining company, Lynus, which is building the world's largest rare earth refinery, and the first built outside of the People's Republic of China (PRC) in three decades. The cost of the plant is estimated at US$230 million (Bradsher 2011). This investment appears as a component of manufacturing FDI. Because of concerns over radioactive contamination, there remains some uncertainty over the future of this project. It is also likely to have limited positive spillovers domestically as an enclave project, given that most of the construction work is being undertaken by migrant labour and a twelve-year tax holiday is in effect. Any spillovers are likely to be negative, in the form of low-level radioactive waste, as was the case some decades ago with the Mitsubishi Chemical refinery in Bukit Merah in north-central Malaysia, which is now one of Asia's largest radioactive waste cleanup sites.

It is still too early to tell if this is a sustainable shift in the trend of FDI decline that started during the AFC, or if it is just a transitory phenomenon. It is also risky to read too much into preliminary estimates since it can take years for the data to settle and be verified as actual investments (Athukorala and Wagle 2011). Some of the apparent increase could also reflect a surge in FDI flows to developing countries in general amid recovery from the GFC. Estimates from UNCTAD

(2011*a*) point to a strong rebound in FDI flows to developing Asia and Latin America recently in the face of significant declines in flows to developed countries. For the first time, developing countries and transition economies absorbed more than half of global FDI flows in 2010. FDI flows to ASEAN more than doubled in 2010 to reach US$79 billion (UNCTAD 2011*b*). In short, the recent uptick in FDI to Malaysia may reflect compositional shifts induced by the GFC that favour regions that continue to grow, such as Asia and Latin America. Taken together, these factors suggest that it is too early to be celebrating a turnaround in Malaysia's FDI fortunes based on preliminary data over the past two years. This is especially the case given that much of the apparent increase can be attributed to investments in the non-traded goods sectors that may soon reach saturation levels, such as in Iskander, or one-off enclave projects whose realization remains uncertain, such as the controversial rare earth refinery near Kuantan.

Foreign Outward Investment

The Malaysian government has been encouraging outflows of FDI for some time now (Menon 2000). Income repatriated from overseas investments — in all sectors except banking, insurance, and sea and air transport — was made tax-exempt in 1995 as an inducement. Malaysia's investments overseas remained low between 1980 and 1992, hovering around US$200 million annually and never exceeding US$300 million in a single year. They increased sharply to just over US$1 billion in 1993 and peaked at US$3.7 billion in 1996. It then fell sharply during the AFC, returning to negligible levels. Outflows of capital from Malaysia started increasing sharply after the AFC, and have grown to the point where Malaysia has been a net exporter of capital since 2005 (see Figure 6.6). During 2006–09, total outflows reached US$40.4 billion, almost double the inflows of US$23.2 billion over the same period. With the gap between inflows and outflows increasing over time, total outflows peaked at almost US$15 billion in 2008. Preliminary estimates from UNCTAD (2012) suggest that outflows have started rising sharply again after the GFC, amounting to US$13.3 billion and US$14.8 billion in 2010 and 2011, respectively. Malaysia is also the only net exporter of capital among the ASEAN countries.

A significant portion of the outflows appear to be taking place in the services sector, which are dominated by oil and gas, as well as

FIGURE 6.6
Outward FDI at Current Prices and Exchange Rates, 1990–2010 for Malaysia, Philippines, and Thailand
(US$ million)

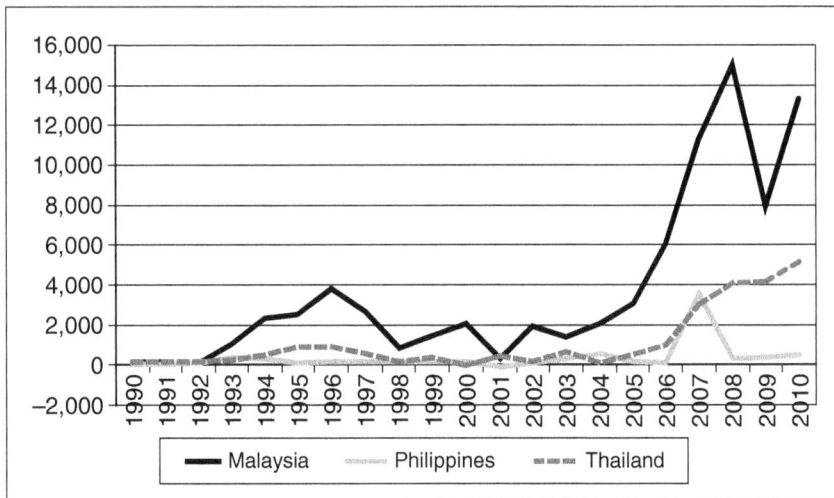

Note: FDI = foreign direct investment.
Sources: UNCTAD, UNCTADstat.

in mining and banking. Earlier it has been noted how there was an unexpected surge in FDI into the agriculture sector in Malaysia in recent years, yet the outflows of capital destined for agriculture are substantially larger, especially with respect to plantations. Furthermore, Petronas has been investing heavily in offshore oil and gas operations in a wide range of countries in several continents, including Australia, Algeria, Chad, Cameroon, Mauritius, and Iraq, as well as closer to home in Indonesia, Myanmar, and Vietnam. Sime Darby is the largest agriculture multinational corporation in the world. Two other Malaysian government-linked corporations (GLCs) are among the world's ten largest in this sector: Kuala Lumpur Kepong (KLK) and Kulim (UNCTAD 2009).[5] There have been increasing levels of outward FDI in the oil palm sector, mostly going to Indonesia due to lower land and labour costs. In a move to diversify horizontally, Sime Darby also purchased rubber plantations in Liberia at a total value of US$800 million in 2009 (UNCTAD 2009). Meanwhile, the MSC Group has investments in mining in Australia, Canada, Indonesia, and the Philippines (UNCTAD 2011b).

Singapore appears to be a large recipient covering a wide range of sectors.[6] A lot of these outward investments in almost all sectors are associated, predictably, with M&A activity.

Outflows of capital are not necessarily a bad thing; to the contrary, they can contribute to a country's wealth if directed toward investments that yield higher returns than are available at home. However, the sheer size of the outflows from Malaysia at the same time that domestic investment continues to dwindle raises concern. A greater cause for concern is that the increase in outflows over time appears to be driven by push rather than pull factors. The growing savings–investment (S–I) gap (see Figures 6.7 and 6.8) mirrors increasing current account surpluses, but there is evidence that capital flight has also increased of late. Dev and Curcio (2011) estimate that illicit capital outflows have more than tripled between 2000 and 2008, rising from about US$22 billion to US$68 billion annually, for a cumulative total of US$291 billion over this period. This places Malaysia behind only the PRC, Russia,

FIGURE 6.7
Malaysia Investment and Savings, 1993–2011
(% of GDP)

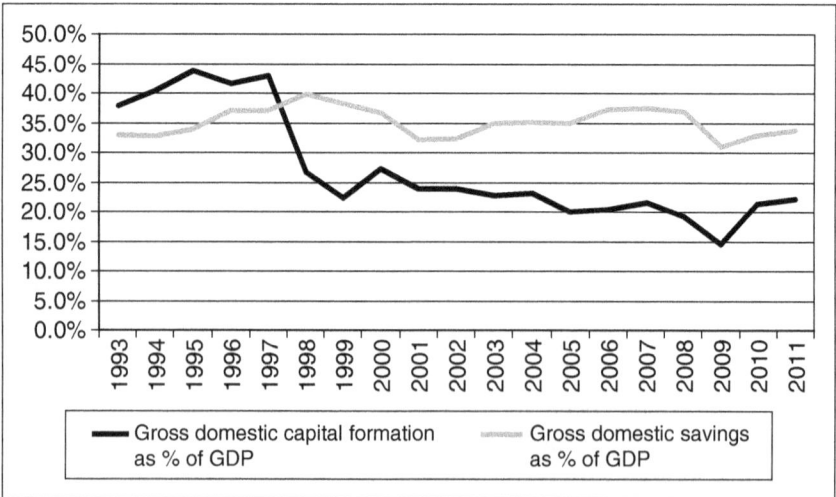

Note: GDP = gross domestic product.
Sources: *Bank Negara Malaysia Annual Report* (various years) and *Bank Negara Malaysia Q1 2012 Bulletin*.

FIGURE 6.8
Malaysia Savings–Investment Gap (Public and Private), 1993–2010

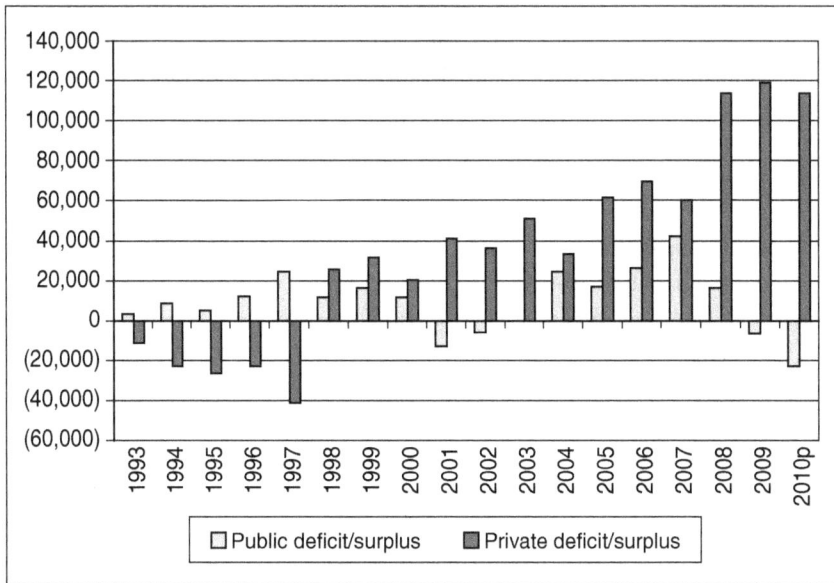

Note: 2010 data are preliminary; 2011 data unavailable.
Sources: Bank Negara Malaysia Annual Report (various years).

Mexico, and Saudi Arabia with respect to illicit outflows. In short, it appears that both foreign and domestic investors are simply abandoning Malaysia.

The Fall in Private Investment: Likely Causes

A number of reasons have been put forward to explain the dismal performance of private investment in Malaysia in the post-AFC era. Some explanations have more validity than others. Many potential explanatory factors existed prior to the AFC and so the challenge is to explain why they should matter now if they had not previously. In what follows, there are reviews of some of the key explanations put forward, assessing their relative merits in accounting for the decline in investment before deciding on what could be considered as the main causes.

During the initial phase of the slowdown in private investment in the immediate aftermath of the AFC, a popular explanation involved the unintended consequences of the capital controls introduced during the AFC — unintended in that they were designed to curb short-term flows, not FDI — and the negative perceptions that they generated. This explanation continued to gather support even as the gradual easing of these controls failed to stem the decline in FDI. But as time went on and FDI continued to fall, it became clear that this explanation could no longer hold water, if it ever did.

Another explanation blames the historic high reliance on FDI itself for its subsequent drop-off. This over-reliance on FDI is seen as having precluded the emergence — or stunted the growth — of domestic firms and innovation.[7] Proponents of this view often draw the contrasting comparison with the Republic of Korea where, apparently, domestic firms grew because they were not crowded out by foreign ones. But Malaysia has some prominent domestic companies, although most of them can hardly be described as private; many are either publicly controlled or are GLCs. In this sense, they bear some resemblance to the *chaebols* in the Republic of Korea, but they are generally considered to be less efficient, lacking the same entrepreneurial drive, more politically constrained because public ownership can be quite high, and less outward-oriented. The government estimates that GLCs employ around 5 per cent of the national workforce and account for approximately 36 per cent and 54 per cent, respectively, of the market capitalization of Bursa Malaysia and the benchmark Kuala Lumpur Composite Index. They can wield significant market power, and therefore can be a deterrent to the entry of private firms.

The NEM (2010, p. 45) is forthright in admitting that "(i)n some industries, heavy government and GLC presence has discouraged private investment". Although GLCs tend to be associated with resource-based, agriculture and services sectors, perhaps because their concentrations in these sectors are particularly high, there is hardly a sector from which they are absent.

While one should hardly blame the lack of FDI for all of Malaysia's current ailments, one cannot look to FDI alone for salvation either. It would appear that the factors affecting FDI and its slowdown may not be that different from those curtailing domestic private investment. It is also more likely that it is domestic GLCs that may be deterring private investment and the entry of new private firms, rather than foreign ones. Furthermore, the pervasiveness of GLCs across almost all sectors, and their ability to exercise not only significant market power but to use their special access to government and regulatory agencies to their favour, suggests that they may present a formidable barrier to both competition and the entry of new private firms. A further disincentive for private firms is illustrated by the links between the NEP and the GLCs in the conduct of business. At present, only firms that meet bumiputera (literally "sons of the soil") equity quotas are allowed to bid for government or GLC procurement contracts. Apart from deterring genuine private sector investment, this system also fails when it comes to meeting its redistributive objectives. This is acknowledged by former Prime Minister Mahathir in his recently released memoirs: "(t)he bumiputera were also selling contracts, licenses, and permits immediately after they were allocated" (2011, p. 468).

Yet another explanation puts the blame on the influx of low-skilled foreign workers, apparently reducing the incentive of multinational corporations to upgrade into higher value-added activities. Although most of the migrant labour is employed in the agriculture and construction sectors, it is sometimes claimed that there is a sufficient inflow of migrant labour into the manufacturing sector to depress domestic wages and hold back the shift from labour-intensive to human capital- and technology-intensive manufacturing activities. Although it is likely that the influx of migrant labour would have affected structural adjustments through factor price changes that influence capital-labour ratios, the extent to which it affected the movement up the value chain is unclear. The absence of such upgrading within manufacturing may have as much to do with the continuing shortage of skilled local labour as it does with the increase in the supply of low-skilled migrant labour. Therefore, the solution to upgrading manufacturing may lie with improving the skill levels of domestic labour rather than simply restricting low-skilled migrant labour.[8] While Malaysia is a net importer of labour, it is a net exporter of skills.

While the migrant labour explanation may not be totally persuasive, it does raise a number of related questions that warrant consideration. For example, what is preventing greater domestic skills enhancement and the development of human capital? And, why is Malaysia a net exporter of skilled labour? Each of these two questions are examined in turn below.

It would appear that a greater investment in education and training is required to address the human capital deficit. But the deficit of skills in Malaysia is not due to any lack of spending; public and private universities and colleges have proliferated throughout Malaysia, and a number of foreign educational institutions have also established campuses in Malaysia. The problem lies with quality, on the one hand, and access on the other. The adage that "quantity has its own quality" is particularly fitting here. Not only has the rapid growth in the number of education and training institutions occurred at the expense of quality, there is also a mismatch between the skills generated in local vocational and higher education institutions, and labour market requirements.[9] NEAC (2010, p. 6) notes that while "(t)he human capital situation in Malaysia is reaching a critical stage... the education system is not producing the skills demanded by firms". This is evidenced by the fact that the highest level of unemployment in Malaysia is among graduates, accounting for about a quarter of the unemployed (Khaled 2009). In October 2009, for instance, there were 81,046 active graduate registrants (on the Labour Exchange) looking for work and another 70,747 active registrants who were diploma holders and also unemployed. Of these, about 90 per cent were reported to be bumiputeras, despite about 80 per cent of appointments in the civil service going to bumiputeras through ethnic quotas (Lee and Nagaraj 2012).

This leads us naturally to the issue of access. Race-based quotas that discriminate in favour of bumiputeras at entry level ensure that access is no longer merit-based. As Woo (2011) puts it, the "education system is still more (of) a socio-political instrument than an economic instrument even though (the) nation-building goal has been achieved". As a result, many (more) qualified candidates are denied access to post-secondary education purely on the basis of race. Or, to turn the argument around, a number of otherwise unqualified or ineligible applicants will gain entry to a post-secondary institution purely on the basis of race. In short, a lower quality of education quality is being provided to less qualified students than would otherwise be the case. It is therefore no surprise that domestic skills enhancement and human capital development have been curbed. This unholy union of mediocrity also accounts for both the high level of unemployment among graduates as well as their racial composition.

Turning to the second question: why is Malaysia a net exporter of skilled labour? There are both push and pull factors at play. Although the two are related and observed outcomes are the result of a summation of the two, there is more that can be done domestically to affect the push rather than the pull. Starting with the pull, there are more countries today that are receptive to migrants than ever before. Industrialized countries such as Australia, Canada, Singapore, and the United States (U.S.) are favoured destinations of professionals and other skilled workers from Malaysia and elsewhere. It is useful to illustrate the push factors by returning to the education system and its flaws. With access restricted and quality declining, an increasing number of non-bumiputera students with the financial wherewithal have been pursuing post-secondary qualifications in the aforementioned countries and the United Kingdom (UK). Many never return. Those who do return quickly find that the restrictions that forced them offshore will continue to affect them, either in gaining employment or in career progression.

Quotas and any other types of selective quantitative restrictions are the most distortionary instruments of protection and they apply not only at entry level to post-secondary education, but continue into the board room and can extend all the way to the factory floor, affecting almost every aspect of economic and social life. These and numerous other distortions that are either directly or indirectly attributable to the workings of the NEP or its reincarnates lie at the very heart of the problem.

Even though the architect of the affirmative action programme was former Prime Minister (PM) Tun Abdul Razak, most of its implementation occurred during the long reign of its main proponent, former Prime Minister Mahathir Mohamad. In his recently published memoirs, Mahathir (2011, p. 39) is now able to admit that the programme "... created a disabling culture of entitlement", and that "many more have been weakened by the privileges that come with positive discrimination". He goes on to lament the failure of the many other discriminatory schemes, starting with the preferential allocation of public share offerings: "almost immediately after the bumiputera were allocated shares, they sold them", and that "this sale of shares for upfront profits frustrated efforts to increase bumiputera ownership of corporate wealth. In fact, this practice increased the disparities in wealth ownership between the bumiputera and non-bumiputera" (pp. 467–68).

Finally, there is acknowledgement of the well-known fact that almost all affirmative action programmes tend to benefit the least worthy within the target group: "... too much of the NEP's benefits would accrue to too small a group of bumiputera investors. Most poor Malays would remain strangers to the benefits ... " (p. 471).

Mahathir (2011, p. 39) also sees a bleak future for bumiputeras because of what the NEP has done to incentives, and the culture of dependency and entitlement that it has inculcated: "I fear for our coming generations. I worry that the children of those who have made it good will take the policy for granted and never learn to be intellectually and economically self-reliant." But the future will be bleak not just for bumiputeras but for all Malaysians, unless the NEP and its distortions are relaxed, and the dominant role of GLCs curtailed. There is no more important policy change required to restore confidence and revive investment than addressing these two inter-related constraints. There is no doubt that there is an increased level of policy unpredictability and political uncertainty in Malaysia today. These factors are deterring foreign investors when once certainty and stability in these areas were hailed as major attractions. But these factors take on a further potency when piled on top of a distorted policy environment. Reducing these uncertainties alone is unlikely to restore the confidence of investors. The underlying system of distortions needs to be overhauled. While both the NEP and GLCs were present long before the AFC, their impacts may have been masked during the heady days of high economic growth leading up to the AFC. Many constraints appear invisible until economic conditions worsen, when they can resurface as binding constraints. The current global environment is also quite different post-AFC, where competition for FDI in the region has been heightened by the growing presence of the PRC and Vietnam, for instance, and where migration options and the mobility of skilled labour are much greater.

Policy Changes to Retain and Revive Private Investment

There is widespread recognition in Malaysia of the challenges required to sustain growth, let alone to break out of the middle income trap by 2020. There is also increasing recognition that many of the country's problems, including the slump in private investment, are rooted in the distortions resulting from the design and implementation of the NEP and its reincarnates. As noted earlier, this has even been acknowledged by the NEP's greatest proponent in his recently released memoirs (Mahathir 2011). Since NEP targets were based on stock rather than flow measures, namely a redistribution of wealth rather than income, many GLCs were created in order to pursue this objective. Over the years the number and influence of the GLCs have grown to such a point where they now dominate many sectors of the economy, creating an uneven playing field that deters the entry of new firms. Levelling the playing field by reducing the market dominance of these GLCs must go hand-in-hand with neutralizing the other distortions of the NEP if private investment is to return to levels projected in the Tenth Malaysia Plan (TMP) to sustain robust growth in the future.

Shortly after assuming office in April 2009, PM Najib Razak began introducing reforms in an attempt to improve Malaysia's competitiveness and investment climate. One of his earliest moves was to open up the financial services industry and some other sectors to foreign investment. In July 2009, the PM established the National Economic Advisory Committee (NAEC) and tasked it with designing a New Economic Model (NEM).

The NEAC produced two reports on the NEM. The first report, released in April 2010, presents an overall framework for transforming Malaysia from a middle income economy into an advanced one by 2020. It provides a diagnosis of the challenges and opportunities facing the Malaysian economy, and recommends eight Strategic Reform Initiatives (SRIs). The second report, released in December 2010, presents the specific policy measures supporting these eight SRIs.

The overall objectives, policy framework, and specific strategies of the NEM were integrated into the Economic Transformation Programme (ETP) and the TMP. The main macroeconomic objectives are to sustain 6 per cent average annual GDP growth on the back of stronger domestic demand, increased private investment, and improved productivity. Gross national income (GNI) per capita is targeted to increase from US$8,000 in 2012 to around US$17,700 in 2020. Private sector participation is underscored as a main driver of growth.

Achieving the 6 per cent annual GDP growth target will require private investment to grow by more than 12 per cent annually over the next five years, a significant and almost unimaginable increase from the 2 per cent annual growth achieved in the Ninth Malaysia Plan.

Private investment's contribution to GDP is targeted to reach almost 20 per cent by 2020, compared with about 10 per cent in 2010. This would be yet another tremendous achievement. With private investment supposed to take centre stage, the government's role will be limited to improving the enabling environment through policy and regulatory changes, investing in areas such as education and infrastructure, and attracting investors through marketing campaigns and fiscal incentives.

The ETP estimates that around 92 per cent of the country's projected investment requirements will need to come from the private sector. These investments will focus on the ETP's twelve National Key Economic Areas (NKEAs) identified as the engines of future growth: (i) oil, gas, and energy; (ii) palm oil; (iii) financial services; (iv) tourism; (v) business services; (vi) electronics and electrical; (vii) wholesale and retail; (viii) education; (ix) healthcare; (x) communications content and infrastructure; (xi) agriculture; and (xii) greater Kuala Lumpur and Klang Valley. Thus far, 113 projects with a total value of MYR177 billion have been announced under the ETP, focused largely on infrastructure, commodity-related investments, and construction. MYR10 billion of investment was realized through October 2011, or 64 per cent of all investments committed for 2011 (IMF 2012). The reforms embedded in the NEM, ETP, and TMP appear, on the surface at least, to signal a departure from the previous government's priorities and approach to development (see Table 6.1). Nevertheless, many of the twelve NKEAs are currently dominated by GLCs. It remains to be seen how much of the investment projects will be truly private rather than government-linked.

The government has had a GLC Transformation Programme in place since 2004. Under the programme, the government completed 36 major divestment transactions between 2004 and December 2010, with total proceeds of MYR24 billion, generating some MYR11.6 billion of gains upon divestment. In 2011, the government announced that it had identified 33 companies under 6 GLICs as ready for divestment. Under the plan to rationalize the portfolio of GLCs, the government announced that it would reduce its stake in 5 of the identified companies, list 7 of them, and sell the remaining 21 companies. Of the 33 GLCs, 24 are expected to be divested by 2012. With all of these completed and planned divestments, the question has to be asked: why has Malaysia continued to struggle with ballooning budget deficits? While it is true

TABLE 6.1
Old versus New Approach to Economic Development in Malaysia

Old Approach	New Approach
Growth primarily through capital accumulation. Focus on investment in production and physical infrastructure in combination with low skilled labour for low value-added exports.	**Growth through productivity.** Focus on innovative processes and cutting-edge technology, supported by healthy levels of private investment and talent, for high value-added goods and services.
Dominant state participation in the economy. Large direct public investment, including through government-linked corporations (GLCs) in selected economic sectors.	Private sector-led growth. Promote competition across and within sectors to revive private investment and market dynamism.
Centralized strategic planning. Guidance and approval from federal authorities for economic decisions.	Localized autonomy in decision-making. Empower state and local authorities to develop and support growth initiatives, and encourage competition between localities.
Balanced regional growth. Disperse economic activities across states to spread benefits from development.	Cluster- and corridor-based economic activities. Concentration of economic activities for economies of scale and better provision of supporting services.
Favour specific industries and firms. Grant preferential treatment in the form of incentives and financing to selected entities.	Favour technologically capable industries and firms. Grant incentives to support innovation and risk-taking to enable entrepreneurs to develop higher value-added products and services.
Export dependence on G-3 (United States, Europe, and Japan) markets. Part of production chain to supply consumer goods and components to traditional markets.	Asia and Middle East orientation. Develop and integrate actively into regional production and financial networks to leverage flows of investment, trade, and ideas.
Restrictions on foreign skilled workers. Fear that foreign talent would displace local workers.	Retain and attract skilled professionals. Embrace talent, both local and foreign, needed to spur an innovative, high value-added economy.

Source: New Economic Model.

that the direct cost of funding NEP-related programmes is high, it also appears that the GLCs are still investing in new sectors during the divestment programme. There has been a spate of acquisitions of late by GLCs in the areas of private sector finance and property development, for instance. Examples include Sime Darby's 30 per cent stake in Penang-based Easter & Oriental, and UEM Land's acquisition of Sunrise to create the largest property development company by market capitalization. Jacobs (2011) highlights many more examples. Another view suggests that GLCs are coming in as a "buyer of last resort" and trying to prop up confidence as private businesses offload their Malaysian investments and look offshore to more conducive investment environments. Whatever the reason, these developments suggest that the divestment programme may more aptly be described as a diversification programme.

The NEM and the NEP

The reforms contained in this new approach appear to involve an attempt to roll back some of the distortions associated with the affirmative action policies established under the NEP. The NEM and TMP shifted the focus of affirmative action to the bottom 40 per cent of the population, while aiming to raise the income levels of all disadvantaged groups, irrespective of race. This appeared to be a revival of the original intent of the NEP, which was the eradication of poverty among the entire population. The emphasis was on market-friendly and transparent affirmative action programmes based on need and merit rather than ethnicity, and meaningful economic participation rather than quotas or targets. Capacity building and skills training were identified as the primary means of assistance.

This development was welcome news indeed. The government appeared to have finally realized that the most important policy change would be a revamping of the NEP, particularly since the goal of reducing inter-ethnic income inequalities had been largely achieved. In its place, intra-ethnic income disparities had worsened, much of which was attributable to the way the NEP was implemented, and a general approach that targeted the worst off was the only way to deal with inequality and the remaining pockets of poverty (Menon 2009). These changes also had the potential to improve the investment climate and stem the outflow of both capital and skilled labour. The question now was whether it could be faithfully implemented.

Things started off well with this new approach. As early as June 2009, the PM had eased the requirement for companies to reserve 30 per cent of their shares for ethnic Malays, one of the core policies of the NEP. The requirement was scrapped for companies already listed on the stock exchange and reduced to 12.5 per cent for initial public offerings, but was retained for strategic industries such as telecommunications, water, and energy. In October 2011, the government announced that the equity requirement would be removed in phases in another seventeen services subsectors in 2012 (EIU 2012).

This is where the good news comes to an end, however. The government has been criticized for backtracking on its commitment to discontinue distortionary affirmative action policies, not just by the opposition parties (Lim 2010), but also by a wide range of commentators (Ahya et al. 2010*a* and 2010*b*, World Bank 2011, Woo 2009 and 2011). The World Bank (2011, p. 40), for instance, was forced to conclude that "limited headway has been made in the implementation of the NEM ... and skepticism abounds with respect to the NEM measures".

There were a number of policy moves that ostensibly contradicted the NEM's intent to focus on merit and need. The TMP itself includes several affirmative action measures that are still targeted at the bumiputera, although these are focused on small and medium-sized enterprises (SMEs). However, the TMP stresses that these measures will now be achieved through more market-friendly approaches.

Although the NEM identifies the key challenges facing Malaysia with its eight SRIs, its implementation and value will remain suspect for as long as the underlying distortions of the NEP remain intact. By failing to address them directly, one has to assume that they will be grandfathered in to pacify vested interests, some of whom are already revolting, and the root causes of the malaise will remain unchecked. Therefore, one is forced to conclude that although appearing detailed and comprehensive, the NEM remains little more than a vision statement that pays lip service to addressing the core underlying problems facing the economy, while remaining unlikely to do so.

Conclusion

Malaysia is an outstanding model of how openness to trade and FDI can transform a poor, agrarian economy into a thriving, manufacturing-based, middle income one in a generation. It is also a success story of how social harmony can be preserved in a multi-racial society, relying on economic openness to sustain growth in the context of an expensive affirmative action programme that also skews incentives. In this sense, the NEP has performed an important signalling role, and has played its part in delivering the peace and stability that has enabled Malaysia to sustain its growth. In the past, such openness resulted in massive inflows of FDI and high rates of economic growth that, when combined with revenues from large oil reserves, augmented the domestic resource base and facilitated a tax-transfer scheme that favoured the majority. All that changed after the AFC, however. FDI flows dropped off sharply and continued to remain low even after recovery. Although some moderation in aggregate investment was to be expected post-AFC, private domestic investment has slumped sharply, as the flight of both capital and skills took hold. If the resource and other costs of the NEP were not a major drag on growth in the past, the trend decline in both domestic and foreign investment, combined with other ongoing adjustments such as out-migration and demographic change, suggests that reform is now critical for sustainability. Muddling through is no longer an option for Malaysia.

The NEP is now past its use-by date. There is increasing recognition that many of Malaysia's economic problems, including the slump in private investment, are rooted in the distortions resulting from the workings and implementation of the NEP and its reincarnates. Since the NEP had as its target a redistribution of wealth rather than income, many GLCs were spawned as vehicles to pursue this objective. There is therefore a clear link between the two. The problems that Malaysia is facing at the moment can also be traced to the workings of not just one or the other, but both. Therefore, any solution must address both constraints. There is little doubt that GLCs have crowded out private investment in a wide range of sectors. It is arguably more important to address the GLC problem for the revival of investment than it is the NEP. It remains to be seen if the plans announced for government divestment in some of these GLCs will progress in a way that removes all barriers that have prevented or discouraged new firms from entering what have been traditional strongholds. Whether divestment proceeds will be channelled back into government involvement in different sectors, as has been happening lately, is another concern. Although the reforms embedded in the NEM, ETP, and TMP signalled a departure from the previous government's priorities and approach to development, implementation has been lacklustre at best and mendacious at worst. The fact that the TMP itself includes several new affirmative action measures is telling.

Unless bold policy changes that neutralize the distortions of the NEP are implemented faithfully and the overwhelming influence of GLCs in the marketplace is curtailed, it is unlikely that private investment will recover. In fact, it could even decline further in the future. The government will then be faced with either a case of slowing growth and rising unemployment, or it will again have to boost public spending in an attempt to offset these effects. If it pursues the latter course, this would further increase the fiscal deficit, probably quite substantially given dwindling domestic reserves. With the budget deficit already at critically high levels, and if the NEP continues to require substantial resources, then the proposed GLC divestment programme may become a necessity if a crisis is to be averted.

Malaysia has always opted for economic expediency during times of impending crises and hopefully this approach will once again prevail. Faced with crises in the past, governments have responded with pragmatism, even loosening some of the more distortionary aspects of the NEP when it was required, although admittedly more so for foreign investors that its own citizenry. Whether the changed political landscape and tighter electoral prospects that prevail today — in the context of a slowing world economy with negative impacts threatening to spill over domestically — will prevent such necessary but risky policy change remains to be seen.

NOTES

1. I am grateful to Prema-Chandra Athukorala, Hal Hill, K.S. Jomo, Greg Lopez, Anant Menon, Ng Thiam Hee, and participants at the Transforming Malaysia: Ideas for the Next Decade workshop (Singapore: Institute of Southeast Asian Studies, 29 September 2011) for useful comments and discussions. Anna Cassandra Melendez provided excellent research assistance. Parts of this chapter draw upon Menon (2014). The views expressed in this

chapter are those of the author and do not necessarily reflect the views and policies of the Asian Development Bank, or its Board of Governors or the governments they represent.

2. The Malaysian experience in attracting FDI up until the mid-1990s is discussed in Athukorala and Menon (1995), and up to the present in Athukorala and Wagle (2011).

3. ASEAN-5 comprises Indonesia, Malaysia, the Philippines, Thailand, and Vietnam.

4. New Straits Times, "Malaysia's FDI up by 12.3% in 2011", 21 February 2012.

5. GLCs are defined as companies that have a primary commercial objective and in which the Government of Malaysia has a direct controlling stake through Khazanah (the main sovereign wealth fund), the Ministry of Finance, Kumpulan Wang Amanah Pencen (National Pension Fund), or Bank Negara Malaysia (BNM). Some GLCs are also controlled by other federal government-linked agencies such as Permodalan Nasional Berhad (PNB), the Employees Provident Fund (EPF), and Tabung Haji. Apart from a percentage of ownership, a controlling stake also refers to the government's ability to appoint board members and senior management, and make major decisions (e.g., contract awards, strategy, restructuring and financing, acquisitions and divestments) for GLCs either directly or through government-linked investment companies.

6. *Asia Sentinel*, "Malaysia's Disastrous Capital Flight", 11 January 2010.

7. This view also ignores the possibility that activities of MNCs could generate knowledge externalities and other spillovers that increase productivity by facilitating the transfer of more efficient technology and management practices from foreign to domestic firms (Menon 1998a).

8. There are also positive elements of labour migration that this critique ignores. As noted earlier, an important implication of the significant inflow of foreign workers has been its effect in mitigating growth in real wages. The concentration of migrant workers in construction and other services has limited the increase in non-traded goods prices. Without migrant labour, the appreciation of the real exchange rate required to facilitate the transfer of labour from the traded to the non-traded sector and meet infrastructure development needs would have had to have been much higher (Athukorala and Menon 1999).

9. Concerns over the quality of education are not limited to post-secondary education, although this is where the deterioration has been most marked. The quality of education at primary and secondary levels has also dropped sharply (Lee and Nagaraj 2012). Addressing the skills shortage will need to look beyond post-secondary education and address underlying problems that begin much earlier in the schooling life of students.

REFERENCES

Ahya, C., D. Tan, and S. Singh. "Malaysia's New Economic Model: Making the Right Noise". Morgan Stanley Global Economic Forum, 2010a.

————. "10th Malaysia Plan: Two Steps Forward, One Step Backward?" Morgan Stanley Global Economic Forum, 2010b.

Asia Sentinel. "Malaysia's Disastrous Capital Flight", 11 January 2010.

Asian Development Bank (ADB). "Malaysia: Interim Country Partnership Strategy Paper". Manila: ADB, 2012.

Athukorala, P. and J. Menon. "Developing with Foreign Investment: Malaysia". Australian Economic Review. 1st Quarter, 1995.

————. "Outward Orientation and Economic Performance: The Malaysian Experience". World Economy, vol. 22, no. 8 (1999): 1119–40.

Athukorala, P. and S. Wagle. "Foreign Direct Investment in Southeast Asia: Is Malaysia Falling Behind?". ASEAN Economic Bulletin, vol. 28, no. 2 (2011): 115–33.

Bhaskaran, M. "Investment Liberalization". Paper presented to the interim workshop on Assessment of Impediments and Actions Required for Achieving an ASEAN Economic Community by 2015. Singapore: Institute of Southeast Asian Studies, 2011.

Bradsher, K. "Taking a Risk for Rare Earths". New York Times, 8 March 2011.

Dev, Kar and Karly Curcio. Illicit Financial Flows from Developing Countries: 2000–2009. Washington, D.C.: Global Financial Integrity, 2011.

Economic Intelligence Unit (EIU). Malaysia Country Report, March 2012.

Fuller, T. "Malaysia Dilutes Its System of Ethnic Preferences". New York Times, 30 June 2009. Available at <http://www.nytimes.com/2009/07/01/world/asia/01malaysia.html>.

Hill, H., T.S. Yean, and R.H.M Zin, eds. Malaysia's Development Challenges: Graduating from the Middle. Oxon: Routledge, 2012.

Hock, L.K. and S. Nagaraj. "The Crisis in Education". In Malaysia's Development Challenges: Graduating from the Middle, edited by H. Hill, T.S. Yean, and R.H.M Zin. Oxon: Routledge, 2012.

IMF. Malaysia 2011 Article IV Consultation. IMF Country Report No. 12/43. February. Washington, D.C.: IMF, 2012.

Jacobs, J. "GLCs versus Private Developers?". The Edge, 29 March 2011. Available at <http://www.theedgemalaysia.com/highlights/193504-glcs-vs-private-developers.html>.

Khaled, M. Opening Speech at the Seminar on Enhancing Graduate Employability: Issues, Concerns, and the Way Forward. Putrajaya, 21 July 2009. Available at <http://khalednordin.com/wp-content/uploads/2009/07/july-21st-2009-seminar-on-enhancing-graduate-employability-issues-concerns-and-the-way-forward.pdf>.

Lee, K.H. and S. Nagaraj. "The Crisis in Education". In *Malaysia's Development Challenges: Graduating from the Middle*, edited by H. Hill, T.S. Yean, and R.H.M. Zin. Oxon: Routledge, 2012.

Lim, K.S. "Tenth Malaysia Plan: Long Live NEP–RIP NEM". Speech Delivered to the Malaysian Parliament on the 10th Malaysia Plan, 21 June 2010.

Menon, J. "Factor Productivity Growth in Foreign and Domestic Firms in Malaysian Manufacturing". *Journal of Asian Economics*, vol. 9, no. 2 (1998): 251–80.

———. "How Open is Malaysia? An Analysis of Trade, Capital, and Labour Flows". *World Economy*, vol. 23, no. 2 (2000): 235–55.

———. "Macroeconomic Management Amid Ethnic Diversity: Fifty Years of Malaysian Experience". *Journal of Asian Economics*, vol. 20, no. 1 (2009): 25–33.

———. "Growth Without Private Investment: What Happened in Malaysia and Can It be Fixed?" *Journal of the Asia Pacific Economy*, vol. 19, no. 2 (2014): 247–71.

Mohamad, Mahathir. *A Doctor in the House: The Memoirs of Tun Dr Mahathir Mohamad*. Kuala Lumpur: MPH Publishing, 2011.

National Economic Advisory Council (NEAC). *New Economic Model (NEM) for Malaysia Parts 1 and 2*. Kuala Lumpur: NEAC, 2010.

New Straits Times. "Malaysia's FDI up by 12.3% in 2011", 21 February 2012.

Star Online. "After Seven Years of Change", 25 June 2011.

United Nations Conference on Trade and Development (UNCTAD). *World Investment Report 2009: Transnational Corporations, Agricultural Production, and Development*. Geneva: UNCTAD, 2009.

———. *Global Investment Trends Monitor*. Geneva: UNCTAD, 2011*a*.

———. *World Investment Report 2011: Non-Equity Modes of International Production and Development*. Geneva: UNCTAD, 2011*b*.

———. *Global Investment Trends Monitor*. Geneva: UNCTAD, 2012.

Woo, W.T. "Getting Malaysia Out of the Middle-Income Trap". Paper presented to the Economic Council Working Group of the Economic Planning Unit of the Prime Minister's Department in Kuala Lumpur, Malaysia, 2009. Available at <http://www.econ.ucdavis.edu/faculty/woo/woo.html>.

———. "Understanding the Middle-Income Trap in Economic Development: The Case of Malaysia". *The 2011 World Economy Asia Lecture*. Globalization and Economic Policy (GEP) conference at the University of Nottingham in Kuala Lumpur, Malaysia, 13 January 2011. Available at <http://www.econ. ucdavis.edu/faculty/woo/woo.html>.

World Bank. *Investing Across Borders 2010: Indicators of Foreign Direct Investment Regulation in 87 Economies*. Washington, D.C.: World Bank, 2010.

———. *Malaysia Economic Monitor*, April 2011. Available at <http://www. worldbank.org/my>. Washington, D.C.: World Bank, 2011.

7

INFRASTRUCTURE IN MALAYSIA
Investment, Growth and Policy Challenges

G. Naidu

Introduction

Since independence, the Malaysian economy has posted impressive rates of growth, in the process undergoing important structural changes (see Table 7.1). Neither the growth of the economy nor its structural transformation, from a predominantly agricultural economy to a manufacturing and service based one, would have been possible without the sustained expansion and modernization of the country's infrastructure.

This chapter describes the development of infrastructure in Malaysia. Infrastructure comprises a wide spectrum of physical facilities and services, ranging from the various types of transport facilities to utilities such as telecommunications, electricity, sewage and water supply. Most types of infrastructure have the common characteristics of being both capital-intensive and long-lasting. There are also important differences between them in terms of industry structure.

TABLE 7.1
Malaysia — An Economic Profile

	2010	
Land Area (km²)	329,876	
Peninsular Malaysia	131,793	
Sabah	73,633	
Sarawak	124,450	
Population Mid-Year (Million)	28.3	
Peninsular Malaysia	22.6	
Sabah	3.2	
Sarawak	2.5	
Population Density (persons per sq. km)	85.8	
Peninsular Malaysia	171.5	
Sabah	43.5	
Sarawak	20.1	
	1990	**2010**
GDP at constant 2000 prices (RM million)	117,839	557,449
Economic Structure (per cent)		
Agriculture	14.1	7.3
Mining	6.1	7.0
Manufacturing	27.3	27.6
Construction	3.4	3.2
Services	49.1	50.8
Per Capita GNP (RM)	6,734	26,420
External Trade		
Exports (RM million)	77,458	754,972
Imports (RM million)	70,365	608,625
Trade Orientation		
Exports/GDP	0.7	1.0
Imports/GDP	0.7	0.8

Sources:
1. Economic Report, Ministry of Finance, Malaysia, Percetakan Nasional Malaysia Berhad (National Printers), various issues.
2. Malaysia, *Yearbook of Statistics*, various years.

Some, for example, are near natural monopolies whilst in others competitive markets are possible. Also infrastructure such as roads and telecommunications are network industries, whereas ports and airports are location specific. Because the sector is very broad and complex, the discussion, of necessity, is broad and addresses cross-cutting and sector-wide issues without going into the specifics of each subsector. Yet another complication with regard to infrastructure in Malaysia arises from the fact that the country comprises three separate physical and political entities.[1] The component parts of the country — Peninsular Malaysia, Sabah and Sarawak — are very different in terms of land area, level of development and population size. The regional disparities render discussion of the country's infrastructure problems and policies somewhat problematic.

In this chapter only some of the important issues pertaining to infrastructure development in Malaysia are addressed. Among the issues discussed are:

- Investment in infrastructure development and the consequent growth of the country's infrastructure stock;
- The sector objectives and strategies of the government; and
- The current and emerging infrastructure challenges.

Investment in Infrastructure

At independence in 1957, Malaya inherited a fairly good set of infrastructure facilities for its immediate needs, albeit highly concentrated along the west coast and also dependent on Singapore for port and airport facilities.[2] Development of infrastructure, especially in Peninsular Malaysia, from 1957 up to 1965 mostly kept abreast of growth in demand: this is borne out by the fact that there were few instances of severe infrastructure shortages or breakdowns even if, as earlier, the spread and coverage of infrastructure was uneven between different regions of the country. (The statistics on infrastructure in Malaysian 1965 just prior to the commencement of the First Malaysia Plan 1966–70 are shown in Table 7.2).[3]

Two objectives have primarily driven the government's infra-structure planning and policy, the first relates to the importance of infrastructure in facilitating economic development, the second being the role of infrastructure in reducing economic imbalances between

TABLE 7.2
Malaysia: Infrastructure Base, 1965

Subsector	1965	Subsector	1965
Roads		**Ports**	
Total Length of Roads (km)	15,256	Number of major ports	2
		Number of Dry Cargo berths	19
Distribution of Roads (%)*			
Peninsular Malaysia	79.8	**Telecommunications****	
Sabah	12.1	Number of Telephone Subscribers	107,000
Sarawak	8.1	Telephones per 100 population	1
		Electricity	
Railways		Electricity Generation Capacity (MW)	336
Length of Railway Tracks (km)			
KTMB	2,115	**Water Resources***	
Sabah Railways	131	Production capacity (mld)	591

Notes: * 1971; ** 1970; *** Peninsular Malaysia.
Source: G. Naidu and Cassey Lee, "Infrastructure in the Economic Development of Malaysia", paper presented at the World Bank Conference on Infrastructure Strategies for East Asia, Singapore, 1994.

different regions of the country. These two motives continue to determine the scale and pattern of infrastructure development in Malaysia.[4]

The development of infrastructure in Malaysia in this section is divided into two phases. The reason for this is that whilst during the first phase (from 1966 to 1990 and coinciding with the First to Fifth Malaysia Plan period) infrastructure development was primarily undertaken by the government, more recently (and as a result of the government's privatization policy) infrastructure development has been by both the public and private sectors.

Infrastructure Development 1966–90 (Pre-Privatization Phase)

The statistics on investment in infrastructure during 1965–90 are summarized in Table 7.3.

A number of conclusions can be drawn from the statistics in the table:

- Between 1966–90, coinciding with the first five Malaysia Plans, the government invested a total of RM60 billion to develop the country's infrastructure;
- Generally, spending on infrastructure increased from one Plan to the next (see Figure 7.1). Major spurts in investment in infrastructure occurred during the Fourth and Fifth Plans (1976–85). The growing amount of investment in infrastructure is evident from the fact that the investment to develop infrastructure during the Fifth Plan at RM25 billion was eighteen times more than the amount spent by the government on infrastructure in the First Plan. Notwithstanding the fact that the statistics in the table are in nominal values, the increases in investment between one Plan period and the subsequent one has been generally very large;
- The infrastructure sector has been the major recipient of development funds. In most Malaysia Plans it has been allocated more than a third of government's total development expenditure, reflecting the high priority the government attached to infrastructure development; and
- As a proportion of GDP, investment in infrastructure during 1966–90 has averaged 5.6 per cent. This is a fairly high percentage of GDP to be allocated towards infrastructure development.

TABLE 7.3
Public Sector Investment in Infrastructure (1966–90)
(RM million)

	1MP (1966–70)	2MP (1971–75)	3MP (1976–80)	4MP (1981–85)	5MP (1986–90)	Sub-total	Annual Average
Transport	**544.9**	**1,233.9**	**2,842.9**	**12,966.0**	**11,216.4**	**28,804.1**	**1,152.2**
Roads	339.9	770.7	1,909.1	7,532.5	6,011.0	16,563.2	662.5
Rail	50.9	29.8	168.4	1,176.7	897.1	2,322.9	92.9
Ports	93.0	251.6	557.1	2,677.3	1,350.6	4,929.6	197.2
Airports	61.1	181.8	208.3	1,579.5	2,957.7	4,988.4	199.5
Urban Transport	–	–	–	–	–	–	–
Utilities	**160.4**	**171.7**	**406.3**	**3,787.5**	**2,524.2**	**7,050.1**	**282.0**
Water Supply	150.8	163.1	337.2	3,393.6	2,467.0	6,511.7	260.5
Sewerage	9.6	8.6	69.1	393.9	57.2	538.4	21.5
Electricity	**530.6**	**122.7**	**1,205.3**	**4,828.7**	**7,013.7**	**13,701.0**	**548.0**
Telecommunications	**146.2**	**152.1**	**1,112.7**	**4,830.1**	**4,210.9**	**10,452.0**	**418.1**
TOTAL	**1,382.1**	**1,680.4**	**5,567.2**	**26,412.3**	**24,965.2**	**60,007.2**	**2,400.3**
Infrastructure Share in Development Expenditure (%)	32.7	17.7	22.9	32.2	46.4	–	–
Infrastructure Investment as Percentage of GDP	2.6	1.9	2.9	7.7	6.2	–	–

Sources: First Malaysia Plan (pp. 69–70), Second Malaysia Plan (pp. 68–71), Third Malaysia Plan (pp. 240–41), Fourth Malaysia Plan (pp. 118–25), Fifth Malaysia Plan (pp. 226–27), Sixth Malaysia Plan (pp. 301, 321, 343).

FIGURE 7.1
Infrastructure Investment, 1966–90

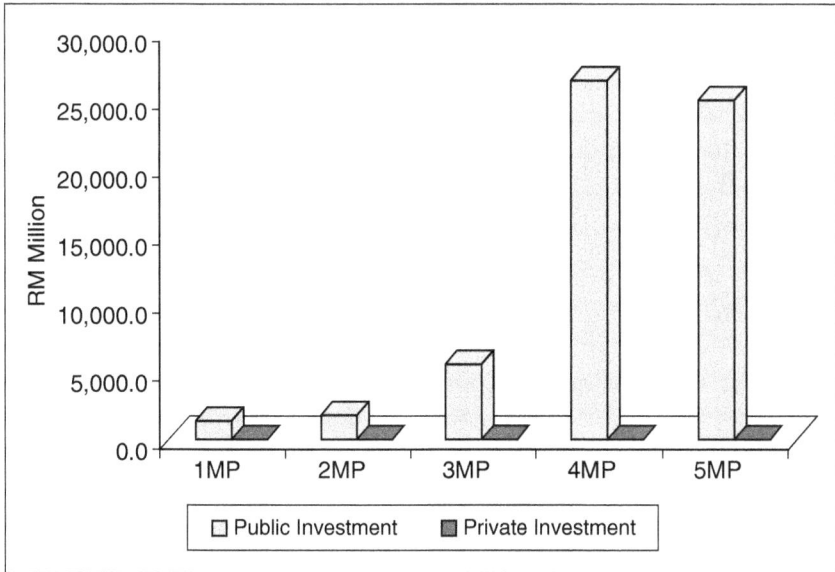

Source: Malaysia Plans (First to Fifth) and Mid-Term Review of the respective Malaysia Plans, Economic Planning Unit, Prime Minister's Department.

Infrastructure Development: 1991–2010 (Private Sector Participation)

Up to Fifth Plan infrastructure development was the responsibility of government. The introduction by the government of its privatization policy in the mid-1980s changed this situation and infrastructure became a focus area for private sector participation. Starting with the Sixth Malaysia Plan (1991–2000) infrastructure development is being undertaken by both the public and private sectors.

The volume and pattern of investment in infrastructure in the country since the implementation of the privatization policy is shown in Table 7.4:

- One fact that emerges is that even with private sector participation in infrastructure development, public sector investment in infrastructure has not decreased. Public sector investment between 1991and 2010 was RM166.5 billion compared to RM60 billion during 1966–90. On an annual measure public sector investment in infrastructure between 1991 and 2010 was RM8.3 billion, compared to an average of RM2.4 billion a year during 1965–90. Even considering that these sums are in nominal values, the increase in public sector spending on infrastructure between 1991 and 2010 over the pre-privatization years was very significant. In short, privatization of infrastructure did not mean a reduction in public sector spending on the sector;

- From the 1990s onwards, private sector resources have supplemented public sector investment in infrastructure, boosting total investment in infrastructure. Statistics on private sector investment in infrastructure, either on an annual or on a five-year basis, are not always available. It is thus not possible to know the actual investment in infrastructure by the private sector. An indication of the role of private sector in infrastructure development, however, can be obtained from the estimated private sector investment in infrastructure during the Seventh Plan (1996–2000). Between 1996 and 2000 the private sector is estimated to have invested RM85.6 billion in infrastructure, which is nearly double the RM49.6 billion spent by public sector on infrastructure during the same period. Of the RM135.3 billion invested in infrastructure in the Seventh Plan, the public sector's share was 36.7 per cent and that of the private sector 63.3 per cent. If similar amounts had been invested by the private sector during the other Malaysia Plans in the post-privatization period — and there is reason to believe this assumption would actually understate private sector investment — it can be surmised that even while public sector was increasing its investment in infrastructure private sector investment was also very substantial, contributing to a significant increase in investment since the introduction of the privatization policy;

- Private sector investment during the Seventh Plan period has far exceeded total public sector investment. In some components of infrastructure, such as transport and telecommunications, the private sector is now the dominant source of finance. The private sector is now the more important source of funding of infrastructure development in the country. The estimated investments of the public and private sectors are illustrated in Figure 7.2; and

TABLE 7.4
Investment in Infrastructure (1991–2010)
(RM million)

	6MP* (1991–95)	7MP (1996–2000)		8MP* (2001–05)	9MP* (2006–10)	Sub-Total*	Annual Average*
		Public Sector	Private Sector				
Transport	**11,594.7**	**20,484.2**	**38,302.7**	**30,936.4**	**30,304.4**	**93,319.7**	**4,666.0**
Road	7,572.6	12,269.5	17,505.0	20,737.5	20,945.5	61,525.1	3,076.3
Rail	1,735.4	5,450.3	10,600.0	5,270.0	3,634.9	16,090.6	804.5
Ports	410.9	1,089.2	4,241.7	2,443.0	1,290.0	5,233.1	261.7
Airports	1,780.6	1,271.2	5,956.0	1,779.3	2,868.5	7,699.6	385.0
Urban	95.2	404.0	–	706.6	1,565.5	2,771.3	138.6
Utilities	**2,796.7**	**3,048.0**	**4,331.1**	**5,964.7**	**17,613.7**	**29,423.1**	**1,471.2**
Water Supply	2,671.9	2,382.7	2,571.7	4,616.8	9,410.1	19,081.5	954.1
Sewerage	124.8	665.3	1,759.4	1,347.9	8,203.6	10,341.6	517.1
Electricity	**17,580.8**	**26,107.2**	**17,576.2**	–	–	**43,688.0**	**2,184.4**
Telecommunication	**39.9**	**4.1**	**25,400.0**	–	–	**44.0**	**2.2**
Total	**32,012.1**	**49,643.5**	**85,610.0**	**36,901.1**	**47,918.1**	**166,474.8**	**8,323.7**

Note: *Excludes private sector investment.
Sources: Seventh Malaysia Plan (Table 11.8, p. 381); Eighth Malaysia Plan (Table 10.8, p. 300); Ninth Malaysia Plan (Table 18.8 p. 390, Table 19.8, p. 410) .

FIGURE 7.2
Infrastructure Investment, 1966–90

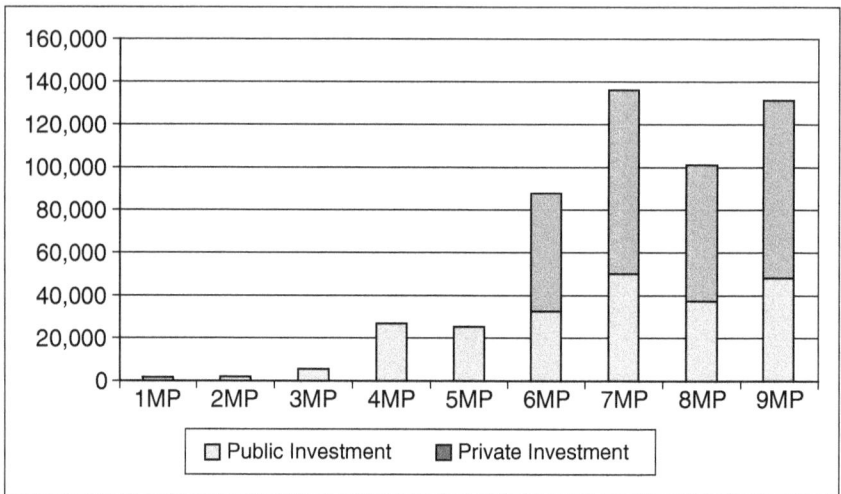

Note: Private sector investment in the Sixth, Eight and Ninth Plans is estimated on the basis of the assumption that the relative shares of public and private sectors in the Plans were the same as in the Seventh Plan.
Sources: Figure 7.1 and Table 7.4.

- The limited information on private sector investment in infrastructure facilities precludes an accurate assessment of investment in infrastructure relative to the country's GDP. In the Seventh Plan, the ratio of investment to GDP was 9.4 per cent compared to an average of 5.7 per cent during the period prior to private sector participation in infrastructure development.

All indications are that the private sector is now the main investor in infrastructure. The focus areas of public and private sector investments in infrastructure can be seen in Table 7.4. Private sector is dominant in electricity and telecommunications. It is also the main investor in nearly all categories of transport infrastructure.

Growth and Modernization of Infrastructure

Investment in infrastructure by the government and since 1990 also by the private sector, has contributed to the expansion and modernization of infrastructure in the country (see Table 7.5). The following points highlight the development of physical infrastructure in the country from 1965 to now.

TABLE 7.5
Malaysia: Infrastructure Growth, 1965–2010

	1965	2005	2010
Roads			
Total Length of Roads (km)	15,256	87,025	135,216
Paved	12,464	67,851	92,438
Gravel	2,107	15,989	16,796
Earth	785	3,185	9,046
Distribution of Roads (%)			
Peninsular Malaysia	79.8	68.6	68.9
Sabah	12.1	18.8	15.8
Sarawak	8.1	12.6	15.3
Railways			
Length of Railway Tracks (km)	1,731	1,920	1,911
KTMB	1,600	1,667	1,658
Sabah Railways	131	131	131
Urban Railways	0	122	122
Ports			
Number of Major Ports	2	8	8
Port Capacity (million tonnes)	n.a.	443	570
Number of Berths	19	233	242
Telecommunications			
Fixed Lines in Operation			
Number of Subscribers (million)	0.1	4.4	4.4
Penetration Rate (%)	1	16.6	15.5
Cellular Phone Subscribers			
Number of Subscribers (million)	0	19.5	33.1
Penetration rate (%)	0	74.1	116.6
Internet Dial-up Subscription			
Number of Subscribers (million)	0	3.7	10.0
Penetration rate (%)	0	13.9	35.0
Internet Broadband Subscription			
Number of Subscribers (million)	0	0.5	2.1
Penetration rate (%)	0	7.9	55.6
Electricity			
Generation Capacity (MW)	336	19,217	24,006
Rural Electrification Coverage (%)			
Malaysia	n.a.	92.9	95.1
Peninsular Malaysia	n.a.	98.6	98.8
Sabah	n.a.	72.8	80.6
Sarawak	n.a.	80.8	89.6
Water Supply			
Production Capacity (mld)	591	14,226	16,077
Supply Coverage (%)			
National	n.a.	95	96.8
Urban	n.a.	98	98
Rural	n.a.	92	95.2

Sources: Table 1, Ninth Malaysia Plan (Table 5.1, p. 135; Table 18.9, p. 377; Table 18.3, p. 379; Table 18.5, p. 386), *Yearbook of Statistics*, Department of Statistics, various years.

(i) Road Network
The expansion of the country's road network is evident from the following:

- The road system of Malaysia has expanded from about 15 thousand km in 1965 to over 135 thousand km in 2010, which is an eight-fold increase in network size;
- There has also been an improvement in the distribution of the road system among the three components parts of the country. In 1965 about 80 per cent of the road network was in Peninsular Malaysia; currently this proportion has come down to below 70 per cent and Sabah and Sarawak have seen their shares in the country's road network increase. Regional disparities, however, still remain and many of the more remote areas in Sarawak and Sabah are still without good access roads; and
- Not only has the size of the road network grown, the main intercity segments of it, comprising mostly the privatized roads, are now two or multi-lane dual carriageways. The North-South Expressway and East Coast Highway are examples of the large number of tolled highways developed by the private sector as BOT projects.

(ii) Railways
The major developments in the rail sector can be summarized as follows:

- The route length of the KTMB network has remained unchanged. The focus of government is on the modernization and capacity expansion of KTMB and not on increasing its network. After decades of under investment, the entire west coastline from Padang Besar on the Thai border to Johor Bahru in the south is being double tracked and electrified. When completed the west coast of Peninsular Malaysia, the most densely populated part of the country, will have a modern railway system;
- The small rail system in Sabah is also being upgraded and rehabilitated, even though the demand for its services is low. The project is being undertaken for social reasons; and
- A major initiative of the government in the rail sector has been the development of an urban railway system. The 1990s saw

the development of an urban rail network comprising two LRT systems, a monorail system and a rail link between KL and the Kuala Lumpur International Airport (KLIA). The primary objective in developing an urban rail system was to reduce congestion on the roads in the Klang Valley. The LRT and monorail systems were developed by the private sector but because of poor financial outcomes the government now owns the network (via Prasarana) and operates the services through RapidKL, another government-owned entity.

(iii) Ports

Ports are critical to the Malaysian economy on account of the country's heavy dependence on trade. The fact that at least nine-tenths of the exports and imports of Malaysia are seaborne explains the importance accorded to the development of ports. The country's ports sector has been substantially expanded to cater for the growth of the country's external trade:

- The expansion of physical capacity of the ports has come about either as a result of the construction of new large terminals — Johor Port, Westports in Klang and Port of Tanjung Pelepas (PTP) being examples of this strategy — or from an expansion of facilities at existing terminals. There are now at least eight major ports in the country compared to only two in as late as 1975;
- The expansion of capacity of the country's ports is evident from the increase in the number of berths, from 19 in 1965 to 242 now. As a result, the total combined handling capacity of Malaysian ports is now almost 600 million tonnes;
- As with other infrastructure, ports in the country have also undergone some changes. Specifically, the construction of container berths and acquisition of high capacity cranes as well as the deepening of draught at many of the country's major ports have been undertaken to deal with the changing composition of the country's exports and imports; and
- Since the 1990s the development of new ports and expansion of existing terminals have been mostly financed by the private sector. Public sector involvement in the development of ports in the country is now quite minimal. All the larger ports in the country are privatized terminals and these handle about 80 per cent or more of the country's exports and imports.

(iv) Telecommunications

The growth of the telecommunications industry has also been very rapid (see Table 7.5). The expansion has been across all components of the telecommunications sector:

- The total number of fixed lines in operation rose from 107 thousand to 4.4 million between 1965 and 2010, raising the penetration rate to 15.5 per cent in 2010 from 1 per cent in 1965;
- In the more recent period, the development of new services rather than fixed line network growth has been the priority. These initiatives include the development of cellular phone infrastructure. Cellular phone subscriptions went up sharply from 19.5 million subscribers in 2005 to 33.1 million subscribers in 2010, increasing the penetration rate from 74.1 per cent to 117 per cent between 2005 and 2010; and
- The provision of requisite infrastructure has also contributed to an increase in internet subscription: dial-up subscriptions went up from 3.7 million in 2005 to 10 million in 2010. Likewise, broadband subscription, which was about half a million in 2005, increased four-fold to 2.1 million in 2010.

In all components of the telecommunications industry, there has been tremendous growth and modernization. Here too, expansion of services and the introduction of new products were largely driven by the private sector.

(v) Electricity

All component parts of the electricity industry have grown from investments made by both the public and private sectors:

- Generation capacity in the sector has risen significantly as a result of investment by the public and private sectors. In 1965, the national electricity generation capacity was 336 MW. In 2005 the total generation capacity was about 19 thousand MW and rose further to 24 thousand MW in 2010. Much of the increase in generation capacity was contributed by the independent power producers (IPPs), sanctioned by the Government under its privatization policy; and
- The development of the electricity sector in the country is also evident from the near total coverage in the urban areas and the increase in coverage in the rural parts of the country.

Rural electrification coverage in Peninsular Malaysia is now 98.8 per cent. In the cases of Sabah and Sarawak the corresponding figures are 80.6 per cent and 89.5 per cent, respectively.

(vi) Water Supply

- In the provision of water too, there has been a very marked improvement. Production capacity in 1965 was 591 million litres a day (mld). In 2010, the production capacity was 27 times higher at 16,077 mld; and
- There has also been an improvement in supply coverage in the rural areas. In 2010, the supply coverage in the rural areas was 95.2 per cent.

The discussion has shown the impact of public sector investment and, since 1990, private sector participation in infrastructure development. The two broad outcomes can be summarized as follows:

- First, the stock of all categories of infrastructure has grown, in most cases capacities have risen manifold; and
- Second, the infrastructure industries have also been modernized in line with technological development and user needs via new types of infrastructure and infrastructure services. Sector upgrading has taken many forms and has occurred in all segments of the sector.

The general conclusion is that, by and large, the supply of infrastructure in the country has kept pace with demand growth.[5] Given the amount of resources expended in the development of infrastructure, this is only to be expected. This positive assessment, however, is not to suggest there are no infrastructure problems in Malaysia. In many parts of the country, infrastructure shortages and service disruptions are not unknown, even if these are infrequent or sporadic. Regional disparities in infrastructure provision continue to exist. Nor is the broad conclusion of infrastructure adequacy intended to imply that mistakes in planning and project implementation have been altogether avoided. The point is that while, by and large, the Government has successfully expanded infrastructure to meet the economic and socio-economic needs of the country, there are still matters related to efficiency in the supply of infrastructure that need to be addressed. These relate to such matters as planning and development of infrastructure, regulation of infrastructure service providers and sale of infrastructure to users.

Infrastructure Sector: Current Plans and Initiatives

The current planning horizon including for infrastructure development in the country is the Tenth Plan, spanning the five-year period 2011–15. Quite unlike the previous Malaysia Plans, however, the Tenth Plan does not provide information on planned public sector and private sector investments in infrastructure. The Tenth Plan only provides a list of major projects to be undertaken by the public and private sectors during the period 2011–15. The Tenth Plan does, however, provide some general and broad directions of infrastructure development up to 2015.

Primarily the infrastructure sector objective of government in the Tenth Plan is to establish a "world class" infrastructure to support growth and productivity. It is not clear what this is supposed to mean and what needs to be done to attain the objectives, and the strategies to attain the objective are also not indicated. The Tenth Plan merely describes a number of projects that are to be undertaken. Essentially, all the projects in the Tenth Plan are intended to increase capacity in their respective sub sectors. The following are the main elements in development of infrastructure in the country up to 2015.

(i) Transport Infrastructure

A number of large projects are indicated in the Tenth Plan with the aim to upgrade transport infrastructure in the country:

- Roads are to be built to provide better access to ports and airports as part of the plans to develop a multimodal transport network in the country. No specific projects are, however, indicated;
- The electrified double tracking of the west coast line of KTMB is to be completed by the end of the Tenth Plan in 2015. It is expected to raise the share of rail in freight transport in Peninsular Malaysia to 10 per cent from the present 1.3 per cent;
- Another physical infrastructure project is the mass rapid transit, My Rapid Transit (MRT), which is intended to further enhance the public transport system in the Klang Valley region;
- In the maritime sector two main initiatives have been indicated. These are the formulation of a national ports policy and capital dredging at some of the major ports in the country to cater for bigger container vessels; and

- Finally, in the airport sector the development of a low cost terminal at KLIA and the upgrading of the Penang International Airport are to be undertaken during the Tenth Plan. These projects are currently underway.

(ii) Telecommunications

As in the earlier Plans, expanding the network is the principal objective of Government in the telecommunications sector. Among the specific details on the development of the telecommunications sector in the Tenth Plan is the raising of household broadband penetration to 75 per cent, from the current 56 per cent level and raising WiFi coverage from the 5,000 hotspots in 2010. Finally, the sector regulator Malaysian Communication and Multimedia Commission (MCMC) is to strengthen the regulatory framework to increase competition in the sector.

(iii) Energy Sector

The main issues to be pursued in the Tenth Plan in the energy sub sector are as follows:

- Formulation of a New Energy Policy focussing on, among others, securing reliable energy supply, energy efficiency, market based energy pricing and stronger governance;
- The development of nuclear energy as an option for electricity generation;
- Transparent sector governance and competitive bidding for all new generation plants to be sanctioned in the future; and
- Renegotiation of the current power purchase agreements (PPAs) between the IPPs and the national electricity company, TNB, to address the high prices being charged by the IPPs.

Aside from the initiatives in the Tenth Plan, the Government is also embarking on the promotion of renewable energy. Towards this end, the Sustainable Energy Development Authority of Malaysia (SEDA) has been established pursuant to the Renewable Energy Act 2011. SEDA's main functions are to promote the development of sustainable energy, to encourage private sector investment in the sustainable energy sector and manage the implementation of the feed in tariff mechanism.

(iv) Sewerage

As for sewerage the objective in the Tenth Plan is to increase coverage and efficiency. The coverage at the start of the Plan was estimated to be 2.541 million Population Equivalent but no targets are indicated.

(v) Water
The focus in the water sector is on:

- Increasing production capacity;
- Ensuring quantity and quality of water supply; and
- Reducing the non revenue water rate (NRW) which at present is 37.2 per cent.

(vi) Rural Infrastructure
The development of rural infrastructure now is being undertaken as part of the Rural Basic Infrastructure NKRA which covers the following: building and upgrading of rural roads, supply of clean and treated water to rural households and supply electricity to rural areas, with particular focus on Sabah and Sarawak. Expanding rural electricity coverage is also to be accorded priority in the Tenth Plan. This task is being spearheaded by PEMANDU.[6] PEMANDU's targets in the development of rural infrastructure which are to be achieved by 2012 are as follows:

- Construction of 7,000 km of new and upgraded roads;
- 140,000 additional households to be provided with 24-hour electricity; and
- 360,000 additional household will have access to clear or treated water.

Infrastructure in Malaysia: Achievements and Emerging Challenges

The development in infrastructure in the country can be summarized in the following points:

- From the perspective of capacity growth, the government's infrastructure development policy has been quite successful. Capacities in all the sub sectors have mostly kept abreast of the growth in demand for the facilities;
- Until the late 1980s, the financing of infrastructure development was almost completely borne by the government. During the period up to the Fifth Plan and even after that, the Malaysian government has continued to spend substantial amounts to develop and modernize infrastructure facilities in the country, giving the sector the highest priority in every Malaysia Plan; and

- Beginning with the Sixth Plan, however, the government has increasingly sanctioned and facilitated private sector participation in infrastructure development and operation. The infusion of private financing has been so large that for some time now private sector investment, in many infrastructure segments, has far exceeded public sector expenditure.

Because of the huge investments by the government as well as the private sector, the capacities of all categories of infrastructure are now many times larger than at the commencement of the First Plan in 1966. The infrastructure of the country has also been modernized and technologically upgraded.

In the development of infrastructure, the Malaysian government had to address a number of issues.

(i) Growing Demand for Infrastructure

The most important issue that the Malaysian government has had to address — and one that continues to drive its infrastructure policy — has been the need to provide adequate infrastructure capacity to meet both the growing domestic demands and the needs of the external sector. All segments of the infrastructure sector have seen significant physical expansion, increased service coverage and higher penetration rates. The government has been generally successful in providing the requisite amount of infrastructure to meet the economic and socio-economic needs of the country. In the process, infrastructure bottlenecks and shortages have also been largely avoided.

While the present infrastructure supply situation in the country is quite good, the expected pace of growth of the Malaysian economy is likely to impose greater and newer demands for investment and improvement of infrastructure facilities in the country. Infrastructure needs will change, in qualitative and quantitative terms. To meet the demands of an economy that intends to become a developed nation by the end of this decade as set out in its Vision 2020, the provision of additional facilities and upgrading existing ones will be a continuing challenge. In this the private sector will continue to play a major role.

(ii) Socio-Economic Considerations

Aside from having to continuously raise infrastructure capacity, a fundamental issue in infrastructure development in the country has been about meeting the socio-economic objective of providing infrastructure for the poorer and less developed parts of the country to, among others, alleviate poverty and enhance economic opportunities for the rural population. In the somewhat complex socio-political situation in the country, the government has to ensure that the provision of infrastructure for the more developed parts of the country has not been at the expense of the less developed regions, the latter consisting of Sabah, Sarawak and also the east coast states of Peninsular Malaysia. The objective is to provide these regions with infrastructure to assist them realize their developmental potential.

In spite of the demands for more infrastructure by the developed regions, progress has been made to provide the less developed parts of the country with infrastructure but clearly this is an on-going exercise and will continue to be a challenge to the government. There is evidence of greater emphasis on rural infrastructure development on the part of the government. In the two states of Sabah and Sarawak, PEMANDU will address their rural infrastructure problems whilst in the east coast states of Peninsular Malaysia, the East Coast Economic Region Development Council (ECERDC) will supplement the government's efforts to rectify the region's infrastructure inadequacies.

(iii) Sector Modernization
Another matter is the modernization of infrastructure facilities to meet new demands from users by adopting new technologies. The government and the private sector operators of infrastructure have had to infuse new technologies into the various segments of infrastructure to avoid obsolescence of facilities. Examples of such measures have been:

- The incorporation of new technologies in the telecommunications industry in the country such as fibre optic cables, cellular mobile phones and broadband internet infrastructure;
- Container berths to replace general cargo facilities at the ports;
- New water treatment and sewerage technologies; and
- EDI facilities for paperless exchange of trade-related documents.

As the economy further transforms by replacing labour intensive industries with high technology ones, infrastructure modernization will acquire importance and urgency.

(iv) Growing Private Sector Participation
Finance infrastructure development is now a shared responsibility of government and the private sector with the latter playing a more important role. A number of factors facilitated private participation in infrastructure development in the country:

- The rapid increase in demand for infrastructure was proving to be beyond the capacity of the government. This was an important reason for the Malaysian government's privatization policy;
- The opportunities for sector unbundling — such as separating generation from transmission and distribution of electricity — opened up some infrastructure sectors for private participation; and
- The recognition that in some infrastructure industries competitive provision of services by the private sector was feasible. This was the case in the telecommunications sub sector.

Currently, large parts of the infrastructure sector have been developed and are being managed by the private sector. Privatization to some extent has allowed the government to direct more resources for the development of infrastructure in the rural areas and in the less developed regions of the country. Private sector participation, already now accounting for about two-third of investment, is poised to increase its share.

(v) Promoting Competition and Strengthening Regulatory Oversight
Promoting efficiency in infrastructure supply and operations is among the concerns of the government. Efficiency is not always easy to achieve, particularly in cases of natural monopoly situations which are not uncommon in the infrastructure industries, and also because, as is the case in Malaysia, mechanisms for sector oversight and regulation are still not well developed. The Malaysian government has, however, taken the following steps to improve efficiency in infrastructure:

- One strategy has been to create competitive supply situations wherever this is possible. The generation segment of the electricity industry and many segments of the telecommunications industry have been deregulated to promote competition;
- In those infrastructure segments where the monopoly element is still significant, the approach has been to establish Key Performance Indicators (KPIs) for industry players to meet. This approach is being extended as evidenced by the formulation and pursuit of its National Key Result Areas (NKRA) programme;
- Strengthening regulatory oversight has been an important facet of the government's intention to enhance efficiency in the supply and distribution of infrastructure services. Towards this end, a regulatory framework is being progressively formulated for the infrastructure sectors (see Table 7.6). It is too early to judge

TABLE 7.6
Infrastructure Regulators

Sector	Regulator	Legislation
Telecommunications	1. Malaysian Communication and Multimedia Commission (MCMC)	1. Communications and Multimedia Act 1998 2. Malaysia Communications and Multimedia Commission Act 1998
Water	1. National Water Services Commission (SPAN)	1. Water Services Industry Act 2006 2. Suruhanjaya Perkhidmatan Air Negara Act 2006
Energy	1. Energy Commission	1. Energy Commission Act 2001 2. Electricity Supply Act 1990 (Amendment) 2001 3. Gas Supply Act 1993 (Amendment) 2001 4. Licensee Supply Regulations 1990 (Amendment) 2002 5. Electricity Regulations 1994 (Amendment) 2003 6. Gas Supply Regulations 1997 (Amendment) 2000 7. Electricity Supply (Compounding of Offences) Regulations 2001 8. Gas Supply (Compoundable Offences) Order 2006 9. Efficient Management of Electricity Energy Regulations 2008

Renewable Energy	1. Sustainable Energy Development Authority of Malaysia (SEDA)	1. Sustainable Energy Development Authority Act 2011 2. Renewable Energy Act 2011
Public Land Transport	1. Land Public Transport Commission (SPAD)	1. Suruhanjaya Pengangkutan Awam Darat Act 2010
Competition	1. Malaysia Competition Commission (MyCC)	1. Competition Commission Act 2010 2. Competition Act 2010
Highways	1. Malaysian Highway Authority (MHA)	1. Highway Authority Malaysia (Incorporation) Act 1980

Ports	1. Port Authorities
	  – Port Klang Authority
	  – Penang Port Commission
	  – Johor Port Authority
	  – Bintulu Port Authority
	  – Kuantan Port Authority
	  – Sabah Port Authority
	  – Miri Port Authority
	  – Kuching Port Authority
	  – Rajang Port Authority
	2. Marine Department
		1. Ports Privatisation Act 1990
		2. Port Authorities Act 1963 (Rev 1992)
		3. Penang Port Commission Act 1955
		4. Bintulu Port Authority Act 1981
		5. Sabah Port Authority Enactment 1967
		6. Sarawak Port Authorities Ordinance 1961
		7. Merchant Shipping Act 1952

Airports	Department of Civil Aviation	1. Civil Aviation Act 1969

Source: Compiled by the author.

the performance of these agencies in regulating the industries under their jurisdiction. But it is still an improvement over the situation until quite recently. The effectiveness of these regulatory agencies has yet to be comprehensively assessed. The basic framework for effective regulatory oversight is being put in place; and

- In the case of projects privatized via BOT and lease-sale arrangements, the regulations are embedded in the contractual agreements and sometimes they include performance standards and other clauses. Many of these agreements have been criticized for being overly tilted in favour of the service providers and against the users. The IPPs and some highway contracts, including the North-South Expressway Concession, are examples over which there is considerable public dissatisfaction about the equity of the contracts. In some, such as the road concessions, vocal public criticism has compelled the government to take steps to delay toll rate increases by compensating the private operators for income loss.

The reason why efficiency is of paramount importance in infrastructure services is because they are an input into all productive activities and inefficiencies in the infrastructure component of the production cycle can raise output costs. If inefficiencies in infrastructure are not rectified, national competitiveness would be compromised.

(vi) User Charges and Infrastructure Tariffs

A contentious issue is the matter of fees charged for the use of infrastructure. Fees for the use of some infrastructure are perceived as being too high. The public, for sure, considers charges for many infrastructure services as too costly, including toll rates on privatized roads, sewerage charges and water rates. The telecommunications and electricity tariffs have also not been spared of similar criticism.

The fact that many of the privatized projects were awarded through direct negotiations rather than via open, competitive tender procedures has contributed to the perception that the user fees of the private operators are high.

The opposite picture emerges in the case of other infrastructure sectors. In some infrastructure entities owned by government, but also including some under private ownership and operations, tariffs are controlled to the extent that tariffs have become misaligned with the costs of service provision. Public transport fares, including hose of the LRT and KTMB and port tariffs, even of those which have been privatized, often remain unchanged for very long periods of time in spite of increasing costs of service provision.

(vii) Promoting Rail Transport

The promotion of rail transport is a new focus of the government's infrastructure policy. The Malaysian economy has evolved to become highly road dependent with rail transport playing a very minor role in both the passenger and freight transport markets in the country. Of late, however, the government appears to want to reverse the past trend and promote rail in both the passenger and freight markets. This is evident from the following:

- The decision to double track and electrify the entire west coast line of KTMB;
- The upgrading of Sabah Railway;
- The proposal to build a high speed rail system between KL and Singapore (Johor Bahru); and
- Assessment of the feasibility of a high speed rail from Tumpat in Kelantan to KL via Kuala Terengganu and Kuantan.

There are a number of reasons why rail transport is beginning to be promoted in the country. First, there are growing concerns about the environment and road transport is a major source of pollution in the country. Second, fuel efficiency is a growing concern and because rail is more fuel-efficient than road transport per unit of output — per passenger km or freight km — the promotion of rail makes economic sense in the long term. Finally, the road accident rates in Malaysia and fatalities from them are among the highest in the world. Rail, as a safer mode of transport, appears to have a strong case over road on the issue of safety.

Notwithstanding the advantages of rail over road, rail operations are very unlikely to be financially viable. This has important consequences for the longer term sustainability of rail transport in the country and would almost certainly require subsidies from government.

(viii) Promoting Public Transport in Urban Areas

To alleviate the growing congestion in Greater KL and the Klang Valley, the government is developing the public transport system in the region.

The measures include:

- Extension of the LRT network;
- Development of the MRT network; and
- Development of Integrated Transport Terminals in the Klang Valley.

The objective is to progressively raise the share of public transport from about 8 per cent in 2010 to 13 per cent in 2012 and to 25 per cent in 2020. The steps being taken in the Klang Valley are to be replicated in the other major urban centres in the country.

There are also proposals to build urban rail systems in the other large conurbations in the country.

(ix) Regional Ambitions

During the early post independence period a large portion of Malaysia's trade was shipped through Singapore Port. Likewise Changi Airport in Singapore functioned as the main international airport for Malaysia. The Malaysian government adopted a set of measures to reduce the country's dependence on transport facilities in Singapore. The matter of dependence on Singapore was addressed in two phases:

- In the first phase the objective was to achieve a high degree of self-sufficiency in port and airport services. This was akin to an import substitution policy. The development of Johor Port and the expansion of Port Klang and Subang Airport were intended to reduce the country's dependence on Singapore for transport infrastructure; and
- More recently the aim has been to go beyond being merely self-sufficient. The government now wants to export its port and airport services. To achieve its regional ambitions the government built the Kuala Lumpur International Airport (KLIA) and promotes it as a regional aviation hub. In the regional market KLIA thus far does not appear to have had much success in becoming a regional aviation hub. In the maritime sector the government has promoted Port Klang as the national load centre and also developed PTP to serve the trans-shipment traffic of the region. The former caters for both national and transhipment traffic whilst PTP primarily serves the regional transhipment market. PTP competes directly with Singapore Port. There has been greater success in the regional ambitions of the country in the maritime sector.

As Malaysia develops to achieve its objective of becoming a developed nation, the demand for infrastructure is likely to both grow rapidly and change in important ways. There are a large numbers of challenges that are likely to emerge in the near and medium term in the development and operation of infrastructure in the country.

The first issue is that the government is unlikely to be able to sustain the high levels of investment in infrastructure as in the past. The limited fiscal space of government will not afford the government with the resources to embark on massive investments in infrastructure. The private sector would thus have to play an even bigger role in infrastructure development than in the past. Creating the right conditions for private sector participation in infrastructure will thus become increasingly important to attract private investment to the sector. Among other measures, a transparent and open bidding for infrastructure projects and concessions will go a long way towards encouraging private participation in infrastructure development and operation.

In the matter of policy implementation, there is urgent need for improvements. Two recent controversies — namely, the award of contract by SEDA for renewable energy supply and the choice of contractor for the LRT expansion project — are examples of one of the basic shortcomings of the government's infrastructure development policy. Specifically, in spite of some improvement in contract awards in recent years, policy implementation still has to be improved if public confidence in infrastructure development policy is to be maintained.

Public sector resources would be needed not only for investment in infrastructure but also for the growing amount of infrastructure subsidies. The manner in which infrastructure has been developed and operated in the country is likely to see an escalation in subsidies for infrastructure. For fiscal reasons and to achieve efficiency, infrastructure subsidies must be progressively reduced. The huge mismatch between user tariffs and cost of services, as in public transport services, will have to be narrowed. Likewise, selective provision of free infrastructure services such as electricity and water has also to be reviewed and where possible reduced. As a general prescription on user tariffs, in all but exceptional cases users must be required to pay the cost of providing the service.

While efforts are now being made to encourage the use of public transport, supporting policies to support the attainment of the objective is still lacking. A whole range of measures can be taken to restrict private car usage in the Klang Valley but thus far these have not been deployed to encourage modal shift from private to public transport.

In the current political scenario in the country and on account of its federal structure, a number of infrastructure related conflicts are emerging between the federal and state governments. The problem with regards to the water industry in Selangor is an indication of the conflicts that could arise between the federal and state governments. Clearly the present framework does not provide proper avenue for resolution of problems such as the current one between Syabas and the Selangor State Government (Syabas was awarded the concession by Federal Government to supply water in the state of Selangor).

A number of legacy issues still exist in the infrastructure sector. These include the inequitable terms and condition in the power purchase agreement of the initial IPP concessions and the toll concession agreements. These legacy issues would have to be resolved to minimize their negative impacts on infrastructure users and sector efficiency.

A number of recent changes have brought the whole matter of planning infrastructure development in Malaysia to the forefront. Over the last two or three years, new agencies have been created to plan and develop infrastructure. These include SPAD (Land Public Transport Commission), PEMANDU with its labs, UKAS and the five regional Corridors. These agencies now appear to be involved in a substantial manner in the planning and implementation of infrastructure projects. The situation that is now developing is quite different from the earlier one in which the Economic Planning Unit (EPU) was the primary central planning agency and decisions on infrastructure development were mostly vested with it. Whether the diffusion is beneficial or detrimental to infrastructure planning is an issue that requires proper evaluation.

Conclusion

A number of conclusions can be drawn from the foregoing description of the growth of infrastructure in the country.

First, there has been immense investment in the development of infrastructure in the country. This has contributed to the growth in the capacity and stock of infrastructure in the country and to its modernization and technical development.

The supply of infrastructure has mostly kept abreast of the demand for infrastructure. In the recent past there have been very few if any instances of infrastructure shortages nor have there been too many cases of excess capacity in the infrastructure sector of the country.

The private sector is now a major player in the development and operation of infrastructure in the country. In the near and medium term the more constrained fiscal position of the government will see the role of the private sector in infrastructure development increase. Unless properly managed, the declining role of the government and the growing importance of private participation can impact on the cost of infrastructure and infrastructure services and on infrastructure development to serve socio-economic objectives.

While privatization has contributed to the growth and development of infrastructure stock in the country, there is no denying that the implementation of the privatization policy has not been always efficiency-inducing. The lack of competitive bidding, the pursuit of inter-ethnic equity goals of the NEP and the willingness of the government to bail out failed privatized projects has, among others, undermined the efficiency gains from privatization being realized.

There are also a number of legacy issues that continue negatively impacting users. These remain unresolved. On a related matter, the effectiveness of new oversight agencies to effectively regulate the infrastructure providers has to be strengthened. There are likely to be new demands for infrastructure as the country develops into a high income economy. These would require improvements in infrastructure sector policy-making and implementation.

NOTES

1. Malaya became an independent nation in August 1957. Sabah and Sarawak joined Malaya to form Malaysia in September 1963.
2. International Bank for Reconstruction and Development (IBRD). *The Economic Development of Malaya*. Baltimore: John Hopkins Press for IBRD, 1955.
3. Since the formation of Malaysia in 1963 ten five-year development plans have been formulated, starting with the First Malaysia Plan of 1966–70 to the ongoing Tenth Malaysia Plan (2011–15).

4. In the early post-independence period national security also had a bearing on the development of infrastructure in the country, particularly roads. Since the end of the communist insurgency this has ceased to be a consideration in infrastructure development.

5 In 2005, it was assessed that sustained investment in infrastructure and efficiency in operations have helped Malaysia achieve considerable competitive advantage across infrastructure sectors, both in international terms and when compared with East Asia's developed economies.

6 The Performance Management and Delivery Unit (PEMANDU) was formally established on 16 September 2009 and is a unit under the Prime Minister's Department. PEMANDU's main role and objective is to oversee implementation and assess progress of the Economic Transformation Programme and the Government Transformation Programme.

REFERENCES

Asian Development Bank, Japan Bank for International Cooperation and The World Bank. *Connecting East Asia: A New Framework for Infrastructure*, 2005.

Department of Statistics, Malaysia. *Yearbook of Statistics*, various years. Kuala Lumpur: Government Printer, various years.

Economic Report, various issues. Kuala Lumpur: Finance Ministry, various years.

International Bank for Reconstruction and Development. *The Economic Development of Malaya*. Baltimore: John Hopkins Press for IBRD, 1955.

Malaysia. *First Malaysia Plan 1966–70*. Kuala Lumpur Government Printer, Malaysia, 1960.

———. *Second Malaysia Plan 1971–75*. Kuala Lumpur Government Printer, Malaysia, 1971.

———. *Third Malaysia Plan 1976–80*. Kuala Lumpur Government Printer, Malaysia, 1976.

———. *Fourth Malaysia Plan 1981–85*. Kuala Lumpur Government Printer, Malaysia, 1981.

———. *Fifth Malaysia Plan 1986–90*. Kuala Lumpur Government Printer, Malaysia, 1986.

———. *Sixth Malaysia Plan 1991–95*. Kuala Lumpur Government Printer, Malaysia, 1991.

———. *Seventh Malaysia Plan 1996–2000*. Kuala Lumpur: Pecetakan Nasional Malaysia Berhad, 1996.

———. *Eighth Malaysia Plan 2001–05*. Kuala Lumpur: Pecetakan Nasional Malaysia Berhad, 2001.

————. *The Third Outline Perspective Plan, 2001–10*. Kuala Lumpur: Pecetakan Nasional Malaysia Berhad, 2001.

————. *Ninth Malaysia Plan 2006–10*.Kuala Lumpur: Pecetakan Nasional Malaysia Berhad, 2006.

————. *Tenth Malaysia Plan 2011–15*. Kuala Lumpur: Pecetakan Nasional Malaysia Berhad, 2010.

Malaysian Institute of Economic Research (MIER). *The Study on Infrastructure Development in Malaysia*. MIER, 2008.

Naidu, G. Infrastructure in Jomo K.S. *Privatizing Malaysia*. Westview Press, Inc., 1994.

Naidu, G. and Cassey Lee. "Infrastructure in the Economic Development of Malaysia". Paper presented at the World Bank Conference on Infrastructure Strategies for East Asia, Singapore, 1994.

————. "The Transition to Privatization: Malaysia". In *Infrastructure Strategies in East Asia: The Untold Story*, edited by Ashoka Mody. The World Bank, 1997.

National Land Public Transport Masterplan, Land Public Transport Commission. December 2011.

Transport Statistics Malaysia, various issues, Ministry of Transport, Malaysia, various years.

Yahya Yaacob and G. Naidu. *Contracting for Private Provision of Infrastructure: The Malaysian Experience*. In *Choices for Efficient Private Provision of Infrastructure in East Asia*, by Harinder Kohli et al. The World Bank, 1997.

8

FINANCIAL REFORMS IN MALAYSIA

G. Sivalingam

Introduction

The focus of this chapter is on financial reforms in Malaysia after the 1997 East Asian Financial Crisis when the economy suffered its worst recession since independence in 1957. The 1997 currency crisis has been seen as a consequence of the fragility of the banking system by those who diagnosed the crisis as being due to short term overborrowing by the banking system (Radelet and Sachs 1998, p. 9) resulting in the twin problems of currency and maturity mismatches (Corsetti 1998, p. 24). However, those who saw it as a consequence of the decline in exports diagnosed the problem as being due to the inability of the countries to finance their external debt because of the widening current account deficit (Corsetti 1998, p. 24; Radelet and Sachs 1998, pp. 19–26).

The tapering of the growth rate of exports as a result of the cyclical downturn in the world electronics industry in 1996 led to the withdrawal of loans by Japanese and European banks, who had provided short term financing to the Malaysian banks. The Malaysian banks were caught because they had used the short term loans to finance long term infrastructure and property development and other lumpy investments.

Foreign Portfolio Investments (FPI), which had peaked in the Kuala Lumpur Stock Exchange (KLSE) in 1993–94, took flight as a result of the banking panic and the subsequent devaluation of the ringgit (Radelet and Sachs 1998, pp. 9–11). This led to the further depreciation of the ringgit, which had an adverse effect on the balance sheet of the corporations (Krugman 1998) and the capital adequacy of the banks.

The Malaysian government however viewed the crisis as being a conspiracy of western hedge funds, western governments and the IMF to impoverish East Asia by creating the conditions for the crisis (Athukorola 2001, pp. 63–66; Mahathir 1998). The Malaysian government view received some academic credibility from the writings of Stiglitz (1998), Bhagwati (1998) and Wade and Veneroso (1998) who elaborated the Treasury-Wall Street Complex theory, whereby the Federal Reserve Bank collaborated with Wall Street by making cheap credit available for hedge funds to invest in East Asia to create a bubble which they could profiteer from being the first one to be out or "sell and run".

The Global Financial Crisis of 2008 did not, however, have such a serious impact on the financial sector of the economy or the Malaysian currency. Financial reforms, especially corporate governance reforms were undertaken on a continuous basis. Attempts were also made to liberalize the services sector and relax equity requirements under the New Economic Policy (NEP) at least in some sectors of the economy. The government also liberalized the banking sector further by issuing licences to foreign banks. The licensing of a new domestic Islamic Bank in 1999 and three new foreign Islamic Banks in 2004 also strengthened, deepened and widened Islamic Banking as a new source of financing for Malaysia.

To place the discussion in perspective, the chapter will discuss the alternative policy prescriptions before it discusses the reforms resulting from the policy prescriptions.

Alternative Policy Recommendations

At the outset of the crisis, the International Monetary Fund (IMF) had the option to bail out the affected East Asian countries by acting as the lender of last resort. Not only did the IMF not choose this option to enable the countries to effectively defend their currencies against the well-financed hedge funds and banks that withdrew their short term loans, but the IMF also with the support of the United States (U.S.) dissuaded Japan from assuming the role of lender of last resort and setting up the Asian Monetary Fund that would be more sensitive to the financing needs of Asian countries. The IMF wanted to restructure the economies so as to transform them from non-market, and in some cases feudal economies, to market economies (Corsetti 1998, pp. 51–52).

The IMF had a calling to eradicate cronyism and corruption which it diagnosed as being some of the root causes of the crisis leading to over investment in infrastructure including property and stocks and shares that had led to the bubble economy (Radelet and Sachs 1998, p. 9). The bubble burst on the expectation of falling export earnings in the near future and this led to panic and herd behaviour among both foreign and domestic investors resulting in the huge capital flight overwhelming inflows of capital (Radelet and Sachs 1998, p. 9). The capital flight caused the interest rate to rise, which resulted in the inability of corporations to service their debt, a consequence of which was the rising Non-Performing Loans (NPLs) in the banking system and the erosion of bank capital. The stock market also crashed because of the massive withdrawals of FPI and the sharp increase in the interest rate. The IMF was of the view that a more transparent competitive market economy would not have created the bubble or created investor panic.

The IMF's prescriptions were consistent with that of its diagnosis. To eliminate corruption and cronyism it wanted to dismantle the social institutions including the NEP that bred corruption and cronyism and resulted in the misallocation of resources (Ang and McKibbin 2007, p. 228). The NEP, which was introduced in 1971 focused on redistributing wealth from the non-Malays including foreigners to the Malays but within the context of a growing economy (Young et al. 1980). The goal of the NEP was to ensure that at least 30 per cent of the wealth of the country was in the hands of the Malays by 1990.

In order to achieve the ownership targets of the NEP, the government directed credit to the Malays to enable them to purchase equity, property and to enter into businesses (Young et al. 1980, pp. 60–96). According to Ang and Mckibbin, in the early 1990s, "most lending was issued for the purchase of shares and real estate property rather than for investment in productive activities. This led to bubbles in the property sector and triggered much speculative activities in the share market prior to the financial crisis of 1997–98" (Ang and McKibbin 2007, p. 228). The Mahathir years were also, according to Haggard (2004, p. 62), "the highpoint of corruption, cronyism and the interpenetration of government, state and party".

In wanting to dismantle the NEP, the IMF was keen to engineer a shift from relationship based banking (Corsetti 1998, p. 23) to rational banking based on neo-classical principles and for project financing to be based on net present value calculations and not on connections. The IMF's suggestions including the need to embark on an austerity drive and increase the interest rate to stop the massive capital flight was initially embraced by the Malaysian government especially the then Minister of Finance (Corsetti et al. 1998*b*, pp. 9–10).

However, the IMF prescription of increasing the interest rate sharply contributed to rising NPL ratios in the banking system as firms defaulted on their loans, thus eroding the capital base of the banks and although there were no bank runs, there were rumours of impending bank runs that were halted by implicit government guarantees to protect all deposits.

The threat of the closure of firms and banks and the threatening political consequences of dismantling the NEP, persuaded Prime Minister Mahathir to abandon the IMF prescriptions and instead of further integrating the Malaysian economy with the world economy, he decided to isolate the economy from global finance and capital movements until the economy stabilized and recovered. Mahathir decided to avoid distress sales of domestic assets and institutions to foreigners as had occurred in Thailand and South Korea (Athukorala 2001, pp. 74–75; Mahathir 1998, pp. 60–61). He was also keen to maintain and implement the NEP and he was encouraged in doing so by Feldstein (1998), who argued that the IMF had no mandate to initiate social engineering in member countries and to change social structures that were inimical to the development of the market economy. Mahathir imposed capital controls in September 1998 and his move was endorsed by Bhagwati (1998), Krugman (1998) and Stiglitz (1998).

In the months before the capital controls were imposed, the National Economic Advisory Council (NEAC) recommended that the government set up three corporations, that is, the Asset Management Corporation (AMC) known as Danaharta, the Danamodal and the Corporate Debt Restructuring Corporation (CDRC) to resolve three problems, that is, rising NPLs, the erosion of the capital base of the banks and the insolvency of large corporations. The chapter will discuss the effort to introduce capital controls and the effects of the setting up of the three corporations (Danharta, Danamodal and CDRC) and the bank mergers before it discusses subsequent measures taken to stabilize and restructure the financial system to ensure its long term sustainability.

Capital Controls

To put a stop to the speculation on the ringgit which was causing its value not only to depreciate but also to be volatile, the Malaysian government in September 1998 instituted capital controls and a fixed exchange rate regime (Ariff and Khalid 2000, p. 157). The Malaysian government also de-internationalized the ringgit to stop the speculation on the ringgit in offshore markets. The economy recovered in 1999, that is, at the same time as the other East Asian countries due to the recovery of the demand for electrical and electronics goods. It is not clear as to whether capital controls gave Malaysia an advantage relative to the other crisis affected countries in East Asia whose economies also recovered at about the same time (Corsetti 1998, p. 48). However, Eichengreen and Leblang (2003, p. 220) are of the view that the net effect of capital controls is "positive in periods of financial instability, when the insulating capacity of controls is precious". At the time the controls were imposed, the NEAC emphasized that it was vital for Malaysia to maintain very high levels of foreign reserves to service the country's external debt. In 2005, Malaysia's total external reserves were about RM265 billion or nearly 7.5 months of retained imports far in excess of the target of 5 months of retained imports set by the NEAC (Bank Negara Malaysia 2008). The capital controls were gradually relaxed and in July 2005, following the lead provided by China, Malaysia switched its exchange rate regime from a fixed exchange rate regime to a managed float. The ringgit, however, remains de-internationalized.

The ringgit has appreciated against the US dollar by about 20 per cent from 2005 to the present. The flexible exchange rate regime has according to the IMF helped Malaysia to overcome the 2008–09 Global Financial Crisis. According to the IMF, the "monetary policy implemented by Bank Negara Malaysia helped soften the impact of the global financial crisis. Specifically, the findings suggest that without the counter-cyclical and discretionary interest rate cuts along exchange rate flexibility, the global financial crisis would have been associated with a much deeper economic contraction in Malaysia" (Harun Alp, Salim Elekdag and Subir Lall 2012, p. 13).

Rationale for Danharta, Danamodal and CDRC

Resolution of Non-Performing Loans (NPLs) of the Banking System

The NEAC recommended the setting up of Danaharta in June 1998 to avert the collapse of the banking system because of rising NPLs in the banking system. The NPLs had increased from 3.7 per cent (on a three-month basis) in 1996 to 13.6 per cent in 1998 (see Table 8.1) Danaharta had two main objectives, that is, (i) acquire the NPLs from the banks so that they can concentrate on lending for economic growth and (ii) to maximize the recovery value of the NPLs. The target was to reduce the NPL ratio to less than 10 per cent and the strategy was to acquire only NPLs worth RM5 million or more. Danaharta hoped to relieve the banking system of at least 70 per cent of all the NPLs in the system. Bank Negara Malaysia also directed the banks to sell their NPLs to Danaharta especially if their NPL ratio was more than 10 per cent. Danaharta acquired the NPLs at a discount and at significantly below market value (Danaharta 2005, p. 19). Danaharta recorded a final loan recovery rate of 58 per cent in 2005 when it was officially closed down (Danaharta 2005, p. 44). Assets that were not converted to cash by Danaharta were handed over to the Ministry of Finance. By 2005, the NPL ratio had been brought down to 5.8 per cent and by 2007 it fell to 3.2 per cent. The gross NPL ratio was brought down further to about 2.2 per cent in 2008 and 1.8 per cent in 2009.

Over the years the provisions to cover for non-performing loans and impaired loans has also been increased. Before the crisis, the provision, for example in 1996, was only about 97 per cent of all NPLs on a three-month basis of the banking system. During the crisis, in 1997, it was increased to about 152 per cent of all NPLs on a three month basis. By 2009, the provisions were a staggering about 348 per cent of the NPLs, indicating an ultra-conservative and cautious posture on the part of the regulators. During the Global Financial Crisis of 2008–09 the provisions ranged between 332 per cent to 348 per cent of all NPLs (see Table 8.1).

TABLE 8.1

Banking System: Outstanding Loan Provisions and NPLs

Year	NPLs-3 Months	Interest-in-Suspense	Specific Provisions	General Provisions	NPL/Total Loans	Total Provision/NPLs	General Provisions/Net Total Loans
1995	14,320	3,939	4,043	4,207	5.5	85.0	1.7
1996	12,480	3,144	3,054	5,854	3.7	96.6	1.8
1997	25,053	2,886	5,402	8,447	4.1	151.4	2.0
1998	76,953	7,377	16,647	8,576	13.6	131.4	2.2
1999	65,540	7,357	17,552	8,016	11.0	151.9	2.2
2000	64,256	8,677	17,901	8,449	9.7	170.8	2.2
2001	76,976	10,039	20,682	8,262	11.5	172.3	2.1
2002	71,693	9,998	18,586	8,729	10.2	187.0	2.1
2003	65,744	9,345	16,417	9,165	8.9	191.9	2.0
2004	60,380	8,469	15,242	9,487	7.5	210.7	1.9
2005	53,570	7,331	14,907	9,427	5.8	224.0	1.8
2006	50,391	6,997	16,034	9,535	4.8	251.9	1.7
2007	41,763	6,031	15,721	10,538	3.2	294.7	1.7
2008	34,983	5,180	13,914	12,057	2.2	332.7	1.7
2009	28,693	3,759	11,146	12,495	1.8	347.5	1.6

Source: Bank Negara Malaysia (2012).

Recapitalization of the Banking System

Danamodal was also set up in 1998 on the recommendation of the NEAC to recapitalize banks whose capital base had been eroded by rising NPLs. The recapitalization was important to enable banks to continue lending for investment projects that were vital to facilitate economic recovery. Although Danamodal had an initial budget of RM16 billion, it only injected RM7.1 billion into ten banks that it considered viable. The banks were to start repaying Danamodal one year after the latter had injected the capital into the banks. The capitalization of the banks helped to improve the Risk Weighted Capital Ratio (RWCR) of the banks from 10.1 per cent in 1998 to 13.2 per cent in 2003. Furthermore, the Core Capital Ratio (CCR) of the banks increased from 9.9 per cent in 1998 to 11 per cent in 2003 (Bank Negara Malaysia 2008). As the Malaysian media, The Star noted, "the banking system appears to be well capitalized with a Core Capital Ratio (CCR) of 12.5 percent and a Risk Weighted Capital Ratio of 14.6 percent in 2011" (24 November 2011).

Restructuring the Debt of the Corporations

Due to the financial crisis, several major corporations were unable to service their debt and this not only threatened the solvency of the corporations but also the banks. The NEAC recommended that the government set up the Corporate Debt Restructuring Corporation (CDRC) in July 1998 to mediate between creditors and debtors. The CDRC was set up in recognition of the fact that the insolvency legislation was inadequate and did not discriminate between viable and non-viable businesses. Corporations that required the assistance of the CDRC would make an application to the CDRC after which the CDRC will evaluate the viability of the application and hold discussions with bankers and shareholders of the corporations before implementing any proposal to restructure the corporation and its debt (Bank Negara Malaysia 2008). The CDRC closed operations after it had assisted in the restructuring of the debt of 48 corporations amounting to RM52.5 billion. It had received 87 applications but rejected 28 applications and transferred 11 applications to Danaharta. It only accepted cases that were viable; had a debt of more than RM100 million; had more than 8 creditors and were not in insolvency administration including liquidation.

Bank Consolidation

The Central Bank of Malaysia had since the mid 1985–86 recession adopted a pro-merger policy because it recognized that "Malaysia had too many small banks to be internationally competitive" (Corsetti et al. 1998a, p. 30). In 1999, the government embarked on a strategy that led to the consolidation of a highly fragmented domestic banking system, which comprised 71 institutions prior to the crisis, to 30 domestic banking institutions organized in ten domestic banking groups by 2002. The target was to increase the capital size of each bank to a minimum of RM2 billion so as to achieve economies of scale.

The bank merger programme was announced by Bank Negara Malaysia on 29 July 1999 and in a sense the merger exercise was not market driven. The consolidation programme launched by Bank Negara Malaysia on 14 February 2000 was focused on forming ten anchor banking group out of the existing 58 financial institutions comprising commercial banks, finance companies and merchant banks. Each emerging anchor banking group will comprise of a commercial bank, finance companies and merchant banks.

The ten anchor banks that emerged as a result of the consolidation or merger exercise that was concluded in 2002 included: Maybank Berhad, Bumiputra Commerce Bank Berhad, RHB Bank Berhad, Public Bank Berhad, Arab-Malaysian Bank Berhad, Hong Leong Bank Berhad, Perwira Affin Bank Berhad, Multipurpose Bank Berhad, Southern Bank Berhad and EON Bank Berhad. Subsequently the reorganized Bumiputra Commerce Bank was renamed Commerce International Merchant Bank (CIMB) and it acquired Southern Bank in 2006, thus bringing down the number of domestic banks to nine. Subsequently in 2011, Hong Leong Bank acquired EON Bank thus lending support of the government's consolidation exercise to increase competition and efficiency in the banking industry by taking advantage of scale economies.

The end result of the merger activities was to increase the concentration of assets in a few banks. The three largest banks accounted for more than 43 per cent of the assets of the banking industry in 2001 (Mathieson and Schinasi 2001, p. 127). By 2010, the three largest domestic banks in Malaysia, that is, Maybank, CIMB and Public Banks accounted 65.6 per cent of the total assets of the domestic conventional banking industry. The actions of the three largest banks that are either

Name of Bank	Asset US$ Billion	Asset RM Billion	Market Capitalization US$ Billion	Market Capitalization RM Billion
Maybank	110.3	330.9	20.7	62.1
CIMB Bank	88.3	264.9	19.5	58.5
Public Bank	74.2	222.6	15.1	45.3
Hong Leong Bank + EON Bank	43.2	129.6	6.4	19.2
AmBank	42.4	127.2	6.1	18.3
RHB Bank	31.6	94.8	5.4	16.2
Hong Leong Bank	27.8	83.4	4.8	14.4
Affin Bank	15.4	46.2	1.6	4.8
EON Bank	15.2	45.6	1.6	4.8
Alliance Bank	10.4	31.2	1.5	4.5
	415.6	1246.8	76.3	228.9

Source: *Annual Reports* of the Domestic Banks in Malaysia, see also <http://1-million-dollar-blog.com/2011-ranking-of-malaysian-banks-based-on-assets-size-market-capitalization/ http://1-million-dollar-blog.com/2011-ranking-of-malaysian-banks-based-on-assets-size-market-capitalization/>.

government linked or close to the government continue to be the major sources of systemic risk in the banking industry.

Measures for Stabilizing and Restructuring the Financial System

Prudential Regulation of Banks

The banks in Malaysia were relatively more effectively regulated by the Central Bank as evidenced by the fact that the ratio of external debt to external reserves in Malaysia was low compared to other crisis affected countries in East Asia at the time of the crisis. In 1997, Malaysia's external debt was only 68 per cent of its external reserves (Bank Negara Malaysia 2008). This was partly because the Central Bank had implemented a policy to approve loans that could generate sufficient foreign exchange to service the debt and repay the principal when due. Although corporations were not permitted to raise funds externally, some of them had accumulated a large amount of foreign debt apparently with the approval of the Central Bank. The bulk of the short term debt, however, was due to borrowings by commercial banks.

To better manage risk and regulate banks, Malaysia decided after the crisis and the Enron scandal to move away from the rules-based to the principle-based regulatory system. Consistent with the adoption of the principle based regulatory system Bank Negara has encouraged the banks and financial institutions to follow procedures laid out by the International Accounting Standards Board (IASB) and not the rules based Financial Accounting Standards Board (FASB).

Malaysia has also adopted a Risk Based Capital Framework and a risk based supervisory regime and had set 2010 as the target date for implementing Basel II although the structure of the banking industry and the economy is not amenable to rapid institutional or social change. As a consequence, the Central Bank has adopted a strategy of more gradual enhancement of the risk management framework of all the banking institutions. By 2011, the banking system was well capitalized with a Core Capital Ratio of 12.5 per cent and a risk weighted capital ratio of 14.6 per cent, which is well above the regulatory minimum level under Basel II and the higher capital requirements under Basel III (*The Star*, 24 November 2011). The banks have also been persuaded to be more market oriented consistent with the third pillar of Basel II that banks should be disciplined by the market and not bailed out by the government. The Central Bank has also increased financial surveillance of the banks. Some of the larger banks are in the process of implementing the Foundation Internal Ratings Based (FIRB) approach for managing credit risk but they initially faced big problems in collecting historical loss data (Global Risk Regulator 2005).

Deposit Insurance

At the outset of the East Asian Financial crisis, Malaysia had no deposit insurance scheme but all bank deposits were protected by an implicit government guarantee. The NEAC recommended the setting up of a deposit insurance corporation along the lines of the Federal Deposit Insurance Corporation (FDIC) in the United States. However, it was not until seven years later, on 1 September 2005, that the Perbadanan

Insurans Deposit Malaysia (PIDM) or the Malaysian Deposit Insurance Corporation (MDIC) was set up as an independent statutory body under the Malaysian Deposit Insurance Corporation Act 2005 which requires all financial institutions to be a member of the MDIC. The deposit insurance system is funded by annual premiums from member institutions and eligible deposits will be insured up to the prescribed limit of RM60,000 per depositor, per member institution inclusive of principal and interest.

Islamic Banking in Malaysia

Malaysia is one of the few countries that has a dual banking system known as the conventional commercial banking system and an Islamic banking system. The first Islamic Bank, the Bank of Islam was established in 1983 under the Islamic Banking Act 1983. The conventional banks were encouraged to open "Islamic Windows" to complement and compete with the Islamic bank in offering syariah compliant services to the Muslim population in Malaysia. In 1999, a second Islamic bank, the Bank Mualamat was licensed and began to operate. At the same time the conventional banks were encouraged to set up Islamic subsidiaries with their own accounting and reporting system. Although three new Islamic banking licences were offered to foreign banks in 2001, they became operational in 2005–06. These new foreign Islamic banks are: the Asian Finance Bank Berhad (2005), the Kuwait Finance House (2005) and the Al Rajhi Bank (2006). There are today 2 full fledged domestic Islamic Banks, 3 foreign Islamic banks and 12 Islamic subsidiaries of domestic commercial banks offering syariah compliant services to the Muslim and non-Muslim population of Malaysia.

Foreign Participation in Financial Services

After the introduction of the NEP in 1971, laws were introduced to limit foreign participation in the financial services sector not only to increase the Malay share of the equity of financial institutions but also to develop domestic financial services providers. The policies are consistent with the Banking and Financial Institutions Act (BAFIA) 1989 and the ten-year Financial Sector Master Plan (FSMP) introduced in 2001. No new licenses have been granted to foreign or local banks except in 2001 when the Bank of China reopened its office in Kuala Lumpur and in 2003 when BNM issued three new Islamic banking licences. The objectives of the FSMP are to enhance the financial infrastructure and to develop the capacity of domestic institutions to compete with foreign firms in a competitive environment (Bank Negara Malaysia 2001). Since 2009, new licences have been given to nine foreign banks and they include: Industrial and Commercial Bank of China (China), Bank of Baroda (India), Andhra Bank (India), Indian Overseas Bank (India), National Bank of Abu Dhabi (UAE), PT Bank Mandiri (Indonesia), Mitzuho Corporate Bank (Japan), Sumitomo Mitsui Banking Corporation (Japan), and PNB Paribas (France). It is expected that the consolidated domestic banking groups will be able to compete with the enlarged foreign competition.

Capital Market Reforms

The ten-year Capital Market Master Plan (CMMP) introduced in 2001 was designed to broaden and deepen the capital market as they have been described as narrow and relatively underdeveloped (de Brouwer 2002, p. 2). The CMMP is also focused on enhancing corporate governance standards; facilitating the entry of foreign financial institutions into the capital market and creating a competitive environment to increase efficiency. The entry of foreign financial institutions into the capital market is expected to provide "an important catalyst for markets to move to best practices" (de Brouwer 2002, p. 2). The Securities Commission is also in the process of implementing a disclosure based regime for listing new firms in the stock exchange.

To facilitate the deepening and widening of the bond market, the government has enhanced the market infrastructure and the legal, administrative and regulatory framework and provided incentives for the development of capital market intermediaries and a reliable market-based benchmark yield curve. Malaysia has also been active in strengthening the demand for ringgit denominated bonds by being an active collaborator in the Asian Bond Fund (ABF) initiative. As a result of these reforms the size of the Malaysian Bond Market has grown by more than 9 per cent per annum between 1997 and 2003 and by more than 10 per cent per annum from 2004 to 2005. As a percentage of GDP, bond financing has nearly doubled from 56 per cent of GDP in 1997 to 93.24 per cent of GDP in 2005 (Bank Negara Malaysia 2008). Malaysia has also emerged as one of the largest issuers of Islamic bonds or *sukuks*. The Second Capital Market Masterplan that was released in 2011 is focused towards (i) strengthening the capital market and grow it to double its size to US$1.9 trillion by 2020 through internationalization, (ii) develop venture capital and private equity industries, (iii) develop the bond market, (iii) offer a greater diversity of products and services and (v) improve corporate governance and investor protection (Securities Commission 2011).

Corporate Governance

There has been a concerted effort since the 1997 East Asian financial crisis, to raise the standards of Corporate Governance to the level of international best practices. International agencies have ranked Malaysia's standards of corporate governance as being relatively high especially in reference to its disclosure regime and the transparency of its accounting standards (World Bank 2000). However, cases of irregularities in financial reporting persist. After the 1997 crisis, the Securities Commission has required listed firms to disclose more information in their annual reports regarding the duties and independence of the directors; the functions of the audit committees; the role of internal auditors; and the quality of audit. Efforts have also been made to raise the level of corporate governance by introducing regulatory reforms such as the revamp of the Listing Requirements of the KLSE and the introduction of new regulations relating to the trading of securities. Institutional reforms introduced to safeguard investors interest include the setting up of the Minority Shareholders Watchdog Group, the Malaysian Institute of Corporate Governance and institutions to train and educate investors (Securities Commission 1999).

Economic Recovery

The Malaysian economy recovered in 1999 after its real GDP contracted by 7.4 per cent in 1998 (see Table 8.3). The recovery in 1999 and 2000 was largely due to the "buoyant world demand for electronics", which was "supported by accommodating macroeconomic policies" (Liu 2001, p. 7). In 2001 real GDP grew by only 0.5 per cent but recovered in 2002 to register a growth of 5.4 per cent and thereafter it has been growing between 5.8 per cent and 6.8 per cent per annum. Unemployment has not been the source of concern and it has declined since the crisis (Liu 2001, p. 7). The current account balance as a

TABLE 8.3
Malaysia: Macroeconomic Indicators

Year	Growth Rate of Real GDP (%)	Current Account Balance (% of GDP)	Growth Rates of Merchandize Exports (%)	Ratio of International Reserves to Imports (Months)	Inflation (%)	Total Debt Service (% of exports of goods and services)	Domestic Bank Credit (% of GDP)	NPL Ratio of the Banks
1990	9.0	−2.1	17.6	5	3.1	12.6	72.7	
1995	9.8	−8.6	25.9	4	4.0	7.0	173.0	
1996	10.0	−3.3	6.0	4	3.4	8.9	193.8	3.8
1997	7.3	−4.4	0.3	3	2.8	7.4	221.8	
1998	−7.4	16.6	−7.0	6	5.2	7.2	216.6	13.6
1999	6.1	15.9	15.9	6	2.8	4.9	197.3	
2000	8.9	9.0	16.1	4	1.5	5.6	186.1	15.4
2001	0.5	7.9	−10.4	5	1.4	6.0	199.5	17.8
2002	5.4	8.0	6.9	5	1.8	7.2	195.8	15.9
2003	5.8	12.1	11.3	7	1.2	7.9	191.7	13.9
2004	6.8	12.1	21.0	8	1.4	6.2	149.5	11.7
2005	5.0	15.0	10.9	8	3.1	5.6	137.0	9.5
2006	5.9	16.7	10.4	8	3.6	3.99	119.0	8.5
2007	6.3	15.9	2.6	8.8	2.0	4.80	113.2	8.2
2008	4.8	17.4	9.7	7.4	5.4	3.62	115.1	2.6
2009	−1.6	16.5	−16.7	9.9	0.6	5.22	137.0	3.7
2010	7.2	11.8	15.7	8.2	1.7	2.7	131.6	3.2

Source: Asian Development Bank (2008).

percentage of GDP has been positive since 1998 after it was negative between 1995 and 1997.

The international reserves of Malaysia have grown tremendously since 2003 and in 2010 they supported more than eight months of imports. The gradual relaxation of capital controls and the move to a managed float of the exchange rate regime helped build investor confidence in the country. Furthermore, as a result of the increasing demand for its agricultural products and the boom in oil prices plus the recovery in the demand for electrical and electronics products helped place Malaysia in a better credit rating (Athukorala 2001, pp. 84–95). The financial system also recovered due to the financial and corporate restructuring efforts of Danaharta, Danamodal and the CDRC. Domestic bank credit as a percentage of GDP has moderated from a high of 221.8 per cent in 1997 to 119 per cent in 2007. However, directed lending does not ensure that bank loans go to the most valued users (Ang and McKibbin 2007). Inflation was brought down from 5.2 per cent in 1998 to –1.7 per cent in 2010. External debt is within manageable limits as total debt service as a percentage of GDP has been brought down from 8.9 per cent in 1996 to 2.7 per cent in 2010. It appears that Malaysia's external vulnerability is well contained.

A Peak into the Future

The Malaysian government in releasing the Second Ten Year Financial Sector Blueprint (2011–20) (Bank Negara Malaysia 2011) in 2011 is upbeat about creating an international financial centre and an Islamic financial centre in Kuala Lumpur. This is despite the fact that Malaysia is a small, open economy dependent on the exports of labour intensive manufactured and primary commodities and oil and hence is vulnerable to fluctuations in the prices of these commodities as the demand for them is not stable even in the short run. The government prides itself in the fact that the Malaysian financial system was resilient during the global financial crisis of 2008 and 2009 as reflected in the low non-performing loan ratios of its banks and the relatively high risk weighted capital ratios and core capital ratios of its banks.

The prospects for the development of Malaysia as a global leader in Islamic finance appears promising because Malaysia is the leader in the world in terms of the amount of *sukuk* or Islamic bonds issued. In furthering the cause of developing Kuala Lumpur as an International

Financial Centre and an Islamic Financial Centre and to give the Islamic finance industry a boost, the Central Bank is expected to set up a single apex authority to interpret the shariah compliance of financial products and instruments. This will considerably reduce transaction costs in the industry.

The main focus of the Second Ten Year Financial Sector Blueprint appears to be to further develop the Malaysian Islamic financial system to enhance its position as the place to issue *sukuk* or Islamic bonds. To attract more oil money and investments from the Middle East, the Second Ten Year Financial Sector Blueprint hopes to develop a wider range of Islamic financial products and instruments while at the same time issuing more new banking licenses to Islamic banks from the Middle East.

The Second Ten Year Financial Sector Blueprint is also headed in the right direction as it focuses on developing human capital and plans to set up another Council, that is, the Financial Services Talent Council to produce highly skilled personnel to drive innovation and increase the efficiency and effectiveness of the intermediation process. This is an uphill task given that Malaysia is not short of training institutions, think-tanks or councils but is mired in relationship banking and pre-occupied with responding to the demands of social capital.

Conclusion

Malaysia has recovered from the East Asian financial crisis of 1997. The banks and the financial institutions have recovered from the effects of the crisis. The reforms instituted since 1997 have reduced the NPLs of the banking system, recapitalized the banks and helped to restructure corporations that were in financial distress. The external reserves of the country have grown over the years and the external debt of the country is manageable. The financial sector and capital sector master plans are being implemented in stages and steps have been taken to implement Basel II in Malaysia. Further research needs to be done on the impact of the reforms on the financial structure as they are being implemented especially in regard to the implementation of Basel II and risk management systems of the banks and the introduction of new regulations and supervision of financial institutions. There are also plans to implement Basel III by the end of 2012. The government has indicated that it is committed to the NEP and that it intends to control the flow of credit to the disadvantaged Malays. This will significantly affect the allocation of credit in the economy but it has been justified in terms of enhancing the political stability of the country. It appears that the "growth with distribution" development strategy initiated in the 1970s will be the preferred strategy of the government.

REFERENCES

Ang, J.B. and W.J. McKibbin. "Financial Liberalization, Financial Sector Development and Growth: Evidence from Malaysia". *Journal of Development Economics* 84 (2007): 215–33.

Ariff, M. and A.M. Khalid. *Liberalization, Growth and the Asian Financial Crisis: Lessons from Developing and Transitional Economies in Asia*. Cheltenham: Edward Elgar, 2000.

Asian Development Bank. *Key Indicators for Asia and the Pacific 2008*. Manila: Asian Development Bank, 2008.

Athukorala, P. *Crisis and Recovery in Malaysia: The Role of Capital Controls*. Cheltenham: Edward Elgar, 2001.

Bank Negara Malaysia. *The Financial Sector Master Plan*. Kuala Lumpur: Government Printer, 2001.

———. *Annual Reports, 1996–2007*. Kuala Lumpur: Government Printer, 2008.

———. *Financial Sector Blueprint, 2011–20*. Kuala Lumpur: Government Printer, 2011.

Bhagwati, J.N. "The Capital Myth: The Difference between Trade in Widgets and Trade in Dollars". *Foreign Affairs* 77 (1998): 7–12.

Corsetti, G. "Interpreting the Asian Financial Crisis: Open Issues in Theory and Policy". *Asian Development Review* 16 (1998): 18–63.

Corsetti, G., P. Pesenti, and N. Roubini. "What Caused the Asian Currency and Financial Crisis? Part I: A Macroeconomic View". NBER Working Paper No. 6833 (1998a).

———. "What Caused the Asian Currency and Financial Crisis: Part II: The Policu Debate". NBER Working Paper No. 6834 (1998b).

Danaharta. *Pengurusan Danaharta Nasional Berhad, Final Report*. Kuala Lumpur: Government Printer, 2005.

de Brouwer, Gordon. *Financial Markets and Policies in East Asia*. London: Routledge, 2002.

Eichengreen, B. and D. Leblang. "Capital Account Liberalization and Growth: Was Mr Mahathir Right?". *International Journal of Finance and Economics* 8 (2003): 205–24.

Feldstein, M. "Refocusing the IMF". *Foreign Affairs* 77 (1998): 20–33.

Global Risk Regulator. Available at <http://www.globalriskregulator.com/archive/February2005-05.html>.

Haggard, S. "Institutions and Growth in East Asia". *Studies in Comparative International Development*, vol. 38, no. 4 (Winter 2004): 53–81.

Harun Alp, Salim Elekdag and Subir Lall. "An Assessment of Malaysian Monetary Policy during the Global Financial Crisis of 2008–2009". International Monetary Fund, January 2012, IMF WP 12/35.

Krugman, P. "Heresy Time". Unpublished manuscript. MA: MIT Cambridge, 1998.

Mahathir, Mohamad. *Currency Turmoil: Selected Speeches and Articles by Prime Minister of Malaysia*. Kuala Lumpur: Limkokwing Integrated, 1998.

Mathieson, D.J. and G. Schinasi. *International Capital Markets: Development, Prospects and Key Policy Issues*. Washington, D.C.: International Monetary Fund, 2001.

Meesook M., I.H. Lee, O. Liu, Y. Khatri, N. Tamirisa, M. Moore and M.H. Krysl. *Malaysia: From Crisis to Recovery*. Washington, D.C.: IMF, 2001.

National Economic Action Council (NEAC). *National Economic Recovery Plan*. Kuala Lumpur: Government Printer, 1998.

Radelet S., and J. Sachs. "The Onset of the East Asian Financial Crisis". NBER Working Paper No. 6680 (1998).

Securities Commission, Malaysia. *The Report on Corporate Governance*. Kuala Lumpur: Government Printer, 1999.

———. *Capital Market Masterplan, Malaysia*. Kuala Lumpur: Government Printer, 2001.

———. *Capital Market Masterplan 2, Malaysia*. Kuala Lumpur: Government Printer, 2011.

Stiglitz, J.E. "Boats, Planes and Capital Flows". *Financial Times*, Wednesday 5 March 1998.

The Star, 24 November 2011.

Wade, R. and F. Veneroso. "The Asian Crisis: The High Debt Model vs The Wall Street-Treasury-IMF Complex". *New Left Review* 50 (1998): 3–23.

World Bank. *Global Economic Prospects and the Developing Countries*. (Washington, D.C.: World Bank, 2000.

Young, K., W.C.F. Bussink, and P. Hassan. *Malaysia: Growth and Equity in a Multiracial Society*. Baltimore: The Johns Hopkins University Press, 1980.

9

ICT IN MALAYSIA'S GROWTH AGENDA[1]

Sharbanom Abu Bakar

Malaysia's ICT Agenda

When Malaysia launched its Vision 2020 in 1991, the aspirations were about becoming a "scientific and progressive society", to develop "an economy that is … able to adapt, innovate and invent …", and "an economy driven by brain power, skills and diligence, in possession of a wealth of information …".

Hence, at the start of the Sixth Malaysia Plan (6MP), during the years from 1991 to 1995, Malaysia was ready to embrace its enviable growth in the electronics manufacturing sector, where information and communications technology (ICT) was recognized widely within the realm of hardware components, rather than as a service; as an "enabler" sector, rather than a driver of economic growth.

ICT assumed this "economic enabler" position in Malaysia's manufacturing sector as the country embarked on its transition from a production-based economy to a knowledge-based economy (K-economy) during the 6MP.[2] This was supported by the introduction of the National Information Technology Council (NITC) during the same period, to ensure that ICT is "well integrated in the socioeconomic fabric of the nation".

The National Information Technology Agenda (NITA) was formulated to realize the core objectives of NITC, during a time when the Malaysian economy was growing at an average gross domestic product (GDP) growth rate of 4.8 per cent. NITA was put together to be the catalyst in transforming Malaysia "into a value-based economy through the development of talent, infrastructure and applications to benefit the Malaysian society". It was also during this period that the Government launched the Multimedia Super Corridor (MSC) project.

MSC Malaysia

MSC Malaysia represents, perhaps the foremost affirmative action to propel ICT into Malaysia's socio-economic fabric — and leapfrog Malaysia's position into the global ICT fraternity. With lofty ambitions as "to create a world-class environment for attracting the best multimedia enterprises to use this region as a test-bed for cutting-edge ICT applications",[3] MSC Malaysia embarked on a frenzy of building a new township complete with the required hard infrastructure, for instance, roadways and telecommunication connectivity, in Cyberjaya, approximately 30 km south of Kuala Lumpur city centre.

Phase 1 (1996–2004) of the MSC Malaysia implementation plan focused on accelerating Malaysia's growth as a global ICT hub by attracting foreign direct investment (FDI); as well as the launch of MSC flagship applications. The development of seven flagship applications, that is, Smart School, Smart Card, Tele-Health, E-Government, Borderless Marketing, World-Wide Web, and R&D Clusters, was regarded as the catalyst to develop a vibrant ICT-friendly environment to accelerate the objectives of Vision 2020. Figure 9.1 illustrates the 3-Phase approach of MSC Malaysia.

By year 2007, MSC Malaysia displayed a mixed bag of results. Four of the flagship applications were on track and received encouraging acceptance from its respective targeted end-users. These were Smart School, Smart Card (MyKad), Tele-Health, and E-Government. Approximately 1,500 MSC-status companies contributed to about RM17.5 billion in sales in 2007. All things considered, MSC Malaysia companies grew 32 per cent in sales since 2002 (from RM4.4 billion to RM17.5 billion).

FIGURE 9.1
Vision, Pre-defined Milestones and Strategic Thrusts of MSC Malaysia

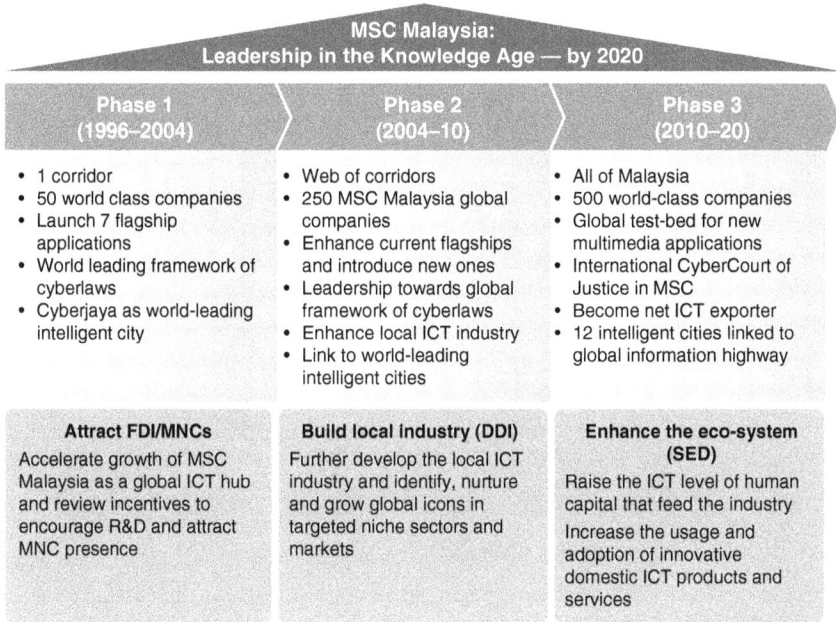

MSC Malaysia: Leadership in the Knowledge Age — by 2020		
Phase 1 (1996–2004)	**Phase 2 (2004–10)**	**Phase 3 (2010–20)**
• 1 corridor • 50 world class companies • Launch 7 flagship applications • World leading framework of cyberlaws • Cyberjaya as world-leading intelligent city	• Web of corridors • 250 MSC Malaysia global companies • Enhance current flagships and introduce new ones • Leadership towards global framework of cyberlaws • Enhance local ICT industry • Link to world-leading intelligent cities	• All of Malaysia • 500 world-class companies • Global test-bed for new multimedia applications • International CyberCourt of Justice in MSC • Become net ICT exporter • 12 intelligent cities linked to global information highway
Attract FDI/MNCs Accelerate growth of MSC Malaysia as a global ICT hub and review incentives to encourage R&D and attract MNC presence	**Build local industry (DDI)** Further develop the local ICT industry and identify, nurture and grow global icons in targeted niche sectors and markets	**Enhance the eco-system (SED)** Raise the ICT level of human capital that feed the industry Increase the usage and adoption of innovative domestic ICT products and services

Source: MDeC.

However, as MSC Malaysia moved into its second phase, there were gaps and relatively new risk factors were identified; including those that stemmed from the global economic meltdown in 2008.

Perhaps the most important yardstick to the success of MSC Malaysia is its contribution to the economy; that is, its ability to create a self-sustaining local ICT industry with the capacity to compete globally. In 2007, the ICT industry contributed approximately RM48 billion, or 9.5 per cent to Malaysia's GDP;[4] whereas the MSC-status companies directly impacted GDP with 1.2 per cent or RM6 billion (see Figure 9.2).

It is encouraging to note that despite the relatively small value in GDP contribution, the MSC-status companies were deriving revenue in areas of Creative Multimedia Content, Shared Services and Outsourcing, and Software and e-Solution; business areas that were virtually unheard of in Malaysia in the early 1990s.

By the year 2007, the economic achievements of MSC Malaysia were bolstered by the accompanying socio-economic benefits through

FIGURE 9.2
Gross Economic Impact of MSC Malaysia was Estimated at
RM8.8 billion in 2007
(Figures in RM billion)

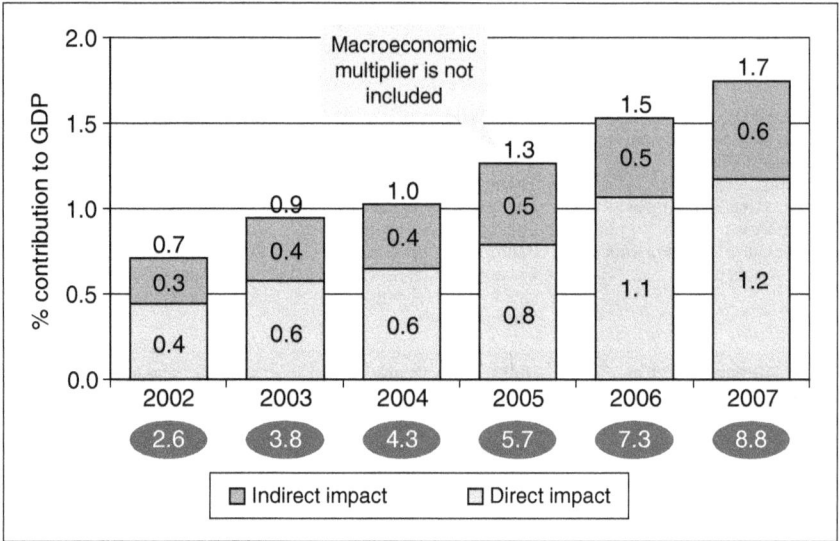

Source: MDeC, BCG (2009).

the creation of high-value jobs, and opportunities for human capital development in the technical skill-set areas. These form the most critical component of MSC Malaysia in ensuring that the local ICT industry is self-sustaining and dynamic enough to handle the rigours of global competition.

Additionally, this is well-aligned with the desired outcome for a knowledge-economy (k-economy); where knowledge, creativity and innovation were recognized as the tools in generating and sustaining growth.

The focus on creation of high-value jobs and human capital development may have been inspired by a 1996 OECD report on "Science, Technology and Industry Outlook", whereby "knowledge-based economies" were described as "economies which are directly based on the production, distribution and use of knowledge and information".[5] The report had suggested that OECD countries require the appropriate organization structures, a skilled workforce, and able management in order to adapt and maintain competitiveness in a k-economy. The most obvious manifestation of this urgency is "the rising human capital levels of the populations and workforces in OECD countries, as measured by educational attainment and is implied by an increased demand for more highly-educated and highly-skilled workers".

Between 2002 and 2007, MSC Malaysia added more than 40,000 highly-skilled ICT workers, or 36 per cent (see Figure 9.3) into the ICT workforce. In fact, the Ninth Malaysia Plan (9MP), during the years 2006 to 2010, placed particular emphasis on ICT training and education to build a pipeline of ICT talents with the required multidisciplinary skills and complex knowledge.

However, 36 per cent growth in the number of knowledge workers when compared to the total labour force was still low compared to OECD standards; 0.5 per cent compared to 3 per cent in OECD 2006.

FIGURE 9.3
High-value Job Creation
(Number of highly skilled local ICT workers in MSC Malaysia increasing from 17,000 in 2002 to almost 60,000 in 2006)

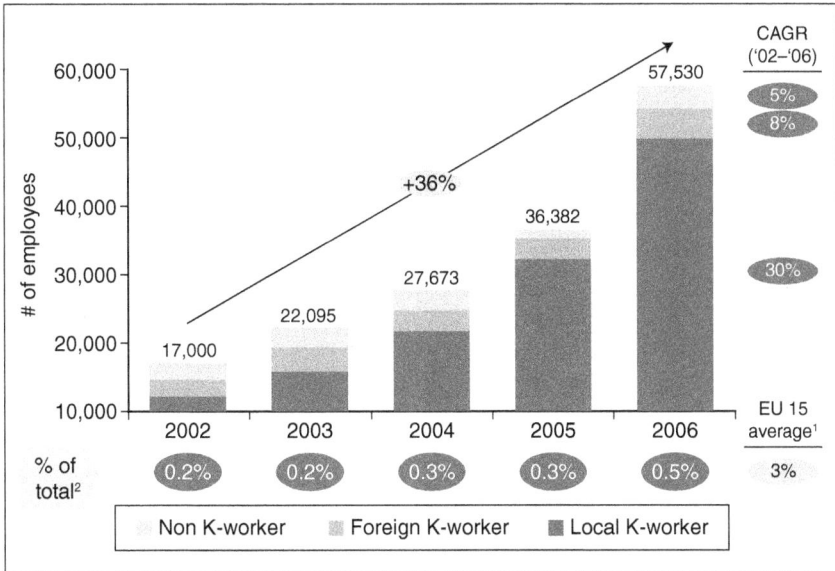

Source: MDeC, BCG (2009).

FIGURE 9.4
ICT Professionals Earn Similar Salaries to other Knowledge Economy
Workers in Other Sectors

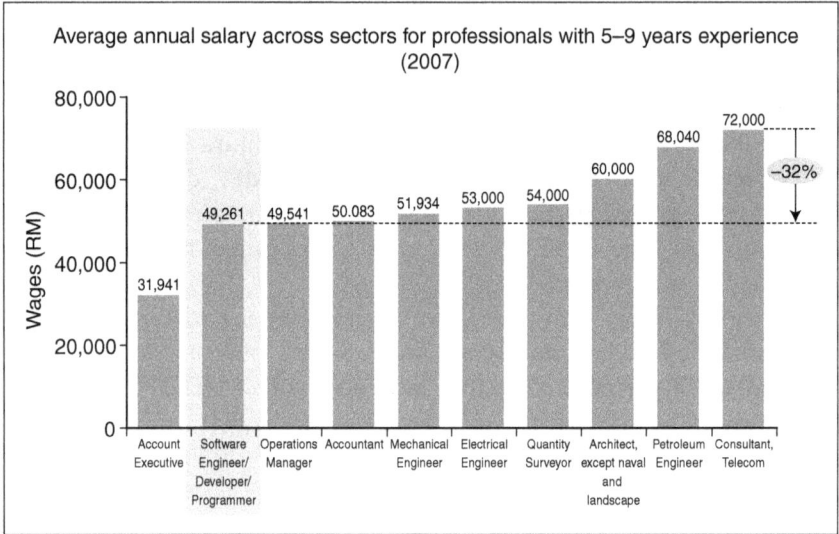

Average annual salary across sectors for professionals with 5–9 years experience (2007)

Source: BCG (2009).

It was heartening to note though, that the salaries for IT workers were comparable to other workers with similar experience in other industries within Malaysia[6] during the same period of 2002 to 2007 (see Figure 9.4). This was during a time when Malaysia was starting to grapple with challenges created by the departure of top Malaysian talents to other countries. The local ICT industry also had to deal with issues over the mismatch of skills and unexpected unemployment among IT graduates.

Perhaps the most striking "unplanned" outcome of MSC Malaysia was the unexpected decrease in the number of ICT graduates from local universities; from 31 per cent in 2002 to 23 per cent in 2007.[7] This was reportedly due to "poor public perception of ICT graduate employability" (see Figure 9.5), despite the existence of 560 new institutes of higher learning (IHLs) since MSC Malaysia was launched in 1996.

Several factors were said to have contributed to this phenomenon, including the limited awareness of ICT as a career option that offer

FIGURE 9.5
**Number of ICT graduates decreasing from 30,000 in 2002
to 17,000 in 2007**

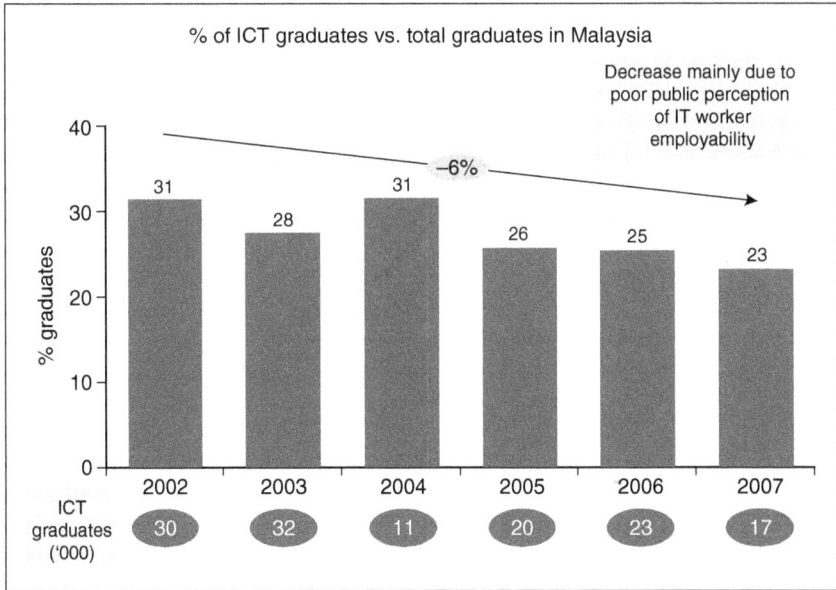

% of ICT graduates vs. total graduates in Malaysia

Decrease mainly due to
poor public perception
of IT worker
employability

−6%

Year	2002	2003	2004	2005	2006	2007
% graduates	31	28	31	26	25	23
ICT graduates ('000)	30	32	11	20	23	17

Source: BCG (2009).

more than just exposure to the use of computer applications in the
school computer labs at public schools; both primary and secondary
levels. It was also suggested that during the same period, ICT had
had to compete with growing interests among undergraduates in
new sectors such as biotechnology and petroleum engineering; among
others, which were regarded as "more prestigious" career choices.

It was unfortunate that a ICT qualification at the time was regarded
as only capable of providing a "single-track" opportunity into the ICT
sector; whereas the skills acquired in the ICT academia are relevant
across all economic sectors, including energy, transport, agriculture;
as economies pursue the need for efficiency and productivity.

Knowledge-Based Economy Master Plan

When the Economic Planning Unit of the Prime Minister's Department
released the K-Economy Master Plan[8] in 2002, Malaysia appeared to be

FIGURE 9.6
Malaysia's Ranking in the World Competitiveness Scoreboard, 1994–2001

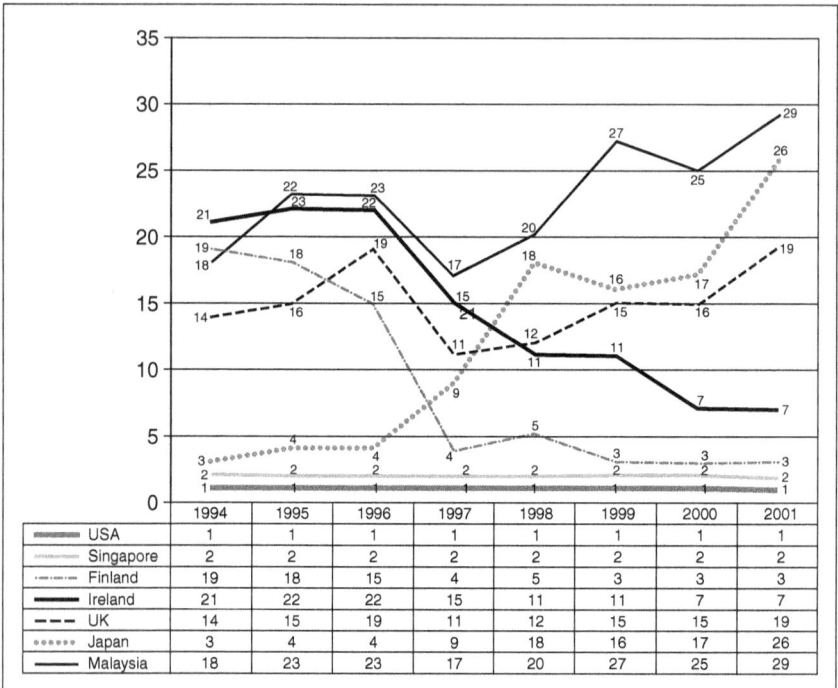

	1994	1995	1996	1997	1998	1999	2000	2001
USA	1	1	1	1	1	1	1	1
Singapore	2	2	2	2	2	2	2	2
Finland	19	18	15	4	5	3	3	3
Ireland	21	22	22	15	11	11	7	7
UK	14	15	19	11	12	15	15	19
Japan	3	4	4	9	18	16	17	26
Malaysia	18	23	23	17	20	27	25	29

Source: The World Competitiveness Yearbook, various issues.

losing ground in its world competitiveness position (see Figure 9.6). While countries such as Ireland and Finland were closing in towards the top ten most competitive countries on the scoreboard that included the United States and Singapore; Malaysia's position worsened from 23rd position in 1996 to 29th in 2001.

This prompted an earnest focus on five factors for the successful shift to a k-economy. These five factors are:

1. Quality of human resources e.g., literacy, secondary and tertiary enrolment, enrolment in science and technology-related subjects;

2. Research & development (R&D) capacity e.g., public/private sector expenditure on R&D, personnel in R&D, patents filed;

3. Availability of infrastructure e.g., digital media, fixed-line telephony, mobile phones, freedom/availability of information;
4. Infrastructure readiness e.g., investment in ICT infrastructure, internet hosts, internet usage;
5. Economic means e.g., availability of k-workers, knowledge-based industries and services, e-commerce, venture capital.

While all the above factors must be addressed collectively, the quality of human resource is perhaps the single most challenging aspect to realize the targets of k-economy. In order to achieve the required level of quality and competency of the k-economy workforce, plans had to include specific initiatives at the primary, secondary, and tertiary levels of education.

However, these have been limited to the learning in school computer labs — using standard computer applications, searching for information, and using social media for effective communication; whereas, these should (perhaps) include topics that introduce students to the growth of businesses on the Internet. For example, the global supply chain put together by multinational logistics companies such as DHL, where packages and documents are tracked at real time and delivered around the world within a committed timeframe. Students can be given early introductions into the systems and tools that support such an operation, for instance.

The government established three focus areas to address the need for quality human resources that can support the move into k-economy. Two of which are on the needs to "upgrade the quality of education at the primary, secondary and tertiary levels ... to foster a cultural and intellectual infrastructure to support lifelong learning"; and "to foster training and re-training for managers and workers ... in order to cope with new demands of technology and markets".

It is conventional wisdom that a nation will not be able to churn out the right skill-sets for a k-economy based on high levels of education alone; especially when there is no clear agreement on the types of competencies and skills that can be taught at institutions of higher-learning. The k-economy labour market typically demands that candidates possess, apart from solid academic performance (knowledge), interpersonal, problem-solving, and ICT skills, among others.

The National Strategic ICT Roadmap released by MOSTI (Ministry of Science, Technology and Innovation) in 2007, for instance, made a

FIGURE 9.7
Scope of Services Science, Management and Engineering (SSME)

Service Science	**Organization** (Manage People) (Productivity++)	***Human Performance Theory*** *Education Social Science* ***Human Capital Management*** *Computer Supported Collaborative Work* ***Computational Organization Theory***
	Process (Manage Information) (Automate++)	*Industrial Engineering Artifical Intelligence* ***Computer Science*** Systems Engineering Operations Research
	Business Value (Manage Capital) (Returns++)	***Management Science*** *MIS* Relationship Marketing ***MBA*** Management of Innovation Law *Game Theory* *Experimental Economics*

Source: *IBM*, 2009.

recommendation on developing an "industry-centric" education that is able to "develop advance concepts such as virtual research and virtual universities, emphasizing collaboration and joint programs".[9] Interestingly, the proposed concept also propagates the need to venture into areas beyond the manufacturing base, and into services science.

Services science education is an interdisciplinary approach to create T-shaped[10] talents. Some of the fields of study included in SSME are Industrial and Systems Engineering, Math and Operations Research, Economics and Social Sciences, and Business and Management (see Figure 9.7). Historically, most scientific research has been geared toward supporting and assisting manufacturing. With SSME, industrial and academic research facilities need to apply more scientific rigour to the practices of services, such as finding better ways to use mathematical optimization to increase productivity and efficiency on demand.

Services Science, Management and Engineering (SSME) is an academic discipline and research area aimed at studying, improving, and teaching services innovation.[11] It is the application and integration of scientific, management and engineering disciplines into tasks that organizations typically perform for others. Cornell University, Massachusetts Institute of Technology, and University of California,

Berkeley are among the universities in the United States that offer SSME in undergraduate and post-graduate programmes.

The SSME approach is in line with the strategic thrusts established in the K-Economy Master Plan 2002 in developing a new generation of knowledge workers by increasing their technical capabilities and managerial skills to create entrepreneurs and techno-preneurs.

National Transformation Policy

In 2010, the Malaysian government continues to address the need for quality human resources through its transformation programmes — Government Transformation Programme (GTP) and Economic Transformation Programme (ETP). While the GTP is "an ambitious, broad based initiative aimed at addressing key areas of concern to the citizens",[12] the ETP is focused on fast-tracking Malaysia to achieve its "high-income nation" status, with a gross national income (GNI) per capita of US$15,000 (as defined by the World Bank) by the year 2020. Malaysia's GNI per capita in 2009 was US$6,700.

In ETP particularly, ICT reinforced its status as an "enabler", with representation in the ETP's National Key Economic Area (NKEA) for Business Services, in the same category with aerospace engineering, green technology and Islamic finance services. This was based on ICT's contribution to GNI, its growth rates in recent pasts, as well as its potential GNI contribution in the coming years.

The Business Services sector in the ETP context is regarded as a highly differentiated industry comprising a range of high value skills and services. A key component of the sector is human capital development, which is essential to nurturing innovation within the country. Most significantly, the sector is central to the needs of raising productivity and enhancing competitiveness of the entire economy. All of the combined initiatives will help reinforce the need for an equitable and inclusive economic and social progress beyond 2020.

In the United States for instance, business services charted higher growth rates than the overall economy during 2002 to 2008; contributing 15 per cent to the GDP in 2005 alone (see Figure 9.8). This is in contrast with the 3 per cent contribution to the Malaysian economy in 2009. The ETP targets that by year 2020, business services as a growing economic sector should be able to contribute approximately RM79 billion in GNI and create 246,000 new jobs.[13]

FIGURE 9.8
Contribution of Business Services in an Economy

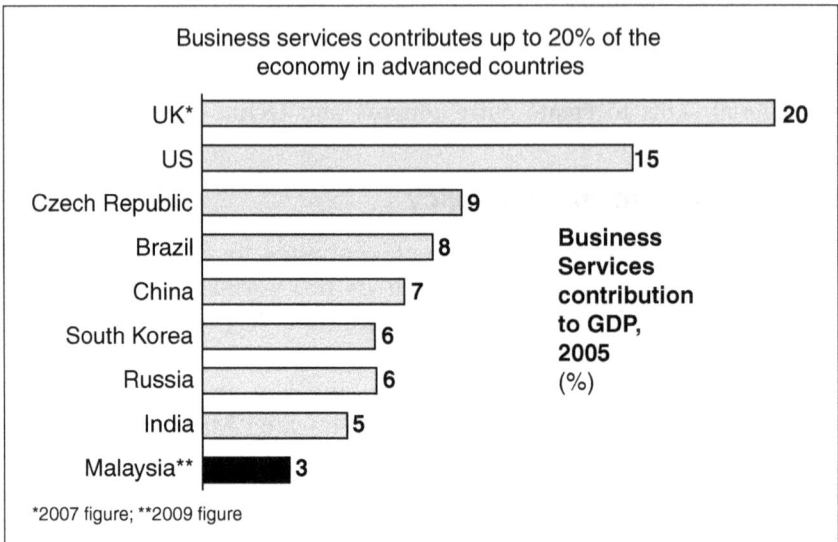

Business services contributes up to 20% of the
economy in advanced countries

UK*		20
US		15
Czech Republic		9
Brazil		8
China		7
South Korea		6
Russia		6
India		5
Malaysia**		3

Business
Services
contribution
to GDP,
2005
(%)

*2007 figure; **2009 figure

Source: *PEMANDU*, 2010.

When ICT was selected as one of the NKEA, there was a deep
focus on business-process outsourcing (BPO); that is "the delegation
of IT-enabled business process to a third party that owns, administers
and manages the process according to a defined set of metrics".[14] Some
of the services include contact centre services, sales and marketing,
accounting and financial services, and HR Management. In this space,
Malaysia has maintained its position as the third most attractive
location for offshore services (after India and China) since 2004[15]
based on three factors, namely cost, people skills and availability, and
business environment.

Meanwhile, the revenues from the outsourcing industry in
2009 was estimated at RM4 billion; although these are not limited
to BPO. However, it became evident that Malaysia is not able to
compete with India and China, especially in terms of economies
of scale.

In order to ensure that the required growth in ICT can happen
in less than a decade, several key drivers for sector growth were

FIGURE 9.9
Malaysia's "Achievements" in the ICT Space

Broadband household penetration rate: **62%** *as of Q2 2011	Mobile penetration rate: **119.2%** *as of Q2 2011	Internet user penetration rate: **62% (17.8 mil)** *as of Q2 2011
eCommerce -2010: **US$36.3B** (B2B = US$31B ; B2C = US$5.2B)	Facebook penetration rate **39.1%** **(11.2 mil)** *as of Q2 2011	Estimated Twitter users: 2010: **86,628** 2011: **303,198**
ICT sector accounted: **9.8%** of GDP *2009	Over **3,000** ICT companies in Malaysia	**10,000 schools** connected to *SchoolNet* in 2010
wireless villages: **115** *as of April 2011 **3,100** *by 2012	Broadband Community Centres **2,598** *as of Q1 2011	online services available via *myGovernment* portal **1,247**

Sources: MDeC, IMD, *World Bank*, United Nations; *The Economist*, ITU Malaysia Internet and E-Commerce 2010–14, *Forecast and Analysis*, IDC June 2010. SocialBakers, Twitter Inc.

identified. Among them, are the increasing broadband penetration and encouraging interests in IT-enabled services, especially across all public services to citizens.

Broadband household penetration rate in Malaysia was 62 per cent at the end of Quarter 2 (April–June) in 2011; well on track to achieve its target of 75 per cent by 2015 (see Figure 9.9). This is well aligned with growths in mobile penetration rate (119 per cent) and number of internet users at 17.8 million. Interestingly, the broadband reach also extended to e-commerce activities that developed into a US$36.3 billion business for Malaysia in 2010.

The e-Commerce sector in particular, is regarded as the new engine that can accelerate the growth of small and medium enterprises (SMEs) in Malaysia. There are approximately 645,000 SMEs operating in Malaysia in 2011, representing 97.3 per cent of total business establishments.[16] Interestingly enough, 90 per cent of these SMEs are classified in the services sector. SMEs contributed 32.7 per cent to the overall GDP in 2012, and the government is targeting an increase to 41 per cent in 2020.

One of the SME development initiatives introduced is to encourage e-Commerce readiness. Based on a 2012 SME ICT usage survey in Malaysia, 70 per cent did not have websites. Additionally, the Associated Chinese Chambers of Commerce and Industry of Malaysia (ACCCIM) reported in its 2012 SMEs survey that the main obstacles faced on e-Commerce adoption range from poor internet bandwidth (30 per cent), followed by expensive set-up cost (25 per cent), and concerns on e-payment security (20 per cent).

Broadband service in Malaysia experienced encouraging growth in the last ten years; moving up from a base of just below 20,000 households in 2002.[17] The use of broadband grew rapidly due to consumer demand pull, supplier competitive push as well as affirmative government policies in the form of the National Broadband Plan (NBP). The strategy behind the NBP promotes a three-pronged approach of strengthening governance, creating supply, and stimulating demand.

As for the interests towards IT-enabled services, it can be attributed to several factors, most notably the emergence of new technologies and focus areas including Service-Oriented Architecture, Cloud Computing, Green IT, Mobile Computing, and Social Media. The infusion of technology has positioned Malaysia in various competitiveness rankings, for instance, the Economist Intelligence Unit's Digital Economy ranking for Malaysia in 2010 was 36th out of 70 nations; behind regional leaders including Hong Kong (7th), Singapore (8th), Taiwan (12th), South Korea (13th), and Japan (16th).[18]

The Digital Economy rankings focus on ways that nations can harness the power of the Internet to improve economic prospects and lives of its citizens. Some of the measures used for considerations include connectivity, business environment, social and cultural environment, legal environment, government policy and vision, as well as consumer and business adoption.

ICT has had a great impact on the Malaysian community. MSC Malaysia's Smart School project has connected 10,000 schools through its SchoolNet programme by 2010 (see Figure 9.9). The programme is a joint collaboration between the government and private sector where broadband infrastructure and internet access are provided to specified school sites using different technologies to suit various locations. The objective is to continuously encourage the use of ICT in education to ensure improved quality of learning for students, enhanced teacher competency, and effectiveness of school administration and management.

SchoolNet network infrastructure was implemented in 2004 to equip up to 10,000 schools with broadband Internet access through a virtual private network. The infrastructure implemented has also created an opportunity for setting up of 2,598 community centres equipped with broadband facilities especially in rural areas around the country (see Figure 9.9). By 2012, 3,100 villages are expected to be connected.

Another area where ICT has become prevalent is the public sector services via the myGovernment portal (<http://www.malaysia.gov. my>). The portal is designed as the single gateway of information and services provided by the government via the Internet. There are links to more than 900 government agencies websites through myGovernment.[19] The portal is an initiative undertaken by the Malaysian Administrative Modernization and Management Planning Unit (MAMPU), a department in the Prime Minister's Office. The portal provides more than 1,260 online services to businesses and citizens including electronic payment services for various statutory and agency fees and charges.

Malaysia's Continuous Journey in ICT

This chapter has attempted to provide an overview of the journey that Malaysia has taken through various Malaysia Plans in positioning ICT in a key role in the economic development and growth. Much of the thought-process and strategies are already in place, spanning almost two decades of concerted efforts that began with the launch of Vision 2020, followed by the inception of MSC Malaysia, the Knowledge-Based Economy Master Plan and now, two parallel tracks of transformation programmes: Government Transformation Programme and Economic Transformation Programme.

Inevitably, these have created mixed results. However, the aim is still the same; albeit repackaged with enhanced emphasis to factor in the evolution of technology, impact of globalization — on the country, companies, and skilled workers — among others.

The challenges remain; in particular, the human capital factor and talent development to meet the demands of technical skill sets required in an advanced economy that is powered by ICT.

NOTES

1. The views expressed in this chapter are those of the author. They do not represent the views of IBM Malaysia and IBM Corporation.
2. Ministry of Science, Technology and Innovation Malaysia (MOSTI): National Strategic ICT Roadmap; MOSTI, MSCTC, IBM; June 2007.
3. MDeC <http://www.mdec.my>.
4. Includes hardware/manufacturing, software/services, and telecommunication.
5. *Source*: OECD, "The Knowledge-based Economy", 1996.
6. *Source*: Payscale; BCG (2009).
7. MOHE, MOE, World Bank, 2007.
8. Foreword by Dr Mahathir bin Mohamad, Minister of Finance, 6 September 2002.
9. Ministry of Science, Technology and Innovation Malaysia (MOSTI): National Strategic ICT Roadmap; MOSTI, MSCTC, IBM; June 2007.
10. A T-shaped person is one who has deep knowledge within one discipline (the vertical bar) and broad knowledge about how it interacts with other disciplines (the horizontal bar), October 2008, available at <https://www. ibm.com/ developerworks/university/spotlights/b_dunn.html>.
11. IBM Services Science Management and Engineering, 2008, available at <http://www. ibm.com/ibm/ideasfromibm/us/compsci/20080728/index. shtml>.
12. PEMANDU, 2012, available at <http://www.pemandu.gov.my/gtp/>.
13. PEMANDU, 2012, available at <http://etp.pemandu.gov.my/>.
14. Gartner (2009).
15. A.T. Kearney Global Services Location Index 2004 and 2005.
16. SME Corporation Malaysia Annual Report, 2011/12.
17. Malaysian Communications and Multimedia Commission; SKMM Publication (2009).
18. The Economist, Economist Intelligence Unit; "Digital Economy Rankings 2010: Beyond E-readiness".
19. National IT Council (NITC), MOSTI (2012), available at <http:ww.nitc. my>.

10

MALAYSIA'S PARTICIPATION IN THE ASEAN ECONOMIC COMMUNITY

Rokiah Alavi

Introduction

The ASEAN Economic Community (AEC) was established in 2007 with the objective to create a single market and production base. The AEC is meant to allow the free movement of goods, services, skilled labour, and capital within the ten ASEAN economies by 2015. Malaysia has given its commitment to ASEAN's initiative to establish a single market, and has consistently been working towards enhancing regional and international linkages to mutually benefit from its trading partners and Asian neighbours. In fact, the AEC's vision and the goals of Malaysia's national economic development plans under the New Economic Model (NEM) are compatible. The vision of the AEC is "to create a highly competitive single market that promotes equitable economic development for member states, as well as facilitating their integration with global economy" (ASEAN Secretariat 2010). This is consistent with the key objective of NEM to develop Malaysia into a "high income nation with inclusiveness and sustainability by 2020" (NEAC 2009). In addition, the NEM highlighted the importance of integration especially with ASEAN countries and Asia through trade and investment in driving the long-term growth of the economy. Hence, it is understandable why Malaysia has been in the forefront in advancing ASEAN's initiative to strengthen regional economic cooperation and convergence.

This chapter intends to study the motivation and prospects for Malaysia in participating in ASEAN Economic Community. The chapter also discusses the progress of Malaysia's implementation of AEC Blueprint and how Malaysia's involvement in ASEAN's initiatives is in line with its economic development objectives. Discussion on the challenges faced by Malaysia in deepening economic integration concludes the chapter.

ASEAN Economic Community

In 1992, the ASEAN leaders announced to form a free trade area, which at that time was seen as a bold and ambitious decision. Throughout the 1970s until the mid-1980s, many ASEAN officials were sceptical over the benefits from economic cooperation and prospects of successful integration (Akrasanee and Stifel 1992). Lack of complementarity and competition for similar developed market were seen as main impediments in establishing economic cooperation. Economic crisis in the mid-1980s and its aftermath policy response triggered the concern among the ASEAN nations to deepen regional economic cooperation. It also made countries in the region to shift their policy emphasis towards more outward-oriented and liberal trade policies. This gave the right atmosphere in ASEAN to jumpstart its economic cooperation plans (Akrasanee and Stifel 1992). The proposal for the ASEAN Free Trade (AFTA), therefore, received full support at the 1992 ASEAN Summit. Since then, economic cooperation initiatives in ASEAN have gained momentum and progressed smoothly ahead. In order to sustain the dynamism and competitiveness of the region, ASEAN leaders foresee that there is a need to graduate ASEAN from an Association to a Community.[1]

To realize this, ASEAN leaders signed the Declaration of the ASEAN (Bali) Concord II, in October 2003, with the intention to create an ASEAN Economic Community by 2020, a target that was subsequently brought forward to 2015 (Soesastro 2007). The historical account of the establishment of AEC is presented in Figure 10.1.

FIGURE 10.1
Historical Account of the Establishment of AEC

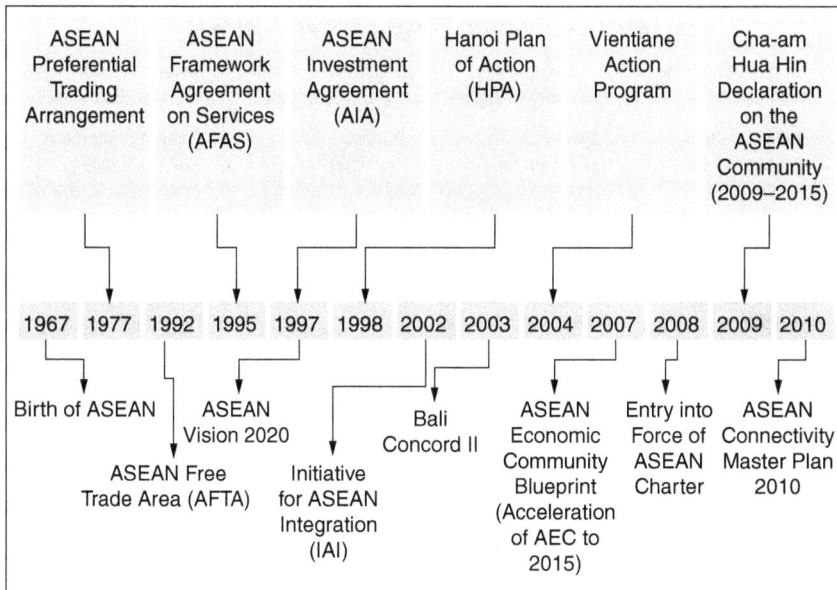

ASEAN Preferential Trading Arrangement	ASEAN Framework Agreement on Services (AFAS)	ASEAN Investment Agreement (AIA)	Hanoi Plan of Action (HPA)	Vientiane Action Program	Cha-am Hua Hin Declaration on the ASEAN Community (2009–2015)

1967 1977 1992 1995 1997 1998 2002 2003 2004 2007 2008 2009 2010

Birth of ASEAN	ASEAN Vision 2020		Bali Concord II	ASEAN Economic Community Blueprint (Acceleration of AEC to 2015)	Entry into Force of ASEAN Charter	ASEAN Connectivity Master Plan 2010
	ASEAN Free Trade Area (AFTA)	Initiative for ASEAN Integration (IAI)				

Source: MITI (2011).

The ASEAN Economic Community is different from the European Economic Community in that the AEC does not require ASEAN member countries to adopt a common external tariff. The development gap within the region warrants different policy needs, and for this reason, the AEC has inbuilt mechanisms to allow policy space and freedom of having own external economic relations (NST 2011).

The ASEAN leaders adopted the AEC Blueprint in 2007. The Blueprint outlines the measures to be taken and the timeline for AEC implementation and is a binding declaration of commitments by all member countries (Soesastro 2007). It categorizes the AEC goals into four areas, namely single market and production base, competitive economic region, equitable economic development, and integration with the global economy (see Figure 10.2). Each goal consists of several core elements and each core element has its objectives, action plans and strategic schedules (Urata and Okabe 2009). These goals are set to be undertaken within a four implementation periods 2008–09, 2010–11,

FIGURE 10.2
ASEAN Economic Community Provisions and Essential Elements

ASEAN ECONOMIC COMMUNITY PROVISIONS			
Single Market and Production Base	Competitive Economic Region	Equitable Economic Development	Integration with the Global Economy
Liberalization and facilitation of free flow of: • Goods • Services • Investment • Skilled labour • Capital • Piority Sectors • Food Agriculture and forestry	Laying the foundation for: • Competition policy • Consumer protection • Intellectual property rights • Ratifying transport agreements • Taxation • E-Commerce	Studies and development of SMEs Initiatives for ASEAN Integration Work Plan 2	Coherent Approach towards External Economic Relations Enhanced participation in global supply networks

Essential Elements towards Realizing the ASEAN Ecomomic Community				
Political will	Coordination and resource mobilization	Implementation of commitments	Capacity building and institutional development	Public–private consultation and engagements

Source: ASEAN Secretariat (2010).

2012–13, and 2014–15 (Soesastro 2007). The Blueprint also includes a commitment to integrate twelve priority sectors: agro-based products, air travel, automotives, e-ASEAN, electronics, fisheries, healthcare, logistics, rubber-based products, textiles and apparel, tourism, and wood-based products. These sectors were expected to achieve accelerated liberalization target by 2010 (logistics in 2013), and accounted for more than 50 per cent of intra-ASEAN trade (WTO Trade Policy Review 2006).

The AEC also addressed concerns related to widening development gap among the ASEAN countries. Initiatives have been taken through Vientiane Plans of Action (VAP) and Vientiane Integration Agenda (VIA), which outlined specific areas and measures to close the development gap in ASEAN, especially through support for promotion of economic growth and expansion of trade and investment (Anthony 2006). ASEAN has agreed on fifteen priorities projects to connect and narrow the gap between old ASEAN members and the CLMV (Cambodia, Laos, Myanmar, Vietnam) countries.[2]

Malaysia's Rationale to Participate in AEC

Malaysia's motivation to participate in the ASEAN Economic Community mainly came as a response to intense competition from the two giant Asian economies, China and India. In addition, Malaysia saw enormous opportunities in the establishment of AEC, particularly in advancing its strategic alliance with China and India as one large and competitive economy. The initiative is expected to benefit Malaysia in terms of improving its attractiveness as FDI destination, reducing cost of doing businesses and in expanding its exports of goods and services. Nevertheless, increased competition for foreign investment and access to export market are essentially the key underlying factors that motivated Malaysia to support the Economic Community initiative.

Malaysia began to feel its attractiveness as an investment destination waning after China emerged as the most competitive location for FDI in the early 1990s. Malaysia also lost to its neighbouring countries as the preferred FDI location, where for one decade FDI inflows to Indonesia, Thailand, and Vietnam surpassed those to Malaysia. India, growing at a faster rate and having recorded commendable export performance, has emerged as another rival. These developments affected Malaysia on whether it could sustain its attractiveness as an FDI destination in the region. Given the importance of FDI in Malaysia's economic development and growth, persistent decline in FDI inflows is seen to have detrimental effects to the country's development plans, particularly its objective to graduate into a high-income nation. China's emergence as economic giant in the region also shrank Malaysia's export market share in the developed countries. These concerns were not peculiar only to Malaysia, but for most countries in the region. One of the responses to these challenges was the proposal to form a single market among the ASEAN countries.

Up to the early 1990s, ASEAN countries have been receiving higher levels of FDI than China (see Figure 10.3). However, China out-performed all countries in the region in 1992, where the FDI inflows jumped almost three fold from US$4,388 million in 1991 to US$11,008 million in 1992. The inflows have continued to climb astoundingly since then. In 1993 and 1994 for instance, the FDI inflows recorded US$33,787 million and US$37,521 million, respectively. In contrast, inflows into ASEAN countries grew at a lower rate, thus widening the annual FDI inflows gap between China and ASEAN countries (see

FIGURE 10.3
FDI Inflows to China, ASEAN and Malaysia, 1990–2010
(US$)

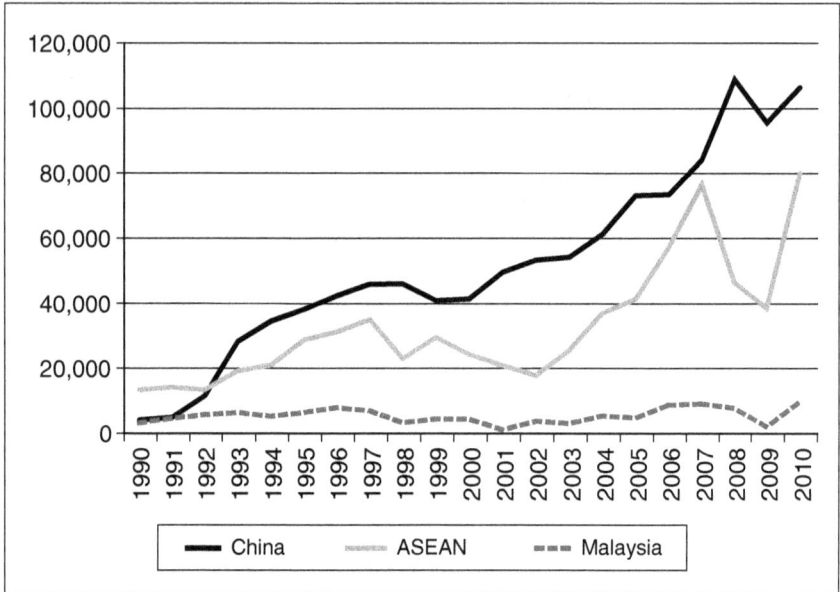

Source: UNCTAD (2011).

Figure 10.3). The FDI inflows gap between China and Malaysia has widened even more.

The FDI trend in the ASEAN countries completely changed after the 1997 crisis. Up to the mid-1990s, Malaysia was the second largest recipient of FDI in the region and accounted for about one-fourth of total FDI inflows to ASEAN (Athukorala 2010). During this period, inflows to Thailand, Indonesia and the Philippines remained below than those into Malaysia, while Singapore has consistently been the leading recipient of FDI (see Figure 10.4). Thailand overtook Malaysia's position as the second largest FDI recipient in the post-crisis period, while Indonesia and Vietnam outperformed Malaysia by 2008.

China's strong growth, large market and competitive economy also brought rapid changes in the global production linkages and

FIGURE 10.4
FDI Trend to Selected ASEAN Countries, 1990–2010

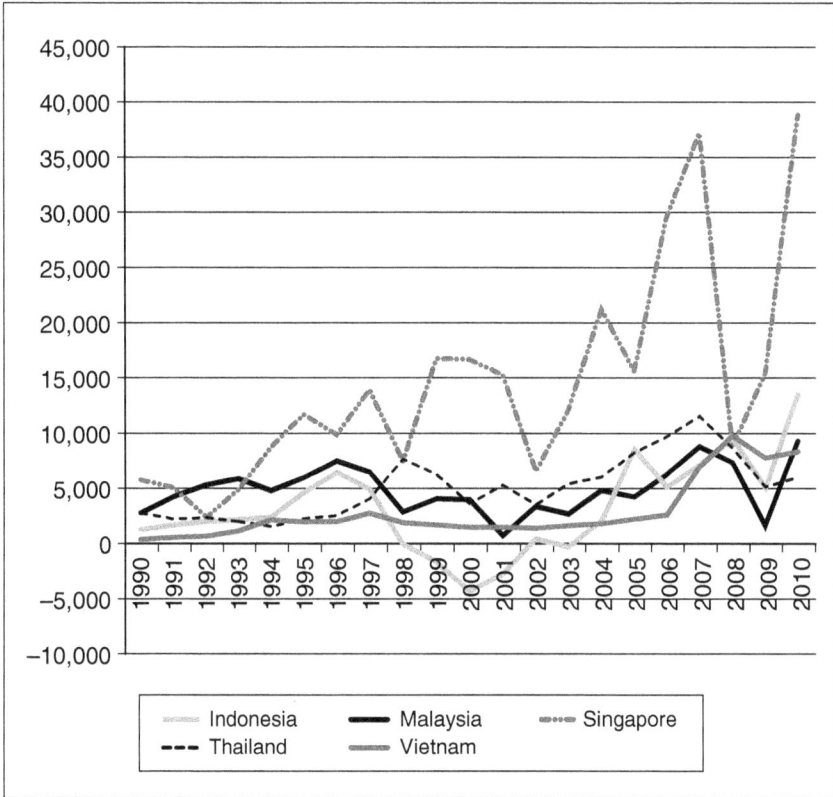

Source: UNCTAD (2011).

direction of trade, particularly within the East Asian region. A distinct structure emerged as regional production networks evolved in East Asia (WTO-IDE-JETRO 2011):

1. East Asian NIEs (except China) involved in the production of sophisticated parts and components, and these intermediate goods are exported to China;

2. China assembles the intermediate goods into final products to be exported to developed countries market for final consumption.

The shift of the core production network activities to China has significantly affected Malaysia's specialization in labour-intensive manufacturing (Tham 2008; Rajah 2011). In early 2000s, about two thirds of Malaysia's net manufactured exports by value competed with China, and Malaysia's complementarities with China are found to be amongst the lowest in the region (Nandan 2006). In response to this, Malaysia repositioned itself to take advantage and mutually benefit from China's growing economy and to reap greater share in the regional production networks. The government changed focus towards high technology manufactured goods and laid strategies to strengthen its complementarities in the regional production networks. Various policy initiatives were drawn under the Industrial Master Plan 3, Economic Transformation Programme and the Tenth Malaysia Plan to shift the economy to be technology and service-driven. For the manufacturing sector, the government placed greater emphasis in promoting investment in new production technology and high-value added sectors, with the objective to move up the value chain and achieve high-income nation status by 2015. This is reflected in the significant increase in FDI in new growth areas, such as renewable energy, aerospace, pharmaceutical, and medical equipment (BNM 2011). There is also a large share of the new investments being channelled into the less capital intensive but high-skilled services sector, such as financial services and shared services operations (BNM 2011).

Participating in ASEAN Economic Community

Under the NEM, regional integration is given emphasis and expected to cover areas wider than just trade and services, i.e. to include research, cultural exchange, education, human resource development, capacity building, infrastructure development and so on. The NEM report stated that "with Malaysia's small domestic market and the potential for a larger contribution from SMEs, scale can be developed through greater integration into regional networks and supply chains which will allow the country to tap into the abundant opportunities emanating from a high growth region" (NEAC 2009). As mentioned earlier, the AEC's goal to achieve competitive economic region and equitable regional development is consistent with Malaysia's aim to be a high-income nation with inclusiveness and sustainability by the year 2020. Therefore, meeting the targets set by the AEC Blueprint has become an integral part of Malaysia's trade policy objectives.

This section intends to evaluate the progress of Malaysia's effort in achieving the AEC goals in creating a single production and market base, i.e. the first pillar of the AEC Blueprint. The analysis is divided into two parts; (1) evaluation on the extent of liberalization in the context of achieving AEC targets; and (2) discussion on the impact liberalization on trade and investment. It is important to note that Malaysia has been progressively liberalizing its trade, investment and labour movement to comply with multilateral, regional, and bilateral agreements, in addition to various autonomous liberalization initiatives.

Free Flow of Goods

Free flow of goods is one of the principal means of achieving a single market and production base (Urata and Okabe 2009). Liberalization efforts covered in the AEC Blueprint in the goods sector include elimination of tariffs and non-tariff measures (NTMs), revising and simplifying rules of origin, trade facilitation measures, customs integration, the ASEAN Single Window, and standards and technical regulations (ASEAN Secretariat 2011a). Since the rules for liberalization of trade in goods are governed by a number of separate regional and bilateral agreements, the ASEAN Economic Ministers signed the ASEAN Trade in Goods Agreement (ATIGA) in 2009 to consolidate these varying legal instruments. ATIGA came into force on 17 May 2010 and contains comprehensive coverage of commitments related to trade in goods, and mechanisms for its implementation as well as institutional arrangements.[3]

Malaysia is committed to progressively liberalize the goods sector in line with the ASEAN Economic Community Blueprint. Under AFTA, Malaysia eliminated duties on 99.5 per cent of its tariff lines in the Inclusion List (see Figure 10.5). However, Malaysia still has 66 tariff lines that have duties range between 5 per cent and 20 per cent (tropical fruits, tobacco, and rice) that will have to be gradually removed by 2015. At the regional level, five ASEAN countries, Malaysia, Thailand, Indonesia, Philippines, and Singapore have eliminated import duties on all products in the Inclusion List (ASEAN

FIGURE 10.5
Average Tariff Rates on Imports from ASEAN, 2000–10

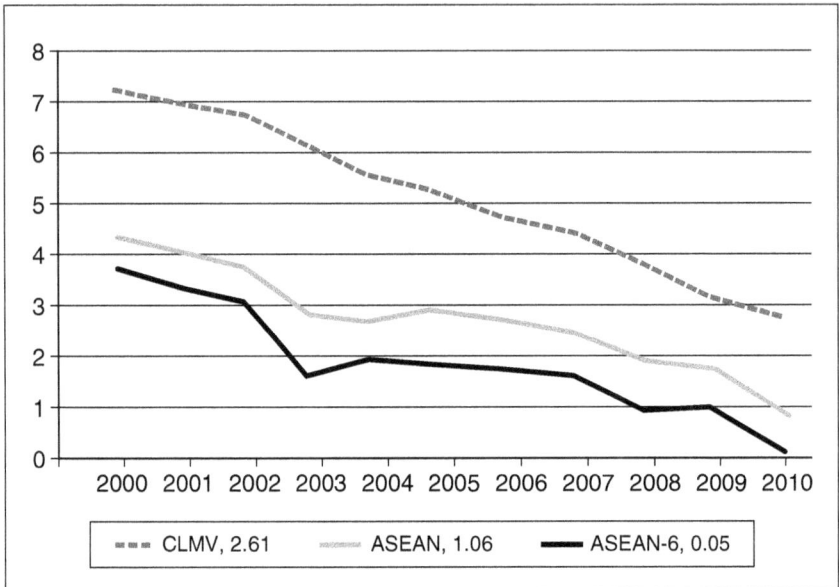

Source: ASEAN Secretariat (2011*c*), ASEAN Community in Figures (ACIF) 2010, Figure 1, p. 30.

Secretariat 2010). Cambodia, Laos, Myanmar, and Vietnam have eliminated tariffs for 46.4 per cent of their tariff lines. In 2010, 78.8 per cent of the tariff lines of ASEAN countries have been fully liberalized,[4] and the average tariff reduced from 4.4 per cent in 2000 to 0.9 per cent in 2009 (ASEAN Secretariat 2009).

The incidence of non-tariff measures such as non-automatic licensing, technical regulations, monopolistic measures, price and quantity measures however are still prevalent in ASEAN countries (ASEAN Secretariat 2009; Ando and Obashi 2009). In Malaysia, large number of products in animals, plants, and food industries are subject to various regulations such as sanitary regulations and technical standards. These measures are applied to over 90 per cent of the tariff lines of animals and animal-origin foods, plants, vegetables and fruits, and animal/ vegetable fats and oils, and more than 80 per cent of the tariff lines of processed food and beverages (Ando and Obashi 2009). Among various types of measures implemented, non-automatic licensing is the most commonly used measure (Hanif et al. 2011 and Ando and Obashi 2009). The task to remove non-tariff barriers (NTBs) is likely to be formidable, not only for Malaysia but also for most of the ASEAN countries (Nandan 2006).

Another important aspect of achieving a single market and production base in ASEAN is trade facilitation. The Asia-Pacific Economic Cooperation (APEC) estimated in 2002 that 5 per cent reduction in trade transaction costs would result in an increase in the GDP by 0.9 per cent. ASEAN's initiatives in trade facilitation among others include the Trade Facilitation Work Programme (2008), the Trade Facilitation Indicators (2009), and the ASEAN Single Window or ASW (2005). ASEAN also launched the ASW Pilot Project and Expanded Data Model (specifying standard data elements for key trade documents).[5] To date, Indonesia, Malaysia, Myanmar, the Philippines, and Thailand have set up respective national working bodies to implement their National Single Window (NSW), which will be integrated to form the ASW (USITC 2010). A NSW is an electronic system to facilitate trade and increase efficiency of the delivery system. Malaysia has progressed commendably in trade facilitation initiatives and has successfully minimized problems related to document processing, cargo inspection at Customs, logistic bottlenecks, and unreliable freight or trade-financing services (UNNext 2010). However, as of March 2010, Singapore was the only member with a fully operational NSW, while Brunei, Indonesia, Malaysia, the Philippines, and Thailand had only partially completed their NSWs (USITC 2010). Malaysia achieved 81 per cent of the NSW implementation requirement and 86 per cent of the transparency and due process criteria (see Table 10.1).

Figure 10.6 presents the trading costs and characteristic of trading environment in ASEAN countries in 2010. There are still great variations among the ASEAN members, in particular with regard to documents needed to export/import as well as days needed to export/import (Sourdin and Pomfret 2009). The range of documents for export and import is between 4 (export — Thailand and Singapore); 3 (import — Thailand) and 10 (Cambodia and Laos PDR). In Malaysia, 7 documents are needed for export and import consignment clearance. The range is much wider for days needed for export and imports. Exporters using Singapore port require 5 days to clear their cargo while it takes only 4 days to import. The longest

TABLE 10.1
Summary of Implementation of ASEAN Single Window (ASW)

	National Policy				
	Overall National Policy	National Single Window	Transparency and Due Process	Regional Cooperation	Total
Brunei	73	73	71	90	76
Cambodia	45	38	57	90	54
Indonesia	78	65	100	90	80
Lao PDR	43	42	43	90	52
Malaysia	83	81	86	90	84
Myanmar	48	50	43	80	54
Philippines	90	92	86	100	92
Singapore	60	62	57	100	68
Thailand	81	78	86	90	83
Vietnam	46	47	43	90	54
Average	64	63	67	91	70

Source: USITC (2010), Table 6.

FIGURE 10.6
Trading Costs and Characteristic of Trading Environment in ASEAN Countries

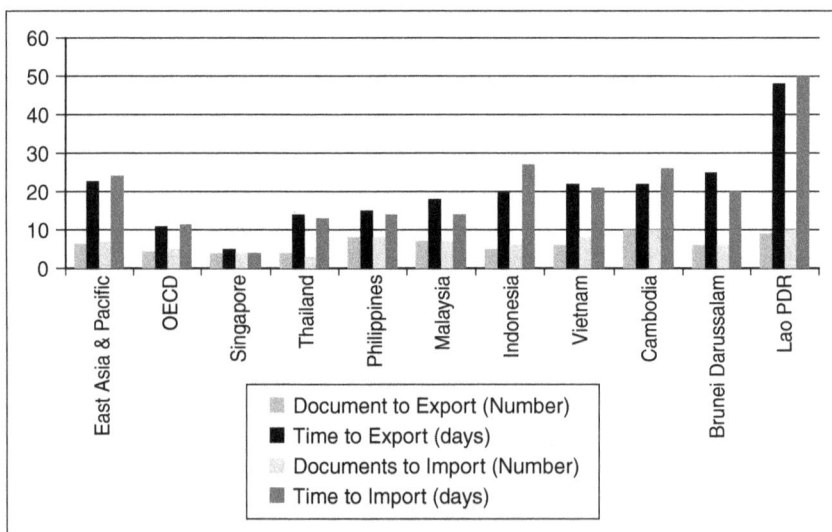

Source: World Bank (2011).

time needed to export/import in the ASEAN region is in Laos, export requires 48 days while import 50 days. It takes about 2 weeks to clear the cargo in Malaysia.

Nevertheless, Malaysia's policy measures to reduce the trading costs have been successful. Sourdin and Pomfret (2009) stated that the trade costs in the original five ASEAN have declined substantially during the 1990s and there is convergence towards Singapore, the lowest cost country in the region (see Figure 10.7). This could be partly due to successful regulatory and administrative reforms in Malaysia with the introduction of PEMUDAH Task Force that have contributed to reduction in the length of time to get permits, release of tax refunds, registration of property, and ease of doing business (see Zakariah et al. 2010).

FIGURE 10.7
Average Costs for Exports in Indonesia, Malaysia, Philippines, Singapore and Thailand, 1990–2008

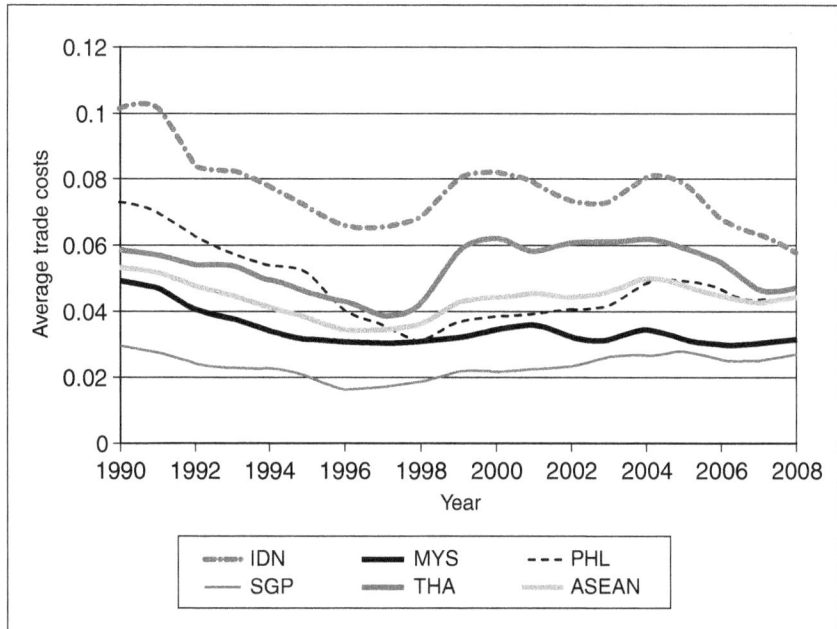

Source: Sourdin and Pomfret (2009), Figure 2.

By the end of the 2000s, Malaysia had caught up with Singapore, and had the lowest cost for exports and imports per container in the region. It is also apparent that there is less trading cost variation among the ASEAN member countries (except for Laos PDR) and the cost in ASEAN countries is much lower than the average cost for Asia Pacific and OECD countries (see Figure 10.8).

Have the initiatives to reduce trading barriers improved Malaysia's trading with ASEAN and regional economies? In the 1980s, more than half of the Malaysian exports were channelled to the U.S., the EU and Japan, while regional demand accounted for only 29.7 per cent of gross exports. Following the intensification of trade integration, East Asia is currently the main export market for Malaysia, accounting for 47.7 per cent of exports in 2010. ASEAN countries remained the leading trade partner of Malaysia, with exports share at about 27 per

FIGURE 10.8
Cost to Export and Import

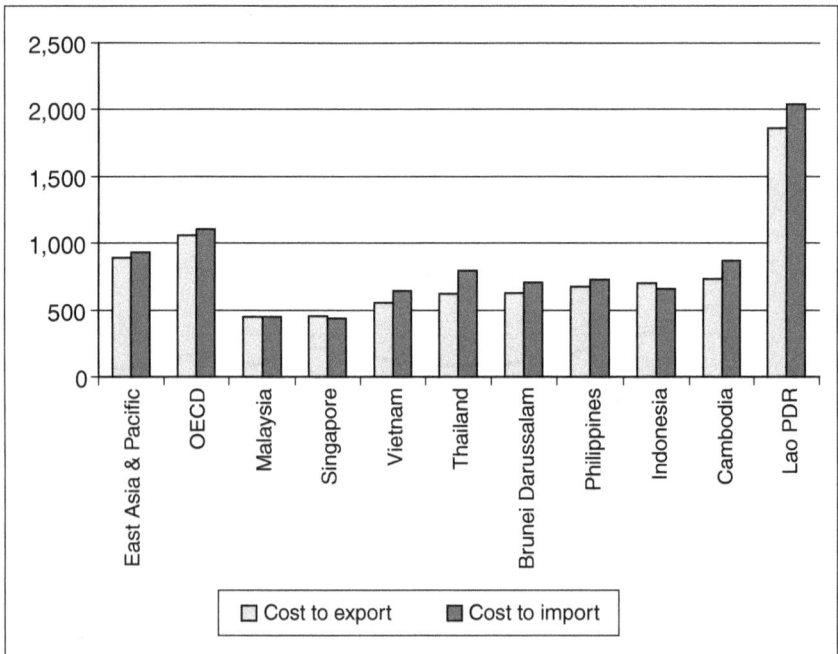

Source: World Bank (2011).

cent of total manufacturing goods trade (see Figure 10.9). However the share of Malaysia's manufacturing exports to ASEAN countries had remained constant for the past one decade. The trend of Malaysia trade share reflects its growing links with China and less reliance on trade with the U.S. and Japan.

Malaysia's imports from regional countries increased to 50.2 per cent of total imports in 2010 from 24.3 per cent in 1980 (BNM 2011). In contrast, the market share for Japan almost halved to 12.6 per cent over the same period (1980: 22.95). In addition, 52.6 per cent of Malaysia's imports of parts and components are from East Asia, compared to 44.8 per cent a decade ago. However, it is to be noted that the change in the trend is largely a result of restructuring of regional production networks.

The CEPT utilization rate is still relatively low but has shown significantly improvement over the years. Malaysia's AFTA CEPT utilization rate by exporters has increased from 3.8 per cent in 1998

FIGURE 10.9
Principal Markets for Manufactured Exports, 2006–10
(% Share of Total Manufacturing Exports)

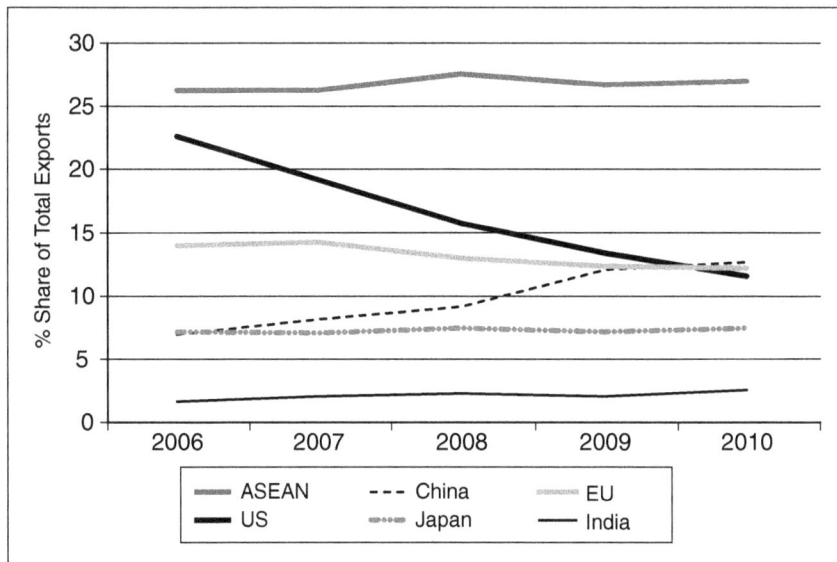

Source: Based on data obtained from Bank Negara Malaysia, *Annual Report 2010*, Table A11.

TABLE 10.2
CEPT Utilization Rate for Exports in Malaysia, 1998–2009
(%)

	1998	2003	2006	2007	2008	2009
Total	1.2	5.3	7.3	8.7	9.4	12.8
Total (Excluding Singapore)	3.8	13.2	16.9	19.3	20.7	27.0

Source: Extracted from Kimura (2010), Table 3.

to 16.9 per cent in 2006, and further increased to 27.0 per cent in 2009 (see Table 10.2).

Factors that have contributed to low CEPT utilization rate include: (i) insignificant difference between CEPT and the MFN rates for most trade items within ASEAN (Ariff 2001), (ii) the main intra-ASEAN export for Malaysia is electrical and electronics, which already have low MFN tariff rates and are exempted from import duties under various incentive schemes (Tham et al. 2008); (iii) lack of knowledge about the use of CEPT; (iv) complicated procedures for obtaining the CEPT certificate of origin (Katsuhide and Shujiro 2009); and (v) unpredictable and inconsistencies in CEPT implementation (Schwarz and Villinger 2004).

Free Flow of Services

The AEC Blueprint provides the parameters for the ASEAN countries to progressively liberalize trade in services through reduction or elimination of trade restrictions. Prior to the adoption of the AEC Blueprint in 2003, the liberalization efforts were undertaken under the ASEAN Framework Agreement on Services (AFAS). ASEAN member states have so far negotiated and signed seven packages under the AFAS, while negotiation for the 8th Package is still on-going. Sectors covered in AFAS are business and professional services, environmental services, healthcare, construction and construction related services, maritime transport services, transport services, distribution services, education services, tourism and related services, financial services, and telecommunication services. As mentioned earlier, the AEC has identified eleven sectors for which liberalization will be accelerated and completed by 2010. Four services sectors, air travel, e-ASEAN, healthcare, and tourism were identified to be included the list. The 12th priority sector, logistics services, came in 2006 (liberalization accelerated to 2013). The target of minimum number of new subsectors to be scheduled in each round is as follows (MITI 2011):

1. 2008 — at least 10 new subsectors
2. 2010 — 15 new subsectors
3. 2012 — 20 new subsectors
4. 2014 — 20 new subsectors
5. 2015 — 7 new subsectors

The services sector is seen to have great potential to contribute significantly to economic growth in both Tenth Malaysia Plan and Industrial Master Plan 3. The services sector is an important component of the national economy, contributing 58 per cent to the GDP in 2010. The government is aiming to tap full potential of the services sector, increasing its share to 65 per cent of GDP by 2020.[6] The Malaysian government has taken various initiatives to liberalize trade in services for the past two decades. In 2009, the government made a significant move in unilaterally liberalizing 27 services subsectors to create conducive environment to attract investments, technology, and create higher value employment opportunities.

However, Malaysia's services sector is still heavily protected and the progress in terms of elimination of trade restrictions is quite limited. This is partly because AFAS has not gone much beyond the GATS, hence, there is lack of motivation to liberalize services trade within AFAS (Corbett 2008). Mahani (2011) highlighted that there are various type of barriers that still exist in Malaysia, among others include licencing requirements, barriers to business and existence of supply capacity namely monopolies, duopolies, and oligopolies in several subsectors. Professional associations like lawyers, nurses, architects, and doctors are still unfavourable to free mobility of professionals from abroad. MITI[7] reported that Malaysia has not met the threshold in the AFAS 7th package and that the country has one of the most protected services sector. There are about 188 different types of measures used in Malaysia and the trade barrier in services can be considered to be among the highest in ASEAN countries (see Table 10.3).

TABLE 10.3
Comparison of Market Access Requirements in AFAS

Country	No. of MA Requirements
Indonesia	206
Philippines	202
Malaysia	188
Vietnam	185
Myanmar	163
Brunei	80
Thailand	73
Lao PDR	51
Singapore	39
Cambodia	20

Source: MITI Official Website.

Nevertheless, Malaysia has made some progress in liberalization of services trade since the AFAS was signed. Thanh and Bartlett (2006) found that there is drop in restrictiveness of about 10 per cent for AFAS as compared with GATS. Malaysia's restrictive index declined from 80 per cent under GATs to 76.3 per cent with further liberalization under AFAS (see Figure 10.10). The level of trade restriction reduction was the highest in Indonesia and the Philippines, with the score reducing by 13 and 14 per cent, respectively. Thailand has the second lowest restrictiveness score after the completion of AFAS Package 4 agreements, at 63.7 per cent (Thanh and Bartlett 2006). Cambodia, being a newcomer in the World Trade Organization (WTO), has the least restrictive services sector in the region.

Services trade is becoming increasingly important for the Malaysia economy and is largely contributed by travel, private healthcare, construction, ICT, and private education sectors. In 2009, Malaysia recorded a stronger trade in services surplus of RM3.2 billion, increasing from 0.7 billion in 2008 (MITI 2010). However, the share of services in total exports has only increased marginally from 12 per cent in 1998 to 14 per cent in 2008 (Mahani 2011). ASEAN has increasingly become an important market for Malaysian service providers. In the case of healthcare services, for example, ASEAN market accounts for 85 to 90 per cent of Malaysia's exports (USITC 2010). Deeper integration

FIGURE 10.10
Level of Restrictions in Services Sector

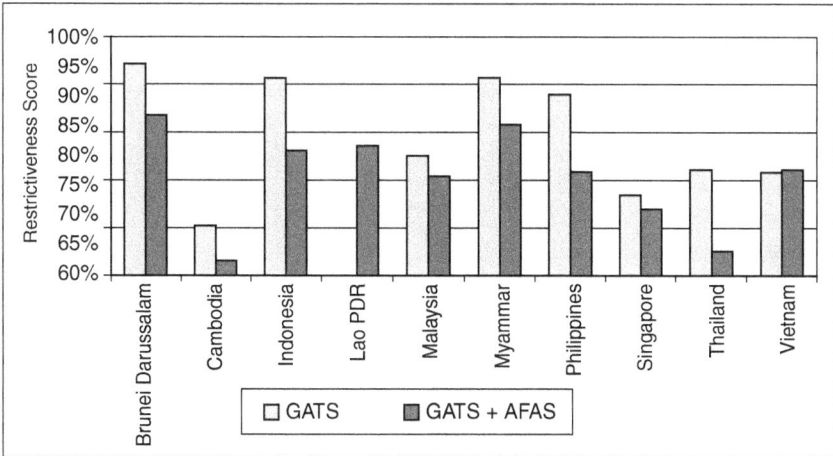

Source: Thanh and Bartlett (2006).

has been developed between Singapore and Malaysia in the healthcare markets in terms of movement of patients, investment, and medical professionals (USITC 2010).

Another successful case is the Malaysian construction sector, which has tapped the overseas markets, particularly ASEAN countries, India, and the Middle East countries. Malaysian companies have shown significant presence in global construction business in terms of total project value, where a total of 23 projects valued at RM14.2 billion were secured by Malaysian contractors abroad in 2009 compared to 50 projects valued at RM9.3 billion in 2008. The focus of overseas projects has mainly been in infrastructure works, such as building and road/highway projects, which are areas of export specialty for Malaysian contractors (CIDB 2007).

Free Flow of Investment

The AEC Blueprint envisaged ASEAN member countries to achieve free and open investment regime by 2015. The existing investment agreements, including investment guarantees, have been enhanced and consolidated into the ASEAN Comprehensive Agreement on Investment (ACIA) to meet challenges of increasing competition for foreign direct investment (ASEAN Secretariat 2011*a*). The ACIA covers all sectors except for most services, which is covered under the AFAS (USITC 2010) and is effective from April 2012. The AEC Blueprint sets targets and parameters on regulations allowing minimum equity ownership for foreign investments in specific industries (see Table 10.4).

Investment climate in Malaysia is liberal and market-oriented. Various policy reforms were undertaken to stimulate FDI, especially after the severe contraction in FDI inflows in 2009. The initiative includes liberalization of 27 services subsectors to allow 100 per cent foreign equity ownership, limit of foreign shareholding in insurance companies, and Islamic and Investment Banks. Equity ownership for foreigners was increased from 49 per cent to 70 per cent for insurance companies, Islamic Banks, and investment banks. In 2010, Foreign Investment Committee's (FIC) investment guidelines were removed to enable faster transactions for acquisitions of interests, mergers, and takeovers of local companies by domestic or foreign parties without FIC approval.

As a response to the growing competition for FDI, the government liberalized investment policies in manufacturing and services sectors and repositioned itself by diverting attention to search for FDI funds from resource rich ASEAN and booming East Asian economies. Malaysia also saw huge potential in the single market initiative in facilitating the expansion of investment opportunities from and to the region.

TABLE 10.4
Equity Targets and Parameters in the AEC Blueprint

	Priority Sectors		
	e-ASEAN (ICT), Tourism, Healthcare, Air-Travel	Logistics	Non-Priority Sectors
End Date for Liberalization	2010	2013	2015
Foreign (ASEAN) Equity Participation	– 49% by 2006 – 51% by 2008 – 70% by 2010	– 49% by 2008 – 51% by 2010 – 70% by 2013	– 30% by 2006 – 49% by 2008 – 51% by 2010

Source: MITI (2011).

To what extent has Malaysia achieved the AEC Blueprint targets for investment liberalization? Dee (2010) found that only Singapore has met the AEC Blueprint target to allow 70 per cent foreign ownership in air services by 2010. In the maritime services, Dee reported that there were no ASEAN countries that have fulfilled the target of 51 per cent foreign equity ownership, while only Singapore and Vietnam achieved the target for telecommunication services. The World Bank (2010) reported that the manufacturing sector is fully open to foreign equity ownership in Malaysia. However, foreign ownership in services sector, electricity, and primary sectors are restrictive (see Table 10.5).

What is the impact? The recent trend of FDI flows to Malaysia clearly shows the impact of the restructuring and liberal investment policies. FDI inflows from the regional countries increased notably, increasing from 10.1 per cent of total FDI inflows in 2001 to almost 30 per cent in 2009 (BNM 2011). Singapore is the leading investor in Malaysia with investment totalling RM46.2 million in 2009, representing 51.4 per cent of total FDI stock from the region (BNM 2011). China's investment increased from RM134.1 million in 2006 (accounting for 0.7 per cent

TABLE 10.5
Malaysia: Foreign Equity Ownership Indexes, 2010

Sectors	Equity Ownership (%)
Mining, Oil and Gas	70
Agriculture and Forestry	85
Light Manufacturing	100
Telecommunication	39.5
Electricity	30
Banking	49
Insurance	49
Transportation	100
Media	65
Sector Group 1 (Construction, Tourism, Retail)	90
Sector Group 2 (Healthcare, Waste Management)	65

Note: 100 = Full Foreign Ownership Allowed
Source: World Bank (2010).

of total investment) to RM1.9 billion in 2007 (5.6 per cent of the total investment). In the first half of 2010, China's investment in Malaysia remained high, accounting for 5.2 per cent of the total investment. Taiwan's share in total investment increased from 2.0 per cent in 2006 to 5.6 per cent in 2010 while Hong Kong's share increased from 0.4 per cent to 4.8 per cent during the same period.[8]

The deepening regional integration and the expanding economic activities provided platform for Malaysian companies to expand investment opportunities in the region. Consequently, there was a gradual increase of net direct investment abroad (DIA) since 2005 and by 2010, it reached RM67.9 billion (BNM 2011). Significant portion of DIAs were within Asia, particularly the ASEAN countries and the Asian Newly Industrialized Economies (NIEs).

Free Flow of Skilled Labour

The Bali Concord II in 2003 called for completion of mutual recognition agreements (MRAs) for qualifications in major professional services by 2008 to facilitate the free movement of professionals and skilled labour. At present, ASEAN has concluded seven MRAs: MRA on Engineering Services signed on 9 December 2005, MRA on Nursing Services signed on 8 December 2006, MRA on Architectural Services and Framework Arrangement in the MRA of Surveying Qualifications both signed on 19 November 2007, MRA on Medical Practitioners, MRA on Dental Practitioners, and MRA Framework on Accountancy Services signed on 26 February 2009.

Common restrictions in Mode 4 supply of services trade among others are language requirement, qualification requirement, commercial presence requirement, subject to domestic regulations, and economic needs tests. Progress in the elimination of restrictions on movement of natural persons and MRAs in AFAS has been very slow mainly because of national sensitivities to the migration issue (Chia 2010). However, Malaysia has made notable progress in this area, where it made commitment in 70 out of the total 104 services sectors that were listed under the seven priority sectors of AFAS (Manning and Bhatnagar 2004). This commitment is ahead of Singapore (60), ahead of Thailand (54), Indonesia (46), the Philippines (38), Brunei (37), Vietnam (34), Laos (29), Cambodia (20), and Myanmar (21). Malaysia has long fully liberalized its policy on the employment of skilled and professional workers in the manufacturing sector, which is in line with

Malaysia's objectives to attract foreign investment and to promote technology transfer (WTO Trade Policy Review 2010).

Manning and Bhatnagar (2004) reported that in 2000, there are about 60,000 skilled and professional workers in Malaysia. These skilled and professional workers originated mostly from outside the ASEAN region and tended to accompany foreign investment into the country. There is also no restriction on the employment of foreign skilled workers in the Multimedia Super Corridor (MSC). As result of this, foreign IT experts especially from India are increasingly being employed in the ICT sector (Manning and Bhatnagar 2004).

Challenges and Concluding Remarks

Malaysia is committed to progressively liberalize selected sectors of the economy in line with the ASEAN Economic Community Blueprint, for freer flow of goods, services and capital by 2015. Malaysia recognizes the benefits of joining AEC. Considerable progress has been achieved in meeting the goals and timelines of the AEC. More than 95 per cent of intra-regional trade in goods is tariff-free while the services sector has been progressively liberalized. Investment rules have been fully liberalized in the manufacturing sector, while regulations on foreign investment in primary and services sectors are gradually being eliminated to attract extra-regional investments and to increase intra-regional investment flows. Trading cost has declined notably since the 1990s. In 2010, Malaysia had the lowest trade cost in the region. Rules and restrictions related to movement of skilled and professional workers are gradually being reduced. ASEAN Secretariat, in March 2012, reported that 67.5 per cent of the measures identified in the AEC Blueprint for the four-year period covering 2008–11 have been implemented by the member countries.

There are some challenges in creating a single ASEAN market with free flow of goods, services and factor of production with equitable income levels. The first concern is related to the implementation aspect of AEC's goals. The goals in the Blueprint are vaguely defined and there are still no concrete milestones to achieve those goals. The target timelines are not mandatory. Thus, the goal-post could be, and in fact has already been, shifted for some provisions in phase one of the Blueprint. Second challenge is that regional economic integration will bring about reforms of domestic policies, changes in governance and transparency. Obviously, there will be resistance by affected parties, monopolists, and lobbyists apprehensive of increased competition and transparency in the economy. In Malaysia, there are some sectors and domestic regulations that are considered sensitive and strategic for national economic development. This will slow down the progress of further liberalization. Hence, the achievement of AEC vision would require strong motivation, political will and leadership.

Another challenge is related to the proliferation of bilateral FTAs in recent years. Malaysia has been actively forming FTA networking since mid-2000s. It has concluded and signed four bilateral Free Trade Agreements (FTAs) with Japan, Pakistan, New Zealand, and Chile. At the regional level, Malaysia and its ASEAN partners concluded five FTAs under ASEAN with China, Korea, Japan, India, and Australia-New Zealand (see Appendix 10.A1). Proliferation of bilateral FTAs is seen by some analysts as a sign of ASEAN's disintegration and divergence from ASEAN's vision to establish a single regional market. But the Malaysian government view bilateral FTAs as an opportunity to gain greater market access and would facilitate and strengthen trade integration within ASEAN. This is because issues that are agreed to in the bilateral FTAs signed by Malaysia have so far been consistent with the commitments made in regional and multilateral trade arrangements.

Furthermore, Malaysia has emphasized on strategic partnership, capacity building, and cooperation with its FTA partners. The trade agreements have been more comprehensive and wide in scope than just liberalizing trade and market access. Building network through FTAs is seen as an effective mechanism to strengthen production capacity, develop integrated production base, intensify human capital development, and improve trade facilitation. Possible negative consequences of complicated Rules of Origin (ROO) arising from bilateral and regional FTAs have received necessary attention and are being addressed in ASEAN.

ASEAN has made significant progress in revising and simplifying the ROO criteria and implementation procedures. Therefore, ROO is expected to be less of an impediment to intra-ASEAN trade in coming years. Furthermore, Estevadeordal, Harris, and Suominen (2007) found that ROO in intra-Asian FTAs tend to be less restrictive and complex than their counterparts in Europe and the Americas (cited in Kimura 2010). Proliferation of bilateral FTAs therefore is not a hindrance to the implementation of AEC Blueprint. In fact, the FTAs will support ASEAN's efforts to build strategic alliance with key economies in the world by further enhancing regional production networks, and improving market access and investment opportunities.

APPENDIX 10.A1
Trade Agreement Signed and Under Negotiation by Malaysia as of December 2011

No.	Trade Agreement	Date Signed
ASEAN Free Trade Agreements		
1.	ASEAN Trade in Goods Agreement (ATIGA) or previously the 1992 CEPT Agreement	26 February 2009
2.	ASEAN Framework on Services	1995
3	ASEAN-China Trade in Goods Agreement	29 November 2004
4.	ASEAN-Korea Trade in Goods Agreement	24 August 2006
5.	ASEAN-China Services Agreement	14 January 2007
6.	ASEAN-Japan Comprehensive Economic partnership	14 April 2009
7.	ASEAN-India Trade in Goods Agreement	13 August 2009
8.	ASEAN-Australia-New Zealand Free Trade Agreement	27 February 2009
Bilateral Free Trade Agreements		
1.	Malaysia-Pakistan Closer Economic Partnership Agreement	8 November 2007
2.	Malaysia-Japan Economic Partnership Agreement	13 December 2005
3.	Malaysia-New Zealand Free Trade Agreement	26 October 2009
4.	Malaysia-Chile Free Trade Agreement	13 May 2010
Free Trade Agreements Under Negotiation		
1.	Malaysia-Turkey	
2.	Malaysia-Australia	
3.	Malaysia-European Free Trade Agreement	
4.	Trade Preferential System-Organisation of Islamic Conference	
5.	Developing Eight (D-8) Preferential Tariff Agreement	
6.	Trans-Pacific Partnership Agreement	

Source: Based on information retrieved from MITI website.

NOTES

1. The ASEAN Community is comprised of three pillars, namely the ASEAN Political-Security Community, ASEAN Economic Community and ASEAN Socio-Cultural Community, all expected to work in tandem in establishing the ASEAN Community (ASEAN Secretariat 2011*a*).
2. *Jakarta Post*, "ASEAN Tries to be United in Facing Rising China", 2011, available at <http://www.thejakarta post.com/news/2011/07/17>.
3. Available at <http://www.asean.org/Fact%20Sheet/AEC/2009-AEC-025.pdf>.
4. MITI AFTA website (accessed 23 September 2011).
5. See USITC (2010) for more discussion on this.
6. Available at <http://etp.pemandu.gov.my>.
7. Sourced from MITI website.
8. Data is extracted from *Economic Report* 2010/11, Ministry of Finance, Malaysia. Data for 2010 are for January to July 2010.

REFERENCES

Akrasanee, N. and D. Stifel. "The Political Economy of the ASEAN Free Trade Area". In *AFTA: The Way Ahead*, edited by P. Imada and S. Naya. Singapore: Institute of Southeast Asian Studies, 1992.

Ando, M. and A. Obashi. "The Pervasiveness of Non-Tariff Measures in ASEAN: Evidences from the Inventory Approach". Paper presented at the Asia-Pacific Trade Economist Conference (ARTNet), Bangkok, Thailand, 2–3 November 2009.

Anthony, M.P. "Bridging Development Gaps in ASEAN: Towards an ASEAN Community". *UNISC Journal*, no. 11 (2006): 37–48.

Ariff, M. "Trade, Investment and Interdependence". In *Reinventing ASEAN*, edited by S.S.C. Tay, J.P. Estanislo and H. Soesastro. Singapore: Institute of Southeast Asian Studies, 2001.

ASEAN Secretariat. *Roadmap for ASEAN Community, 2009–15*. Jakarta, 2009.

――――. *ASEAN Economic Scoreboard: Charting Progress Toward Regional Economic Integration*. Jakarta, 2010.

――――. *ASEAN Economic Community Factbook*. Jakarta, 2011*a*.

――――. "ASEAN Integration in Trade in Services: Development, Challenges and Way Forward". Jakarta, 2011*b*.

――――. *ASEAN Community in Figures (ACIF) 2010* (2011*c*).

Athukorala, P.C. "Production Networks and Trade Patterns in East: Regionalism or Globalisation?". ADB Working Paper Series in Regional Economic Integration, no. 56 (August 2010).

BNM. *Bank Negara Annual Report 2010*. Kuala Lumpur: Central Bank of Malaysia, 2011.

Chia, S.Y. "Free Flow of Skilled Labor in the ASEAN Economic Community". ERIA Research, No. 3. Jakarta: Economic Research Institute for ASEAN and East Asia, 2010. Available at <http://www.eria.org>.

CIDB. *CIBD Annual Report*. Kuala Lumpur: Construction Industry Development Board, 2007.

Corbett, J. and S. Umezaki. "Overview: Deepening East Asian Economic Integration". In *Deepening East Asian Economic Integration*, edited by Jenny Corbett and So Umezaki. Jakarta: Economic Research Institute for ASEAN and East Asia (ERIA) Research Project Report 2008. Available at <http://www.eria.org/pdf/research/y2008/no1/DEI-00-Front_Cover.pdf>.

Dee, P. "Services Liberalization toward the ASEAN Economic Community". ERIA Research, no. 3. Jakarta: Economic Research Institute for ASEAN and East Asia, 2010. Available at <http://www.eria.org>.

Estevadeordal, A., J. Harris and K. Suominen. "Multilateralizing Preferential Rules of Origin Around the World". Paper presented at WTO/HEI/NCCR Conference on Multeralizing Regionalism, Geneva, Switzerland, 10–12 September 2007. Available at <http://www.wto.org/english/tratop_e/region_e/conference_sept07e.htm>.

Hanif, A., R. Alavi, G. Mat Ghani G., and J. Duasa. "The Determinants of Non-Tariff Barriers in Malaysia's Manufacturing Sector". Paper presented at 2011 International Conference on Economics and Business Information, IPDER, vol. 9. Thailand: Bangkok, 2011.

Katsuhide, T. and U. Shujiro. "On the Use of FTAs by Japanese Firms: Further Evidence". RIETI Discussion Paper Series 09-E-028. Japan: The Research Institute of Economy, Trade and Industry, 2009. Available at <http://www.rieti.go.jp>.

Kimura, F. "FTA Networking in East Asia and Asia-Pacific: Where Are We Going?". ERIA Policy Paper. Jakarta: Economic Research Institute for ASEAN and East Asia, 2010. Available at <http://www.eria.org>.

Mahani, Z.A. "Growing Trade in Services in APEC Economies: Malaysian Experiences", 2011. Available at <http://www.sincpec.sg/docs/pecc_conf_29300611/PS2_S1_Mahani_ppt.pdf>.

Manning, C. and P. Bhatnagar. "Liberalizing and Facilitating the Movement of Individual Service Providers under AFAS: Implication for Labour and Immigration Policies and Procedures in ASEAN". REPSF Project, no. 2 (2004).

MITI. *International Trade and Industry Report*. Ministry of International Trade and Industry, Malaysia, 2010.

———. "AEC and Malaysia's FTAs Initiatives: Opportunities and Benefits". Seminar on ASEAN Economic Community, organized by the Ministry of International Trade and Industry (MITI) and the Asean-Business Advisory Council (ABAC), Kuala Lumpur, 17 March 2011.

Nandan, G. *ASEAN: Building an Economic Community*. Economic Analytical Unit, Department of Foreign Affairs, AusAID, Australian Government, 2006. Available at <http://www.dfat.au/eau>.

NEAC. *New Economic Model for Malaysia*. Putrajaya: National Economic Advisory Council, 2009.

NST. "ASEAN Economic Community: Myth or Reality?", by Rebecca Fatima Sta Maria. *New Straits Times*, 28 February 2011.

Rajah, R. "Industrial Policy and Industrialization". In *Malaysian Economy: Unfolding Growth and Social Change*, edited by R. Rasiah. Kuala Lumpur: Oxford University Press, 2011.

Schwarz, A. and R. Villinger. "Integrating Southeast Asia's Economies". *The McKinsey Quarterly*, vol. 1 (2004): 1–10.

Soesastro, H. "Implementing the ASEAN Economic Community (AEC) Blueprint". In *Deepening Economic Integration in East Asia: ASEAN Economic Community and Beyond*, edited by Hadi Soesastro. ERIA Research Project, nos. 1–2. Jakarta: Economic Research Institute for ASEAN and East Asia, 2007. Available at <http://www.eria.org>.

Sourdin, P. and R. Pomfret. "Trade Facilitation toward the ASEAN Economic Community". ERIA Research, no. 3. Jakarta: Economic Research Institute for ASEAN and East Asia, 2009. Available at <http://www.eria.org>.

Tham, S.Y. "ASEAN Economic Cooperation: Moving Towards an ASEAN Economic Community". In *Community in ASEAN: Ideas and Practices*, edited by Tham Siew Yean, Lee Poh Ping and Norani Othman. Bangi: Penerbit Universiti Kebangsaan Malaysia, 2008.

Thanh, V.T. and P. Bartlett. *Ten Years of ASEAN Framework Agreement on Services (AFAS): An Assessment*. REPSF Project, no. 05/004 (2006). Available at <http://www.aseansec.org/aadcp/repsf/docs/05-004-FinalReport.pdf>.

United Nations Conference on Trade and Development (UNCTAD). *World Investment Report 2011: Non-Equity Modes of International Production and Development*. Geneva: UNCTAD, 2011.

UNNext. "Towards a Single Window Trading Environment: Case of Malaysia's National Single Window". United Nations Network of Experts for Paperless Trade in Asia and the Pacific. Brief no. 4, July 2010.

Urata, S. and Okabe M. "Overview: Tracing the Progress toward the ASEAN Economic Community". ERIA Research Project, no. 3. Jakarta: Economic Research Institute for ASEAN and East Asia, 2009. Available at <http://www.eria.org>.

USITC. "ASEAN: Regional Trends in Economic Integration, Export Competitiveness, and Inbound Investment for Selected Industries". USITC Publication 4176. Washington, D.C.: United States International Trade Commission, August 2010.

World Bank. *Investing Cross Border 2010: Indicators for Foreign Direct Investment Regulation in 87 Countries.* Washington, D.C.: World Bank, 2010.

————. *Ease of Doing Business.* Washington, D.C.: World Bank, 2011. Available at <http://www.doingbusiness.org/>.

WTO Trade Policy Review. *Economy Gains from Openness to Trade and Investment and Prudent Management.* Geneva: World Trade Organization, 2006. Available at <http://www.wto.org/english/tratop_e/tpr_e/tp257_e.htm>.

————. *Malaysia: Further Trade-related Reforms Would Help Long-term Economic Growth.* Geneva: World Trade Organisation, 2010. Available at <http://www.wto.org/english/tratop_e/tpr_e/tp325_e.htm>.

WTO-IDE-JETRO. *Trade Patterns and Global Value Chains in East Asia: From Trade in Goods to Trade in Tasks*, 2011. Available at <http://www.ide.go.jp/English/Press/pdf/20110606_news.pdf>.

Zakariah, A., et al. *ERIA Study to Further Improve the ASEAN Economic Community Scorecard: The Malaysia Country Report.* Kuala Lumpur: Malaysia Institute of Economic Research and Jakarta: Economic Research Institute for ASEAN and East Asia, 2010.

Commentary 2

Political Economy and Foreign Policy

Johan Saravanamuttu

Malaysia has always pursued developmental goals in foreign policy. In the flush of independence, Prime Minister Tunku Abdul Rahman espoused a *laissez-faire* foreign policy posture to attract foreign investment. This was changed under the Tun Razak tenure to policy stances which stressed the control of national resources, such as oil, to a more directed investment policy geared to implement the New Economy Policy (NEP) introduced in 1971. Under the leadership of Mahathir Mohamad, the "Look East Policy" was launched in 1981, aimed not just at emulating the East Asian work ethnic, but also at attracting a massive influx of Japanese investment. In more recent times, two premiers, Abdullah Badawi and Najib Razak, have capitalized on Malaysia's good relations with China to win a number of highly lucrative investment projects from the rising Asian economic giant. In April 2011, Chinese Premier Wen Jiabao's visit to Malaysia saw the signing of a slew of agreements worth one billion US dollars, among which were: a contract between China's Huandian Engineers and Malaysia's Janakuasa for a coaled-fired plant; a pact between ZTE Corporation and DiGi to supply telecommunications infrastructure; and an MOU to build 6.5 km tunnel between Penang Island and the mainland by Beijing's Urban Construction Group Company.

In this article, we will examine trade policy in the current era of a globalized world economy underpinned by neo-liberalism. Malaysia's trading policies have been geared to its development needs and increasingly to its changing and transformed industrialized economy. Thus, its Ministry of International trade and Industry (MITI) has been actively negotiating and signing bilateral and multilateral Free Trade Agreements (FTAs) with important trading partners. This is to ensure that Malaysian goods and services do not face unfair competition abroad and can enjoy, as much as possible, "most favoured nation" treatment in world markets.

Malaysia's stance on FTAs took a radical shift in the early 2000s, demonstrated by MITI moving in the direction of WTO-plus bilateral FTAs. Since 2002, it has been actively pursuing FTAs with a host of countries, and by the middle of 2008, Malaysia concluded two bilateral FTAs with Japan and Pakistan. The negotiation for an FTA with the U.S., which started in 2006, was stalled in 2008 and Malaysia has instead seemingly opted to join the U.S.-sponsored Trans-Pacific Partnership (TPP). According to reports, Malaysia and the US were unable to resolve many contentious issues, in particular, those related to the NEP and more open government procurement policies. However, under the TPP, the government procurement issue is being pursued.

In October 2005, Malaysia concluded a significant FTA with Japan, which goes by the name Japan-Malaysia Economic Partnership Agreement (JMEPA). The JMEPA allows Malaysia to maintain, if not expand, its share of the Japanese market for Malaysian exports through preferential tariff treatment and technical collaboration. The cooperation and collaboration activities envisaged under the JMEPA would promote the growth of new sectors such as high-tech industries, including biotechnology, services including manufacturing related services, and ICT and multimedia. For SMEs, economic and technical cooperation would facilitate quality enhancement, vendor development, and inclusion of Malaysian SMEs into the manufacturing supply chain of Japanese multinational companies.

The second FTA was concluded in January 2008 with Pakistan. This agreement enables the Malaysian business community to use Pakistan as the springboard to expand their business with Pakistan's trading partners in the South Asia region. In recent years, the number of successes in bilateral FTAs has increased sharply, such as, with New Zealand (2009), India (2011), Australia (2012), and Chile (2012). At the point of writing, bilateral FTA negotiations are ongoing with the European Union (EU) and Turkey.

There are also various plurilateral FTAs to which Malaysia is a party. The major ones involve Malaysia as a member of ASEAN. The on-going ASEAN FTA proposals are with India, Japan, EU, Korea, China, and Australia and New Zealand. The ASEAN-Japan negotiations appear to have gone some distance. Negotiations on ASEAN-Japan Comprehensive Economic Partnership Agreement (AJCEP), which commenced in April 2005, were concluded in December 2007. ASEAN member states and Japan undertook domestic clearance for the signing of AJCEP Agreement and, after eleven rounds of negotiations over four years, the agreement came into force on April 2008.

The highly significant ASEAN-China FTA is progressing with several protocols already signed under a Framework Agreement, which came into force on 1 July 2003. This is an umbrella agreement which provides general provision on the establishment of an ASEAN-China Free Trade Area (ACFTA) within ten years by pursuing progressive elimination of tariffs and non-tariff barriers; progressive liberalization of trade in services and investment; strengthening trade facilitation measures; and economic cooperation in other areas of common interest. MITI argues that the ASEAN-China FTA will bring into Malaysia's orbit an economic region with 1.7 billion consumers, regional GDP of about US$2 trillion and total trade estimated at US$1.23 trillion. It will be the biggest and largest FTA among developing countries. With market access opportunities to a population of 1.2 billion, preferential trade for Malaysian products will increase immensely.

Along with its various bilateral and plurilateral FTAs, whether concluded or not, Malaysia has evidently worked along with its ASEAN members to move towards concluding the ASEAN Free Trade Area Agreement (AFTA) scheduled for 2015. The AFTA project has gone through considerable metamorphosis and is now anchored on the creation of an ASEAN Economic Community. Economists have made the point that, with the proliferation of FTAs in East Asia, ASEAN's own integration appears to be derailed. Economists generally still consider FTAs, whether bilateral or plurilateral, to be only a "second best" strategy of the neo-liberal world order. The "noodle bowl" of FTAs may turn out to be counter-productive to such groupings as ASEAN, which may eventually want to integrate regionally into a single market like the EU.

Malaysia's stance on ASEAN integration is perhaps fraught with such a dilemma. Should it move along with its Southeast Asian economic partners or go at it alone and along with the countries with which it has apparent political affinity? Such hedging is clearly evident in Malaysia's foreign economic relations in general. An example of such hedging was the July 2006 ratification of the Preferential Tariff Agreement (PTA) with eight Islamic countries, namely, Bangladesh, Indonesia, Iran, Malaysia, Egypt, Nigeria, Pakistan, and Turkey. As with FTAs, MITI argues that the implementation of the D-8 PTA would enable Malaysian exporters to enjoy preferential tariff treatment for selected products in the market of the participating members and enable exporters to gain competitive advantage over similar products originating from non-participating countries. However, to astute observers, it would seem that the major consideration for such a move was a political-cultural one rather than an economic one.

It should be stressed that Malaysia's primary and most important economic relationships in trade and investment are still with the global economic powerhouses of U.S., EU, Japan, and increasingly China. This has meant that in terms of political economy, both its postures and strategies towards these states remained stable. Malaysia's move to negotiate an FTA with the U.S. should be appreciated in these terms; so too, should the FTA with Japan and the ongoing one with the EU. As such, China will no doubt feature prominently in Malaysia's foreign economic policies, one way or another in the near future.

PART II

Politics, Decentralization and Environment

11

PRISONS TO MIND IN MALAYSIA'S NATION BUILDING

Ooi Kee Beng

Introduction

The thrust of the argument in this chapter builds on the idea that Malaysian nation building has been occurring in an atmosphere of conservatism and compromise. Undoubtedly, there were many parties involved that were correctly called radical, but these were successfully neutralized in the run-up to Independence. This was best noted in how the Alliance Model easily overshadowed the option embodied in Onn Ja'afar's Independence of Malaya Party or the communist path.

However, the Alliance Model, built around the three parties — United Malays National Organisation (UMNO), Malayan Chinese Association (MCA) and Malayan Indian Congress (MIC) — fossilized racial categories in a system of apparent inter-racial cooperation under Malay leadership. More importantly, the major controversial points of the Constitution were hammered out under its watch, leading to the myth of The Social Contract, where the Chinese and Indian parties purportedly accepted perpetual Malay dominance in exchange for citizenship in the new country.

Despite the relative lack of violence, Malaysian independence occurred in an atmosphere of severe crisis and strategic compromise. What need discussing are thus the origins of the discursive structure of Malaysian politics. Let's go back in time to the pre-Merdeka era, at least for a while, to determine the strong trends that have continued to form the country's self-image to this day.

Colonial Retreat vs Communist Ascendance

The British Malayan colonies changed colonial hands in 1942, along with most of East Asia. The Japanese Occupation saw the strong rise in relevance of the Malayan Communist Party, which received support from the British through Force 136, and which drew inspiration from the Chinese Communist Party in China. The Malayan Peoples' Anti-Japanese Army (MPAJA) was formed in June or July 1942, and when demobilized after the War, it boasted 6,000 to 7,000 members (Cheah 1987, pp. 61–75).

In 1945, the Malayan colonies switched colonial hands again, back to the British. But things had changed. The population had been radicalized and parties other than the Malayan Communist Party (MCP) would soon make themselves felt, such as the pan-Indonesia Partai Kebangsaan Melayu Malaya (PKMM) and UMNO.

The toppling and execution of traditional leaders in western Sumatra in April 1946 in the "Sumatra Social Revolution" could not but have put a scare into the British as well as the Malay aristocrats on the peninsula (Kahin 2003, pp. 178–83; Reid 1971, p. 22). To what extent this spelled the end for the Malayan Union, and persuaded the British to negotiate so hurriedly with conservative Malay leaders remains unclear. But the wisdom of avoiding social revolutions at a time when China was falling into communist hands and relations with the MCP were souring would have been obvious to the besieged colonists.

In any case, British post-War colonial politics went from being egalitarian to racialist at lightning speed. Already in July, not long after the killing of rajas took place in East Sumatra, a Working Committee consisting of six British representatives, four representatives of the Rulers and two UMNO men, was immediately formed to discuss constitutional proposals made by the Sultan of Perak. This hurriedly met on 6 August, but had to take a break after 16 August for

Ramadhan month. In any case, after only four meetings, its final report was ready on 18 November, but was kept secret until 24 December 1946. Opposition from a group of parties such as the Malayan Democratic Union (MDU), the Straits Chinese British Association, the Indian Chamber of Commerce, the General Labour Union under the umbrella organizations of AMCJA and PUTERA (Pusat Tenaga Rakyat) — especially through the general strike of 20 October 1947 — delayed the Federation of Malaya from replacing the Malayan Union until 21 January 1948 (Simandjuntak 1969, pp. 35–52; Harper 1999, pp. 89–90).

Communist insurgence began when the MCP tactic of gaining control over trade unions was foiled by restrictions placed on union officials, and by the disappearance of MCP secretary-general Lai Teck. The subsequent declaration of the Emergency by the British on 18 June 1948 set the backdrop for the process of independence that would be granted within ten years, and which left a legacy of ill foreboding in the country.

Without doubt, the assassination by the MCP of British High Commissioner Sir Henry Gurney in October 1951 made the British more than willing to welcome the Alliance Model that emerged in the Kuala Lumpur Municipal Election in February 1952 through cooperation between Selangor UMNO and the Kuala Lumpur MCA. The latter party was formed on 27 February 1949, with British prodding, to counteract MCP influence in Chinese communities.

Communal Ceasefire or Social Contract?

The history of Malaysia is thus very much a history of how different interests negotiated among themselves or fought themselves to a ceasefire. What is now popularly called The Social Contract is archetypical of this development, of the restrictive state of mind it fostered, and of the vested interests it protected. In governance, a crisis mentality became the norm, as can be seen in the number of emergency legislations that have appeared and that have never been repealed. (At the moment of writing, the government of Najib Abdul Razak is in the process of ending three emergency declarations).

The Social Contract refers commonly to an undocumented purported and conceptually dubious agreement between the MCA, UMNO, and the MIC which nevertheless facilitated the transfer of political power from the worried and harried British to a coalition of conservatives on 31 August 1957. However, several major points for the Federal Constitution of the new country, which came into effect on 27 August that year, were already granted relevance on 21 January 1948 in the Federation of Malaya Agreement. For example, the safeguarding of the special position of the Malays in Article 153 was taken from clause 19(1)(d) of the Agreement.

In essence, Malaysia is the Improbable Country, a tapestry of disparate colonial parts sewn together; leaving it fixated even today with the stitches and not with the whole. The national discourse became more concerned with negotiating separateness between the communities than with overcoming it.

Constitutional Amendments and Extended Coalitionism

This communal ceasefire was not an easy one and by 1969, it had failed to satisfy anyone. After inter-communal rioting left hundreds dead on 13 May that year, a concerted attempt orchestrated by UMNO and its allies was undertaken to restructure the political arena and to rewrite the rules of engagement between political opponents.

The coalition was expanded to absorb as many opposition parties as possible, turning the Alliance into the Barisan Nasional (BN). The only major party that kept out was the Democratic Action Party. This expansion neutralized the opposition politics that had been so rampant in the 1960s, and the impetus for political conflicts in the country would thereafter come mainly as a result of splits within UMNO.

Concentration of power was also evident in changes brought about within UMNO itself. When Tun Abdul Razak Hussein became Prime Minister on 22 September 1970, the party experienced profound changes immediately. The term of the Majlis Tertinggi (Supreme Council) was raised from one to three years, even as the Council gained the critical power to choose party candidates for elections. More significant was the establishment of bureaus within the party, placed under the Council, to work in tandem with government agencies. All in all, seven bureaus came into being: Politics, Finance, Education, Labour and Labour Union, Religion, Culture and Social Welfare, and Economics. This concept of kerajaan berparti ("government with the party") tied the governmental structure tightly to the party apparatus (Torii 1997, p. 221).

Why Malaysian politics is fixated with the two-thirds majority in parliament or at state level stems from the fact that constitutional amendments were so frequently made from the very start that even Mahathir Mohamed, who later as Prime Minister would paradoxically be responsible for many such measures, complained about the abuse of the Constitution in his book, *The Malay Dilemma* published in 1970 — just before the greatest amendments were to be made by Tun Abdul Razak — that "the manner, the frequency and the trivial reasons for altering the Constitution reduced this supreme law of the nation to a useless scrap of paper" (Mahathir 1970, p. 11).

Crisis legislations, originating with the Emergency, continued as the policy of preference throughout Malaysia's history, reflecting and exacerbating the ad hoc and tapestry nature of the country. The Constitution (Amendment) Act of 1971 was passed as a prerequisite for parliamentarism being reinstated. The Act restricted free speech, limiting the privileges of parliamentarians and assemblymen; defining the scope of official usage of the national language; and enhancing the status of bumiputeras.

What is most interesting is that until 2012 no crisis legislation had ever been repealed.[1] Apart from the 1971 Act mentioned above, such laws include the following (Lee 1995, pp. 106–25):

1. The Internal Security Act 1960;
2. The Emergency (Federal Constitution and Constitution of Sarawak) Act 1966, aimed at solving a constitutional deadlock which gives the Governor absolute discretion to convene Sarawak's Council Negri and dismiss the Chief Minister following a vote of no confidence in the Council;
3. The Emergency (Essential Powers) Ordinance No. 2, 1969, which placed all powers with the Director of Operations of the National Operations Council;
4. The Sedition Act of 1948, amended in 1971, making seditious any statement questioning Article 153 safeguarding bumiputera and Malay rights;
5. The University and University Colleges Act 1971; amended in April 2010 to allow appeals;
6. The Official Secrets Act of 1972;
7. The Emergency Powers (Kelantan) Act of 1977 which imposed federal rule in the state;
8. The Printing Presses and Publications Act 1984.

The framework within which the New Economic Policy (NEP) was implemented was therefore a narrow one with a series of harsh laws being passed to limit civil rights, but a broad one where UMNO's ability to penetrate society and the civil service was concerned. When the Barisan Nasional came into being just before the 1974 general elections, the constitutional and bureaucratic structure for centralization of power was already in place, turbocharged by the new ethos of Malay-first economic development. The deep penetration of the NEP into Malaysian life has continued to this day.

The NEP ethos was a broad one that strengthened the stranglehold on public discourses that constitutional amendments and UMNO dominance already exerted. The balancing between inter-racial wealth and national economic growth encouraged political correctness — which over time functioned as an umbrella hiding weaknesses in the system, such as rising corruption, rampant inefficiency, resource wastage, nonchalant monitoring of policies, and increasing divisions between individuals of different ethnicity.

Centralism vs Federalism

At this point, let's move the analysis to the present time. With the success of the opposition parties in the general elections of 2008, major ills in the system became evident. First, power had become centralized in the hands of UMNO to a larger degree than had been obvious to the general population. This was already apparent in the steady abolishment of local elections, which became complete in 1976 when the Local Government Act was passed (Tennant 1973, p. 347; Goh 2005, pp. 55–58). Control over the civil service had always been policy where UMNO was concerned. In fact, the MCA and the MIC had "tacitly agreed" to UMNO demands to retain the British practice of having a four-to-one ratio in the Malayan Civil Service in favour of Malays. Today, the ratio is tilted even further in that direction (Means 1970, p. 198). While the NEP sought to push Malays into fields where they were underrepresented, no outflow of Malays from areas where they were overrepresented took place. Where the civil service in general was concerned, as was the case with the military, the paramilitary, the police and even the judiciary, the NEP ambition "to reduce and eventually eliminate the identification of race with economic function" was ignored.

To be sure, many Malay leaders did not see the NEP as a temporary affirmative action programme aimed at dissipating socio-economically defined racial divisions, but as the concrete formulation of the indeterminate "special position" expressed in Article 153 of the Constitution. UMNO's wish for permanent power could therefore ride steadily on the back of the wish for permanent special rights for the Malays.

Creedism or Racialism?

Racialism is undeniably a key element in Malaysian politics, starting with the country's Constitution itself, which has the dubious distinction of carrying something so contingent as the definition of a race. Article 160 states that "'Malay' means a person who professes the religion of Islam, habitually speaks the Malay language, conforms to Malay custom" (see Federal Constitution 2006). This is further institutionalized in the race-based structure of all the parties that formed the first independent Malayan government. With the implementation of the NEP in 1970, and despite the fact that the NEP's success would logically be measured by the disappearance of race-profession stereo-typing, race became an ever more relevant factor in Malaysian life.

This observation is uncontroversial as such. With the widespread Islamization that successively took place, especially during the Mahathir Mohamed era, more and more conflicts are better understood as expressions of creedism rather than racism. Since the Malay "race" is defined through Islam and all marriages with Malays involve obligatory conversion on the part of a non-Muslim spouse, it may be analytically more fruitful to recognize that the active element in the inter-communal equation is now religion more than race.

More and more controversies in Malaysia are now taking on a religious aspect. The Hindu Rights Action Force (Hindraf) that managed to attract Indians away from the BN in the 2008 elections was the most dramatic of these. Any plan to demolish a Hindu temple is now a potential hot potato. Issues such as the ban on the import of Malay bibles, the ban on the use of the word "Allah" by non-Muslims, or the astounding claims made by Malay right-wingers about a Malaysian Christian conspiracy to turn Muslim Malaysia into a Christian state, which led to a raid on a church for having Muslim guests for dinner, are becoming common.

The defining of race through religion is a potent strategy which began as a defensive measure, but which through the shift in political focus from blood ties to faith affiliation has become a concept with a strong capacity to offend.

With the return of opposition politics and the control won by opposition parties in four states, issues of governance have become major points of contention. State governments have to compete with policies to show how enlightened their rule is. This comes in the wake of endless criticism about the abuse of power that the BN has over the years been accused of. Competence, accountability, and transparency are some terms bandied around, and corruption, politics of patronage and money politics are now major subjects of public discussion.

Such criticism tends to consider the problem as structural, considering how long the BN has been unchallenged. The cynicism that pervades the country makes piecemeal reforms from the federal government suspect. In that sense, Malaysia finds itself in a position where only major overhauls are credible.

Conclusion — Breaking Trends

The 2008 and 2013 election results mean that the BN is more than ever dependent on UMNO, a party which has never commanded a simple majority of the votes. So far, allies such as the MCA, the Parti Gerakan Rakyat, the MIC, or the People's Progressive Party, have failed to show any sign of revival. This means that the BN is becoming more and more synonymous with UMNO. The unique system of representation through race-parties that the Alliance, and then the BN, owes for its success in the past is therefore badly corroded. For now, what the BN seems able to manage to do is hold its positions. No advancements have been obvious since 8 March 2008.

In the 1950s, colonialism (western influence falling like a pack of cards, with India, Indonesia, and China leading the way), communism (local effects of the global Cold War), communalism (race-based consociationalism and language use) and constitutionalism (elections and the Reid Commission) were the major issues that had to be handled in preparation for independence.

In the 1960s, the Confrontation with Indonesia and the Federation of Malaysia formed with Singapore, Sabah, and Sarawak were major political concerns. After 1969, the NEP changed the whole equation and heightened ethnic consciousness even further. Islamization was, in many ways, a function of the racial divide.

Politics in Malaysia in the near future is expected to involve dimensions such as the following: centralism versus federalism; creedism versus multiculturalism (1Malay versus 1Malaysia/Bangsa Malaysia); good governance and its links to economic growth; institutional corruption and degradation; rule of law versus power abuses; universal values vs ethnonational/national values; and social justice and welfare measures.

There is no doubt that Malaysia now has a two-coalition system, fuelled by the increasing urbanization of an ever younger Malay community. East Malaysian ethnographies and concerns are also playing a more significant role in federal discourses, along with civil society's growth in the wake of the return of opposition politics.

What seems most significant though is that new means of communication — Internet, SMS, Facebook, and Twitter — are changing how people communicate with each other, foreboding a return of debate culture and more lively journalism to Malaysia.

In more concrete terms, the continual budget deficits and the increasing national debt, along with the tendency to retain subsidies, spells ill for the country. Given the strong and sustained political contention from the opposition, the government has been tempted to make full use of the national budget in order to win votes. Even the Minister in the Prime Minister's Department, Idris Jala, has at least twice warned that the country could go bankrupt by 2019 if the deficits continue. This deviates tragically from the goal announced in 1990 by former Prime Minister Mahathir Mohamad that the country would reach advanced nation status by 2020 (*The Malaysian Insider*, 28 May 2010).

To an extent, a stand-off between the two political camps has been in place since 2008. As long as this situation remains, the government will try to reform as cautiously as possible without upsetting its core supporters. As long as it does that, the opposition can continue to sell itself as the champions of change. Shifts in support have been marginal, except in Johor state, and unless dramatic changes occur in general elections in the near future, Malaysia will remain unable to act decisively in making changes that the new global economic structure requires.

NOTE

1. Prime Minister Najib Razak repealed the Emergency Ordinance of 1969, as
   well as the Internal Security Act 1960 which was replaced with the Peaceful
   Assembly Act 2012. The University and University Colleges Act was also
   amended to allow students to participate in political activities.

REFERENCES

Goh Ban Lee. "The Demise of Local Government Elections and Urban Politics".
   In *Elections and Democracy in Malaysia*, edited by Mavis Puthucheary and
   Norani Othman. Bangi: Penerbit Universiti Kebangsaan Malaysia, 2005.
Harding, Andrew. *Law, Government and the Constitution in Malaysia*. Kuala
   Lumpur/The Hague: Malayan Law Journal/Kulwer Law International,
   1996.
Harper, T.N. *The End of Empire and the Making of Malaysia*. Cambridge
   University Press, 1999.
Kahin, George McTurnan. *Nationalism and Revolution in Indonesia*. Southeast
   Asia Programme Publications, Cornell University, 2003.
Laws of Malaysia — Federal Constitution. Kuala Lumpur: The Commissioner
   of Law Revision, Malaysia, 2006.
Lee, H.P. *Constitutional Conflicts in Contemporary Malaysia*. Kuala Lumpur: Oxford
   University Press, 1995.
Mahathir Mohamed. *The Malay Dilemma*. Petaling Jaya: Federal Publications,
   1970 (1981).
"Malaysia faces bankruptcy unless it...". *The Malaysian Insider*, 28 May 2010.
Means, Gordon P. *Malaysian Politics*. London: Hodder and Stoughton, 1970
   (1976).
Pua, Tony. *The Tiger that Lost Its Roar: A Tale of Malaysia's Political Economy*.
   Kuala Lumpur: Democratic Action Party, 2011.
Reid, Anthony. "The Birth of the Republic in Sumatra". In *Indonesia*, vol. 12.
   Cornell University: Southeast Asia Program Publications, 1971.
Tennant, Paul. "The Decline of Elective Local Government in Malaysia". *Asian
   Survey*, vol. 13, no. 4 (April 1973): 347–65.
The Federation of Malaya Agreement 1948. Kuala Lumpur: Government Press,
   1956.
Torii, Takashi. "The New Economic Policy and the United Malays National
   Organization — With Special Reference to the Restructuring of Malaysian
   Society". *In the Developing Economies*, vol. 35, issue 3 (September 1997):
   209–39.
Simandjuntak, B. *Malayan Federalism 1945–63*. A Study of Federal Problems in a
   Plural Society. Kuala Lumpur and Singapore: Oxford University Press, 1969.

Commentary 3

"New Politics" in Malaysia:
Towards Transformative Development?

Bridget Welsh

After the opposition in the March 2008 General Elections broke the two-thirds hold of the incumbent National Front (Barisan Nasional or BN) coalition had in parliament, the country has entered an era of "new politics". In parliament and on cyberspace, political discussions have blossomed. The opposition which took over the helm of four state governments gained an opportunity to showcase its governance. Pressure was placed on the BN, dominated by the United Malays National Organization (UMNO), to improve performance, and for the country's sixth Premier Najib Tun Razak, to win a political mandate nationally and within his own party. His political campaign has extended over three years, as all eyes have focused on the upcoming 13th General Elections which have to be held before June 2013. Simultaneously, politics have widened beyond the narrow political arena to extend to everyday events, from scandal revelations to tweeting debates. Civil society, in movements such as Bersih, have become active voices of change for reform. This intensive "new politics" from 2008 to 2012 — pluralism, more robust checks and balances, greater competition, more uncertainty and more political activity — are part of the broader political transformation taking place.

Few have looked at the development impact of Malaysia's contemporary political climate. Has "new politics" left an imprint, and, if so, what is it? Are there distinct patterns emerging in Malaysia's political economy in this period that will affect its development trajectory? While it is still early days, there are trends that have emerged that are changing Malaysia development approach since 2008, and, in the longer term, are likely to shape its future.

(1) Broadening of Economic Policy First of all, rising competition in Malaysia's politics has introduced a more substantive public discussion of economic policy. Open discussions are taking place over questions of subsidies, housing, transportation and government procurement,

among others. Noticeably, the discussion has moved away from a New Economic Policy-centred myopia.

The focal point on economic matters continues to be the annual budget, which has become more contentious with the presentation of alternative budgets. Politicians now openly analyse economic problems and solutions as part of their "normal" activities, such as the debates between UMNO Youth Chief Khairy Jamaluddin and Parti Keadilan Rakyat (PKR) leader Rafizi Ramli in 2012. While the discussions remain narrowly confined to political actors and range in quality, the broadening has made an impact: "new politics" has enlarged policy engagement.

(2) *Inequality Centre Stage*   Perhaps the most prominent arena where the discussion has widened is income inequality. The chapters in this book argue that inequality has moved from between ethnic groups to within ethnic communities. In Malaysia's era of "new politics", we have seen further evolution in the thinking over inequality, and the related issue of poverty. Politicians, especially from the opposition, are putting the issue of inequality back on the table, without using the ethnic lens. Drawing from reports by the World Bank on income disparities, attention has centred on the 53 per cent of households making under RM3,000. Inequality's political prominence has also brought to the fore regional disparities, notably the higher incidence of lower incomes in East Malaysia. Finally, the government itself has become more transparent and sanguine in its analysis of the household survey, publishing the *Household Incomes and Basic Amenities Survey Report* of 2009 that acknowledged the rising numbers of poverty and the reversal of Malaysia's impressive trend in poverty reduction. Inequality has come on the agenda in a different manner, reflecting growing sophistication of analysis as well as more open appreciation of the problem that not all Malaysians are benefitting currently.

(3) *Rise of Populist Policies*   With the greater focus on inequality, politicians have embraced populist solutions. The fact is that the majority of voters are in the lower income households. Responding to policies floated initially by the opposition, the BN government has opened the floodgate to be seen to redress the conditions of the disadvantaged. The classic example is the introduction of the cash transfer 1Malaysia People's Assistance Programme or BR1M, which distributed funds to 5.2 million households in 2011–12.

This practice of politicians trying to be "popular" is not uncommon, but what distinguishes the form that has evolved in post-2008 Malaysia is that there is competition between the different players to outdo the other in the distributive initiatives. Car prices, senior citizen benefits, scholarships, and recently smart phone offers are all aimed at wooing support for the next polls. This is as much a reflection of political insecurity as it is uncertainty. There is also a distinct move away from vulnerable communities towards "politically vulnerable" communities, as concerns with safety nets and livelihood sustainability have been ignored.

(4) "Look East" Policy   The populist wooing has led to a new trajectory in policy focus, greater inclusion of East Malaysia development in national discussions. In the 1980s, Dr Mahathir announced a Look East Policy centred on following the example of East Asian countries, especially Japan. Post-2008, political competition has evoked a domestic Look East variant, where consideration of the resource rents (the share of oil royalty), customary land rights, infrastructural development and transitions outside of natural resource economies have taken on national prominence. The reason is simple — these are the fixed deposit seats. Over a third of the BN is from Sabah and Sarawak and there has been an concerted effort to weaken the BN hold in these states, from the September 16th projection of a new government in 2008 to the more recent former-BN MPs to the opposition.

Beyond politics, the East Malaysian states have brought home the development challenges Malaysia is facing to move toward new sources of economic growth beyond natural resources, to generate jobs with decent salaries and to improve the provision of services. More Malaysians are now aware of the unique circumstances of these states, but also empathize with the commonalities in their experiences, notably a heavy dependence on a narrow range of commodities and oil and gas revenue.

(5) Development as Cash Transfers   The harder questions have only started to be asked. One of the implications of Malaysia's greater populism is that an increasing share of the development budget is being allocated to cash transfers, more than half of the 2013 development budget for example. The debate on these programmes in the development community varies, but there is consensus that these measures are not sustainable and are best used in post-emergency

measures. Since 2008, the Najib administration has used these initiatives to such a degree that they have become the norm and dominant mode of his development policy.

The political dimension to these payouts is clear as they are carefully calibrated and targeted. Internationally, the consensus is that development should not be tied directly to political support, but this is a dominant theme in Malaysian politics. The regime relies heavily on its development record for support. They have long procured the view that the people should be "grateful" to the government for doing its job.

There are additional concerns with cash transfers. No attention has been paid to the context where funds are being allocated. Are the funds being spent on value-added items that generate better quality of life for families or are they being blown on unnecessary consumables? The early evidence of BR1M suggests that much of the funds were quickly dispersed to pay outstanding debts or make purchases on non-necessary items. There has not been carefully monitoring of these transfers and this lack of monitoring suggests that little interest has been placed on how the funds actually improve conditions for families.

There is another side-effect — the reinforcement of dependence on government. Malaysia already has a long tradition of public sector allocations, entrenched in the New Economic Policy from the 1970s. The contemporary cash transfers deepen the sense of entitlement, as they have not been accompanied by supporting initiatives to generate jobs and raise incomes. One-off assistance is shallow and practised long-term, harmful. Cash transfers appear to be part of a political post-2008 emergency rather than a coherent development strategy focused on addressing welfare.

(5) Missing the Money   The use of cash transfers should be seen in the context of concerns about the pattern of government spending. The country has engaged in deficit spending for fifteen years, since the onset of the Asian financial crisis of 1997–98 and resulting political challenge to Dr Mahathir. While the federal deficit in 2013 is estimated at 4 per cent of GDP, the overall public deficit is much higher at 10.5 per cent of GDP. This excludes additional contingent liabilities. The high spending on the cash transfers only serves to enhance the larger fiscal challenges, particularly since Malaysia has a narrow tax base.

Malaysia has also faced the problem of capital flight after 2008, directly tied to the political unknowns. In the last year there has been a disinvestment from government-linked stocks. The trend has been accompanied by a decline in investment into Malaysia, where the country does not compare well with regional neighbours such as Indonesia, Singapore or Thailand. Individual states, such as Penang, have bucked this trend, but there appears to be a shortfall of money coming into the country. The FDI has not responded to the incentives provided, in part because there has been a lack of substantive reforms in public sector spending. The political uncertainty is a contributing factor.

This is enhanced by the challenges of human development, where there are missing people who are part of Malaysia's brain drain. Over 1 million have left the country, many of the most talented. Malaysia faces the challenge of providing skill sets to business, shaped in part by the limitations on its education sector.

Towards Development?

Malaysia's leadership has used the framework of transformation in its Economic Transformation Programme (ETP). Yet, the political conditions for genuine transformation are not yet present. While Malaysia's "new policies" has brought to the fore more breadth in the discussion of economic policy, moved it out of its focus on the NEP, drew attention to East Malaysia and put inequality centre-stage, the policies adopted to address development have been blinded by a narrow political focus. They are short-term and if repeated create conditions within the public sector and in society for making genuinely transformative development harder to achieve.

Longer term, substantive reforms are crucial. There is a need to move Malaysia's financial dependence on resource rents towards a more diverse revenue base. There is also a need to harness and hone human capital domestically. And finally, there is a need to reduce the state's involvement in the economy towards sustainable growth, while involving the more vibrant domestic private sector with greater opportunities for all Malaysians.

12

MALAYSIA'S FEDERAL SYSTEM: STIFLING LOCAL INITIATIVE?

Francis E. Hutchinson

The Malaysian state is usually portrayed as centralized, top-heavy, and far-reaching. Bureaucrats in the powerful Prime Minister's Office or Economic Planning Unit design ambitious programmes for the country, then government agencies headquartered in the nation's capital implement them in all corners of Malaysia, from Perlis to Sabah.

While true to a certain extent, this depiction overlooks the fact that Malaysia has a federal government structure. In addition to a central government centred in Putrajaya, the country has thirteen state governments that are responsible for particular jurisdictions; receive revenue from specific sources; and have constitutionally-stipulated responsibilities. They are important providers of goods and services, and can play a role in creating an enabling environment for business.

However, Malaysia's governance structure is heavily weighted towards the federal government, which receives the bulk of revenue and is responsible for most public services. In fact, the country is one of the world's most centralized federations, with the centre receiving almost 90 per cent of all government revenue. And, above and beyond duties for fiscal, monetary, and trade policy, the federal government is responsible for most types of infrastructure, science and technology policy, and all levels of education.

While the image of a strong central state may hold appeal, an excessive concentration of responsibilities may not always be optimal. Public finance literature holds that an appropriate attribution of responsibilities and revenue sources between levels of government can enhance welfare. For example, while some services benefit from economies of scale and are best provided nationally, others require detailed knowledge of local conditions and are best supplied locally.

Over the past thirty years, a "Silent Revolution" of decentralization has swept the globe, as sub-national governments have been empowered with additional responsibilities, autonomy, and revenue. However, Malaysia constitutes an important exception. Unlike neighbouring Philippines or Indonesia, that had to construct new levels of government to decentralize, it already has an established federal system.

Despite this, Malaysia has continued to centralize responsibilities at the national level. If it continues, this trend will stifle the vital role that state governments can play in creating an enabling environment for business and leveraging local-level knowledge to foster economic growth. While not overly glamorous, their responsibilities for the provision of local services and investor liaison — as well as their ability to read the local economic context and make strategic investments to diminish risk in new sectors — are vital over the long term.

This chapter is comprised of five sections. Following this introduction, the next section will briefly review theories of federalism and the role they attribute to sub-national governments, particularly with regard to economic policy. The third section will look at how Malaysia's federal system was designed and why it is so heavily oriented towards the centre. Drawing on the cases of two of Malaysia's most industrialized states, the fourth section will look at whether state governments can still play a role in fostering economic growth within their jurisdictions. The final section will advance some proposals for preserving the country's federal system.

Federalism

The aim of federal systems of government is to combine the centralized management of national issues with some element of self-rule among a country's constituent units, such as states or provinces. According to Bednar, the formal criteria for forming a federation are having constitutionally-recognized: territorially-exclusive constituent units; independent sources of authority for both federal and state governments; and policy sovereignty for each level of government.[1]

However, beyond these stipulations, federal systems vary widely in how they distribute revenue sources and responsibilities between central and provincial or state-level governments. The optimal media will vary between countries, as the central and local provision of services offer different advantages.

Fiscal federalism literature argues that responsibilities for service provision should be apportioned according to whether their benefits will be felt at the national or local level. For example, public goods associated with economic and political stability and sovereignty are felt at the national level, and are therefore best provided by the central government. Conversely, those goods and services that provide localized benefits are best provided by sub-national governments. This is because the level of government closest to end-users will have more information on their needs and the optimal combination of services and taxes for that jurisdiction.[2] Similarly, with regard to revenue, the centre should be attributed sources that are generalized in nature, such as income from tariffs, or distributive, such as income tax, as they can be implemented nationally. Conversely, states should receive income from production and consumption, which are localized.[3]

Above and beyond this dynamic, there are a number of reasons that argue in favour of a substantial role for state or provincial governments.

First, sub-national governments are subject to the disciplines of the market-place to a greater degree than their national counterparts. Tiebout argues that, assuming perfect information, citizens and firms compare the tax burdens and service delivery options of their constituency with others. They will then "vote with their feet" for the most beneficial combination of services and taxes. This competition between sub-national units will improve distributive efficiency as they will be subject to quasi-market pressures, and public goods and services will be parcelled out according to local needs and preferences.[4]

Second, the relative costs and benefits of services provided by sub-national governments are more visible to end-users, and citizens are also better positioned to monitor government performance and ensure the effective delivery of services. Furthermore, government officials at the sub-national level will have more direct incentives to perform due to their proximity to end-users.[5]

Third, while technological changes have heightened competition and made investments more mobile, economic activity, particularly the knowledge-intensive variety, remains very sensitive to geography and its local institutional contexts. This is because firms do not develop new products and processes in isolation, but rather through contact and communication with other firms, as well as research institutes, technology centres, capital providers, and government agencies. Furthermore, they are also affected by local norms and traditions regarding inter-firm relations, acceptable business practices, and perceptions of quality. Because of their deeper knowledge of the local environment and their proximity to local firms, sub-national governments are in a unique position to shape and mould the institutional context in a way that supports economic activity.[6]

Fourth, greater knowledge of the local environment and more freedom in policy-making can enable policy-makers to more easily tailor measures to leverage their state's comparative advantage. This can enable states or provinces to specialize in producing certain goods and services, which in turn can result in a more diversified and stable national economy.[7]

Because of these reasons, national governments have sought to devolve responsibilities to lower levels of government. In some cases, this has been through the introduction of decentralization measures, as in the case of the Philippines and Indonesia. In others, such as India, it has been through a generalized "rolling back" of national-level regulatory frameworks that has allowed sub-national governments to move in. In still other cases, such as China, provincial or state-level governments were given financial incentives for achieving higher growth rates in their jurisdictions.[8]

Malaysia's Federal System

As mentioned, Malaysia is a centralized federation, with responsibilities and revenue sources geared strongly towards the federal government. In fact, the country has been described as having "a centralized unitary system with federal features".[9]

However, when viewed from a historical perspective, the central government is actually the newest aspect of Malaysia's governance system. Constructed in the aftermath of the Second World War and in the run-up to independence in 1957, the new nation and its federal government brought together a varied group of political units — including some that had been in existence for centuries.[10]

While these different political units or "mini-states" had a range of attributes and leadership structures, it was in these smaller governments that Malaysia's founding fathers earned the administrative experience that enabled them to helm the country's transition to Merdeka. For example, Tunku Abdul Rahman, Malaya's first Prime Minister, was a district officer in Kedah's government. Onn Jaafar, the founder of UMNO, was a district officer and then Mentri Besar of Johor. Tun Abdul Razak, the second Prime Minister, was state secretary of the government of Pahang.[11]

Given this historical antecedent, it is worth asking why the federation that emerged was so centralized. This is because the structure of the emerging central government was influenced by British interests, nationalist aims, and pre-existing political institutions. The British and the emerging Malay nationalist elite desired a strong central government to drive economic development and to handle the Emergency.[12] However, the sultans at the head of nine states were politically important and commanded widespread support among the Malay population — and many of the nationalist elite were themselves members of the aristocracy.[13]

As a result, after considerable bargaining, the body charged with drafting Malaya's constitution, the Reid Commission, was tasked with providing for "a strong central government with states and settlements enjoying a measure of autonomy".[14] Under this arrangement, sultans and state governments were retained as part of Malaya's governance structure, but with responsibilities restricted to land and religious matters.

In 1963, the federation was subsequently enlarged with the incorporation of Singapore, Sarawak, and Sabah, and its name was altered to become Malaysia. In recognition of their different economic structures and desire for greater autonomy, these states were given additional revenues and responsibilities. While Singapore's association with the Federation ended in 1965, Sabah and Sarawak have remained in it and retain a slightly wider set of responsibilities and revenue sources than their counterparts on the peninsula.

Due to the particular historical context within which the Federation of Malaysia was formed, it has a number of structural tensions.

The first is the disproportionate share of responsibilities attributed to the federal government. Beyond the responsibilities for external affairs, defence, and finance, the Constitution attributes to the centre aspects such as: internal security; trade, commerce, and industry; most types of infrastructure; transport; health and medicine; as well as education at all levels. For their part, state governments are responsible for: land management; agriculture and forestry; and local government and services (such as maintenance of smaller roads, licencing of establishments, and managing market-places). Housing, as well as town and country planning are listed as shared responsibilities.[15]

It is worth asking whether the centralized provision of so many public services is optimal. It is hard to argue that policy-makers in Putrajaya are in the best position to ascertain efficient bus routes in Penang, or that urban planning in Seremban needs to be carried out jointly with the federal government. These are tasks that require considerable local-level knowledge and social capital with end-users to be carried out effectively.

The second tension relates to financing. The Constitution attributes the bulk of revenue sources to the federal government, including taxes on income, capital gains, and consumption, as well as tariffs. Thus, over the 2000–04 period, the centre received 86 per cent of total government revenue before inter-governmental transfers, making Malaysia one of the most heavily centralized federations in fiscal terms in the world.[16] To put things in perspective, the budget for the Prime Minister's Office alone is more than ten times the budget of the entire Penang state government.[17]

In contrast, state governments are dependent on smaller, less flexible revenue sources such as those accruing from land, forestry and mines, as well as entertainment. State governments can create subsidiaries that operate on a for-profit basis, the proceeds of which can be used to cross-subsidize other activities. Beyond this, the Constitution stipulates that states receive a series of federal grants, including two pegged to their population and road network, among others. However, state governments are subject to a hard budget constraint as they are forbidden from imposing taxes or taking out loans without federal government approval.[18]

This gives rise to two issues. First, the preponderance of revenue from inflexible resources such as timber, tin, and oil, means that states have differing levels of income based on their natural endowments. Second, the relative paucity of revenue sources means that state governments have become increasingly reliant on federal transfers to remain solvent. Initially this comprised grants but, over time, has come to increasingly consist of loans, compromising the autonomy of states.[19]

In some cases, state governments have opted to cede relatively expensive aspects of public services such as water infrastructure to the federal government.

In addition, central control over the allocation of resources is increased by two additional mechanisms. First, the National Finance Council has the mandate to coordinate financial relations between the centre and the states. The Council is comprised of the Prime Minister, federal ministers he appoints, and a representative from each state. However, the Council's recommendations are not binding, as ultimate responsibility regarding revisions rests in the hands of the Prime Minister.[20]

Second, the federal government is responsible for development planning. While state governments do provide inputs and make requests, the central government ultimately decides how the allocation of big-ticket infrastructure items — such as highways, bridges, ports, and airports — should be apportioned between states.[21] The capital intensity of these investments is very high, making the federal government the prime economic actor at the state level. For example, over the 1985–99 period, federal government development expenditure was 4.5 times the expenditure of all state governments put together.[22]

The third tension relates to the balance of power between federal and state governments. A number of articles in the Constitution enable the federal government to over-ride state-level policies in certain circumstances. For example, the centre can, even in domains attributed to the states, intervene in the "national interest" or ensure "uniformity of laws". And, despite land being a state government prerogative, the central government can acquire state land for national programmes. Furthermore, if a state of emergency is declared, the central government has free hand to make laws at the state level — which has been used twice.[23]

In addition, there are no real safeguards to protect state rights from being further eroded through amendments to the Constitution. Depending on the nature of the amendment, a simple majority or two-thirds majority in both houses of parliament is necessary.[24] However, no mechanisms for doing the same are available to states. In addition, the Senate (Dewan Negara) is meant to act as a check on the lower house. The original allocation of seats, which are appointive, had a majority allocated to representatives named by the states. However, it is now comprised of a majority of representatives appointed by the King upon the recommendation of the Prime Minister. At present, states nominate 26 senators and the centre, 44.[25]

Despite the design of Malaysia's federal system being very centralized at its inception, revenue sources and responsibilities have continued to gravitate to the national level over the past decades, regardless of the implications for effective service delivery. Facilitated by the structural imbalances outlined above, this has been driven by Malaysia's political dynamics.

The foremost political dynamic is the long-running dominance of the current ruling coalition, Barisan Nasional, at both the federal and state level. Within the coalition, a disproportionate amount of power is held by its largest member, the United Malays National Organization (UMNO). Despite having fourteen constituent members, Barisan Nasional has been very successful at preserving internal cohesion, enabling consultation yet diluting the ability of smaller members to bargain for concession.[26]

While both levels of government theoretically have sovereign control over responsibilities that are uniquely attributed to them, party hierarchy linking central and state leaders means this line is blurred.[27] For example, Barisan Nasional leaders at the national level approve the candidates of coalition members at the state level. And, with a few exceptions, Chief Ministers and Mentris Besar are UMNO party members. Where this is the case, UMNO can use party discipline to ensure central directives are followed.[28]

The Role of State Governments

Given the overwhelming role attributed to the federal government in Malaysia, it is worth asking whether state governments retain any relevance. An analysis of the practical implications of their responsibilities as well as available empirical evidence suggests that state governments can and do play a fundamental role, particularly insofar as fostering economic growth within their jurisdictions. By delivering local government services effectively, addressing market failures, and diminishing risk for investments in new sectors, state governments play a key role in moulding the everyday environment in which firms work. The next paragraphs will illustrate these points, where appropriate, with practical examples from Penang and Johor, two of Malaysia's most dynamic and industrialized states.

Despite the creation of a National Land Council to harmonize policy, state governments still retain responsibility for land issues at an operational level, handling matters such as land law, as well as the acquisition and alienation of land for private or public use.[29] State governments have thus emerged as important real estate players, controlling sizeable land banks for industrial and commercial use. These attributes have also made state governments well-placed to assume investor liaison and marketing functions, which they have through the establishment of specialized agencies and promotion bodies. In addition, the complexities involved in mastering thirteen different legal frameworks relating to land has made federal government agencies, such as the Malaysian Industrial Development Authority, reluctant to assume control over investment liaison functions related to real estate.[30]

The Constitution also attributes the responsibility for local governments and the provision of local public services to state governments. In addition to maintaining roads, drains, and lighting, this involves issues such as land zoning, and approving building permissions, business licences, and certificates of safety for commercial premises.[31]

Furthermore, state governments are important consumers in the local economy. Above and beyond directly employing significant numbers of workers, they also generate substantial demand for goods and services. Through decisions to undertake public works projects directly or through sub-contracting, fund public services such as bus services or welfare programmes, and have open and transparent procurement policies, state governments can substantially shape the local environment for business.[32] For example, upon assuming power in 2008, the new administration in Penang decreed the use of an open tender system for all state government procurement. Over two-and-a-half years, just one state body, the Penang Development Corporation, awarded more than RM260 million to local contractors under this new system.[33]

Thus, through their responsibilities for land issues and local government services, state governments can influence the operating environment within which firms operate. In addition, they are also responsible for the local regulatory environment that is crucial for business, particularly at start-up. However, state governments can also affect the context for business in more far-reaching ways.

In the late 1960s and early 1970s, state economic development corporations (SEDCs) were set up across Malaysia. Inspired by Singapore's Economic Development Board, the federal government set up these organizations with a remit to promote industrialization and entrepreneurship at the local level.[34] The SEDCs were originally under the exclusive control of state governments but, after 1974, were supervised by the federal Ministry of Public Enterprises.[35] However, state governments retained more influence over the day-to-day activities of these corporations as chairmanship of the board of directors was retained by the Chief Minister or Mentri Besar of each state.

Capitalizing on their prerogative to alienate land and then sell it, the SEDCs used the proceeds to cross-subsidize investments in new areas or to implement market-complementing measures. Some state governments used this capital to diversify their economies through diminishing risk for investors seeking to move into new sectors. Others, in comparison, sought to accumulate assets directly, often focusing on short-term and more profitable activities.

An indication of the extent to which the business environment can be shaped by these measures is shown by Tables 12.1 and 12.2, which set out the results of a survey conducted among more than 110 local and international firms operating in the electronics sector in Penang and Johor. Carried out in 2001, the results provide an illustrative, if somewhat dated, snapshot of the operating environment for the electronics sector — an export-oriented sector with demanding requirements for efficiency and the constant acquisition of new technological capabilities, and thus one acutely responsive to its surrounding context.[36]

Table 12.1 shows the ratings on a Likert scale by the firms of a range of public goods and services provided by the federal government. Overall, the scores range between 2 and 3.5 on the scale, indicating a moderate level of service provision. A notable exception is venture capital, which was rated very poorly in both states, perhaps reflecting the traditional concentration of finance in Kuala Lumpur. With regard to the two states, the ratings for Penang tend to be slightly higher than those for Johor. However, with two exceptions, the disparities are less than 0.5 of a point. Thus, the federal provision of services such as secondary education, education, security, telecommunications, and R&D incentives is largely the same in the two states.

TABLE 12.1
Ratings of the Business Environment in Penang and Johor, 2001
(Federal Government-related Responsibilities)

	Foreign		Local	
	Johor	Penang	Johor	Penang
Secondary school	2.98	3.11	2.77	2.86
Health care	3.11	3.15	3.19	3.17
Security	2.75	3.12	2.98	3.25
Telecommunications	3.23	3.17	3.05	3.47
Customs	3.12	3.95	2.81	3.12
Transport	2.21	3.87	2.11	3.45
R&D incentives	2.45	2.55	2.11	2.57
Venture capital	1.55	1.87	1.88	2.11

Source: Extracted from UNU-MERIT, WB, DFID Survey (2004) in Rasiah (2008), pp. 140, 143, N=113.

However, transport and customs stand out as areas where the business environment differs significantly between the two states. With regard to transport, both local and foreign firms rated Penang more highly. This could be due to the state's larger and more well-connected airport. In contrast, Johor's airport has found it hard to attract international carriers, particularly given the proximity of Singapore's Changi airport. Foreign firms also took issue with the quality of customs services in Johor relative to Penang. This could be because Johor functions as a gateway to Peninsular Malaysia from Singapore, resulting in larger bottlenecks and delays.[37] However, Penang acts as a conduit only for the northern region of the country, entailing a lower volume of traffic.

These two issues notwithstanding, the context for business insofar as federally-provided public goods and services are concerned is quite similar in the two states. However, when those aspects of the business environment that map more closely onto state-level responsibilities are scrutinized, the picture changes notably. While the overall scores tend to remain in the middle, the gap between the two states widens notably in Penang's favour with all rankings, bar one, higher by more than half a point. The following paragraphs will explore state government policies as they relate to these rubrics.

TABLE 12.2
Ratings of the Business Environment in Penang and Johor, 2001
(State Government-related Responsibilities)

	Foreign		Local	
	Johor	Penang	Johor	Penang
State development authority	2.35	3.57	2.11	2.63
Training institutions	2.01	3.98	2.15	3.33
Supply of skilled labour	1.67	2.25	1.55	2.01
Industry associations	2.17	3.67	2.05	3.25

Source: Extracted from UNU-MERIT, WB, DFID Survey (2004) in Rasiah (2008), pp. 140, 143, N=113.

State Development Authority

Firms in Penang, particularly foreign ones, gave their state development authority a substantially higher rating than did those in Johor. This is most likely reflective of the different approaches taken by the two governments to promote growth.

From 1970 onwards, the Penang state government moved aggressively to promote manufacturing. Perceiving the opportunities offered by the internationalization of the electronics sector, it embarked on an aggressive marketing drive, targeting small US-based firms. Through its SEDC, it moved to provide infrastructure for investors, including industrial parks, land, and low-cost housing. It also pioneered the building of free trade zones in Malaysia, setting up the first in the country in 1972. The state government invested substantial amounts in a variety of start-ups, including ship-building, food-processing, textiles, electronics, and high quality glass fabrication.[38] Some of these worked, and others failed, but in key cases, these strategic investments served to diminish risk in new sectors. For example, the first electronics firm in the state was not a multinational, but one owned by the state government.[39] This, along with the state government's commitment to meeting international investors' needs, was key in attracting the first flagship firms.[40]

In the 1980s, the state government focused its energies on the most successful manufacturing subsectors that had emerged, making strategic investments in more technology-intensive operations, such as precision engineering and biotechnology. In addition, Penang's SEDC acted as an intermediary between multinational corporations and local firms, seeking to encourage subcontracting and technology transfer. It also moved to boost local capabilities through establishing a training institute and clinic for local firms. In the 1990s, the state government changed focus again towards supporting sectors for manufacturing such as logistics, and on fostering the growth of its private education sector in order to deepen its skill base.[41]

Relative to its counterpart in Johor, the Penang SEDC maintained a much smaller portfolio of firms, geared more to opening up new sectors as opposed to accumulating assets. In 2002, the Penang SEDC had an investment portfolio worth RM266 million, with investments in 57 firms in addition to shares in 11 publicly-listed firms.[42]

Part of the organization's effectiveness may have lain in the state government's participatory planning processes. The state government's three development plans have had substantial input from prominent industrialists as well as the local academic community.[43] In addition, the state government institutionalized a series of committees with the "captains" of industry, such as the Penang Economic Council (1991–93), Penang Industrial Council (1993–99), and Penang Competitiveness Committee (2002). That said, the membership of these councils was comprised of larger firms, and the state government has been criticized for neglecting the needs of smaller firms — which is reflected in the lower ratings given to the state development authority by local firms.

Johor, for its part, has also pursued an ambitious strategy. Upon its inception, the Johor SEDC was given primary responsibility for developing the state's land bank and generating revenue. In line with its mandate, it acquired private land and converted it for industrial use. Its business model with regard to potential investors was based on offering land in attractive locations accompanied by streamlined business processes, rather than using low cost as an incentive to attract investment.[44] The profits from this were used to cross-subsidize a range of strategic investments in new sectors.[45]

This focus, along with sizeable oil palm plantations and a highly leveraged growth strategy, initially worked well, allowing the SEDC to expand rapidly. By 1996, the Johor SEDC was at the heart of a conglomerate with 19 divisions, assets worth RM7.4 billion, a turnover of RM2.83 billion, and 4 firms listed on the Kuala Lumpur stock exchange. It attempted to directly attain market leadership in the oil palm, restaurant, healthcare, and hospitality sectors.[46]

However, the Johor SEDC was hard hit by the 1997/98 financial crisis, losing RM680 million in 1997 and a further RM630 million the following year. In 1998, its total debt reached RM10 billion, and it had to liquidate 35 subsidiaries and request federal government's help to restructure its debt. Following this, it closed a number of its divisions, sold many offshore holdings, and re-focused its energies on a reduced set of sectors.[47] At present, there are discussions about divesting some of the conglomerate's assets to pay off an estimated RM6.6 billion in debt.[48]

At present, the SEDC is focused on the agriculture, property development, healthcare, and hospitality sectors. It remains a major player in the state's economy with a stable of more than 280 firms, including 8 companies listed on the Kuala Lumpur Stock Exchange, and 65,000 employees in Malaysia and overseas. However, none of these initiatives have targeted either the electronics sector or any of its downstream activities. This is despite state government plans to foster excellence in the electronics sector, as well as supporting industries such as automation and precision engineering.[49]

Regarding planning processes, Johor's have tended to be state-led, with emphasis placed on investments in infrastructure, accumulation of assets, and state initiatives to address perceived policy needs. In addition, these plans have not been carried out by local stakeholders, but have been sub-contracted to professional consulting firms outside the state.[50]

Training Provision

This different focus also permeated through other aspects of state government activity, as is seen in the two governments' approaches to training provision. The Penang state government was an early innovator in the area of adult education and workforce training. During the 1980s, the state government became aware of emerging skills shortages in the manufacturing sector. After consultation with the private sector, it established the Penang Skills Development Centre (PSDC) in 1989 with a mandate to provide technical training to high school graduates, unemployed degree-holders, and the existing workforce in the electronics industry.

The PSDC is industry-driven, as partner organizations — which are largely comprised of electronics firms — manage the organization. Under this model, client companies pool their resources, including equipment, to provide training on industry-specific issues. Over the 1989–2000 period, the Centre carried out 4,000 training courses for 75,000 students.[51] Based on the PSDC's success, skills development centres have subsequently been set up in other states in Malaysia, and the Centre's model has also been replicated in other countries. By late 2010, the PSDC had trained some 150,000 people.[52]

Following Penang's example, Johor established its own skills development centre (JSDC) in 1993. Over the past eighteen years, the JSDC has trained some 35,000 workers in a range of industry-relevant courses. However, the Centre has not managed to reach the same level of quality instruction or communication with industry.[53] It has a more reduced set of programmes, which are less technically sophisticated and focus more on heavy industry. A key difference from its Penang counterpart is that it is not industry-led or managed, and thus has more difficulty ensuring constant input from the private sector regarding the curriculum.

The Johor SEDC, for its part, has two subsidiaries, the Entrepreneurial Development Unit and the Institute of Management Development, both of which are geared to providing a range of technical and managerial courses. However, they are limited to Bumiputeras, thus excluding the majority of the manufacturing sector, which is estimated to be 80 per cent non-Malay.[54]

Skilled Labour

University education is a federal government responsibility. However, federal policies regarding university education have favoured Johor over Penang, thus strongly suggesting that it has been state government policies in the latter that have boosted its ratings.

Regarding federal policies, Johor houses two federally-funded technology universities, both with a special emphasis on engineering — a crucial human resource for the electronics sector. This includes the Universiti Teknologi Malaysia, which is the oldest and most prestigious public institution for engineering in the country.[55] In contrast, Penang has only one university, whose disciplinary focus centres on science, particularly pharmaceutical studies.[56] Of crucial importance, the university's engineering department was actually located in another state until 2001.[57]

With regard to local initiative, the state government of Penang has taken a proactive role in encouraging the development of education. In 1997, it established a coordination body, the Penang Education Consultative Council: to monitor the growth of the sector, promote the state as a centre for education, and attempt to ensure that private institutions are of acceptable quality.[58] In addition, the Penang SEDC has emerged as an important player in the private education sector, investing in two of the state's highest quality private colleges offering engineering courses.[59] The Penang Skills Development Centre is also very active in the higher education sector. It offers its students a range of diploma programmes in technical subjects that can be built on to pursue undergraduate or master's degrees in eighteen partner universities in

Malaysia, Australia, Ireland and the United Kingdom.[60] More recently, in 2006, the then-ruling party at the state level established one of only two open universities in Malaysia, Wawasan Open University, which focuses on technology and business administration.

State government activity in this sector in Johor has been less developed, even in recent years. The Johor state government has funded the creation of an Industrial Technology Institute which provides: diplomas in a range of engineering disciplines in conjunction with the Technology University; as well as a number of qualifications of a vocational nature.[61] The links with the local university are promising; however, there is little evidence of industry input into the curriculum or choice of courses. The Johor Skills Development Centre, for its part, offers diploma programmes that can be transferred to one local university with which there is no formal agreement. The Johor SEDC has a College of Nursing and Health Science, with campuses in Kuala Lumpur and Johor Bahru.[62]

Industry Associations

The situation regarding industry associations is also different in the two locations. Malaysia has a range of well-established country-wide business associations such as the ethnic chambers of commerce and the Federation of Malaysian Manufacturers. However, Penang's more private-sector focused approach has fostered the development of a range of industry associations, with potentially positive effects for inter-firm linkages and collective learning. In contrast, the emergence of industry associations is still in its infancy in Johor.

Penang's most well-known industry association is FREPENCA (The Free Industrial Zone, Penang, Companies' Association), which is comprised of some sixty multinationals and large local firms who collectively employ some 60,000 people.[63] Established in 1978 by some of the first electronics firms in the state, FREPENCA has been a crucial mechanism through which the state government has been able to communicate with the private sector. In addition to generating valuable feedback and statistics on investment trends and policy needs, the association has also worked with the state government to address issues such as security, transport, infrastructure, and labour.[64]

Other business associations in Penang's ecosystem include the Small and Medium Enterprises Association (SAMENTA), whose membership is comprised of some 200 firms in the manufacturing and services sector, and the Penang Foundry and Engineering Industries Association (PENFEIA) which also has some 200 members in the foundry and engineering sectors.[65]

In recent years, the state government has taken this further. Over the 2005–07 period, it established the Radio Frequency Cluster, the Software Consortium of Penang (SCoPe), the Penang Automation Cluster (PAC), and Techbiz, a cluster for Bumiputera businessmen in the ICT sector. These clusters were created with the aim of generating contacts and synergy between firm owners, as well as serving as a collective means of marketing Penang talent to MNCs. Some of these consortia, such as SCoPe, are very active and organize a range of technical and promotion events.[66] The consortia have been good mechanisms for member firms to articulate their concerns and exchange industry information. That said, interest from MNCs has been limited, and attempts at creating collaborative relations has not met with much success due to the fact that many members are, in fact, competitors.[67] Notwithstanding this, these organizations do enable the state to market specific capabilities, and provide a forum for industry-specific issues to be identified.

Given its focus on the acquisition of assets, the Johor state government has had less interface with the private sector, particularly in manufacturing. Actually, rather than seeking to communicate with the established private sector, the SEDC has been attempting to encourage the emergence of new entrepreneurs. Thus, it established the Johor Business and Industry Club (BISTARI) in 1991 for Bumiputeras to meet and exchange ideas, accompanied by a business centre with information on how to start-up businesses. In 2001, this was complemented by the Malaysian Islamic Chamber of Commerce.[68] While these initiatives are promising, neither the Johor state government or its SEDC have established mechanisms for reaching out to the segments of the local manufacturing sector that are not Malay.

The most promising instance of dialogue and cooperation for firms in the manufacturing sector has emerged organically. The SME Association of South Johor was established in 2001, and has 500 members from the southern part of the state in a range of sectors, including E&E. Its goals are to give SMEs a bigger voice, make linkages between the government and the private sector, and bolster capabilities through providing information. The association holds training sessions in English and Chinese on government grants and loans, marketing techniques, and accounting techniques. In addition, its President is an adviser for the Johor State Government's training institute, the Johor Skills Development Centre.[69]

However, for much of the manufacturing sector in Johor, there has been a feeling that communicating and articulating the private sector's issues need to be improved. For example, a 2006 survey found that 89 per cent of respondents supported the establishment of an electronics cluster association with the aim of articulating issues facing the sector as a whole.[70]

Thus, despite increasing centralization, state governments can and do play an important role in the country's economy. While all firm-owners would like more highways and international flight connections, it is quite likely that the problems they face on a daily basis are about more mundane matters. This includes securing reliable and reasonably-priced land, obtaining permits quickly, meeting new clients, or accessing information on market and technological trends. These issues are particularly important for smaller firms, who have limited in-house capabilities and are more affected by the surrounding environment than large companies or multinational corporations.

Conclusion

Despite a structural bias towards — and a subsequent concentration of power in — the centre, Malaysia is blessed with a federal system. In a context where countries around the region are seeking to benefit from a more decentralized system of administration, Malaysia already has a federal system where state governments can and do play a significant role. Through managing land, facilitating investment, formulating local-level economic plans, and making strategic investments in new sectors, state governments can mould the local institutional environment in important ways.

However, looking forward, current national plans do not bode well for the health of federalism in the country. Policy frameworks such as the Tenth Malaysia Plan, New Economic Model, and Economic Transformation Programme have the potential to further undercut the effective functioning of state governments. The establishment of economic corridors, which are federally appointed regulatory agencies to facilitate investment outside the Klang Valley, cut across state boundaries and intrude on areas of established competence of state governments. In addition, the stated policy of further federal control over public services such as water and solid waste management also reduces the sphere of influence that sub-national governments have.[71]

Given what is known about the effective functioning of federal systems, it is likely that Malaysia will reap decreasing returns in terms of productivity and efficiency, should it proceed to centralize further. Thus, rather than seeking to further reduce the room for manoeuvre of state governments, Malaysia may well gain more from revitalizing them.

The most effective means of revitalizing initiative at the state level is to increase the incentives for performance. At present, rankings of investor inflows to each state are published yearly, but current fiscal arrangements mean this has no impact on centre-state transfers. Thus, state governments have no direct incentive to engage in their investor liaison roles. In contrast, in India, state governments derive more than half of their total revenues from sales taxes generated in their jurisdiction.[72] Revenue of this type is relatively stable, generated locally, and is influenced by investment inflows. Alternatively, incentives could be linked even more directly to investment promotion, through federal grants to states that are tied to the amount of investment they generate. Malaysia's federal system already has at least two such pro-rata grant structures in place.

In addition, the incentive for state governments to perform has been reduced by federal government expansion into areas of their competence such as water and solid waste management. This has frequently taken the form of privatization, where the responsibility for state government provided public services is transferred to private sector firms under federal supervision. Thus, in 1993 one consortium was awarded a 28-year concession to operate, maintain, and manage sewerage systems in 143 local authorities. In 2011, three firms were given 22-year concessions to provide solid waste management services in 8 states and federal territories.[73]

This drive overlooks very real success stories such as the Pihak Berkuasa Air (PBA) Holdings Berhad, a publicly-listed corporation that supplies water to Penang and is majority-owned by the Penang state government. Despite water bills for 80 per cent of Penang's registered domestic water users being subsidised and the commercial water tariff being among the lowest in Asia, PBA still generates a profit.[74] Thus, while the federal government may choose to pursue the further privatization of utilities, this should not overlook existing success stories. Indeed, there is no reason why state governments should be precluded from competing with private service providers for business.

Increasing transparency and accountability at the state level can also improve performance. Countries such as Mexico, India, Indonesia, and the Philippines have begun yearly ranking exercises of the business environments in municipalities and states or provinces. These exercises have proven very effective at encouraging regulatory reforms, through highlighting bottlenecks and pinpointing comparative inefficiencies, as well as naming and shaming the lowest performers. For example, 13 out of 20 cities surveyed in the Philippines carried out regulatory reforms in the year following the first subnational business survey.[75]

At present, Malaysia has carried out a local government ranking exercise. However, no such analogous exercise has been carried out for state governments. In addition, the establishment of growth corridors looks to further reduce the accountability of state governments through adding an additional bureaucratic layer between the centre and states. Alternatively, ranking or rating exercises can be carried out at the state level, but for different public services. Under these "report card" initiatives, citizens "grade" their local public services according to their efficiency, effectiveness, and quality of service.

Last, the potential for innovation and policy transfer can be encouraged and systematized by a more regular incorporation of state-level development plans into the federal government's Malaysia Plans. Many state-level plans have been financed exclusively by state governments, drawing on extensive local level knowledge and social capital. Yet, it is a frequent refrain from state government officials that their planning processes are by-passed by federal planning machinery.[76] These plans, accompanied by transparent key performance indicators, would greatly enrich plans at both the state and national levels.

During its drive to decentralize, Indonesia had to construct a multi-levelled system of governance, a process that some have likened to "building the ship while sailing it". Malaysia for its part, has the ship, but risks leaving it in the dock.

NOTES

1. Jenna Bednar, *The Robust Federation: Principles of Design* (Cambridge University Press, 2009), pp. 18–19.
2. Wallace E. Oates, "An Essay on Fiscal Federalism", *Journal of Economic Literature*, vol. XXXVII (September 1999): 1122.
3. Richard A. Musgrave and Peggy B. Musgrave, *Public Finance in Theory and Practice*, 5th ed. (New York: McGraw-Hill Book Company, 1989), p. 459.
4. Charles M. Tiebout, "A Pure Theory of Local Expenditures", *The Journal of Political Economy*, vol. 64, no. 5 (1956).
5. Vito Tanzi, "Fiscal Federalism and Decentralization: A Review of Some Efficiency and Macroeconomic Aspects", *Annual World Bank Conference on Development Economics* (Washington, D.C.: World Bank, 1995), p. 300.
6. Michael Storper and Allen J. Scott, "The Wealth of Regions: Market Forces and Policy Imperatives in Local and Global Context", *Futures*, vol. 27, no. 5 (1995); Allen J. Scott and Michael Storper, "Regions, Globalization, Development", *Regional Studies*, vol. 37, nos. 6–7 (2003).
7. Gareth Williams, Pierre Landell-Mills, and Alex Duncan, *Uneven Growth within Low-income Countries: Does It Matter and Can Governments Do Anything Effective?*, The Policy Practice published papers (Oxford: The Policy Practice Limited, 2005), p. 18.
8. Lloyd I. Rudolph and Susan H. Rudolph, "The Iconization of Chandrababu: Sharing Sovereignty in India's Federal Market Economy", *Economic and Political Weekly*, 5 May 2001, p. 1542; Yang Yao, "The Political Economy of Government Policies toward Regional Inequality in China", in *Reshaping Economic Geography in East Asia*, edited by Yukon Huang and Alessandro Magnoli Bocchi (Washington, D.C.: World Bank, 2009), p. 201.
9. Francis Loh Kok Wah, "Federation of Malaysia", in *Foreign Relations in Federal Countries*, edited by Hans Michelmann (Montreal: McGill-Queen's University Press, 2009), p. 195.
10. These units or "mini-states" can be grouped into five. The Settlements of Penang and Malacca were ruled directly by the British as Crown Colonies. The Federated Malay States of Perak, Selangor, Negri Sembilan, and Pahang, were protectorates ruled by Sultans who had paramount authority over matters of religion and custom, but were treaty-bound to accept British advice in all other matters. Their administration was centralized in Kuala Lumpur. The Unfederated States of Perlis, Kedah, Kelantan, Trengganu, and Johor were also protectorates. But, while their treaty obligations were similar to those in Federated Malay States, their later incorporation into the British Empire meant that their administrations developed more endogenously. Sabah was administered by a private firm, the British North Borneo Company, and Sarawak was ruled by the Brooke dynasty, who were British subjects.

11. John Funston, *Malay Politics in Malaysia: A Study of UMNO and PAS* (Kuala Lumpur: Hienemann Educational Books (Pte.) Ltd., 1980), pp. 109–16.

12. Walter Holzhausen, *Federal Finance in Malaysia: The Theory and Problems of Federal/State Government Financial Relations in a Developing Country* (Kuala Lumpur: Penerbit Universiti Malaya, 1974), p. 12.

13. The standard works on this issue are: A.J. Stockwell, *British Policy and Malay Politics during the Malayan Union Experiment 1942–1948*, The Malaysian Branch of the Royal Asiatic Society, Monograph no. 8 (Kuala Lumpur: JMBRAS, 1979); James de V. Allen, *The Malayan Union* (New Haven: Yale University Press, 1967); and Albert Lau, *The Malayan Union Controversy 1942–48* (Singapore: Oxford University Press, 1990).

14. *Report of the Federation of Malaya Constitutional Commission* (Kuala Lumpur: Government Press, 1957), p. 6 in B.H. Shafruddin, *The Federal Factor in the Government and Politics of Peninsular Malaysia* (Singapore: Oxford University Press, 1987), p. 2.

15. Ninth Schedule of the Constitution of Malaysia.

16. Harihar Bhattacharyya, *Federalism in Asia: India, Pakistan, and Malaysia* (New York: Routledge 2010), p. 83.

17. In 2012, the figures for each were RM13.5 billion and RM900 million, respectively. Tricia Yeoh, "What's in the Budget for State Governments?". *Penang Economic Monthly*, issue 11.11 (November 2011): 44.

18. Tenth Schedule of the Constitution of Malaysia; Abdul Rahim Anuar, "Fiscal Decentralization in Malaysia", *Hitotsubashi Journal of Economics* 41 (2000): 88–89.

19. Abdul Rahim Anuar, "Fiscal Decentralization in Malaysia", *Hitotsubashi Journal of Economics* 41 (2000): 88–89.

20. B.H. Shafruddin, *The Federal Factor in the Government and Politics of Peninsular Malaysia* (Singapore: Oxford University Press, 1987), p. 98.

21. B.H. Shafruddin, *The Federal Factor in the Government and Politics of Peninsular Malaysia* (Singapore: Oxford University Press, 1987), pp. 184–86.

22. Jomo K.S. and Wee Chong Hui, "The Political Economy of Malaysian Federalism: Economic Development, Public Policy and Conflict Containment", Discussion Paper no. 2002/113 (Helsinki: World Institute for Development Economics Research, 2002), p. 29.

23. B.H. Shafruddin, "Malaysia Centre-state Relations by Design and Process", in *Between Centre and State: Federalism in Perspective*, edited by B.H. Shafruddin and Iftikhar A.M.Z. Fadzli (Kuala Lumpur: Institute of Strategic and International Studies, 1987), pp. 8–10.

24. Up to 2007, the Constitution had been amended some fifty times. J.C. Fong, *Constitutional Federalism in Malaysia* (Kuala Lumpur: Sweet and Maxwell Asia, 2006), pp. 198, 211.

25. Available at <http://www.parlimen.gov.my/index.php?uweb=dn&lang=en> (accessed 13 February 2012).

26. Harold Crouch, *Government and Society in Malaysia* (Singapore: Talisman Publishing, 1996), p. 34.

27. Harihar Bhattacharyya, *Federalism in Asia: India, Pakistan, and Malaysia* (New York: Routledge, 2010), p. 118.

28. Francis Loh Kok Wah, "Federation of Malaysia", in *Foreign Relations in Federal Countries*, edited by Hans Michelmann (Montreal: McGill-Queens University Press, 2009), p. 194.

29. This is an example of the erosion of states' rights. In 1960, the Constitution was amended to provide for the creation of the National Council for Local Government. Despite local government being the prerogative of state governments, the Council was established to "formulate ... a national policy for promotion, development, and control of local government". The Council brings together one representative from each state and the same number from the centre. Assuming all centrally-appointed representatives vote in line with federal prerogatives, only one vote from a state government is needed to make a policy change in line with central interests. B.H. Shafruddin, *The Federal Factor in the Government and Politics of Peninsular Malaysia* (Singapore: Oxford University Press, 1987), p. 17; J.C. Fong, *Constitutional Federalism in Malaysia* (Kuala Lumpur: Sweet and Maxwell Asia, 2006), p. 244. Sabah and Sarawak have representatives on this council, but they do not vote.

30. Interview with former senior official of the Penang Development Corporation, Penang, 3 November 2011.

31. Available at <http://www.jsic.com.my/linkpage04/getting_start.php> (accessed 15 February 2012).

32. Liew Chin Tong and Francis E. Hutchinson, "Implementing Pro-Employment Policies at the Sub-national Level", in *Pilot Studies for a New Penang*, edited by Ooi Kee Beng and Goh Ban Lee (Singapore: Institute of Southeast Asian Studies, 2010), pp. 122–25.

33. Zairil Khir Johari, "Entering New Territory with Open Tenders", *Penang Economic Monthly*, issue 10.11 (October 2011): 11.

34. See for example, the Johor State Economic Development Corporation Enactment 1968, p. 7.

35. Chet Singh, "Corporate Planning and SEDCs: The Penang Experience", in *Corporate Planning* (Kuala Lumpur: Kementerian Perusahaan Awam, 1979), p. 3.

36. State-level business surveys are a rarity in Malaysia. Following the establishment of growth corridors in 2006, this trend looks to worsen as surveys are now conducted for corridors, which cut across state boundaries. See for

example World Bank, *Malaysia Productivity and Investment Climate Assessment Update* (Washington, D.C.: World Bank, 2009).

37. It is likely that this would have improved in Johor with the establishment of the state's third port, Port Tanjung Pelepas, in October 1999.

38. PDC, *Annual Report 1977* (Penang: Penang Development Corporation, 1978), p. 13; PDC, *Annual Report 1980* (Penang: Penang Development Corporation, 1981), p. 23.

39. Penelco was wholly-owned by the PDC and manufactured kit transistors and radios. It was in operation from 1970–75. PDC, *Annual Report 1979* (Penang: Penang Development Corporation, 1980), p. 12. While it was ultimately dissolved, it was key in convincing the first electronics firms like Clarion and Hewlett-Packard that manufacturing operations were viable in Penang.

40. Andy Grove, Chairman of Intel relates that his decision to invest in Penang was sealed when the Penang Development Corporation laid a road overnight to enable him to inspect a potential building site (*The Edge*, 27 April 2003).

41. Francis E. Hutchinson, "'Developmental States' and Economic Growth at the Sub-national Level: The Case of Penang", in *Southeast Asian Affairs 2008*, edited by Daljit Singh and Tin Maung Maung Than (Singapore: Institute of Southeast Asian Studies, 2009), p. 230.

42. PDC, *Annual Report 2002* (Penang: Penang Development Corporation, 2002), p. 34. This has remained constant in recent years. In 2009, the portfolio was worth 218 million and comprised 39 firms.

43. The Penang state government has had historic links with Universiti Sains Malaysia through the Centre for Policy Studies, and academics as well as leading industrialists were involved in its state-level planning exercises in 1991 and 2001.

44. Interview with Tan Sri Ali Hashim, former CEO of JCorp, Kuala Lumpur, 5 September 2011.

45. Dato Mohd Ali Hashim, "The Johor State Economic Development Corporation as a Successful Corporate Organisation and an Islamic Business Institution", paper presented to the Islamic Development Bank, Nomination for the Islamic Development Bank Award in Islamic Economics, March 1993, p. 3.

46. Johor Corporation, *1996 Annual Report* (Johor Bahru: Johor Corporation, 1997), p. 86; Johor Corporation, *1997 Annual Report* (Johor Bahru: Johor Corporation, 1998), p. 70.

47. Johor Corporation, *1998 Annual Report* (Johor Bahru: Johor Corporation, 1998), p. 77; interview with Tan Sri Ali Hashim, former CEO of JCorp, Kuala Lumpur, 5 September 2011; *The Edge*, 7 January 2011.

48. JCorp, *Annual Report 2010* (Johor Bahru: JCorp, 2011), p. 5.

49. RMA Perunding Bersatu, *Johor Operational Master Plan Study* (Johor Bahru: State Economic Planning Unit, 1996), pp. 6–19.

50. The two principal consultants are the Malaysian Institute of Economic Research and RMA Perunding Bersatu Sdn Bhd — both in Kuala Lumpur. The recent exception is the 2006 Comprehensive Development Plan for South Johor, which was carried out by Khazanah, which is the investment arm of the federal government.

51. Interview with Boonler Somchit, Executive Director, Penang Skills Development Centre, Penang, 24 February 2004.

52. Poh Heem Heem and Tan Yin Hooi, "Penang in the New Asian Economy: Skills Development and Future Human Resource Challenges", in *Catching the Wind: Penang in a Rising Asia*, edited by Francis E. Hutchinson and Johan Saravanamuttu (Singapore: Institute of Southeast Asian Studies, 2012).

53. Rajah Rasiah, "Industrial Clustering of Electronics Firms in Indonesia and Malaysia", in *Production Networks and Industrial Clusters: Integrating Economies in Southeast Asia*, edited by Ikuo Kuroiwa and Toh Mun Heng (Singapore: IDE/Institute of Southeast Asian Studies, 2008).

54. Background Industrial Surveys for SJER Development Master Plan Study, RMA Perunding Bersatu 2006.

55. Available at <http://www.utm.my/about/brief-history-of-utm/> (accessed 22 February 2012).

56. Interview with Dr Molly N.N. Lee, Associate Professor of Education Studies, USM, Penang, 17 February 2004.

57. Available at <http://www.eng.usm.my/v3/index.php?option=com_content &view=article&id=54&Itemid=98&lang=en> (accessed 22 February 2012).

58. Available at <http://www.penangeducation.org.my/about-us/about-penang-education-council> (accessed 22 February 2012).

59. Disted-Stamford and INTI College.

60. Available at <http://www.psdc.org.my/html/default.aspx?ID=9&PID=44> (accessed 22 February 2012).

61. Available at <http://itpypj.edu.my/v3/bm/kursus> (accessed 29 September 2011).

62. Interview with Tan Sri Ali Hashim, former CEO of JCorp, Kuala Lumpur, 5 September 2011; JCorp, *2008 Annual Report* (Johor Bahru: Johor Corporation, 2009), p. 67.

63. Free Industrial Zone, Penang, Companies' Association.

64. Interview with Honorary Treasurer, FREPENCA, Penang, 5 February 2004.

65. Interview with a PENFEIA representative, Penang, 23 April 2009.

66. Interview with industry observers BB and BC, Penang, 18 March 2009.

67. PSDC, "Technology Roadmap for the Electrical and Electronics Industry of

Penang" (Penang: Penang Skills Development Corporation, 2007).
68. JCorp, *Annual Report 2002* (Johor Bahru: JCorp, 2003).
69. Interview with SMEASJ President, Pasir Gudang, 21 April 2010. Another interesting business association is the South Johor Foundry and Engineering Industries Association, which has some 400 members, many of whom are in supporting industries in the manufacturing sector. Interviews with SJFEIA members, Skudai, 23 June 2010.
70. Background Industrial Surveys for SJER Development Master Plan Study, RMA Perunding Bersatu 2006.
71. See, for example, the Penang State Government's "Penang Blueprint: A Blueprint for Change" (draft version) (Penang: Socio-economic and Environmental Research Institute, 2011).
72. Harihar Bhattacharyya, *Federalism in Asia: India, Pakistan, and Malaysia* (New York: Routledge, 2010), p. 125.
73. Jeff Tan, *Privatization in Malaysia: Regulation, Rent-seeking, and Policy Failure* (Abingdon: Routledge, 2008), p. 84; *The Edge* (19 November 2011).
74. Jaseni Maidinsa, "PBA Holdings Bhd: The Road to Privatisation, Corporatisation and Beyond". In *Catching the Wind: Penang in a Rising Asia*, edited by Francis E. Hutchinson and Johan Saravanamuttu (Singapore: Institute of Southeast Asian Studies, 2012).
75. World Bank, *Doing Business in the Philippines* (Washington, D.C.: International Bank for Reconstruction and Development), p. 9.
76. Interviews with: State Executive Councillor, Penang State Government, 2 April 2004; and senior Johor Civil Servant, Johor Bahru, 22 June 2010.

REFERENCES

Secondary Sources:

Anuar, Abdul Rahim. "Fiscal Decentralization in Malaysia". *Hitotsubashi Journal of Economics* 41 (2000).

Bednar, Jenna. *The Robust Federation: Principles of Design*. New York: Cambridge University Press, 2009.

Bhattacharyya, Harihar. *Federalism in Asia: India, Pakistan, and Malaysia*. New York: Routledge, 2010.

Crouch, Harold. *Government and Society in Malaysia*. Singapore: Talisman Publishing, 1996.

de V. Allen, James. *The Malayan Union*. New Haven: Yale University Press, 1967.

Fong, J.C. *Constitutional Federalism in Malaysia*. Kuala Lumpur: Sweet and Maxwell Asia, 2006.

Funston, John. *Malay Politics in Malaysia: A Study of UMNO and PAS*. Kuala

Lumpur: Hienemann Educational Books (Pte.) Ltd., 1980.

Hashim, Mohd Ali. "The Johor State Economic Development Corporation as a Successful Corporate Organisation and an Islamic Business Institution". Paper presented to the Islamic Development Bank, Nomination for the Islamic Development Bank Award in Islamic Economics, March 1993.

Holzhausen, Walter. *Federal Finance in Malaysia: The Theory and Problems of Federal/State Government Financial Relations in a Developing Country*. Kuala Lumpur: Penerbit Universiti Malaya, 1974.

Hutchinson, Francis E. "'Developmental States' and Economic Growth at the Sub-national Level: The Case of Penang". In *Southeast Asian Affairs 2008*, edited by Daljit Singh and Tin Maung Maung Than. Singapore: Institute of Southeast Asian Studies, 2009.

Jomo K.S. and Wee Chong Hui. "The Political Economy of Malaysian Federalism: Economic Development, Public Policy and Conflict Containment". Discussion Paper No. 2002/113. Helsinki: World Institute for Development Economics Research, 2002.

Khir Johari, Zairil. "Entering New Territory with Open Tenders". *Penang Economic Monthly*, issue 10.11, October 2011.

Lau, Albert. *The Malayan Union Controversy 1942–48*. Singapore: Oxford University Press, 1990.

Liew Chin Tong and Francis E. Hutchinson. "Implementing Pro-Employment Policies at the Sub-national Level". In *Pilot Studies for a New Penang*, edited by Ooi Kee Beng and Goh Ban Lee. Singapore: Institute of Southeast Asian Studies, 2010.

Loh, Francis. "Federation of Malaysia". In *Foreign Relations in Federal Countries*, edited by Hans Michelmann. Montreal: McGill-Queen's University Press, 2009.

Maidinsa, Jaseni. "PBA Holdings Bhd: The Road to Privatisation, Corporatisation and Beyond". In *Catching the Wind: Penang in a Rising Asia*, edited by Francis E. Hutchinson and Johan Saravanamuttu. Singapore: Institute of Southeast Asian Studies, 2012.

Musgrave, Richard A. and Peggy B. Musgrave. *Public Finance in Theory and Practice*, 5th ed. New York: McGraw-Hill Book Company, 1989.

Oates, Wallace E. "An Essay on Fiscal Federalism". *Journal of Economic Literature*. vol. XXXVII (September 1999).

Poh Heem Heem and Tan Yin Hooi. "Penang in the New Asian Economy: Skills Development and Future Human Resource Challenges". In *Catching the Wind: Penang in a Rising Asia*, edited by Francis E. Hutchinson and Johan Saravanamuttu. Singapore: Institute of Southeast Asian Studies, 2012.

Rasiah, Rajah. "Industrial Clustering of Electronics Firms in Indonesia and Malaysia". In *Production Networks and Industrial Clusters: Integrating Economies in Southeast Asia*, edited by Ikuo Kuroiwa and Toh Mun Heng. Singapore:

IDE/Institute of Southeast Asian Studies, 2008.

Rudolph, Lloyd I. and Susan H. Rudolph. "The Iconization of Chandrababu: Sharing Sovereignty in India's Federal Market Economy". *Economic and Political Weekly*, 5 May 2001.

Scott, Allen J. and Michael Storper. "Regions, Globalization, Development". *Regional Studies*, vol. 37, nos. 6–7 (2003).

Shafruddin, B.H. *The Federal Factor in the Government and Politics of Peninsular Malaysia*. Singapore: Oxford University Press, 1987.

———. "Malaysia Centre-State Relations by Design And Process". In *Between Centre and State: Federalism in Perspective*, edited by B.H. Shafruddin and Iftikhar A.M.Z. Fadzli. Kuala Lumpur: Institute of Strategic and International Studies, 1987.

Singh, Chet. "Corporate Planning and SEDCs: The Penang Experience". In *Corporate Planning*. Kuala Lumpur: Kementerian Perusahaan Awam, 1979.

Stockwell, A.J. *British Policy and Malay Politics during the Malayan Union Experiment 1942–1948*. The Malaysian Branch of the Royal Asiatic Society, Monograph no. 8. Kuala Lumpur: JMBRAS, 1979.

Storper, Michael and Allen J. Scott. "The Wealth of Regions: Market Forces and Policy Imperatives in Local and Global Context". *Futures*, vol. 27, no. 5 (1995).

Tan, Jeff. *Privatization in Malaysia: Regulation, Rent-seeking, and Policy Failure*. Abingdon: Routledge, 2008.

Tanzi, Vito. "Fiscal Federalism and Decentralization: A Review of Some Efficiency and Macroeconomic Aspects". *Annual World Bank Conference on Development Economics*. Washington, D.C.: World Bank, 1995.

Tiebout, Charles M. "A Pure Theory of Local Expenditures". *The Journal of Political Economy*, vol. 64, no. 5 (1956).

Williams, Gareth, Pierre Landell-Mills, and Alex Duncan. "Uneven Growth within Low-income Countries: Does It Matter and Can Governments Do Anything Effective?". The Policy Practice published papers. Oxford: The Policy Practice Limited, 2005.

World Bank. *Doing Business in the Philippines*. Washington, D.C.: International Bank for Reconstruction and Development, 2009.

———. *Malaysia Productivity and Investment Climate Assessment Update*. Washington, D.C.: World Bank, 2009.

Yang Yao. "The Political Economy of Government Policies toward Regional Inequality in China". In *Reshaping Economic Geography in East Asia*, edited by Yukon Huang and Alessandro Magnoli Bocchi. Washington, D.C.: World Bank, 2009.

Yeoh, Tricia. "What's in the Budget for State Governments?". *Penang Economic Monthly*, issue 11.11 (November 2011).

Primary Sources:

Background Industrial Surveys for SJER Development Master Plan Study. RMA Perunding Bersatu, 2006.

The Constitution of Malaysia.

Johor State Economic Development Corporation Enactment, no. 4, 1968.

Johor Corporation/JCorp. *Annual Report*. Johor Bahru: Johor Corporation/JCorp, various years.

PDC. *Annual Report*. Penang: Penang Development Corporation, various years.

PSDC. "Technology Roadmap for the Electrical and Electronics Industry of Penang". Penang: Penang Skills Development Corporation, 2007.

RMA Perunding Bersatu. *Johor Operational Master Plan Study*. Johor Bahru: State Economic Planning Unit, 1996.

Periodicals:

The Edge, 7 January 2011.

The Edge, 27 April 2003.

Interviews:

Molly N.N. Lee, Associate Professor of Education Studies, Universiti Sains Malaysia, Penang, 17 February 2004.

Boonler Somchit, Executive Director, Penang Skills Development Centre, Penang, 24 February 2004.

Tan Sri Ali Hashim, former CEO of JCorp, Kuala Lumpur, 5 September 2011.

Former senior official of the Penang Development Corporation, Penang, 3 November 2011.

Honorary Treasurer, FREPENCA, Penang, 5 February 2004.

Industry observers BB and BC, Penang, 18 March 2009.

Representative, PENFEIA, Penang, 23 April 2009.

State Executive Councillor, Penang State Government, Penang, 2 April 2004.

President, SME Association of South Johor, Pasir Gudang, 21 April 2010.

Senior Johor Civil Servant, Johor Bahru, 22 June 2010.

Commentry 4

Fifteen Consecutive Years of Budget Deficits, and Counting ...

Teh Chi-Chang

It has been fifteen years since the federal government delivered a Budget surplus. The last year of surplus was in 1997, the year the Asian currency and economic crises erupted. Subsequent to that, the federal government has incurred a Budget deficit every year, through the economic cycles of recovery and prosperity and despite the windfall to revenues from high commodity prices.

This article will not delve into the economic merits, or not, of running deficits for fifteen consecutive years, even while neighbours such as Indonesia, Thailand and Singapore reported at least occasional surpluses. Rather, it will focus on the budgetary processes — particularly the budgetary indiscipline displayed by the federal government and its consequences, and suggest remedial measures.

The federal government has consistently exceeded its stated Budget. As shown in Figure 12.1, since 1999, actual expenditure every year has been higher than budgeted. The sole exception was in 2009 when the sub-prime crisis was resolved faster than anticipated. Surprisingly, the subsequent years of 2010 and 2011 also saw government expenditure over-runs of 6–7 per cent above the original Budgets, despite relatively benign economic conditions.

Another noteworthy point is that federal government expenditure growth has outpaced economic growth, as measured by GDP. Between 1997 and 2011, federal government expenditure grew by a compound average growth rate of 10.2 per cent. GDP grew by just 8.2 per cent. Put another way, by 2011, federal government expenditure had grown to 27 per cent of GDP, from just 21 per cent in 1997.

This ever-increasing expenditure has been partly paid for by the windfall from high oil prices. In addition to the automatic revenue transfers that accrue to the government from the taxes, royalties and duties levied on higher oil prices, the federal government has been demanding increasingly higher levels of dividend payouts from Petroliam Nasional Berhad, the national oil company better known as Petronas.

FIGURE 12.1
The Federal Government Has Consistently Exceeded Its Stated Budget

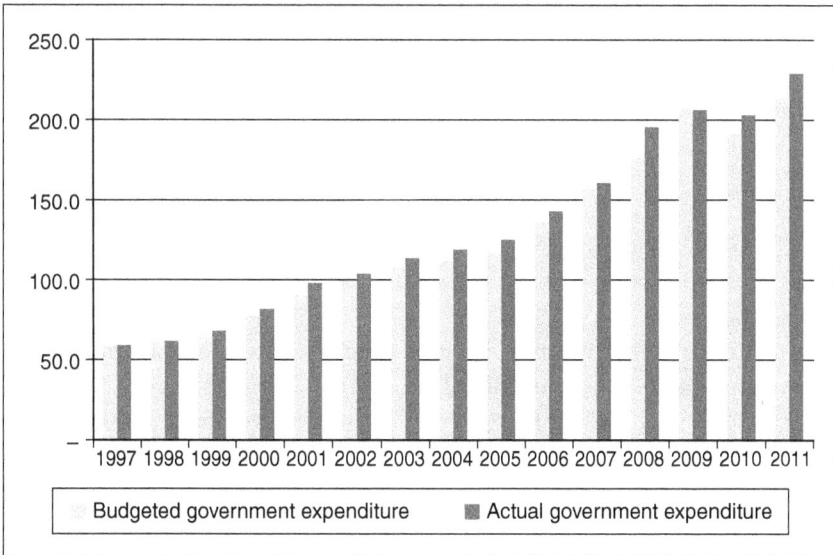

Source: *Economic Reports*, Ministry of Finance.

In 2011, Petronas paid 55 per cent of its net profit to the government. This is far higher than the 38 per cent average paid by other national oil corporations. If taxes and royalties are included, the percentage paid to the government rises to 75 per cent of its net profit, totalling RM66 billion.

Petroleum-related income accounted for RM56 billion or 35 per cent of federal government revenues in 2010, the latest year for which official data is currently available. We estimate it will be of a similar level in 2011. Just a few years earlier, in 2003, Petronas contributed only about RM22 billion of 21 per cent of federal government revenue.

The federal government budget understates the actual contribution by Petronas, as it does not include direct subsidies borne by Petronas. In its financial year ended March 2011, Petronas also directly subsidized the cheap gas supplied to independent power producers and other industries, which amounted to RM20 billion[1] on top of the taxes, royalties and dividends it paid to the government.

Nevertheless, even with the oil revenue windfall, the increasing dividends drawn from Petronas by the federal government and the direct subsidy burden borne by Petronas, the overall annual Budget has still been in deficit. The manifestation of this deficit is the fast-growing national debt. As of end 2011, federal government debt totalled RM456 billion. This is nearly double the RM229 billion level in 2005. Put another way, the federal government has added on more debt in the last six years than in the 48 years following independence in 1957.

The total national debt now stands at nearly 54 per cent of GDP. This is very near the 55 per cent federal government funding limit under the Loan (Local) Act 1959 and Government Funding Act 1983. The national debt number, in fact, understates the true picture. It does not include contingent liabilities which the federal government is ultimately responsible for. Examples of such contingent liabilities are the debt raised by statutory bodies such as Port Klang Free Zone and the RM300 million borrowed by the Federal Territories Foundation from the Employees Provident Fund to provide financing for purchasers of low-cost housing.

Such contingent liabilities have risen dramatically in the last two years. The 2011 level of RM117 billion is a record high. It is a 21 per cent increase from RM97 billion in 2010, which was, in turn, a 15 per cent increase from RM84 billion in 2010.

If the contingent liabilities are included, the effective debt level as of end 2011 would be RM573 billion, or 67 per cent of GDP. On a per capita basis, the RM573 billion effective debt is equivalent to RM20,000 for each and every Malaysian.[2] The debt does not appear to have been invested in development projects that have significantly improved the capital or human resource stock of the country.

Quite the reverse appears true. Malaysian households are increasingly dependent on federal government subsidies. Last year, in May 2011, Prime Minister Dato' Sri Najib Razak lectured Malaysians on kicking their addiction to subsidies, going so far as equating subsidies with opium.[3] However, he has presided over a federal government that has more than tripled the amount spent on subsidies. The federal government subsidy bill is expected to hit RM33 billion in 2012, a massive 40 per cent increase over RM24 billion in 2011, and more than three times the RM10 billion total in 2008 just before Dato Sri Najib assumed the premiership.[4]

Forty per cent of Malaysian households subsist on monthly incomes averaging RM1,500 per month,[5] or RM50 per day. The pervasiveness of low-incomes was made obvious in the Bantuan Rakyat 1Malaysia (BR1M) scheme under which households earning less than RM3,000 per month were given a RM500 one-off welfare payment. As of June 2012, more than RM2 billion had been distributed to 4.7 million households.[6] This means that over ⅔ rds — 69 per cent — of the 6.8 million Malaysian households[7] qualify for welfare support.

The prognosis does not look good for increasing income levels in future. The workforce is poorly qualified. Seventy-seven per cent — more than ¾ rds — of the workforce, has SPM (Sijil Pelajaran Malaysia, roughly equivalent to the British ('O'-Levels) qualifications, at best.[8] Local graduates are ill-matched to the jobs available. ¼ of local graduates remain unemployed six months after graduation.[9] Recipients of PTPTN (Perbadanan Tabung Pendidikan Nasional) study loans for higher education are paying back less than ½ the amounts they owe.[10]

Private investment too, is severely lagging. In October 2010, the federal government launched the ambitious Economic Transformation Programme (ETP), which aims to take Malaysia to high-income status by 2020.[11] The ETP identified twelve National Key Economic Areas (NKEAs)[12] with strong growth potential. Within these twelve NKEAs, 131 Entry Point Projects (EPPs) were selected to "kick-start the programme".

The ETP was supposed to be private-sector driven. It targeted a 60 : 32 : 8 spread of investments between the private sector, government-linked corporations (GLCs) and the government. However, a year later, by the end of 2011, the government and GLCs were still the main investors. The 25 per cent government share of committed investments was more than three times the 8 per cent target. The private sector share was just 35 per cent, well under the 60 per cent target.[13]

The picture is even more sobering from the perspective of actual investments. Actual ETP investments from all sources — private and government/GLCs — in 2011 totalled just RM12 billion, a mere 7 per cent of the RM179 billion committed investments that PEMANDU, the government agency driving the ETP,[14] prefers to highlight. This very slow rate of investment is concerning, particularly when being "shovel-ready", ie., ready for implementation was part of the criteria for the selection of EPPs.[15]

Is there a way out of this morass? The deficit is a function of federal government revenues and expenditure. Curtailing it requires higher levels of the former, and lower levels of the latter. Raising significant amounts of revenue in the near-term is daunting. Much of the workforce is poorly qualified and lowly paid, the tax base is narrow (just 1.7 million of a 12 million workforce pay taxes[16]), new private investment is weak, and Petronas is already tightly squeezed. Coupled with the turbulent global economic environment, the outlook for tax receipts is fair, at best.

On the expenditure side, the routine flouting of annual Budgets must be broken. The government must adhere to the Budgets it presents unless there are extremely extenuating circumstances. A step towards this would be the separation of the roles of Prime Minister and Finance Minister. These are roles analogous to Chief Executive Officer (CEO) and Chief Financial Officer (CFO). In the corporate sector, shareholders would never tolerate the CEO also holding the CFO position. However, no eyebrows have been raised in Malaysia at the same person holding both roles in government.

The last time the federal government had a Budget surplus was in 1997, which was also the last year when the positions of Prime Minister and Finance Minister were held by separate individuals.[17] Since then, Prime Ministers Mahathir, Abdullah and Najib have concurrently held the Finance Minister position. A strong Finance Minister would be a first-step in ensuring Budgets are adhered to rather than routinely flouted.

The second major step would be to crack down on wastage and procurement inefficiencies. Every year, the report of the Auditor-General presents a litany of profligate spending and mismanagement. And, every year, hardly any action is taken. For example, no corruption was found in the recent case of marine police procuring a pair of binoculars for RM56,000 that should have cost just RM1,000.[18]

In the longer-term, substantive discussions and consultations must be conducted with key stakeholders to create policies and effectively execute measures to clarify Budgetary choices, reduce the burgeoning subsidy bill, and create a conducive environment for private enterprise and rising household incomes.

13

THE ENVIRONMENT

Wee Chong Hui

Introduction

The Malaysian Federation covers around 330,803 square kilometres of land between 1° and 7° latitude north of the equator at longitude 100° and 119° east. Comprising the peninsular states, and Sabah and Sarawak on the north of Borneo Island, with the two regions separated by the South China Sea, it has 4,675 kilometre of coastline. It is amongst the top twenty countries for the most endangered amphibian, mammal, and conifer species (United Nations 2011, pp. 111–12), providing the only habitat to certain species. Malaysia is known for its tropical timber. It is a leading exporter of palm oil. Besides other industrial crops, food and other agricultural produce, it exports tin, crude petroleum, and liquefied natural gas. Most of its petroleum resources are in its continental shelf.

Malaysia has a population of 28.3 million, with a favourable population density of 85,400 persons per square kilometre. It has used its natural resources to achieve enviable socio-economic development. The government has launched ten five-year development plans, which have been guided by longer term policies formulated in response to national and international socio-economic conditions as the country is increasingly globalized.

Similar to the international community, Malaysia has been concerned about the environment and sustainable development. Malaysia's economic successes have increased expectations of continuing economic growth and its accompanying pressures on the environment. Malaysian official inclusion of social concerns exerts further demands. Its traditional community participation in the village is evolving into national and international networks with improving electronic connectivity, and the necessary government consultation with the public compounds environmental challenges. The current uncertain world economic outlook further exacerbates the urgency.

This chapter examines the state of the Malaysian environment and activities affecting it. It explores government policies and programmes. It takes stock of the constraints influencing Malaysia's achievements before exploring strategies for achieving inclusive sustainable development. The analysis is based on the aspirations for economic growth, equity, socio-political development, and sound management of the natural environment. It emphasizes human well-being over the generations, and the environment is taken as the means towards this end.

Socio-Economic Background

Malaysia had a per capita gross national income (GNI) of RM26,175 in 2010 (or US$11,800 at US$1 = RM2.3624). Its gross domestic product (GDP) growth averaged over 6 per cent for 1970–2000 and approximately 5 per cent for 2000–10. Its unemployment rate is low by international standard — falling from 8 per cent in 1970 to 5.1 per cent in 1990 and 3.4 per cent in 2010. The incidence of poverty amongst Malaysian citizens fell from 12.4 per cent in 1989 to 3.8 per cent in 2010. The Gini coefficient for Malaysian citizens is high, increasing from 0.422 in 1989 to 0.461 in 2002 and 2004 before falling to 0.441 in 2009 (Economic Planning Unit, Malaysia — EPU).

Malaysia has diversified from a predominantly primary economy at its formation in 1963. Agriculture, fishing, forestry, mining and quarrying generated more than 35 per cent of GDP and 50 per cent of employment in the mid-1960s. By 1970, GDP from the primary sector was about 27 per cent while employment was 42 per cent. In 2010, it accounted for 16 per cent and 12 per cent respectively. During this period, GDP from manufacturing grew from less than 10 per cent to 26 per cent, while employment in manufacturing grew from less than 10 per cent to 28 per cent. The tertiary sector contributed slightly more than 50 per cent of GDP throughout, with its share of employment increasing from about 40 per cent to 70 per cent (various Malaysia plan documents).

Export of goods and services valued slightly more than GNI in 2010. The major primary commodities — oil palm, rubber, saw logs, sawn timber, tin, crude petroleum and condensates, and liquefied natural gas — earned 18 per cent of exports. Resource-based and non-resource based manufactures earned over 60 per cent. These exports have grown with production with time (Department of Statistics, Malaysia — DOS).

Urbanization has more than doubled from 25 per cent in 1970 to the current 71 per cent. Urban manufacturing started drawing the young and increasingly educated rural Malays and indigenes from the late 1960s. The trend aligned the industrialization policies and objective of increasing indigenous participation to reflect their population under the New Economic Policy (1971–90) and similar intent in the National Development Policy (1991–2000), National Vision Policy (1991–2010) and Vision 2020. Urban supporting services provided further pull, while relatively low wages and returns to smallholder agriculture provided the push for the migration.

Malaysia is a plural society. The 2010 estimates of citizens in the country were 54.5 per cent Malay, 11.8 per cent indigenous peoples of Sabah, Sarawak and Orang Asli of the peninsula, 24.8 per cent Chinese, 7.4 per cent Indians and 1.4 per cent others. The rural population has been predominantly Malays and other indigenes (DOS). The urban population was traditionally Chinese engaged in trading and backyard industries, but more reflective of Malaysian pluralism today.

Malaysia ranks 9th among 133 countries for the Environmental Performance Index and its ecological footprint indicates consumption of 2.5 hectares a person in 2005, below the global average of 2.7 hectares. However, this is above the sustainable threshold of 2.1 hectare (United Nations 2011, p. 103).

Land Constraint

Forested area recorded some 55 per cent in 2010, a decrease of 7 per cent in 46 years, from 62 per cent in 1964 (see Table 13.1). This is above the 50 per cent government commitment for forest cover, although forest diversity has been proposed as an improved indicator. In fact, among 20 countries, Malaysia is 6th for the largest number of threatened mammal (70 species) and 16th for the largest number of threatened birds (42 species) (United Nations 2011, p. 113).

TABLE 13.1
Forested Area, 1964–2010

	Area, 2009 (sq. km)	Forested area (%)				
		1964	1988	1998	2009	2010
More developed states, P. Malaysia:						
Johor	19,210		29.3	26.4	25.3	
Melaka	1,664		5.4	4.0	3.2	
N. Sembilan	6,686		29.6	26.5	24.1	
Perak	21,035		52.4	50.9	49.2	
P. Pinang	1,048		7.0	7.0	7.4	
Selangor	8,104		35.6	32.0	30.6	
Federal territories	383	69.7	–	0.2	9.7	44.5
Less developed states, P. Malaysia:						
Kedah	9,500		39.2	36.6	36.4	
Kelantan	15,099		61.8	59.9	57.5	
Pahang	36,137		61.7	54.4	57.2	
Perlis	821		13.0	14.5	13.6	
Terengganu	13,035		51.8	51.6	50.2	
Less developed states, Borneo Island:						
Sabah	73,631	n.a.	60.9	60.2	58.4	58.4
Sarawak	124,450	73.0	75.8	67.4	64.8	64.8
Malaysia	330,803	62.1	61.5	56.6	55.2	55.2

Note: n.a. – not available
Source: Calculated with data from *State/District Data Bank, Malaysia*, various issues.

Forested areas in 2010 consist of permanent forest reserves (39.6 per cent), wildlife reserves (3.4 per cent) and stateland (12.2 per cent). The permanent forest reserves are further categorized into production forest (25.2 per cent) and protected forest (14.4 per cent), the latter for conservation and slightly above the 10 per cent global modernization target (United Nations 2011, p. 105). The reserves include inland forest (91.1 per cent), peat swamp forest (3.9 per cent), mangrove forest (3.6 per cent), and plantation (1.4 per cent) (DOS). Land and forests are constitutionally under state government jurisdiction. The state government decides and can reverse decisions on the use of stateland and certain reserves, including switching to other government revenue-generating uses.

The peninsular forested area decreased from 70 per cent in 1963 to 45 per cent in 2009. States with urbanization exceeding 60 per cent, such as the officially categorized "more developed states" of Johor, Melaka, N. Sembilan, Perak, P. Pinang and Selangor, and the "less developed state" of Kedah, are less than 50 per cent forested. Forest revenues have been important for the other "less developed states" which experienced the fastest deforestation, i.e. Sarawak (11 per cent of forested area), Pahang (4.5 per cent), Kelantan (5.3 per cent), Sabah (2.5 per cent), and Terengganu (1.6 per cent), although petroleum royalty has also been important for Sarawak, Sabah, and Terengganu. Finally, the smallest state, Perlis, was less than 15 per cent forested.

Timber Industry

The timber industry has moderated over the years. Log production increased from 28.0 million cubic metres in 1980 to 40.1 million cubic metres, before decreasing to 17.6 million cubic metres in 2010. Saw logs export was RM2,142 million in 2010, compared to a peak of RM4,546 million in 1993. Sawn timber exports was RM3,245 million, compared to RM4,356 in 1989 (Bank Negara Malaysia).

Deforestation proceeded earlier in the peninsula, where logs crossed state boundaries in opposite directions concurrently as sellers maximized personal returns over social optimality. Illegal logging was especially problematic at times of high timber prices. Currently, most logging is in Sabah and Sarawak. British multinational companies spurred the log export boom in the latter states in the 1960s, and local timber concessionaries took over from the late 1980s. Timber processing is a major export-oriented manufacturing industry in these states, although the major portion of revenues has been reaped by concessionaries rather than relatively low-waged employees. Monocrop replanting with fast-growing species has been implemented to feed the industries. Nationwide, high value rattan are planted inland and mangrove in the coastal areas. Nurseries have also been developed.

Logging has caused soil erosion and water pollution, said to affect rural household water supply and fish harvests along the river. There were also indigenous claims over some forests and land for communal use besides commercial logging and oil palm plantation. The breakdown of negotiations have led to timber blockades in Sarawak. Today, legal recourse through the court is more frequent. The Human Rights Commission has had dialogues with the indigenous peoples of Sabah and Sarawak on land issues and native customary rights (NCR). The government is surveying communal land, but its implication in limiting future claims of communal rights has been raised.

Agriculture

The percentage of area under rice appears to have changed minimally (see Table 13.2). Although the use of pesticides have increased yield, it has led to diminished harvests of rice-field fishery by farmers. Wet rice

TABLE 13.2
Area and Percentage of Land under Selected Crops, 1980–2009
(square kilometres)

Year	Rice (all seasons)	Rubber Estates	Rubber Smallholdings	Oil Palm Estates	Oil Palm Smallholdings
1980	7,168	5,107	14,939	5,473	4,760
	(2%)	(2%)	(5%)	(2%)	(1%)
1990	6,806	14,880	3,487	7,121	11,174
	(2%)	(5%)	(1%)	(2%)	(3%)
2000	6,987	1,238	13,069	20,242	13,525
	(2%)	–	(4%)	(6%)	(4%)
2009	6,749	4,850	10,093	28,072	18,840
	(2%)	(1%)	(3%)	(8%)	(6%)

Source: Malaysia, *Yearbook of Statistics*, various years.

smallholdings of the peninsular Malays experienced land pressure as the population increased. There has been concern over the conversion of rice to tobacco planting when tobacco gave higher returns. However, the exodus of youths in search of urban prospects from the 1980s led to labour shortage and abandoned rice farms.

Indigenous slash and burn hill rice had suited the local environment. Natural fertilizer excluded the need for fertilizer imports and the land rejuvenated during fallow. However, the fallow period shortened with increasing population pressure and contests for land from other industries. Subsequently the urban drift reduced hill rice planting. The government's latest option is to encourage rice planting by private companies towards 60 per cent self-sufficiency for national food security.

Natural rubber is a foreign exchange earner and a local industrial input. Smallholder rubber has contributed to household income. Rubber plantations provide employment, although at relatively low wage. The recent declines of rubber price limit its competition for land. There have been substantial research on rubber and rubber wood had been used for furniture as wood from natural forest depleted.

The decline in the area under rubber parallels an increase in the area under oil palm, the "golden crop". Land development schemes under the Federal Land Development Authority (FELDA) in the peninsula helped reduce the incidence of poverty among the landless. The schemes supply fresh fruit bunches for processing by FELDA's mills, which have an advantage over other mills that have been experiencing shortages in recent years.

Since the 1980s, the extension in oil palm area is mainly in Sabah and Sarawak. Oil palm has been planted in logged over area, while the sale of timber extracted before planting adds revenues. In Sarawak, the State Government introduces the Konsep Baru (literally translated as "New Concept") of developing NCR land, whereby land is charged to private companies for the long term development of oil palm for profit-sharing between landowners and the financing companies. The concept provides a solution to land shortage besides offering financial returns to NCR land. However, there have been diverse opinions of landowners and the companies for certain ventures over time and disputes have been brought to court.

Burning to clear the land for planting also causes air pollution, while effluent discharge from palm oil mills pollutes the river. Heavy fines for waste discharge above the permissible level have reportedly led to the mills improving their treatment facilities, and many Malaysian companies are members of the Roundtable on Sustainable Palm Oil (RSPO). However, RSPO has experienced mixed responses to its initiatives. Major producing Indonesian companies have also withdrawn from RSPO, while the Malaysian government is working on its own palm oil certification.

Aquaculture has been developed as an added alternative to sea fishery, integrated with cropping and animal husbandry to maximize the utilization of resources (e.g. papaya planting on the bunds of fish ponds, use of animal waste for feed). The use of closed tin mines also optimizes on scarce land.

Construction

However, highways and urbanization have been competing for scarce land. Conspicuous consumption exacerbated with accelerated economic growth in the early 1990s, catapulting demand and subsequent speculation for commercial space, and transportation links between townships. Meanwhile, housing needs intensified with the increase in population and affluence. The congestion has been challenging. Planting at highways comes after various catastrophes from landslides due to construction on hill-slopes.

Energy Constraints and Pollution

The demand for energy grew with the economy. In 2007, energy use in 2007 was 1.632 million tonnes of oil equivalent (mtoe) per million persons, an increase of 28.2 per cent from 2000. This is behind Brunei (1.925 mtoe, decrease of 9.7 per cent) and Singapore (2.880 mtoe, decrease of 54.2 per cent), and above those for Philippines (0.260 mtoe, 17.7 per cent), Indonesia (0.643 mtoe, 12.2 per cent), and Thailand (1.092 mtoe, 34.7 per cent) (United Nations 2011, Table 7.7). Malaysia's carbon dioxide emission then was 6.7 tonne per person and 1.3 tonne per US$1,000 GDP, higher than the world averages of 4.35 and 0.75 respectively (*The Tenth Malaysia Plan* –10MP). In 2005, most of the demand was for industries (38.2 per cent), transport (37.8 per cent), and residential and commercial uses (12.5 per cent) (Hamdan Mokhtar 2002). Of the 1,906 petajoules forecasted for commercial demand in 2011, 55 per cent are from petroleum products, 17 per cent from electricity, 24 per cent from natural gas and 4 per cent from coal and coke. In 2010, 106,291 gigawatt hours of electricity was generated, predominantly from gas (59 per cent), coal (34 per cent) and hydro-dam (6 per cent) (EPU).

Malaysia has 21,500 cubic metres of water per capita per year. Management includes ensuring logistically sufficient supply — including handling drought-prone areas — and flood control. Over 90 per cent of its raw water supply is from rivers. The peninsular demand for water in 2010 was 33,100 million cubic metres, of which 54 cent was for irrigation. Some 95 per cent of households are supplied with water (10MP). It is noteworthy that water is also needed for producing biomass and biogas for electricity and hydroelectricity options that are being explored.

In 2008, 6 per cent of river basins monitored were polluted, showing a decline from 10 per cent in 2005. Most were clean (49 per cent) or slightly polluted (45 per cent) in terms of ammoniacal nitrogen, suspended solids and heavy metals such as arsenic, cadmium, lead, mercury, and zinc. Heavy metal concentrations were within acceptable values and decreasing. The ammoniacal nitrogen pollutant was traced to domestic sewerage, animal waste and industrial effluents, while suspended solids, to soil erosion and sedimentation from highland development, logging, and clearing for mining (10MP; DOS 2009).

Certain marine fishery resources have been depleting due to over-fishing from increases in fisherman population, including illegal foreign fishermen, and the use of fishing technology, developed without appropriate consideration on environmental impacts or before comprehensive research on the matter. The monitored marine environment that continues into international waters contained suspended solids, oil and grease, and escherichia coli exceeding the recommended Interim Marine Water Quality Standards, although all heavy metals except for lead were below the recommendations. There were no tarball residues found by monitoring stations at coastal areas and estuaries. Pollution resulted from oil spill from grounding and illegal discharge from vessels, pipeline rupture, explosion, fire, and overfilling. Pressure increased with cargo throughput growth (7.3 per cent), comprising both imports (54.8 per cent) and exports (45.2 per cent) (DOS 2009).

Monitored air quality ranges from good to moderate, except for higher air pollution index on intermittent days in Selangor and Sarawak due to peat swamp fires and transboundary haze. The levels of ozone, lead, carbon monoxide, sulphur dioxide, nitrogen dioxide and particulate matter have been below the Malaysian Ambient Air Quality Guidelines. The major sources of pollution were motor vehicles, power plants and industries, emitting 80, 11 and 7 per cent of the tonnage of pollutants, respectively in 2008.

The switch to natural gas for vehicle and industries reduces sulphur dioxide pollutant. Enhanced enforcement also reduces the emission of black smoke from vehicles. About 70 per cent of nitrogen dioxide was from power stations and industries. The less stringent environmental regulations in the early years were attractive to foreign manufacturing, which created employment and export-led growth. Nonetheless, Malaysia has tightened control over the years and revised the quantum of fines and penalties. There was already increased compliance to more than 80 per cent for 21 industries, except for the 71 per cent compliance for non-metallic mineral industries in 2008 (DOS 2009).

Natural radiation is generally at an acceptable level. However, there is a US$100 million cleanup for a rare earth refinery in the Bukit Merah Mines, which residents blamed for birth defects and eight leukaemia cases within five years in a community of 11,000, which had no leukaemia cases "after many years". In May 2011, there were also protests against the proposed Lynas rare earth refinery in Kuantan. The assistance of the International Atomic Energy Agency (IAEA) was enlisted. The IAEA Mission reported that there was no non-compliance affecting the safety aspects of the project then — 40 per cent completed for siting and construction. The company, Lynas, is to provide a second radioactive impact assessment (RIA) to account for pre-operation, operation and de-commissioning for consideration for further licensing by the Malaysian authority.

In fact, the Mission recommends, inter alia, that (1) The Malaysian Atomic Energy Licensing Board (AELB) requires Lynas to: (a) submit a plan for long term waste management, (b) submit a plan for managing the waste from the decommissioning and dismantling of the plant at the end of its life and (c) contribute to a fund for long term management of waste, including de-commissioning and remediation; (2) Regular RIA are conducted, and the exposure and environmental monitoring results used for more accurate assessment of doses to the worker and members of the public, with dose reduction where appropriate; and (3) AELB should have the resources, competence and independence to regulate the Lynas project (IAEA 2011). The independence of AELB aligns the Malaysian promotion of governance.

Environmental Initiatives

Malaysia has long recognized the need for sustainable development. It gazetted its first protected area in 1902 and enacted its Wildlife Protection Act, 1972. In 1977, it acceded to the Convention on International Trade in Endangered Species of Wild Flora and Fauna (CITES). More concerted efforts were made from the mid-1980s in consideration of the long term conservation versus shorter term, but great financial gains from logging. In 1989, it acceded to agreements on the protection of the ozone layer. In the 1990s, it acceded to agreements on the movements and disposal of hazardous wastes, and on wetlands and waterfowl habitat; it also ratified agreements on biodiversity and climate change (see United Nations 2011, Table 7.1).

The National Policy on the Environment (2002) integrates sustainable economic, social, and cultural development goals of the past decades with environmental conservation. It focuses on natural resource and environmental management, including the prevention and control of pollution, the strengthening of institutional capacity, education, and awareness. Subsequently, the National Green Technology (2009) aims to ensure sustainable development by developing roadmaps to guide the application of green technologies in various sectors including power generation, transport, and construction.

Meanwhile, the National Climate Change Policy (2009) not only identifies options and strategies for a low-carbon economy. Relevant legislations and policies are streamlined and coordinated, while inter-ministerial and cross-sectoral committees are established to drive and facilitate the implementation of adaptation and mitigation measures (10MP: Table 6-2). Policy instruments on forestry, agriculture, biodiversity, human settlements and urban planning, sanitation and water, energy and transport, and climate change have been formulated over the years (see also United Nations 2011, Table 7.2).

The Awareness, Faculty, Finance, Infrastructure, Research and Marketing (AFFIRM) Framework outlines an ecosystem for environmental sustainability. The government will coopt the private sector and civil society to increase awareness of the collective environmental responsibility. It will introduce green topics in school and university curriculums and a system for the formulation of grading and certification mechanism for competency in green technology. A green technology soft loan fund of RM5.1 billion has been set up for companies supplying and utilizing green technology, whereby the government bears 2 per cent of the interest rate and guarantees 60 per cent financing, with the remaining 40 per cent from banking institutions. Green infrastructure will be pioneered in Putraaya and Cyberjaya for the formulation of country-wide guidelines. Research, development, and commercialization of green technology by local research centres and industries, and their collaborations with foreign universities and multinational corporations are also promoted. Research has been conducted to improve efficiency in use (e.g. studies are on water cycle to improve harvest and use) and environmental quality (e.g. of water). An eco-labelling scheme and matching international standards will be developed to increase export competitiveness and support the government's green procurement initiative.

The Tenth Malaysia Plan, 2011–15

The last of the four strategic thrusts to achieve Vision 2020 launched in June 2010, the 10MP, states the agenda of protecting the environmental quality of life and caring for the environment, while harnessing economic value from the process (p. 297). Efforts are also focussed on developing a climate resilient growth strategy and enhancing conservation of the physical and biological ecology.

Environment Enhancing the Quality of Life

Urban conurbation of compact mix-use neighbourhood of residential, retail and office with open space, green corridors, and facilities for community interactions are to be built around public transport system. The mass rapid transit system for the capital city of Kuala Lumpur and bus rapid transit aims to shorten travel time. Besides private transport, public transport has developed from taxis and buses to light rail transit.

The government aims for efficient and sustainable water service. It invests in reducing non-revenue water such as reducing water leakages through maintenance and repairs, and reducing thefts. The proposed repairs of water tanks in low cost houses with support from a house maintenance fund to be established encompasses the objective of assistance for low income groups. A tariff mechanism to fully recover cost, beyond the 78 per cent of operating expenditure for 2009, is to be phased in so that there are funds for investments. Water and sewerage services are to be integrated to facilitate the accounting of water use, while industrial recycling water is encouraged through tax rebate.

Developing a Climate Resilient Growth Strategy

Climate adaptation efforts aim to protect Malaysia from the risks of climate change, and mitigation efforts aim to reduce Malaysia's carbon footprint. Measures to be taken to evaluate trade-offs in handling risks include developing risk assessment framework and prioritizing measures to address risks, implementing policy decision frameworks to ensure that infrastructural investments are climate resilient, and enhancing capacity in climate prediction and modelling for local application. Efforts to reduce Malaysia's carbon footprint focuses on energy generation and efficiency, solid waste management, air quality, and forest conservation.

While continuing to prospect for and improve production technology in petroleum resources under the purview and management of the federal-owned Petroliam Nasional Berhad, the government initiates renewable energy programmes. Biomass, biogas, mini-hydro and solar resources are considered renewable "for a more sustainable energy supply". The 2015 target from such sources is 985 MW, i.e., 5.5 per cent of electricity generation. A renewable energy fund for investment incentives in renewable energy will be set up from a feed-in-tariff of 1 per cent from electricity consumers.

Energy saving of 4,000 kilo tonnes of oil equivalent is targeted through low energy appliances as well as guidelines for buildings and townships. Amongst the proposals are increased energy performance labelling for appliances to facilitate informed decisions on their use and restricting the manufacture, import and sale of appliances to a minimum energy standard. Labelling is to be increased from air conditioner, fan, refrigerator, and television and to rice cooker, electric kettle, microwave, dishwasher, washing machine, and clothes dryer. It is hoped that incandescent light bulbs will be phased out in residential areas to reduce annual carbon emissions by 723,000 tonnes and energy use by 1,074 gigawatts. Energy efficient motors, pumps and variable speed controls in industries are identified for the industries.

To allow for the integration of renewable energy systems and energy saving features in buildings, the Uniform Building By-Laws are revised to incorporate the Malaysian Standard: Code of Practice of Energy Efficiency and Renewable Energy. The adoption of the consumption benchmark, Green Building Index is to be widened. Tax incentives are proposed for green buildings (e.g., with solar energy panel, thermal insulated roof for air-conditioned buildings, and also rain harvesting facilities and water conservation features). In September 2010, government offices were directed to keep air conditions at a maximum of 24°C. The promotion of green township will start with Putrajaya and Guidelines, using guidelines and rating scales based on carbon footprint benchmark.

Solid waste management aims to reduce the emission of greenhouse gases through the 3R programme — reducing, reusing, and recycling. The option for compulsory separation of organic waste at the household level is being reviewed for: (1) converting organic waste to compost for use, (2) reducing waste disposal at landfills, and (3) recovering methane from landfills to generate energy. Others include building material recovery facilities, thermal treatment plants, and the recycling of non-organic waste. A deposit is to be made by manufacturers to refund consumers for returning their used recyclable items. The current federalization of integrated solid waste management and public cleansing services are said to improve efficiency in scale management while reducing financial strain on local authorities, which undertook such responsibilities in the past.

Improved standards aim to further reduce emissions from vehicles and industries, the latter also encouraged to self-regulate with control and monitoring systems and audits in line with corporate social responsibility. The government has used satellite monitoring of burning and permitted staggered open burning, the licences also issued in consideration of seasonal influences. It is also proposing an ASEAN haze fire handling programme and strengthening sustainable peatland management to prevent fires. The Federal Government will encourage state governments to gazette forests, especially water catchment areas, as protected areas. INFAPRO in the Danum Valley, Sabah, is one of the international pioneering carbon trading projects, where logged-over forest is rehabilitated with trees providing effective carbon fixing. Tree planting by the public at large is also encouraged.

Conservation

Conservation efforts are to be directed towards forest and wildlife, as well as sustainable and safe utilization of resources. The Common Vision on Biodiversity adopts a three-pronged implementation approach and outreach strategy of strengthening the protected areas system, managing landscapes and seascapes for biodiversity, and mainstreaming diversity. The Central Forest Spine of 4.32 million hectares in the peninsular and the Heart of Borneo of 6.0 million hectares in Sabah and Sarawak are earmarked to house diversity and habitats meant to serve as biodiversity reservoirs and watershed areas, with eco-tourism potentials. Ecological linkages within these areas aim to "reconnect fragmented forest complexes to allow the movement of wildlife and biological processes" and reduce human-wildlife conflicts. The intensification of wildlife management and the protection of endangered species under CITES also include public-private partnerships for flagship species of orang utan, tiger, tapir, and gaur.

Inland waters, human physical settlements and urban areas are also linked to the shoreline and marine resources. Studies on pollution include the carrying capacities of rivers and maximum allowable discharge of pollutants. The water quality index has been revised. Meanwhile, coastal management includes mangrove planting, while marine parks conserve representative significant offshore ecosystem. Coral reefs where commercial fish live, breed, feed, and grow are protected to ensure their contributions to fishery resources. Biodiversity data are to be similarly linked and integrated to develop a one-stop database in future.

The government recognizes that local communities can contribute towards conservation and nature tourism, and possess traditional knowledge with potentials for the development of medicinal, pharmaceutical, nutraceutical and bio-technical products. It will co-opt the communities in conservation and formulate and implement a framework for knowledge sharing (e.g. ecotourism involving the Tagal system amongst the Dusuns in Sabah, where river fishing was traditionally prohibited for 1–2 years for river cleanliness and sustainable fish stocks). At the same time, safety in the transfer, handling, and use of technology and bio-safety are also prioritized.

Discussion

Malaysian agendas, plans and strategies have usually been commendable. The challenge has always lied in enforcement, including the indifference of the government employees concerned, poor coordination between government agencies, weakness and oversight in implementation capacities, and legal loopholes in implementation. The challenge is all the more since the Malaysian environmental programmes, as for many other countries, are relatively new. Governance has been undermined by rent-seeking, and there are rent-seekers, motivated enough by enormous gains from previous acts, to continue activities causing environmental catastrophes such as deforestation, precarious construction or dumping of hazardous waste.

The 10MP is launched in an uncertain world economic outlook, affecting the Malaysian open economy. From the general election of 2008, Malaysian federalism also seems to be charting a new direction, towards a two-party system. Constitutionally, the next general election is to be held before 2013, but the latest rumours have it in 2012. Although environmental conservation may be publicly highlighted in the current political-economic situation, power plays have dissipated concerted efforts and actions towards long term sustainability. The usual mid-term review of the 10MP may be another commendable report, adding another set of short-term mitigation measures fraught with limitations to the long road to sustainable development.

While the political players may be pre-occupied with the macro political-economic distractions, government employees can dutifully undertake their responsibilities and the civil society can play its role in environmental sustainability. The latest Auditor-General's reports indicate the neglect of appropriate financial procedures (*Sun Daily* 2011). Government financial sustainability not only reflects efficiency in the management of limited resources accessible to the government, government efficiency directs the economy to sustainable development within environmental constraints.

For example, the government controlled the prices of petroleum products from 1982 and taxes on producers are adjusted to compensate for the difference between control price and market price. The rising price of petroleum imposes a fiscal constraint because of fuel subsidies even though Malaysia earns more revenue from petroleum resources. In 2010, subsidies for liquefied petroleum gas, diesel, and petrol totalled

RM10,000 million or 6.2 per cent of federal government revenue (Treasury, Malaysia). However, only one third* of the subsidy is enjoyed by the needy (*Sin Chew Jit Poh* 2010). Since subsidization for the middle and high income groups leads to unnecessary consumption, the government proposes to reduce subsidization, while still prioritizing the welfare of low income groups. As most electricity is produced from subsidized gas, poor households consuming below RM20 of electricity per month are exempted from payment. There is lower subsidy for petrol of higher quality (RON97), which is also managed on a monthly float. The government is also paying attention to the retention of subsidies for its intended use by Malaysian vehicles (rather than Singaporean, entering through Johor) and for Malaysian fishery (rather than have subsidized petrol illegally sold to Thai fishermen). The above commendable programmes require commitment to enforcement on the part of government employees.

The corrective actions recommended by the Auditor-General (AG) were taken by the government agencies concerned. The AG has said that proactive supervision and monitoring were preferred to corrective measures (*Sun Daily* 2011). The Government Transformation Programme (GTP), the second strategic thrust to achieve Vision 2020 launched in January 2010, states that the government is the custodian of public interest and its official principles include "Upholds the highest level of integrity", embodying ethical conduct and good governance. If the AG were given a chance to continue performing his duties in line with the GTP, the Malaysian environmental agenda would have brighter prospects.

Participation

The environment is a collective responsibility and local participation can be mobilized through the local authorities, at the same time handling the fiscal constraints of the local authorities. Local authorities have small revenue bases and budget constraints. The Malaysian traditional communal activity, "gotong royong", of cleaning public places has had the advantage of clearing them of solid waste and saving cost on the part of the local authorities.

In fact, the local authorities replace local governments after local elections were suspended from 1964. Some local authorities reported that representatives of various interest groups such as political parties, women's groups, youth organizations, welfare organizations and other non-governmental organizations '(NGOs) sit in their committees to ensure their respective interests. However, significant political parties outside the ruling coalition have not been mentioned. Attention has been drawn to the advisory role of the committees and the authorities' prerogative not to follow their advices. The committee meetings organized by the authorities are also generally closed to the public, and minutes of the meetings are confidential.

The proposed urban conurbation has to be enlivened with a sense of belonging, ownership, and responsibility. Beyond the cleansing "gotong royong" for public places are the principles of participative consultation to conserve a liveable environment in the spirit of Local Agenda 21, which all local authorities adopted in 2000. The re-instatement of elections for local governments would also facilitate participation at the local level. Meanwhile NGOs should engage with the authorities for improved environmental management. Reducing consumption should be promoted to be at par with recycling and reusing to limit the expansion of brownfields.

More than indigenous knowledge on conservation and potential values of green products is living in the natural environment collect-ively shared by the present and future generations. Indigenous com-munities in Sarawak have forests for communal use such as hunting, gathering and fishing, and timber for housing for generations. Traditionally, everyone is a custodian of the forest environment for common good, similar to newer official conservation efforts to date. There is a need to preserve the culture to enhance official efforts, including the environment in which the culture is practised and conserved.

Economic empowerment is also necessary for community involve-ments in conservation. Low income groups would be too concerned with increasing income to be involved. Since the majority depends on employment for income, continuous efforts should be made to improve employment conditions.

Federal-State Relations

Malaysia is a centralized federation and the narrow revenue base of the state governments risk over-exploitation of land and forest, the jurisdictions of which are vested in the state governments. Decentralization which empowers the state governments financially will reduce the pressure on these natural resources.

Generally, decentralization also promotes participation in environmental responsibilities. However, recent moves towards centralization include the federalization of water supplies and the integration solid waste management and public cleansing services in the peninsular states, where they are handled by local authorities. The federalization of water involves privatization, and services have been found wanting. There have been suggestions that the Federal Government pays interested state governments to supply water instead of private suppliers for the services. The federalization of solid waste management and public cleansing integrate these services, with the local authorities paying the same rate as they did previously, while the Federal Government pays the extra charge. This applies for in all peninsular states except three states which applied for exemption. These three states are the states of Penang, Selangor and Perak, the former two being led independently by the opposition and the latter under the opposition before some opposition-supported State Assemblymen declared support for the ruling coalition. These states are amongst the more developed states and should be capable of handling the services.

The Federal Government and the state government have to collaborate for sound environmental management. While decentralization may empower state governments generally in keeping with the spirit of federalism, environmental impact is widespread and the Federal Government has to contribute its more comprehensive perspective and provide the necessary support to guide the state governments. In 1995, for example, the Federal Minister of Science, Technology and Environment issues an order so that the public need not be consulted on the environmental impact assessment for the controversial Bakun dam in Sarawak, unlike for dams elsewhere. Although this may appear to recognize the Sarawak ordinance concerned at that time, it is timely to reverse the order in the interest of environmentally sustainable development for all. At the same time, the Federal Government can compensate the state for benefits foregone from projects which would otherwise contradict national environmental goals.

Conclusions

Having achieved enviable socio-economic development, Malaysia envisions a developed country status by 2020. Malaysia is blessed with natural endowments, and it declares noble goals of environmental sustainability and plans impressive frameworks, strategies and programmes, and mechanisms to achieve these goals. However, the government has not always promoted integrity, accountability or participation, or let participation develop unfettered in contradiction to the *1Malaysia Concept* of "People First, Performance Now", launched in 2009 as the first strategic thrust to achieve Vision 2020. The empowering participation of stakeholders is the challenging task ahead. The various groups have to dialogue with each other and to be mutually supportive towards equitable socio-economic development.

The development of communication has facilitated and will continue to facilitate participation for environmentally sustainable development. Communication creates awareness and stimulates concern. Interest groups in substantial numbers can be easily mobilized via virtual communication. Hence, they can make more effective demands. With leadership and organization, the current situation is opportune for the agenda on environmentally sustainable development.

There are conflicting demands on the finite environment, at least within the urgent timeframe of technological progress. Urgent attention is required on the conservation of forest resources and gene pools, sufficient supplies of energy and clean water, and the prevention of water and air pollution. As Malaysia aspires for economic growth, transport and communication infrastructure, industries, township and residential projects compete for its forested land and adversely affect water catchment for human and industrial needs. The increasing commercial and household demands for energy strain resources, and, together with growing industries and human settlements, degrade water and air resources for a long term liveable quality of life.

The Economic Transformation Programme to achieve The New Economic Model of a high income, inclusive and sustainable nation, the third strategic thrust to achieve Vision 2020, was launched in March 2010. Since its formation in 1963, the Malaysian economic growth has been based on conspicuous consumption. The acculturation of the concept of environmentally sustainable development is now necessary to achieve its environmental goals, hence requiring social transformation.

There is a need for a social policy of participation in environmentally sustainable development and its operationalization. Besides collective responsibility for environmental protection and conservation, an environmentally sustainable state of development, with measurable indicators, has to be continuously formulated for social acceptance, support and participation.

In environmental conservation, national boundaries are porous. Malaysia should intensify efforts in international cooperation on technology sharing, support in environmental management and collective responsibility. Carbon trading better captures environmental costs worldwide. Malaysia has one of the remaining tropical rainforests with a large gene pool and contribution as carbon sink. The burden of custody should not lie on Malaysia alone. Besides conservation and research on Malaysian natural endowments supported by the international community, there is a need for support for improving the quality of life otherwise foregone by its peoples in environmental conservation for the benefit of the seamless world.

REFERENCES

Bank Negara Malaysia. *Monthly Statistical Bulletin*, various years.
Department of Statistics (DOS), Malaysia. *Compendium of Environmental Statistics, Malaysia, 2009*.
———. *State/District Data Bank, Malaysia*, various years.
———. *Yearbook of Statistics, Malaysia*, various years.
Economic Planning Unit, Malaysia. Available at <http://www.epu.gov.my/c/document_library/get_file?uuid=bc7fof87-72d4-48d8-8c8f-65920e480783&groupId=34492> (accessed 29 November 2011).
Hamdan Mokhtar. "Malaysian Energy Situation". Seminar on "COGEN 3: A Business Facilitator", Grand Bluewave Hotel, Shah Alam, Malaysia, 2–3 September 2002.
International Atomic Energy (IAEA). "Report of the International Mission on Review of the Safety Aspects of a Proposed Rare Earth Processing Facility (the Lynas Project)", 2011.

Sin Che Jit Poh. "Subsidy Rationalisation a Bold Step for Future: Najib".
    Available at <http://www.mysinchew.com/node/41933> (accessed 8 August
    2011).
The Sun Daily. "AG Report 2010; Better Performance Overall amid Areas of
    concern". Available at <http://www.thesundaily.my/news/197863> (accessed
    29 November 2011).
Treasury, Malaysia. *Economic Report, Malaysia*, various years.
United Nations. *Malaysia, The Millennium Development Goals at 2010*. United
    Nations, 2011.

PART III

Social Issues

14

MALAYSIA'S EDUCATION, OFF COURSE
Heady Growth, Systemic Woes, Small Fixes

Hwok-Aun Lee

Introduction

Education, economy, and society interact in mutual relationship, but in recent decades increasing attention has been cast in the direction of academia's contribution to economic growth and social development. This is partly a natural outcome of Malaysia's climb up the development ladder, where policy focus broadens from providing universal basic schooling to generating mass higher education and addressing both the quantity and quality of learning. Policy rhetoric has acknowledged, in line with the need to shift away from low-wage and labour-intensive production, that Malaysia must transit toward more skill- and knowledge-intensive output and cultivate a more innovative economy. Visions of a more integrated society and a more mature democracy have also been projected, most notably in Vision 2020. Education institutions play a paramount role in these processes, both to transform themselves and to facilitate multifaceted transformation, particularly in light of aspirations to be a knowledge-based economy.

Malaysia has made considerable quantitative gains, attaining near universal primary schooling and high secondary enrolment rates and steadily expanding tertiary education. However, the quality of educational institutions has fallen short, even regressed, in terms of mass generation of a skilled and innovative workforce and a knowledge-oriented society. Growth in educational provision has facilitated the rise to an upper middle income economy, but mediocrity in educational outcomes constitutes a major barrier to Malaysia's goal of attaining a high income economy and broad socio-political development. The fundamental problem lies in a systemic decline in the teaching profession and the failure to attract capable entrants, exacerbated by a drift toward redressing the education malaise through marginal and mechanical solutions.

From the early 1990s, Malaysia embarked on a new phase of development, in which the balance between growth and equity tilted more toward the former. The main thrust of the New Economic Policy (NEP) from 1971 was to restructure the economy, predominantly through interracial redistribution and affirmative action programmes favouring the majority Bumiputera. Preferential programmes remained decidedly intact beyond the NEP's official closure in 1990, but education policy became increasingly framed in terms of human capital or human resource development. There was no shortage of rhetoric, targets, programmes, and institutional changes in line with lofty national ambitions. The Education Act 1996, repealing the Education Act 1961, expressed in its preamble, a "vital role" for education in "achieving the country's vision of attaining the status of a fully developed nation" and "the mission to develop a world-class quality education system which will realize the full potential of the individual and fulfill the aspiration of the Malaysian nation". Curriculum reforms in 1995 and 1999 introduced content-based and outcome-based learning, as new concepts and approaches gained currency (UNESCO 2011). The National Education Blueprint (2006–10), and the more ambitious Malaysia Education Blueprint 2013–25, both set out, among various objectives, to rejuvenate national schools and transform the education system in a more balanced and holistic direction (Ministry of Education 2006, 2013).

Two decades from the 1990s shift, education statistics continue to accumulate, but indications abound that the projected transformation has lost direction and momentum. Malaysia continues to occupy the "middle income" bracket internationally — presently in the upper middle regions — both in terms of relative income per capita as well as in a multidimensional profile of socio-economic attainments, institutional depth, technological capability, and democratic empowerment. It has become commonplace to hear public outcry and official acknowledgement of the manifold shortcomings of students and graduates — saliently, their lack of critical and creative thinking skills, technical and communication abilities, English proficiency, as well as racial integration. Much breath and ink continue to be spent articulating the need to shift to higher gears of production, and greater generation, and sophistication of knowledge, innovation, and civic engagement. The transformations certainly require much time, yet there is a palpable sense that more progress could and should have materialized, particularly when Malaysia's achievements are compared to those of high-performing Asian countries. Not only has Malaysia been relatively surpassed, systemic decline in public institutions has arguably curtailed education standards in an absolute sense (Cheong et al. 2011, p. 180).

The following sections appraise Malaysia's achievements and shortfalls in education, and reflect on the prospects for the education system to contribute toward socio-economic development and national transformation. Schools and academies have not been renovated into the envisioned, dynamic nodes of learning and knowledge generation, while continuous increase in educational provision and socio-economic conditions raise demands for quality education. Indeed, rapid supply growth has undermined the capacity of education institutions to contribute to the broad transformation of Malaysian economy and society. In addition, the education system, while commissioned to play a unifying role, is in some ways separating society. This malaise, I argue, is rooted in the quality of teaching personnel and a widespread loss of confidence in public education, and has been aggravated by hasty policy and pursuit of speedy results that trump thorough analysis and systemic reform. All in all, Malaysia's education saga in the recent past is one of growth without transformation. The lack of political will to grapple with systemic issues darkens the prospects for transformation in the coming decade.

The Growth Record: Expansion and Expenses

Education indicators trace Malaysia's steady growth in schooling provision and rapid expansion of higher education over the past two
decades. The country almost reached universal primary schooling by
the 1990s, registering a net enrolment rate of 93 per cent in 1993 and
96 per cent over 2005–09.[1] Secondary school enrolment continued to
increase, from 1990 to the late 2000s, although Malaysia's performance
in this regard trails that of Indonesia and Thailand, according to official
sources (see Table 14.1). Away from the spotlight, secondary school
incompletion, especially the dropout rate for boys, continues to be a
major problem (Cheong et al. 2011, p. 169).

Public spending on education, as a proportion of GDP, is substantially
higher in Malaysia than in these Southeast Asian neighbours, as well
as other upper middle income countries such as Brazil and Chile (see
Table 14.2). Notably, Malaysia allocates to tertiary education larger
proportions of the total education budget, and spends more per
student. In development planning, the country has consistently and
increasingly allocated resources to the education sector, through public
expenditures and private sector collaboration (Cheong et al. 2011, p. 166).
Significant areas of spending include construction of school facilities,
information technology, and teacher training, especially to serve rural
communities. By 1998, only 5 per cent of primary school teachers
were considered inadequately trained. The secondary school pupil-
teacher ratio improved from 27.3 in 1980 to 20.4 in 1990, and continued
to decline to 14.2 in 2008 (Leete 2007, p. 195).

The education headline of the last twenty years in Malaysia, as
well as in other upper middle income countries, is the rapid expansion
of higher education (see Table 14.1). Public institutions swelled, with
enrolment increasing from 7.1 per cent of the 20–24 year-old population
to 15.5 per cent in 2000, then growing more moderately to 20.2 per
cent in 2010 (see Table 14.3). The Private Higher Educational Institutions
Act (1996) permitted degree-conferring domestic private higher education institutions (HEIs), beyond the then existing matriculation, transfer
or twinning programmes with overseas institutions. Hot on the heels
of the Act, degree-level enrolment hit 60,000 in 2000, further ballooning
to 111,000 in 2005 and 228,000 in 2010. Correspondingly, gross
enrolment rates burgeoned from 9.6 per cent in 2000 to 19.6 per cent in
2010. Private HEIs presently account for almost half of all certificates,
diplomas and degrees (see Table 14.3).

TABLE 14.1
Gross Secondary and Tertiary Enrolment Rates, Selected Countries

	Secondary Schooling			Tertiary Education		
	1990	2000	2008	1990	2000	2008
Brazil	–	104.2	100.8	10.8	17.8	34.4
Chile	78.2	82.7	90.4	21.3[2]	37.3	54.8
Indonesia	48.0	56.2	74.4	8.7	14.8[1]	21.3
Malaysia	56.0	65.0	68.7	7.3	25.5	36.5
Thailand	29.1	63.2[1]	74.3	16.1	41.2	44.7
South Korea	92.6	97.2	97.2	36.8	83.2	98.1

Notes: 2001[1]; 1991[2].
Source: *World Bank*, <http://www.databank.worldbank.org>.

TABLE 14.2
Education Spending and R&D Participation, Selected Countries

	Public Spending on Education (% GDP)	Public Spending per Pupil as a % of GDP per Capita				Researchers in R&D (Per Million People)	
		All Levels		Tertiary Level			
	1998–2007	2000	2008	2000	2008	2000	2006
Brazil	4.4	12.4	18.1	55.5	29.6[2]	384	620
Chile	3.7	14.7	12.7	19.4	11.5	413	833[5]
Indonesia	3.0[1]	10.5	14.2	n.a.	18.7	n.a.	n.a.
Malaysia	6.2	21.6	15.0	81.1	33.9	276	372
Thailand	4.5	21.1	16.6	36.0	22.0	281[4]	311[6]
South Korea	4.1	16.9	20.5	8.4[3]	9.0	2,919	4,187

Notes: 2001–07[1]; 2007[2]; 1999[3]; 2001[4]; 2004[5]; 2005[6].
Source: *World Bank*, <http://www.databank.worldbank.org>.

TABLE 14.3
Malaysia's Gross Enrolment in Higher Education
(per 20–24 year-old population)

	1990	1995	2000	2005	2010
Public institutions	7.1	9.5	15.5	18.0	20.2
Private institutions	n.a.	n.a.	9.6	11.0	19.6

Note: Includes certificate, diploma, undergraduate degree and teacher training programmes.
Sources: Malaysia (2000), Malaysia (2005), Malaysia (2010).

Higher education policy placed emphasis on research, postgraduate programmes and internationalization, and yielded significant growth in these areas. Over 2000–10, postgraduate enrolment increased by 11.4 per cent per year, compared to 8.4 per cent at the undergraduate level. International students comprise an increasing, albeit still small, proportion of enrolment, mostly in private HEIs.[2] The proportion of undergraduates studying abroad, an exceptionally high figure in the 1980s and 1990s and a feature of Malaysia's educational landscape, was naturally impacted by the proliferation of more affordable opportunities at home. Malaysians enrolled in overseas universities, as a proportion of the higher education student population, dropped from 31.6 per cent in 1990 to 15.3 per cent in 2001, 7.3 per cent in 2010 (Wan 2007).[3]

Affirmative action measures in secondary and higher education have maintained their role of promoting Bumiputera attainment. Some main instruments were expanded, especially in the late 1990s, while accommodations were also made for non-Bumiputera participation. Matriculation colleges, which were fully Bumiputera until the introduction of a 10 per cent non-Bumiputera quota in 2003, saw enrolment burgeon from 9,010 in 1990 to 46,501 in 2000, before settling in the 50,000–55,000 range over 2005–10. MARA junior science colleges — also exclusively Bumiputera until a 10 per cent non-Bumiputera allocation in 2002 — saw enrolment climb steeply from 15,400 in 2000 to 36,100 in 2010. Among Malaysian students overseas, those registered as sponsored, a disproportionate majority of whom are presumably Bumiputera students funded by public sources, numbered 28,291 in 2010, or 35.7 per cent of Malaysians studying abroad.[4] Matriculation programmes and government agency scholarships are mainstays of affirmative action, and have evidently facilitated Bumiputera educational attainment (Loo 2007). However, the quality of education in these domestic institutions remains wanting. Consequently, they are ineffective at cultivating a sufficient mass of capable, self-dependent, and confident Bumiputera, constricting the scope for fundamental reform and rollback of these preferential programmes.

The expansion of education translates into a more qualified labour force. From 1990 to 2010, the share of workforce with only primary schooling fell from 34.6 per cent to 13.2 per cent, while the proportions with secondary schooling and with tertiary education rose, respectively, from 46.8 per cent to 58.0 per cent and from 8.8 per cent to 26.2 per cent.[5] Growth in educational provision and implementation of affirmative action has promoted access to tertiary education, although the Indian and non-Malay Bumiputera communities still lag in this regard. In 2010, the proportion of the labour force with tertiary education was highest for Malays (29.9 per cent), followed by Chinese (25.1 per cent), Indians (23.1 per cent) and non-Malay Bumiputera (15.2 per cent). On the whole, these achievements have helped foster economic growth and Malaysia's international position in the upper middle income strata. Expansion in the workforce's educational profile sustained manufacturing output and exports and enabled the growth of service industries. The next stage of transformation, however, entails much more substantial change, and on that score Malaysia has fallen far short.

The Transformation Record: Systemic Decline, Marginal Remedies

The foremost shortfall — indeed, an abject failure — of Malaysia's education system is the continuous, unmitigated decline of the teaching profession, a vocation that has witnessed its esteem and the quality of entrants spiral downwards. This root issue must be mentioned at the outset of this discussion, because it has also been one of the most overlooked elements of reform, often relegated to an afterthought, or even when acknowledged as a major problem, it is deemed remediable by mechanical alterations or marginal fixes. There are around 175,000 applicants to teachers training programmes and 20,000 new placements per year. It continues to be a popular career option and the pool may be wide — but it is exceedingly shallow. In 2010, a miniscule 3 per cent of applicants to the postgraduate teaching programme earned a combined grade point average (CGPA) above 3.5 out of 4.0 (Malaysia 2010, p. 206). High CPGAs alone do not make good teachers, and training and experience can improve pedagogical effectiveness, but the staggeringly low entry bar emphatically reflects the mediocre base on which Malaysia is building its teaching corps.

The decline in quality of teaching, although widely perceived and officially acknowledged, is not readily measured or tracked over time. National examination results continue to be decorated annually with stellar performances of top scorers. But other trends suggest deterioration in standards and loss of confidence in the national schooling system. Malaysia's performance in the international Trends in Mathematics and Science Study (TIMSS) reveals precipitous drop in scores — the largest regression among all countries participating in the survey. Malaysia fares especially poorly against other high growth East Asian countries, including Thailand (see Table 14.4). A major factor in the strong preference for vernacular, especially Chinese medium, schools over national schools is the experience or perception of lax standards and less capable or under-motivated teachers in the latter.[6] The drop in Malaysian students' abilities in mathematics and science, and widespread rejection of national schools for those who can opt out — including a significant segment of non-Chinese — undermine the transformation that the education system is supposed to foster toward a knowledge-oriented economy and more integrated society.

The descent of education confounds the increasing policy attention it has received, and the measures taken ostensibly to cultivate technical, language and thinking abilities necessary for socio-economic transformation. However, many interventions have been hastily conceived and politically influenced, notably in the latter years of the Mahathir administration. A salient example is the abrupt switch to teaching mathematics and science in English in 2003 (widely known by its Malay acronym, PPSMI). The programmes encountered the foreseeable problem of inadequately equipped teachers, to which the response was

TABLE 14.4
Trends in Mathematics and Science Study
(TIMSS), Eighth Grade Cohort Average Score

	1999	2003	2007	2011
Mathematics				
Malaysia	492	510	471	426
Singapore	568	578	567	590
South Korea	549	558	553	560
Taiwan	569	571	561	564
Thailand	482	n.a.	471	451
Science				
Malaysia	519	508	474	440
Singapore	604	605	593	611
South Korea	587	589	597	609
Taiwan	585	585	598	609
Thailand	467	n.a.	441	427

Source: Mullis, Martin, Foy and Arora (2012*a*, 2012*b*).

large supplies of multimedia materials and training modules, which in turn took teachers away from their classrooms. The policy was scrapped in 2009, mainly due to ethno-nationalistic pressure and political posturing, but without any robust benefit-cost evaluation of the programme. As noted above, national examination results and international test scores indicate varying trends, with the former showing continual progress in mathematical and scientific education while the latter indicates otherwise. Tellingly, in November 2008, then Education Minister Hishammuddin Hussein extolled Malaysia's examination results as evidence of PPSMI's success, only for his successor, Muhyiddin Yassin, to refer to Malaysia's TIMSS standings in July 2009, a mere eight months later, as proof that PPSMI was foundering.

Another case originates in Mahathir's pronouncement of "meritocracy" in university admissions in 2002. Thus, grades from the difficult national examination system, through which non-Bumiputera enter university, were deemed equal to grades from less demanding matriculation programmes, which cater to the vast majority of Bumiputera students. The relationships between affirmative action and educational outcomes are undoubtedly complex and under-explored. Nonetheless, available research has found that university students who entered through matriculation colleges demonstrate less academic ability than those, mainly non-Bumiputera, who passed through the national schooling system (Tan and Santhiram 2009; Haliza et al. 2009). The virtually unchanged racial composition of entering university cohorts thus continues to create illusions of equal qualification and successful education policies, and ultimately undermines transformation.

Education featured even more prominently in the post-Mahathir policy discourses. Abdullah Badawi predicated his administration on reviving education from its desultory state, and created the Ministry of Higher Education to specifically oversee tertiary education, while primary and secondary schooling remained under the Ministry of Education's purview (Abdullah 2004, Malaysia 2005). Administrative reshuffle and sweeping action plans, however, bore insubstantial results. The Najib Razak administration designated education a national key result area (NKRA), and the Tenth Malaysia Plan (2011–15) highlighted the specific problem of teacher quality. However, proposed policies refrained from systemic reforms, preferring instead to rely on road shows to promote the current remuneration package to potential recruits, and profiling novel and potentially impactful but small-scale programmes, such as Teach for Malaysia and trust schools. The government aims to convince potential applicants of the esteem in the teaching profession, and to inform them of the market competitiveness of starting salaries, seemingly oblivious to the contradiction between attempting to attract intelligent youth while treating them as impressionable, and the high likelihood that highly capable ones will weigh career earnings, not just starting pay, in their decisions (Malaysia 2010, p. 207). On the whole, the vicious cycle of a weakening teaching corps and deteriorating education persists.

The cumulative feedback loop of low esteem of the teaching profession and dim profile of entrants is exceedingly difficult to break, especially in a top-down and centralized manner characteristic of governance in Malaysia. While pursuing teaching reforms that intend to facilitate more creative and critical thinking, executive order and bureaucratic supervision have increasingly crept into the system, predisposed more toward extracting output than attracting talent. The allocation of public funds in primary and secondary schooling offers a general indication of such a shift, with the share of administrative departments in federal operating expenditures growing from 3.0 per cent in 1992 to 4.7 per cent in 2000 to 7.6 per cent in 2010.[7] Since 2004, a few notable interventions include programmes to increase the proportion of degree-holding teachers and the introduction of Excellent Teacher and Excellent Principal awards (Ministry of Education 2008, UNESCO 2011). While these measures likely yield some benefits, they remain focused on quantitative gain administered by centralized authority, and are limited to exceptional successes. The potential gains from greater school autonomy and teacher autonomy and better rewards across the board remain largely untapped. The Education Blueprint 2013–25 makes commitments to empower district officers and principals, but remains silent on teachers. The school-based assessment scheme introduced in 2011, ostensibly to reduce the weight of examinations, compelled teachers to score students according to a standardized, elaborate and onerous matrix of developmental criteria and personal attributes, provoking public dissent from the typically docile teaching workforce.

The imperative of revitalizing teaching and schooling is under-scored by the presence of systemically reproducing class and regional inequalities. Examination results are significantly worse for rural students, and influenced by socio-economic background — income, access to books and tuition classes outside of school, and parents' education (Osman Rani and Rasiah 2011). The dilemma is not new, yet probably more pressing than ever. Students from households with fewer resources to supplement in-school instruction are most dependent on, but are worse served by, the public schools they attend. The urban-rural and class divides stand to be perpetuated, so long as disparities in extra-schooling resources and urbanization of better educated parents persist, while the schooling system remains incapable of overcoming these obstacles. The apparent adequacy of urban extra-school facilities and intractability of the decline in the national schooling system may exacerbate the tendency to avoid dealing with root causes.

The labour market offers another window into the condition of graduates. The unemployment rate of the tertiary educated labour force has been consistently higher than that of less qualified workers.[8] Compounding this issue is the reality that graduate unemployment disproportionately affects the Bumiputera community. Within the tertiary educated labour force, non-Malay Bumiputera register the highest unemployment rate, at 9.5 per cent in 2007, followed by 4.3 per cent for Malays, 4.0 per cent for Indians and 2.2 per cent for Chinese. Employer and employee surveys consistently find that graduates, particularly from public higher education institutions (where the vast majority of Bumiputera obtain degrees), substantially fail to meet the mark, especially in terms of English proficiency, communication skills and technical knowledge (World Bank 2004; World Bank 2009; Quah 2009; Jobstreet 2005). Bumiputera graduates of public universities are much more dependent on public sector employment, which reflects, contrary to the objective of affirmative action, lesser mobility in private sector labour markets (Lee 2012). In a massive, but stopgap, effort to enhance their employability, the government spent RM415 million over 2001–05 to retrain 40,000 graduates (Cheong et al. 2011, p. 172).

The employment situation of Malaysian graduates has been and remains a crucial issue, but broader, systemic deficiencies in the tertiary education system on the whole, whether involving public or private institutions, impact on the prospects for socio-economic transformation. The development of research universities and growth in science and engineering fields will play major roles towards that end. The government has availed substantial funds for research, and increased competition in accessing the funds. However, Malaysia still lags in research and development participation (see Table 14.2), which accordingly translates into low R&D output as well. On the enrolment side, while policy has emphasized the sciences since 1980s, the ratio of science to arts enrolment has persisted at around 60–40 (Leete 2007, p. 209). Indeed, only 36 per cent of all tertiary students in 2010 were in science and engineering subjects. This drop from previous proportions derives considerably from the massive expansion of private HEIs, which heavily invested in lower cost programmes like business and professional qualifications, such that only 28 per cent of enrolment is in science and engineering.[9]

Overall, the dispersion of deficiencies across private and public institution, and considerably higher regard for overseas degrees, underscore the systemic dimension to the lack of socio-economic transformation in Malaysia's institutes of higher learning. In large-scale employer and employee surveys conducted by the World Bank in 2002 and 2007, 30–33 per cent of respondent firms considered foreign-trained Malaysian workers better qualified than Malaysian-trained ones (World Bank 2005; World Bank 2009).[10] As with basic schooling, the dynamism and capability of personnel is also essential to quality higher education, and cannot be inspired or induced through the current, vigorous regime of monitoring standard procedures and attention to procedural compliance over academic content.[11] The calibre of educators and researchers in higher education, analogous to the situation among school teachers, is generally perceived to have declined. This is not surprising. It follows, from the scholastic deterioration of the schooling system and the absence of a culture of learning in examination-centric and intellectually stifling environments, that higher education will suffer constraints in the quantity and quality of academic staff.

Furthermore, Malaysia loses many highly qualified citizens through "brain drain". This dilemma warrants mention here, particularly from the perspective of young adults who study abroad and do not return to Malaysia to work — as differentiable from issues of the Malaysian diaspora. The World Bank's (2011, p. 98) widely circulated report and survey findings on brain drain estimates the number of tertiary educated Malaysian-born migrants, aged twenty-five and above, at close to 280,000 in 2010, a sizable proportion of which are presumably affected by the current education malaise. The survey found that career prospects, remuneration and social injustice and corruption to be the strongest factors.[12] Nonetheless, while it is informative, the complexity of factors urges caution in interpreting the causes of brain drain. Many questions remain unanswered. For instance, while a significant portion of survey respondents disapprove of affirmative action in public institutions, it is unclear whether abolishing affirmative action will cause them to pursue higher education in public universities and employment in the public sector. The impact of education quality remains to be examined in detail, but labour market premiums attached to overseas degrees over local degrees suggest that the languishing reputation of domestic tertiary institutes impacts on the depletion of talent, particularly in the form of Malaysians not returning after studying overseas.

The education system plays a key role in national unity. Indeed, the most politically weighty issues in education revolve around integration and equitable access. However, available indications point to a deepening of the 'dual-tracking' phenomenon — the majority of Bumiputera passing through national and residential schools and public higher education, and non-Bumiputera overwhelmingly opting for vernacular schools and largely advancing to private higher institutes (Cheong et al. 2011). Various outcomes result from this inclination of large sections of Malaysia's main ethnic groups to follow their own, non-intersecting educational and social trajectories. First, social separation reduces the scope for interaction and integration, especially between ethnic groups. Chinese-medium schools are the predominant choice of Chinese; the corollary occurs for Indians and Tamil-medium schools and Bumiputera and national schools. This trend stems from a range of reasons, among the most salient of which is the quality of instruction, although the efficacy of "national-type" schools in inculcating critical and creative thinking is also questionable. Second, Bumiputera students remain under-challenged in sequestered environments, especially at the matriculation level, while generous scholarship programmes possibly leave the community more stratified by educational attainment. Despatching the best scholars to study abroad leaves the less capable Bumiputera students in the domestic public institutions.

Conclusions

Among pre-requisites for engendering and sustaining transformation in Malaysia's education system, surely the state of the educating professions precedes other factors. While the relationship between educator attributes and learning outcomes has yet to be rigorously examined in Malaysia, the importance of an effective teaching corps to realize the needed reforms is readily deducible from the continuing inefficacy of decades-long interventions and investments in curriculum, infrastructure, and training that have failed to yield the necessary and desired fruit. The perceived stasis or regression in the quality of school leavers and university graduates, despite generous attention to the problem, underscores the foremost transformation that needs to take place in education: attracting the bright, curious and committed to careers in teaching, research, and other roles in education.

Unfortunately, this premise rests uncomfortably with the current state of policy-making and its predilection for quick fixes — even in the face of admitted deficiencies in critical thinking and creativity, which by definition cannot be resolved through formulaic, standardized and top-down enforcement. While much attention and resources have been allocated towards making national schools competitive against vernacular or private schools, the cause of making teaching a vocation of choice has been tepidly greeted. As noted above, a candid and bold admission of the dire condition of entrants to teachers training could only be met with feeble attempts to sell the current pay and benefits package without altering its contents. Likewise, students' lack of thinking skills has become a commonplace remark in officialdom, but school curricula continue to dictate content and allow derisory room for debate. University students remain under the yoke of the Universities and University Colleges Act, the Aku Janjioath, and other tools of control that curtail critical thinking.[13]

Malaysia must be galvanized around a national project of reversing the decay in education, beginning with the public schools. The concomitant issues of national unity, brain drain, and affirmative action also substantively hinge on arresting and reversing the slide in public education institutions. This will entail difficult decisions be made, in terms of the allocation of education funds, specifically to avail more for teacher's salaries and benefits. The relatively heavy spending in tertiary education, alongside persistent national under-achievement in secondary school enrolment and completion, warrant examination of the distribution of spending between education levels. Another important area concerns the extent to which Malaysia's highly staffed public sector and administrative positions consume resources that could otherwise be directly committed to educational work.

Raising the quality of teaching professionals, of course, is one element of a set of necessary change. Esteem, dynamism, and commitment on the job significantly derive from institutional and individual autonomy.

The increasing weight attached to performance auditing warrants reconsideration, taking cognisance of the need to balance policies that extract effort and target-meeting against those that give space for capable teachers, academicians, and students to thrive. Without political will and bold leadership, these necessary transformations will fail to materialize and academic mediocrity will persist. And it is impossible to envisage Malaysia as a knowledge-based economy and advanced nation without an excellent national education system.

NOTES

1. As Leete (2007) points out, this ratio only captures public schooling and thus understates enrolment. The total figure, including private schools, would be higher and closer to universal schooling.
2. In 2010, international students constituted 11.2 per cent of private HEI enrolment, compared to 4.4 per cent for public HEIs.
3. Absolute numbers also declined, from 104,000 in 2001 to 79,000 in 2010 (Wan 2007).
4. Public Service Department (JPA) scholarships get into the public limelight annually, disproportionate to its scale of operation (around 1,500 new scholars per year), partly because of the intense competition and high expectations and its distinct political symbolism. This chapter omits the JPA scholarship scheme because it comprises a minute fraction of every age cohort, and it unavoidably draws in socio-political issues that lie beyond our scope.
5. *Yearbook of Statistics* and *Labor Force Survey Report*, various years.
6. Koh Lay Chin, "Chinese Medium Schools to the Rescue", *The Nut Graph*, 9 March 2010, available at <http://www.thenutgraph.com/chinese-medium-schools-to-the-rescue>.
7. Author's calculations from the *Federal Government Financial Statements* (various years).
8. Author's calculations from the *Labour Force Survey Report*.
9. Author's calculations from Ministry of Higher Education (2010).
10. The Malaysia Productivity and Investment Climate Surveys of manufacturing and service firms obtained samples of 1,151 firms in 2002 and 1,418 firms in 2007, from regions of Peninsular Malaysia.
11. The Malaysian Qualification Agency (MQA) monitors higher education through auditing adherence to an elaborate schema for course and programme design, content and teaching modes. While it has greater authority and clearer frameworks than its predecessor, the National Accreditation Board (LAN), the MQA overwhelmingly stresses uniformity and compliance with

standardized forms and procedures, over academic content and scholastic quality.

12. While the sample size was small — around 200 — and disproportionately represented by younger adults, its findings are consistent with other surveys and inductive observations on the subject, which also tend to draw participation from younger Malaysians abroad.

13. The Universities and University Colleges Act (UUCA) — due to be amended in 2012 — and the *AkuJanji* (Malay for "I promise") students' oath of conduct constrict academic freedom by suffusing a climate of compliance and pre-empting or punishing public expression of dissent. While most attention has typically fixed on the UUCA's restrictions against students' political participation, broader restriction of student expression and assembly have more pervasive consequences.

References

Abdullah bin Haji Ahmad Badawi. Opening Address At The Malaysian Education Summit, Sunway Lagoon Resort Hotel, Kuala Lumpur, 27 April 2004. Available at <http://www.pmo.gov.my/ucapan/?m=p&p=paklah&id=2840>.

Account General of Malaysia. *Federal Government Financial Statements*. Putrajaya: Account General of Malaysia, various years.

Cheong, Kee-Cheok, Viswanathan Selvaratnam and Kim-Leng Goh. "Education and Human Capital Formation". In *Malaysian Economy: Unfolding Growth and Social Change*, edited by R. Rasiah. Oxford University Press, 2011.

Department of Statistics. *Labour Force Survey Report*. Putrajaya: Government Printer, various years.

———. *Yearbook of Statistics*. Putrajaya: Government Printer, various years.

Haliza Othman et al. "A Comparative Study of Engineering Students on their Pre-university Results with their First-year Performance at FKAB, UKM". Paper presented at the 2009 Teaching and Learning Congress, National University of Malaysia, Bangi. Available at <http://pkukmweb.ukm.my/~upak/pdffile/PeKA09/P3/28.pdf> (accessed 15 October 2010).

Jobstreet. "Survey of Managers on Reasons why They did not Hire Some Fresh Graduates". Available at <http://pesona.mmu.edu.my/~ytbau/tes3211/job_survey_2005.pdf> (accessed 20 July 2009).

Lee, Hwok-Aun. "Affirmative Action in Malaysia: Education and Employment Outcomes since the 1990s". *Journal of Contemporary Asia*, vol. 42, no. 2 (2012): 230–54.

Leete, Richard. *From Kampung to Twin Towers: 50 Years of Economic and Social Development*. Petaling Jaya: Oxford Fajar, 2007.

Loo, Seng Piew. "Schooling in Malaysia". In *Going to School in East Asia*, edited by Gerald A. Postigliane and Jason Tan. Westport, CT: Greenwood, 2007.

Malaysia. *Eighth Malaysia Plan, 2001–05*. Kuala Lumpur: Government Printer, 2000.

———. *Ninth Malaysia Plan, 2006–10*. Kuala Lumpur: Government Printer, 2005.

———. *Tenth Malaysia Plan, 2011–15*. Kuala Lumpur: Government Printer, 2010.

Ministry of Education. *Education Development Blueprint, 2006–10*. Putrajaya: Ministry of Education, 2006.

———. *Malaysia Education for All: Mid-term Assessment Report 2000–07*. Putrajaya: Ministry of Education, 2008.

———. *Malaysia Education Blueprint 2013–25 (Preschool to Post-Secondary Education)*. Putrajaya: Ministry of Education, 2013.

Ministry of Higher Education. *Higher Education Indicators*. Putrajaya: Ministry of Higher Education, 2010.

Mullis, I.V.S., M.O. Martin, P. Foy, and A. Arora. *TIMSS International Results in Mathematics*. Chestnut Hill, MA: TIMSS & PIRLS International Study Center, Boston College, 2012*a*.

———. *TIMSS International Results in Science*. Chestnut Hill, MA: TIMSS & PIRLS International Study Center, Boston College, 2012*b*.

Osman Rani Hassan and Rajah Rasiah. "Poverty and Student Performance in Malaysia". *International Journal of Institutions and Economies*, vol. 3, no. 1 (2000): 61–76.

Quah, Chun Ho, et al. "Employers' Preference for Foreign-Trained Graduates: Myth or Reality?". *European Journal of Scientific Research*, vol. 34, no. 3 (2009): 372–83.

Tan, Yao Sua and Santhiram R. Raman. *The Transformation from Elitist to Mass Higher Education in Malaysia: Problems and Challenges*. CenPRIS Working Paper 101/09. UniversitiSains Malaysia, 2000.

UNESCO. *World Data on Education: Malaysia (Seventh Edition)*. International Bureau of Education, 2011. Available at <http://www.ibe.unesco.org>.

Wan, Chang Da. "Public and Private Higher Education Institutions in Malaysia: Competing, Complementary or Crossbreeds as Education Providers". *Kajian Malaysia*, vol. 25, no. 1 (2007): 1–14.

World Bank. *Malaysia: Firm Competitiveness, Investment Climate, and Growth*. Poverty Reduction, Economic Management and Financial Sector Unit (PREM), East Asia and Pacific Region. Report No. 26841-MA, 2005.

———. *Malaysia: Productivity and Investment Climate Assessment Update*. Poverty Reduction, Economic Management and Financial Sector Unit (PREM), East Asia and Pacific Region. Report No. 49137-MY, 2009.

———. *Malaysia Economic Monitor: Brain Drain*. Bangkok: World Bank, 2011.

15

GROWTH AND CHANGE IN FINANCING MALAYSIAN HIGHER EDUCATION

Lee Hock Guan

By the 1980s, a combination of rising per unit-student cost and accelerating demand for higher education had pressured European states to question whether they could afford to maintain their largely public supported higher educational systems. By the first decade of the twenty-first century, in more and more countries, massification[1] of higher education had brought about a funding crisis in higher education (Hahn 2007; Woodhall 2007). Numerous countries found it increasingly difficult to sustain higher educational systems substantially, if not totally, funded by public revenues. To curtail government funding, many countries turned to the "private sector — represented by households, businesses and philanthropists — [to take on] even greater responsibility for the costs of higher education" (Hahn 2007, p. 3). Except for United States and a handful of other countries where historically private finance has played a large role in the provision of higher education, many countries adopted varying cost-sharing[2] systems to support mass higher education (Johnstone 2009; Johnstone, Arora and Experton 1998).

For the developing world, several distinctive factors have contributed to their crisis of financing higher education, such as; "pressures for enrolment expansion given the relatively low enrolment ratios", "higher education has been the fastest-growing segment of the education sector", "rapid increase has driven high levels of subsidization", and public budget allocation limitations (World Bank 1994, p. 2). With the ascendance of neo-liberalism and its promotion of the market and privatization since the 1980s, the prevailing solution adopted is to diversify public higher education's sources of funding and to expand the privatization of higher education. The World Bank indeed advocates "mobilizing greater private financing, including cost sharing with students", to support higher education (World Bank 1994, p. 40).

Malaysia too experienced several of the distinctive factors that led to higher education funding crisis in the developing world; it rapidly raised the enrolment ratios from low to high, public spending on higher education grew much faster than for primary and secondary, public higher institutions were and remain largely subsidized by the government, and the switch from elite to mass higher education. Similarly, the Malaysian government adopted a cost sharing system to finance higher education where increasingly students and parents are responsible for the cost as well. However, the growth and pattern of financing higher education is also shaped by the politics and political system of a country. In Malaysia, rampant racial politics has entrenched an excessively racialized political system where the government intervened in equity and access to higher education to ensure that the higher education enrolment would reflect the country's racial breakdown. Privatization and massification of higher education have been subjected to racially structured policies to advance and protect Malay enrolment and participation. In short, race-based policies to entrench Malay enrolment and participation in higher education have significantly shaped the growth and pattern of financing students enrolled in both public and private higher education.

Shifting Trends in Financing Higher Education

In brief, financing higher education in Malaysia is enmeshed with two major state objectives that have influenced the development of higher education (Sharom 1980). Since the First Malaysia Plan (1966–70), the state has assigned to higher education a central role in producing trained and skilled Malaysians to meet the manpower needs of the economy. After the May 1969 riots, higher education was also tasked with rectifying the "existing imbalances in educational opportunities among racial and income groups" (Third Malaysia Plan, p. 39). Until the 1990s, the two objectives were pursued in the milieu of an elite higher educational system, monopolized by government-supported public colleges and universities. In the 1990s, growing concern over the shortage of highly educated and skilled manpower critical towards the growth of a knowledge economy led the government to transform the elite higher educational system into a mass system (Santhiram and Tan 2009).

During the NEP period (1971–90), due to the elite higher educational system's limited enrolment capacity, many qualified Malaysians could not gain access to study in the local public institutions. For many better qualified Chinese and Indian students, they were denied admission into local public higher institutions because of mandated racial quota admission policy to raise Malay enrolment to at least be equal to, if not more than, their proportion of the total population. Limited enrolment capacity also meant that Malaysia was dependent on overseas higher education to absorb qualified Malaysians who failed to gain admission into local institutions and also to enable Malaysians to pursue courses which were not offered locally especially in science and technology fields.

From 1978 to 1985, the number of Malaysians studying overseas grew by an annual average of 9 per cent from 36,000 in 1978 to 39,908 in 1980, 58,000 in 1983 and 60,000 in 1985 (Fifth Malaysia Plan, p. 489). In 1980, Malaysians studying overseas amounted to 51.2 per cent of total higher education enrolment, and in 1985 the figure was 46.2 per cent. Chinese students constituted the majority of Malaysians studying overseas followed by Malays and Indians; in 1983, the ethnic breakdown was 63.3 per cent Chinese, 18.9 per cent Malays and 15 per cent Indians (Fourth Malaysia Plan, p. 361). By the early 1980s, the government had grown apprehensive over the high financial costs of sending Malaysians to study overseas; the estimated outflow of foreign exchange was about RM1.2 billion a year from 1981–85 (Fifth Malaysia Plan, p. 489). Moreover, the government was shouldering a sizable financial burden as it was sponsoring a large number of the Malaysians studying overseas; 8,700 (22 per cent of total overseas students) in 1980 and 12,800 (22.1 per cent) in 1983. In line with the policy to upgrade Malay enrolment, Malay students received most of the state scholarships and loans, mainly provided by Public Service Department (PSD) and Indigenous People's Trust Council (MARA), while most of the Chinese and Indian students were self-funded.

An economic slump in the mid-1980s and the Australian and British states' decisions to charge foreign students studying in their higher education institutions full fees pressured the government to introduce measures to reduce the cost of financing Malaysians to study abroad. Racial considerations significantly influenced the ways the measures to reduce both public and private sources of funding overseas study were put into practice. Local public higher educational system's enrolment capacity was increased by expanding existing public higher education facilities and by building new institutions. Facilities to offer programmes to pre-university students especially for government-sponsored students in order to reduce the time they would have to study abroad were introduced (Fourth Malaysia Plan, p. 361). Selected public higher education institutions established pre-university and twinning and credit transfer programmes for government-sponsored students.

In 1985, the Mahathir administration assigned to Institut Teknologi MARA (ITM) the task of starting preparatory programmes for government-sponsored students bound for overseas. ITM played a pioneering role in establishing twinning and credit transfers programmes with American counterparts, with Midwest Universities Consortium for International Activities (MUCIA) from 1985 to 1992 and Texas International Education Consortium (TIEC) from 1985 to 1988 (MUCIA 1987; Faridahanim, et al. 2000). Predictably, Malay students were the principal beneficiary of the expanded enrolment in the local public higher educational system and the various government-funded preparatory and twinning and credit transfer programmes.

Taking into account the balance of payment deficit problem and the manpower needs of the economy, the Mahathir administration also permitted the private sector to expand and establish pre-university and twinning and credit transfer programs.[3] Private higher education provided an alternative cheaper route to pursue an overseas education for many qualified Chinese and Indian students who were denied admission into local public higher education institutions because of mandated racial quota policy. Consequently, the financial burden of studying in local private higher education institutions was shouldered by the Chinese and Indian students and their parents[4] (Lee 1999). Because of the higher cost of studying in the private higher education institutions, the majority of the private sector's Chinese and Indians students would come from the higher income groups.

The 1997 Asian financial crisis further hastened the government's plan to radically reform the Malaysian higher educational system. Aware of the huge public expenditure increasing the higher education enrolment would incur led the government "to relinquish its role as the main provider of higher education by encouraging public institutions to seek revenue elsewhere and by pressing the private sector to set up independent higher education institutions" (Johari Mat 2003, p. 1). Thus mass higher education was implemented through expanding and upgrading of old public higher education institutions and the building of new ones, and the issuing of new licences to increase the number of private higher institutions. A variety of private higher education institutions was established; foreign university campuses, government linked corporations supported, political parties linked, etc. (Tengku Shamsul Bahrin 2011). Consequently, higher education enrolment rate for the cohort 17–23 years increased from 2.9 per cent in 1990 to 29 per cent in 2003 and to close to 40 per cent in 2010.

With the establishment of mass higher education, the government also radically modified the pattern of financing Malay students especially by switching gradually to a cost sharing system with Malay students and parents contributing an increasing share of the cost. For example, MARA financial aid scheme was converted in January 1998 to a 100 per cent loan scheme except for loans given out under the Excellent Student Scheme where students can apply to convert their loans to scholarships based on their examination results.[5] Policy-makers, however, recognized that in a cost sharing system, many qualified Malays from lower incomes might not be able to continue with their studies as they would not afford it. This could result in Malay enrolment falling below their ratio of the population. The *Perbadanan Tabung Pendidikan Tinggi Nasional* (PTPTN) was established in part to ensure that there would be loans available for most qualified Malay students to afford both public and private higher education, and in part to maintain the government targeted racial composition of enrolment in higher education.

In the transition from elite to mass higher education then, the government-supported public higher education system state was replaced by a blend of highly government-supported public and largely privately-funded private higher education institutions. Due to mandated racial quota admission policy to public higher institutions, Malays were the primary beneficiary of largely government funded public higher education system. Various local pre-university programmes in public institutions were set up for usually government-supported students to reduce the time they would study abroad. Also, government scholarships and loans for higher education continue to disproportionately benefit Malays and increasingly Malay owned private higher education institutions too.[6] With the transition to mass higher education, the state adopted a cost sharing system that resulted in privatizing the cost of higher education to an increasing number of students and parents including among the Malays. The government adopted a gradualist privatization scheme where initially the private higher education sector largely enrolled privately funded Chinese students, and later, after the establishment of a mass higher educational system, the private sector enrolled both PTPTN-supported Malay students and largely privately funded non-Malay students.

Public Higher Education Expenditure[7]

Education has consistently received generous public funding in Malaysia and accounted for a high and increasing share of the government's total expenditure. Since 1970, as a percentage of Gross Domestic Product (GDP), education expenditure has typically ranged between 4 to 6 per cent; in 2009, it was about 5.8 per cent of GDP or 19 per cent of total public expenditure. In the 1970s and 1980s, because of the prevailing opinion that primary and secondary education will give higher rates of returns, the two levels received the bigger share of the public educational expenditure.[8] Since the 1990s, with the emphasis on increasing enrolment at the higher education level, public spending on higher education has been growing at a faster rate than the spending for primary and secondary education.

From the Fifth to Eighth Malaysia Plans, development expenditure for higher education average about 34 per cent of the total educational development expenditure, reaching an all time high of 43.5 per cent in the Sixth Malaysia Plan (see Table 15.1). However, its share fell to 25 per cent in the Seventh Malaysia Plan largely because of the fiscal contraction triggered by the 1997 Asian financial crisis. In the Eighth and Ninth Malaysia Plans, the spending on developing the higher education sector was raised back to 35.3 per cent and 39.8 per cent respectively. In absolute terms, government development expenditure for higher education increased from RM1.7 billion in 5MP (1986–90) to RM5.0 billion in 7MP (1996–2000) and RM16.1 billion in 9MP (2006–10).

While increasing privatization has helped to ease government higher education spending, nevertheless, from 1994 to 1998, total public spending on higher education grew at 11 per cent per year on average, compared to 9 per cent for secondary education and 4 per cent for primary education. In 1998, higher educational budget took up 20 per cent of the total educational expenditure, and between 2007 and 2010 it averaged about 37.7 per cent of the total educational expenditure or 6.3 per cent of the total public expenditure. In 2005, the government allocated about 2.7 per cent of its GDP towards higher education, and in 2010 the figure was 1.69 per cent of GDP. Malaysia's spending on higher education measured in terms of public expenditure per student is about RM22,021 or 49.4 per cent of GDP per capita is among the highest in Asia, if not the world, and compares favourably to the top OECD performers (see Table 15.2).

TABLE 15.1
Federal Government Development Expenditure on
Education and Training
(in MYR million)

Malaysia Plan	Education Expenditure (a)	Higher Education Expenditure (b)	b/a (%)
5th (1986–90)	5,382	1,727	32.1
6th (1991–95)	6,982	3,039	43.5
7th (1996–2000)	19,724	5,005	25.4
8th (2001–05)	37,922	13,404	35.3
9th*(2006–10)	40,357	16,069	39.8

Note: * allocation
Source: Various Malaysia Plans.

TABLE 15.2
Higher Education Expenditure in 2007, or Latest Year Available

Country	Public Expenditure per Student as % of GDP per Capita	Public Expenditure per Student PPP US$	Country	Public Expenditure per Student as % of GDP per Capita	Public Expenditure per Student PPP US$
Norway	47.1	25,191	Malaysia	49.4	6,673
Sweden	39.0	14,312	South Korea	8.8	2,355
United Kingdom	24.8	8,346	Singapore	26.9	13,238
United States	22.4	9,700	Indonesia	16.1	696
Australia	21.0	7,348	Thailand	23.0	1,774
Japan	20.1	6,431	Vietnam	61.7	1,717

Source: UNESCO Global Education Digest, 2009.

Thus while privatization of higher education has transferred part
of the financial burden to students and parents, government higher
education spending has continued to account for a high and increasing proportion of the government's total expenditure. The main reason
that government higher education spending remains substantial is
because the local public institutions account for at least half the total
enrolment and continue to be very dependent on government funds.
On average, the government subsidizes between 80 to 95 per cent of
the tuition fee students have to pay; Table 15.3 shows the costs borne
by the government for selected fields of study (*Bernama*, 15 April 2012,
<http://www.my.news.yahoo.com/govt-bears-85-95-per-cent-tuition-fee-
163208770.html>). Indeed, tuition subsidy in Malaysia is one of the
highest in the world.

Through corporatization, the government has tried to enable public
higher education institutions to diversify their income mechanisms and
resources, but without removing the substantial tuition fees subsidies.
For various reasons, public higher institutions have been unsuccessful
in weaning away from their heavy dependence on public funding.[9]
Since Malay enrolment in public higher institutions represents more
than their proportion of the total population, in 2008 Malay enrolment
made up more than 80 per cent of total enrolment in public higher
educational system,[10] then the community has disproportionately
benefited from public spending on higher education. Moreover, while
Malay students continue to be the principal beneficiary, it is also
a fact that children of the middle and upper Malay classes would

TABLE 15.3
Tuition Fees Charged for Selected Courses at Public Universities, 2005
(in MYR)

Field of Study	Cost for Programme	Tuition Fees Paid by Student	Cost Born by Government
Business management	21,582	4,700 (22%)	16,882 (78%)
Engineering	53,130	6,500 (17%)	46,630 (83%)
Medicine	275,518	9,800 (4%)	265,718 (96%)
Science	48,512	5,000 (10%)	43,512 (90%)
Arts	20,551	4,200 (20%)	16,351 (80%)

Source: Ministry of Higher Education.

have disproportionately benefited since the selection criterion remains largely income-blind. Studies indeed have shown that subsidies to higher education in Malaysia has been, and probably remains, regressive with students from better-off incomes background, across ethnic groups, benefiting the most (Mehmet 1986; Hammer et al. 1995).

Growth of National Student Loans

Undoubtedly, the establishment of the national student loans scheme PTPTN has contributed to enhancing access to higher education across ethnicity and class and thus to the successful massification and privatization of higher education. A government subsidized student loan scheme, in theory the PTPTN loans are to help to subsidize part of the tuition fees and living expenses especially for students from lower income groups. Students from both private and public higher institutions are eligible to apply for loans, and the amount differs according to institutions, field of study and, in recent years,[11] income of parents of the students as well.

The PTPTN has contributed significantly to the expansion of first the public higher education sector and, since 2000, the private higher education sector. In 1997, the PTPTN financed slightly more than 12,000 students which totalled nearly RM220 million (see Table 15.4).

TABLE 15.4
Allocation of the National Higher Education Fund, Selected Years

Year	Student Enrolment		Total No. of Students	Proportion of Students from Private	Amount RM
	Public Sector	Private Sector			
1997	11,905	179	12,084	1.5%	219.5
1999	76,389	6,769	83,158	8.1%	1,683.6
2001	84,306	26,338	110,644	23.8%	2,134.1
2002	86,186	19,591	105,077	18.5%	1,981.2
2003	86,057	26,564	112,621	23.6%	1,863.4
2004	88,282	30,829	119,111	25.9%	2,268.4
2005	98,755	45,704	144,459	31.6%	2,762.9
Total	635,208	164,978	800,186	20.6%	15,138.3

Source: Ministry of Higher Education.

In 1999, the total number of students the PTPTN funded dramatically increased to 83,158 and the amount needed to nearly RM1.9 billion. Since then, the number of students annually receiving subsidized loans from PTPTN and in parallel the annual loan allocation, except for the years 2002 and 2003, has steady increased. In 2005, a total of 144,459 students received a total of nearly RM2.8 billion, and the government announced in 2010 that the PTPTN has approved 238,722 loans using an allocation of RM6.04 billion.

PTPTN's contribution to the growth of both the public and private higher education sector in the country is overwhelming. In 2000, about 32.3 per cent of students enrolled in public higher education received PTPTN funding and in 2005 the figure was reduced to 25.6 per cent. This reduction is due to the diversion of loans to finance students enrolled in the private higher education; the proportion of subsidized students in private higher education has increased from 1.8 per cent in 1997 to 8.8 per cent in 2000 and almost 30 per cent by 2005 (see Table 15.4). By 2011, the government announced that private higher institution students receiving PTPTN loans made up 40 per cent of the recipients. The total of number of students enrolled in the private higher education receiving PTPTN loans has increased from 179 in 1997 to 8,286 in 2000, 45,704 in 2005 and 88,834 in 2011.

Although students enrolled in private higher education institutions made up about one third of the total number of students receiving PTPTN subsidized loans in 2005, the percentage of financial allocation to support the private students has exceeded the 30 per cent student proportion because of the generally higher fees charged by private higher education institutions. Thus, while 37.9 per cent and 38.1 per cent of the PTPTN loans were given out to private sector students, in terms of amount, they constituted the bigger share of loans given out, 58.13 per cent and 55.76 per cent respectively. In absolute amount, the PTPTN loaned out RM3.5 billion and RM3.1 billion to private sector students in 2010 and 2011 compared to the smaller amount of RM2.5 billion and RM2.4 billion respectively to public sector students. The average loan per private sector student is RM38,000 in 2010 and RM35,000 in 2011 compared to RM17,000 and RM18,000 for public sector students respectively.

Officially, the PTPTN eligibility is colour-blind, but, in practice, the allocation has followed a clearly race-based quota policy; as of April 2010, out of the 1.5 million students who have received PTPTN loans, 70 per cent went to Malay students, 18 per cent Chinese students,

5 per cent Indian students and 7 per cent other races (SASSY MP, 4 July 2010). While the PTPTN was initially established with the aim of supporting students who gained admission to public higher institutions, since 2001, an increasing percentage of the loans has been funnelled to private sector students. However, not all private higher institutions have equally benefited from the PTPTN funds precisely because funds have been used to facilitate especially the enrolment of Malay students in and to support Malay-owned private higher institutions. For Malay students receiving PTPTN loans, they have limited freedom of choice in terms of selecting the private college to enrol. This is because, until recently, most loans given out to Malay students are applied by and channelled through the operators of private colleges and universities. Public financing such as PTPTN has also been manipulated for the purpose of increasing Malay ownership of the private higher education sector. Towards the end of the 1990s, the government was becoming perturbed by the small representation of Malays enrolled in the rapidly growing private higher education sector. It was not for the lack of qualifications that Malay students were not enrolling in the local private higher education institutions, but because most of them could not afford to pay the higher access costs. It was in part to increase Malay enrolment in the private higher education sector that the PTPTN has diverted a substantial portion of its funds to finance the enrolment of Malay students in the private higher education sector.

In part attracted by the business potential in operating private higher education institutions, especially after 1996, an increasing number of Malay-owned private colleges and universities were established. By 2002, there were an estimated 186 Malay-owned private universities and colleges, excluding the private universities established by government-linked companies, with Malay/bumiputra student accounting for nearly 90 per cent of the enrolment (*Berita Harian*, 17 June 2002). In 2010, there were an estimated 60,000 Malay/bumiputra students enrolled in 120 Malay-owned private colleges with at least 20,000 of the students receiving PTPTN loans alone (*Utusan Malaysia*, 22 April 2010). It is clear then that without the substantial financing from PTPTN and MARA, quite a number of Malay owned private higher educational institutions would have difficulty enrolling sufficient students to remain financially viable.

Various weaknesses in the organizational design and implementation of the PTPTN have been identified; repayment ratios, default rates, administration cost and efficiency (World Bank 2007; Hua and Ziderman 2008). The World Bank (2007) has also voiced its concern over the sustainability of the PTPTN in the future if no remedial steps are taken to strengthen the financing scheme; indeed, the Auditor General of Malaysia estimated that the PTPTN's deficit would balloon to RM43 billion by 2020. That increasingly the PTPTN loans have been diverted to support the private higher education sector especially the Malay-owned institutions have raised concern over issues such as the quality of education provided by the private sector and the questionable long run sustainability of private higher institutions that depend largely on PTPTN sponsored students.

Conclusions

Since the 1990s, Malaysian education policy has been driven by an ambitious plan to raise the higher education enrolment from around 10 per cent in 1990 to 40 per cent by 2010. To achieve this ambitious plan, the inherited British elitist higher education was transformed into a mass higher education system. Massification of higher education sector was pursued through a two-pronged strategy; liberalizing higher education to private providers and expanding the public higher education sector. The existing cost sharing scheme has enhanced the access to higher education across all ethnic groups and to a certain extent across classes as well since the PTPTN subsidized loans would have enabled more students from lower income groups to enrol in especially private higher institutions.

However, mandated racial quota policies to advance Malay enrolment and participation have affected the equity and access to and thus financing of higher education. Overall, government spending on higher education has disproportionately benefited the Malays because the latter comprised more than 80 per cent of the enrolment in local public higher education institutions and are also the main beneficiary of public scholarships and subsidized PTPTN loans. Disproportionately more Malay students have received the subsidized PTPTN loans and policy-makers have also used PTPTN to support Malay-owned private higher institutions. In contrast, only the selected top Chinese and Indian students would be awarded the limited government sponsored merit-based scholarships while other qualified Chinese and Indian students access to public scholarships and subsidize PTPTN loans continue to be regulated by a tacit racial quota policy.

With the success of the NEP, intra-Malay educational inequalities have widened with children of especially the higher income Malays disproportionately benefiting from the racial policies which remain largely income-blind. On the one hand, the PTPTN and MARA loans are financially unsustainable in part because higher incomes Malays have used them to secure cheap loans to finance their children's higher education. In addition, across ethnic groups the financing policy that increasingly shifts responsibility to students and parents would make it ever more difficult for lower-income students to attend higher education and become a major financial burden for middle income Malaysians. And if they manage to secure PTPTN loans, frequently lower-income students would find it difficult to repay the loans such that there would be more and more student loan debt and defaults. Given the growing income differentiation and inequity in Malaysia, and in the Malay community in particular, the financing of higher education should be modified to be less race-based and more income-sensitive in order to help students from the lowest socio-economic across all ethnic groups.

NOTES

1. The classification of higher educational system into elite (less than 15 per cent of higher education age cohort), mass (15–30 per cent) and universal more than 50 per cent) by Martin Trow in 1974. See Trow (2005).
2. In 1986, D. Bruce Johnstone introduced his influential concept of "cost-sharing" which claims that all costs of higher education are "borne by a combination of four sources of finance: (i) taxpayers, (ii) parents, (iii) students and (iv) private institutions/donors" (cited in Woodhall 2007, p. 22).
3. The previously private higher education sector which mainly offered commerce, vocational and technical courses for students who could not obtain places in the local public higher education institutions was converted into an alternative system to obtain foreign tertiary qualifications at highly discounted prices.
4. Among the Chinese students, they could take study loan from the KOPERASI JAYADIRI MALAYSIA BERHAD (KOJADI), established on 12 March 1981. KOJADI was established with the aim of providing educational loans to

needy students, largely Chinese, to pursue higher education. In addition, banks also started to offer "education savings or investment schemes" for mainly Chinese and Indian parents to invest ahead for their children's education in private higher education.

5. MARA Study Loan Scheme was first introduced in 1966 when MARA was formed. The financial assistance was then given out in the form of full scholarships. From 1968, the financial aid for college was divided into two types. MARA scholarships with a 25 per cent repayment and MARA study loans with a 100 per cent repayment. From 1 January 1985 until 31 December 1997, the financial aid was in the form of convertible loans. Students who obtained good grades upon graduation were eligible to apply to convert their MARA study loans to MARA scholarships.

6. Until recently, the PSD "routinely award 80 per cent of overseas scholarships to Bumiputra and the remainder 20 per cent to non-Bumiputra students" (Foong 2008, p. 21). In its recent selection criterion, the PSD has divided its 1,500 overseas scholarships into; 300 (20 per cent) merit, 60 (5 per cent) Sarawak bumiputeras, 60 (5 per cent) Sabah Bumiputeras, 144 (10 per cent) socially handicapped, and the bulk 720 (60 per cent) ethnic composition of society. Without fail a disproportionate percentage of the merit-based were awarded to non-Malays; in 2010, 20 per cent went to bumiputeras and 80 per cent to non-bumiputeras. Unsurprisingly, the vast majority of the rest of the PSD overseas scholarships were awarded to Malay/bumiputera students (ibid). PSD's race-based selection process is most evident in its allocation for local degree and diploma programmes where it adhered strictly to the ethnic composition of society where the recipients are consistently 70 per cent bumiputera and 30 percent non-bumiputera (Fong 2008, p. 21).

7. This does not include public funded scholarships, local state expenditure on higher education and the funding by other government bodies such as MARA and PSD.

8. For an interesting assessment of the contribution of economic thinking to education, see Woodhall (2007).

9. Several other problems with the existing pattern of public spending on higher education have been raised by the 2007 World Bank Report.

10. This includes enrolment in community colleges, polytechnics, and universities and university colleges especially Universiti Teknologi MARA.

11. PTPTN recently introduced a variable loan structure based on student's parents' income: RM5,001 and above — tuition fees, (b) RM4,001–RM5,000 — partial loans, and (c) RM4,000 and below — full loans.

REFERENCES

Altbach, Philip. "The Logic of Mass Higher Education". *Tertiary Education and Management* 10 (Spring 1999): 107–24.

Faridahanim Mohd Jaafar, Zaini Abdullah, and Jamaliah Mohd Khalili. "An Analytical Survey on College Students Experiences: The Quality of Efforts Exerted and Their Perception of the Gains". The Case of PPP/ITM American Degree Programme. Shah Alam, Selangor: Bureau of Research and Consultancy, UniTM, June 2000.

Foong Kee Kuan. "Funding Higher Education in Malaysia". Australia, Canberra, East Asia Bureau of Economic Research Working Paper no. 44 (2008).

Hahn, Ryan. *The Global State of Higher Education and the Rise of Private Finance.* Washington, D.C.: Institute For Higher Education Policy, 2007.

Hua Shen and Adrian Ziderman. *Student Loans Repayment and Recovery: International Comparison.* Germany: Bonn, Institute for the Study of Labor no. 3588 (2008).

Jeffrey S. Hammer, Ijaz Nabi, and James A. Cercone. "Distributional Effects of Social Sector Expenditures in Malaysia". In *Public Spending and the Poor: Theory and Evidence,* edited by van de Walle, Dominique and Kimberly Nead. Baltimore and London: The Johns Hopkins University Press for the World Bank, 1995.

Johari Mat. "Distance Education Public Policy and Practice in the Higher Education: The Case of Malaysia (Part II)". Unpublished paper delivered at the Revista Brasileira de Aprendizagem Aberta e a Distância, São Paulo, September 2003.

Johnstone, D. Bruce. "Worldwide Trends in Financing Higher Education: A Conceptual Framework". In *Financing Access and Equity in Higher Education,* edited by Jane Knight. Rotterdam: Sense Publishers, 2009.

Johnstone, D. Bruce, Alka Arora and William Experton. *The Financing and Management of Higher Education: A Status Report on Worldwide Reforms.* Washington, D.C.: The World Bank, 1998.

Lee, Molly. "Private Higher Education in Malaysia". Monograph Series no. 2. Penang: School of Educational Studies, Universiti Sains Malaysia, 1999.

Malaysia. Malaysia Plans (various five-year plans). Kuala Lumpur: Government Printers Malaysia, various years.

Mehmet, Ozay. *Human Capital Formation in Malaysian Universities: A Socio-economic Profile of the 1983 Graduates.* Institute of Advanced Studies, University of Malaya, 1983.

Midwest Universities Consortium for International Activities. *The ITM/ MUCIA Program in Malaysia: Cooperation in Higher Education, East Lansing.* Michigan: MUCIA, May 1987.

Ministry of Higher Education, Malaysia. Available at <http://www.mohe.gov.my>.

Mohd Fuad Razali. "PTPTN Untungkan Pelajar Bukan Bumiputera". *Berita Harian*, 17 June 2002.

Santhiram, R. and Tan Yao Sua. "The Transformation from Elitist to Mass Higher Education in Malaysia: Problems and Challenges". *Journal of Applied Research in Education*, vol. 13, nos. 124–39 (2009).

SASSY MP. "Jawapan Menteri Pengajian Tinggi Mengenai Jumlah Pembiayaan Kepada Peminjam PTPTN Mengikut Kaum dan Negeri". Available at <http://teresakok.com/2010/07/14/jawapan-menteri-pengajian-tinggi-mengenai-jumlah-pembiayaan-kepada-peminjam-ptptn-mengikut-kaum-negeri/> (accessed 20 August 2012).

Sharom Ahmat. *Nation Building and the University in Developing Countries: The Case of Malaysia, Higher Education* 9 (1980): 721–41.

Tengku Shamsul Bahrin. *Private Higher Education in Transition: A Personal Perspective in Malaysia — Policies and Issues in Economic Development*. Kuala Lumpur: ISIS, 2011.

Trow, Martin. "Reflections on the Transition from Elite to Mass to Universal Access in Modern Societies since WWII". In *International Handbook of Higher Education*, edited by James J.F. Forest and Philip G. Altbach. NYC: Springer International Handbooks of Education, vol. 18, 2005.

UNESCO. *Global Education Digest 2009: Comparing Education Statistics Across the World*. Canada: Montreal, UNESCO Institute for Statistics, 2009.

Marzita Abdullah. "IPTS bumiputera terancam — 30 buah di jangka 'gulung tikar' dan menjejaskan masa depan 8,000 pelajar". *Utusan Malaysia*, 22 April 2010.

Woodhall, Maureen. *Funding Higher Education: The Contribution of Economic Thinking to Debate and Policy Development*. Education Working Paper Series no. 8. Washington, D.C.: World Bank, 2007.

World Bank. *Higher Education: The Lessons of Experience*. Washington, D.C.: The World Bank, 1994.

———. *Malaysia and the Knowledge Economy: Building a World-Class Higher Education*. Washington, D.C.: Human Development Sector Reports, no. 40397 (2007).

16

INCOME INEQUALITY
A Drag on being a Developed Nation?

Ragayah Haji Mat Zin

Introduction

Income distribution has always been a core and prioritized issue in Malaysian economic development. Although inequality (as measured by the Gini ratio) was rising prior to 1976, it was reduced by about 16.6 per cent by the end of the New Economic Policy 1971–90 (NEP). However, inequality has fluctuated in the last twenty years and currently remains at the same level as in 1990. The persistent high inequality can be an obstacle to eradicate absolute poverty, improve inclusiveness (Bourguignon 2003, p. 6) and can threaten economic growth. Although Malaysia has successfully reduced absolute overall poverty incidence to 3.8 per cent in 2009, there are still geographical areas with high concentrations of poverty. Moreover, Malaysia's income disparity is not only much higher than that of many developed countries in the world, but also relative to its neighbours — Indonesia, Philippines, and Thailand (World Bank 2011, p. 73) which have much lower per capita incomes than Malaysia.

Given the above concerns, this chapter aims to examine the Malaysian income distribution status, attempt to explain the reasons for the changes in the last twenty years, and propose some recommendations to improve the situation. For this purpose, the next section analyses the trends and patterns of overall, rural, urban, and ethnic inequality. Some of the indicators of inequality will also be decomposed into "within group" and "between group" components to give a deeper understanding of the income distribution situation. Section 3 offers several explanations regarding the changes in income distribution, while Section 4 will provide some policy recommendations to narrow income inequality in Malaysia. Section 5 concludes the chapter.

Trends in Income Inequality

Table 16.1 shows that the Gini ratio reflecting the overall income distribution rose from 0.513 in 1970 to 0.557 in 1976, falling to 0.442 at the end of the NEP period, and thereafter oscillating to reach 0.441 in 2007. Table 16.1 also shows that income distribution in both the rural and urban areas exhibit similar trends over the NEP period. The Gini ratio for rural households rose between 1970 and 1976 but fell thereafter to 0.401 by 1992. It also exhibited fluctuating values after this, falling to its lowest level in 2007 but rising again to 0.407 in 2009. The urban Gini ratio also followed the same pattern, but generally at a higher level, reaching its lowest level in 1997, then widening again to reach a local peak (0.444) in 2004, before moderating to 0.423 in 2009.

Income disparities between urban and rural areas remain high. It managed to come down to 1.7 in 1990, but rose again to 2.11 in 2002 and 2004 before falling to 1.91 in 2007 and 1.85 in 2009. The decompositions of the inequality measures show that most of the inequality is explained by the "within group" component and a much smaller proportion is explained by the "between group" component, that is, within the urban or the rural areas themselves, rather than due to the urban-rural differences (Ragayah 2009).

Examining the values of the Gini for the various states reveals that, with a few exceptions, states with high inequality tend to have high incidence of poverty. Hence, states like Sabah, Sarawak, Perlis, Kelantan, and Terengganu have relatively high inequality, while the rest with higher mean monthly household incomes have relatively lower Gini,

TABLE 16.1
Malaysia: Gini Coefficient by Ethnicity, Strata and State, 1970–2009

	1970[a]	1974[a]	1976[a]	1979	1984	1987[b]	1989	1992	1995	1997	1999	2002	2004	2007	2009
Malaysia	0.513	0.530	0.557	0.505	0.483	0.456	0.442	0.459	0.456	0.459	0.443	0.461	0.462	0.441	0.441
Ethnic															
Bumiputra	0.466	0.476	0.506	0.468	0.464	0.447	0.429	0.442	0.441	0.448	0.433	0.435	0.452	0.430	0.440
Chinese	0.466	0.520	0.541	0.474	0.452	0.428	0.419	0.420	0.428	0.416	0.434	0.455	0.446	0.432	0.425
Indians	0.472	0.451	0.509	0.460	0.419	0.402	0.390	0.402	0.404	0.409	0.413	0.399	0.425	0.414	0.424
Others	0.667	0.665	0.630	0.598	0.570	0.663	0.404	0.556	0.414	0.555	0.393	0.449	0.462	0.545	0.495
Strata															
Urban	n.a.	0.541	0.531	0.491	0.468	0.449	0.444	0.439	0.431	0.427	0.432	0.439	0.444	0.427	0.423
Rural	n.a.	0.473	0.540	0.471	0.450	0.427	0.416	0.401	0.410	0.424	0.421	0.405	0.397	0.388	0.407
State															
Johor	n.a.	0.439	0.469	0.442	0.404	0.386	0.381	0.423	0.399	0.397	0.386	0.408	0.395	0.368	0.393
Kedah	n.a.	0.523	0.497	0.468	0.476	0.434	0.428	0.433	0.406	0.429	0.409	0.426	0.387	0.392	0.408
Kelantan	n.a.	0.612	0.505	0.438	0.464	0.414	0.407	0.451	0.442	0.442	0.424	0.444	0.416	0.368	0.428
Melaka	n.a.	0.506	0.558	0.472	0.438	0.403	0.396	0.397	0.399	0.371	0.399	0.386	0.352	0.380	0.372
N Sembilan	n.a.	0.465	0.490	0.432	0.422	0.431	0.366	0.406	0.384	0.408	0.392	0.401	0.380	0.385	0.372
Pahang	n.a.	0.445	0.384	0.478	0.416	0.372	0.350	0.369	0.373	0.359	0.332	0.404	0.389	0.380	0.382
Penang	n.a.	0.597	0.608	0.492	0.452	0.422	0.406	0.412	0.405	0.398	0.399	0.435	0.398	0.411	0.419
Perak	n.a.	0.452	0.525	0.447	0.428	0.410	0.421	0.399	0.397	0.381	0.387	0.417	0.393	0.399	0.400
Perlis	n.a.	0.425	0.498	0.440	0.459	0.408	0.377	0.415	0.379	0.412	0.394	0.437	0.423	0.454	0.434
Selangor	n.a.	0.507	0.516	0.505	0.481	0.462	0.444	0.446	0.424	0.409	0.394	0.423	0.443	0.418	0.424
Terengganu	n.a.	0.502	0.482	0.458	0.461	0.478	0.459	0.448	0.464	0.466	0.440	0.424	0.443	0.399	0.418
Sabah/FT Labuan	—	—	—	0.490	0.491	0.467	0.459	0.468	0.448	0.454	0.448	0.465	0.477	0.450	0.453
Sarawak	—	—	—	0.501	0.498	0.465	0.441	0.467	0.440	0.447	0.407	0.445	0.440	0.442	0.448
F.T. KL	—	—	—	—	0.486	0.465	0.428	0.443	0.423	0.417	0.414	0.448	0.467	0.446	0.374
F.T. Putrajaya	—	—	—	—	—	—	—	—	—	—	—	—	—	0.362	0.342

Notes:

[a] Refers to Peninsular Malaysia only;

[b] Starting 1989, data is based on Malaysian citizens;

[c] From 1999 onwards, calculation of poverty is based on 2005 Methodology.

Source: Ragayah (2009); Economic Planning Unit, *Socio-Economic Statistics: Household Income and Poverty*, 2011, available at <http://www.epu.gov.my/household-income-poverty> (accessed 5 August 2011).

except for Selangor and Penang. In the former states, certain portions of the population remain trapped in pockets of poverty, engaging in poorly paid occupations such as small-scale agriculture, fishing, and low-end services, and have relatively low levels of education and skills, while certain sections of society, such as senior government officers, business owners, and executives, earn relatively high incomes. Foreign direct investment (FDI) or manufacturing activities are scarce in these states. While Terengganu, Sabah, and Sarawak have oil and gas (and had timber earlier on), the benefits have not trickled down to the bottom. Sabah also continues to face influx of illegal migrants from the Philippines and Indonesia, and Sarawak is encumbered by poor rural infrastructure.

An important aspect of income inequality in Malaysia is ethnic income distribution. In 1970, the degree of inequality among the major ethnic groups in Peninsular Malaysia was highest among the Indians, followed by the Malays/Bumiputeras and the Chinese. By 1976, inequalities among the three races peaked with the disparity being highest among the Chinese, followed by the Indians and the Bumiputeras, respectively. Income disparities of all the three ethnic groups improved to reach the lowest levels for the Bumiputeras and the Indians in 1989, but all three experienced vacillating trends after that with the Chinese experiencing their lowest disparity in 1997. Except for the Chinese, both the Bumiputeras and the Indians are experiencing widening income distribution in the last few years. After 1979, with the exception of 2002 when Chinese inequality was the highest, Bumiputera income inequality stayed the highest, followed by the Chinese and the Indians, respectively. The decomposition indices for the ethnic inequality also reveal that most of the inequality in Malaysia is accounted for by the "intra-" or "within group" component and a much smaller proportion is explained by the "inter-" or "between group" component (Ragayah 2009). If we use the Theil index for decomposition, the between group component has been declining from 10.06 per cent in 1995 to 5.43 per cent in 2007.

Factors Explaining Income Distribution

During the NEP period, various government interventions are said to have had an impact on growth, poverty and equity, including rural development, education and employment, export-oriented industrialization, as well as restructuring of equity ownership and asset accumulation. While it can be said that rural development programmes do improve the income and welfare of the rural households, their efficacy in achieving this objective, as well as redistribution of income, can still be improved. Moreover, while these programmes helped in poverty eradication, studies have shown that they were not as effective in redistributing income among the rural households since their benefits are rather unequally distributed. It was other measures that were more responsible for the drop in the Gini ratio in the rural areas, including the provision and quota for education and the rapid growth brought about by industrialization and structural change that provided employment for both the rapidly increasing rural labour as well as the urban poor. Moreover, the tightening of the labour market in the late 1970s and early 1980s, as well as the revision of the government sector salary structure that proportionately favoured the lower income groups, resulted in reducing the poverty incidence and improving income distribution in the urban areas. The restructuring of asset ownership, financial and physical, favouring Bumiputeras also helped to redress the imbalances in the ownership of assets and wealth in all sectors of the society. Overall, it can be said that Malaysia was successful in moderating income inequalities during the NEP period.

In order to explain the fluctuating disparity in the last twenty years, Gill and Kharas (2007, p. 3) proposed five major drivers of inequalities — trade and globalization, labour market reform, the formation of clusters and agglomeration effects, the process of fiscal decentralization and impediments to the process of internal migration. Labour market reform and fiscal decentralization are not relevant to Malaysia, although labour market policies have a large impact on Malaysian income distribution.

Trade and Globalization

In order to diversify the economy from being too dependent on agriculture and primary commodities, the government encouraged FDI and export-oriented manufacturing after 1968. While government intervened via licencing and quotas, private sector development was encouraged in these export-oriented industries through the provision of various incentives. Since the 1990s, the labour-intensive export-oriented industrialization approach could no longer be sustained for labour-scarce Malaysia. Hence, Malaysia has been upgrading, albeit slowly, her industrialization development to that which is more capital- and technology-intensive. Moreover, production and trade have also been expanding. Consequently, this development raised the demand for skilled and highly educated workers as the economy moves up the value chain. Since the supply of this type of workers lagged behind their demand, these skilled workers were able to command an increasing premium over the unskilled workers. The shortage of skilled workers was worsened by the relatively substantial brain drain that was concurrently happening, particularly in the 1990s. At the same time, the divergence of the wages of skilled and unskilled workers were said to have been enhanced by the massive entry of unskilled foreign labour into the Malaysian economy that dampened the wages of unskilled labour (Ishak 2000; Ragayah 1998). However, the mushrooming of tertiary institutions after 1996 and the slower growth ameliorated the situation.

The liberalization of the NEP requirements to stimulate the economy after the mid-1980s recession eased the 30 per cent equity to be owned by Bumiputeras, which resulted in non-Bumiputera average income rising faster than Bumiputera average income. This, together with the acceleration of privatization to step up the creation of the Bumiputera Commercial and Industrial Community, might also have contributed to the subsequent widening of income inequality, with inequality being highest among the Bumiputera community.

What is puzzling is that the data on salaries and wages in the manufacturing sector (which accounts for about 28 per cent of total employment in the last decade) does not seem to support this argument for the period 1989–99, as the shares of earnings for the lower income groups have generally been increasing relative to the professional group in the managerial and professional category (see Table 16.2). However, between 1999 and 2004, the ratio of the managerial and professional group average income to that of the average income of the production workers directly employed or through labour contractors showed an increasing trend, which could explain the widening inequality in the urban areas as well as the country as a whole. The opposite happened in the last two years, which is consistent with falling inequality.

TABLE 16.2
Ratio of Salaries and Wages to the Managerial and Professional Group by Job Category in the Manufacturing Sector, 1989–2008

Year	Managerial & Professional		Technical & Supervisory (RM)	Clerical & Related Occupation (RM)	General Workers		Production/Operative Workers Directly Employed			Production Workers Employed Through Labour Contractors		
	Professional (RM)	Non-professional (RM)			Driver (RM)	Others (RM)	Skilled (RM)	S-Skilled (RM)	Unskilled (RM)	Skilled (RM)	S-Skilled (RM)	Unskilled (RM)
1989	1.000	0.6004	0.2877	0.1914	0.1693	0.1161	0.1399	0.0978	0.0847	0.1781	0.1252	0.0827
1990	1.000	0.6326	0.2977	0.2017	0.1743	0.1201	0.1466	0.1091	0.0887	0.1987	0.1445	0.0949
1991	1.000	0.6313	0.2924	0.1912	0.1671	0.1176	0.1453	0.1078	0.0865	0.1943	0.1250	0.0934
1992	1.000	0.6230	0.2998	0.1897	0.1686	0.1231	0.1506	0.1155	0.0903	0.1867	0.1320	0.0872
1993	1.000	0.6306	0.3128	0.1988	0.1728	0.1248	0.1618	0.1184	0.0988	0.2028	0.1309	0.0980
1994	1.000	0.6607	0.3162	0.2011	0.1722	0.1224	0.1632	0.1210	0.1009	0.2102	0.1319	0.0989
1995	1.000	0.6500	0.3303	0.2099	0.1913	0.1313	0.1731	0.1301	0.1033	0.2332	0.1310	0.1040
1996	1.000	0.6176	0.3363	0.2083	0.1904	0.1354	0.1756	0.1326	0.1081	0.2413	0.1305	0.0995
1998	1.000	0.6372	0.3403	0.2154	0.1772	0.1440	0.1794	0.1376	0.1128	0.1952	0.1436	0.1088
2000	1.000		0.4124	0.2679	0.1959			0.1780		0.1871		
2001	1.000		0.4065	0.2749	0.1966			0.1720		0.1875		
2002	1.000		0.3947	0.2669	0.1838			0.1692		0.1662		
2003	1.000		0.3901	0.2702	0.1801			0.1640		0.1800		
2004	1.000		0.3980	0.2765	0.1875			0.1653		0.1747		
2005	1.000		n.a.	n.a.	n.a.			n.a.		n.a.		
2006	1.000		n.a.	n.a.	n.a.			n.a.		n.a.		
2007	1.000		0.4298	0.2771	0.1998			0.1797		0.1669		
2008	1.000		0.4374	0.2837	0.2014			0.1778		0.1747		

Source: Calculated from Malaysia, *Annual Survey of Manufacturing Industries*, Department of Statistics, various issues.

Labour Market Policies

Malaysia has long followed policies that restrain labour organizations in an effort, *inter alia*, to increase both foreign and domestic invest-ment and production. Arbitrary arrest and detention without trial have long been used against labour, while 1967 Industrial Relations Act (IRA) prohibited unions from engaging in collective bargaining and strikes over issues involving job promotion, transfers, recruitment, retrenchment, dismissal, reinstatement, allocation of duties, and strikes related to such matters (Rasiah and Zulkifly 1998, p. 74). Moreover, unions lose the right to strike once a dispute is referred to the industrial court. These restrictions crippled labour mobilization and greatly reduced its influence on workers' wages and welfare.

As labour scarcity emerged and real wages started to rise in the 1980s, the government allowed the import of foreign workers. The influx of legal foreign workers peaked in 2008 and was estimated to have decreased to 1.8 million in 2010 accounting for 15.5 per cent of the total employment in 2010. Large-scale low-wage migration into Malaysia used to be conducive to overall economic growth, to increasing returns in capital, but resulted in increased disparity in incomes. Since the late 1990s, the policies on foreign workers have become incoherent and run counter to the national objective of achiev-ing high-income status (NEAC 2010, p. 126). Ragayah (1998, 2002, pp. 59–60) has argued that easily available foreign workers discouraged employers from developing more technologically intensive methods of production and from providing skill training to their workers, thereby, keeping productivity and wages low. Thus, while immigrant labour did contribute to keeping Malaysian exports competitive in the short and medium-term, there may be a price to pay in the long run as firms face increasingly severe shortages of skilled personnel and fall behind in technology development. This low returns on education in Malaysia — both as a result of deficiencies in skills formation as well as inefficiencies in firm productivity — is one of the major causes of the brain drain (World Bank 2011, p. 75). Moreover, Tham and Liew (2004) have shown that foreign workers have a negative impact on competitiveness and with lower productivity than local workers, while Tham and Liew (2010) shows that firms use foreign workers to increase their competitiveness by lowering unit labour through decreasing the salaries and wages for all workers (both native and foreign) by more

TABLE 16.3
Share of GDP Component of Selected Countries, 2005

Countries	Compensation of Employees %	Gross Operating Surplus/Gross Mixed Income %	Taxes Less Subsidies on Production and Imports %
Malaysia	28.0	67.1	4.9
Philippines*	27.8	64.0	8.2
Korea	45.8	43.0	11.2
Canada	50.6	38.1	11.3
Japan	51.5	40.4	7.7
United Kingdom	54.5	33.5	12.1
United States	56.9	36.6	7.0

Note: * Refer to data for 2006.
Source: Razaman Ridzuan and Syed Ibrahim Mohd Jamaluddin (2009).

than the decrease in labour productivity, thus, suppressing wages and stretching income inequality. In other words, workers are paid below their productivity, resulting in compensation paid to employees being only 28.0 per cent (see Table 16.3) compared to over 50 per cent in most high income countries. Malaysia's level is only at about the same as that of the Philippines.

The World Bank (2010, pp. 80–81) also found that Malaysian workers do not get a fair share of output due to various non-competitive aspects of the market including excessive bureaucratic red-tape, regulatory burdens, and tax-related costs, all of which dissuade investment, new firm creation, and firm operation. Although Malaysia has improved in its competitiveness ranking, it is still behind neighbouring countries like Singapore, Hong Kong and Thailand in terms of the ease of setting up a new firm. Thus, existing firms can keep wages low without worrying that their workers would leave for a new firm.

Constraints on the Process of Internal Migration

Migration is one of the ways to pare off inequality between rural and urban areas. However, the costs of migrating are high and unaffordable to many of the poor. These local workers have to compete for the limited number of decently remunerated low-skill jobs with the foreign workers and they may end up not improving their economic situation. Consequently, poverty incidence persists and inequality continues to be high.

For most of the years during the last two decades, the percentage of urban-rural migration in the two top occupational categories, the professional, technical, and related workers as well as the administrative and managerial workers, generally exceeded the percentage of rural-urban migration, resulting in a net urban-rural migration of these groups (see Table 16.4). At the same time, the percentage of rural-urban migration of the lowest occupational category, the production and related workers, transport equipment operators and labourers, exceeded the percentage of urban-rural migration for most years of the first decade, resulting in net inflows into the urban areas of this category of workers. This process would then leave behind the really poor. High migration costs can lead to geographic poverty traps, as the poor are impeded from taking advantage of economic opportunities elsewhere. Thus, the combined inflow of the professional, technical, and related workers into the rural areas would surely widen its income disparities. However, the migration trends of the last several years until 2008 show that urban-rural migration of both the bottom groups tend to exceed the rural-urban migration, which might boost up the average incomes of the lower classes of households, contributing to improving income distribution in the rural areas.

Formation of Clusters and Agglomeration Effects

Rising inequality since the end of the NEP could also be attributed to the difference in the growth rates of rural compared to urban incomes due to the lag in the growth of the agriculture sector, while there was robust growth in the major urban clusters enabling the tapping of scale economies and agglomeration effects. Although there are attempts to revitalize agriculture, productivity growth of the sector is still sluggish. This subsector continues to face the problems of uneconomic farm size that hinders technology transfer as well as labour shortage, ageing farm labour, and declining competitiveness of the smallholder unit of production.

Fortunately, sometimes the rural sector experience good luck in the commodity market. Rural poverty during the 1997–98 financial

TABLE 16.4
Percentage Distribution of Employed Internal Migrants by Occupation and Migration Direction

Occupation	1992		1993		1995		1996		1997		1998		1999		2000	
	U-R	R-U	U-R	R-U	U-R	R-U	U-R	R-U	U-R	R-U	U-R	R-U	U-R	R-U	U-R	R-U
Professional, technical and related workers	13.4	9.0	13.3	10.3	18.5	11.8	15.0	11.6	16.7	17.9	16.7	13.7	12.5	12.3	18.7	11.8
Administrative and managerial workers	1.8	1.6	0.9	1.7	5.3	2.7	3.3	1.8	3.7	2.5	5.2	3.3	3.9	1.6	3.4	1.8
Clerical and related workers	9.1	6.8	7.8	8.1	9.1	8.8	13.1	12.0	8.7	11.6	13.7	10.5	9.2	13.5	10.3	9.2
Sales workers	5.8	5.4	5.0	4.5	7.8	9.3	8.4	7.7	6.6	7.8	8.0	9.7	7.0	10.2	6.1	8.9
Service workers	14.8	18.1	13.8	17.0	11.5	16.4	11.2	18.9	9.7	16.5	11.8	14.8	10.4	15.4	13.4	19.5
Agricultural, animal husbandry and forestry workers, fishermen and hunters	15.4	3.4	16.1	2.6	10.7	2.3	10.6	2.3	8.3	3.3	12.6	1.6	17.1	1.7	7.6	2.5
Production and related workers, transport equipment operators and labourers	39.7	55.7	43.1	55.8	37.1	48.7	38.4	45.7	46.3	40.4	32.0	46.4	39.9	45.3	40.5	46.3
Total	100.0	100.0	100.0	100.0	100.0	100.0	100.0	100.0	100.0	100.0	100.0	100.0	100.0	100.0	100.0	100.0

TABLE 16.4 (*Cont'd*)

Occupation	2001		2002		2003		2007		2008		2009–10	
	U-R	R-U	U-R	R-U	U-R	R-U	U-R	R-U	U-R	R-U	U-R	R-U
Legislators, senior officials & managers	3.5	2.9	4.0	3.9	3.2	5.8	5.9	1.7	5.5	1.4	2.9	4.0
Professionals	9.8	4.1	5.4	7.4	8.5	2.5	12.8	9.5	9.5	6.9	8.0	5.4
Technician & associate professionals	18.6	12.9	14.6	12.8	18.0	15.2	22.0	12.9	14.4	11.4	19.6	17.7
Clerical workers	6.3	7.3	5.4	6.3	5.7	7.8	6.2	8.1	7.8	12.0	5.8	12.0
Service workers & shop & market sales workers	12.5	18.8	13.4	19.0	14.0	17.5	6.6	17.9	21.8	32.1	14.0	15.6
Skilled agricultural & fishery workers	10.7	2.7	13.0	2.2	9.5	3.7	10.2	2.1	10.7	0.6	13.7	1.0
Craft & related trades workers	11.5	20.0	15.3	20.2	13.8	20.2	12.3	27.2	11.7	17.8	9.8	14.1
Plant & machine operators & assemblers	15.0	21.3	14.0	16.7	12.2	12.8	11.5	9.9	6.5	9.0	14.8	12.1
Elementary occupations	12.1	10.1	14.9	11.5	15.1	14.5	12.4	10.7	12.1	8.7	11.4	18.0
Total	100.0	100.0	100.0	100.0	100.0	100.0	100.0	100.0	100.0	100.0	100.0	100.0

Note: U-R: Urban-Rural   R-U: Rural-Urban

Source: Malaysia, *Migration Survey Report*, Department of Statistics, various years.

crisis declined more rapidly than urban poverty, due to the resurgence of rural income as world-price declines of commodities produced by rural households were limited by depreciation of the exchange rate that increased the ringgit price of commodities, which in some cases led to increased output. Between 2004 and 2007, the surge in the palm oil and rubber prices also boosted rural income, whereby the bottom 40 per cent rural income group had the fastest rise in their mean monthly income (26.9 per cent), compared to 19.4 per cent for the middle 40 per cent and 20.6 per cent for the top 20 per cent of rural households. Unfortunately, both palm oil and rubber prices plunged in 2009 due to the global financial crisis, resulting in increasing disparity between the top 20 per cent households in the rural areas that experienced a 15.6 per cent jump in income between 2007 and 2009, compared to 9.9 per cent of the middle 40 per cent and 3.9 per cent of the bottom 40 per cent of rural households. Among the urban households, the mean monthly income of the bottom 40 per cent rose the highest between 2004 and 2009 compared to that of the top 20 per cent and middle 40 per cent of households. These differential rates of increase would definitely contribute towards explaining the recent movements in income inequality.

State-government-party Collusion

Another source of inequality is state-government-party collusion (Abdul Rahman Embong 2008) or corruption, cronyism, and nepotism (Gill and Kharas 2007, p. 1), which has been documented by Gomez (1990, 1994), Gomez and Jomo (1997) and Saravanamuttu (2009). This is defined as the "ownership and control of the economy by political parties such as UMNO, MCA and MIC". It also connotes linkages of parties to noted business tycoons or "cronies", many of whom are engaged in rent-seeking enterprises, with the leaders of the ruling parties using their political clout and influence to earn enormous rents for themselves or their political cronies and families. In some cases, the linkage between personal and family assets becomes rather conflated with that of the political party which the political leader controls. This phenomenon transcends ethnicity, as described in a case study by Morishita (2009) and enabled a selected section of the Malaysian society to accumulate income and wealth very rapidly, thus accentuating inequality.

Policy Suggestions for Improving Income Distribution[1]

Malaysia is aspiring to be a high income nation that is inclusive and sustainable by 2020. However, in order to be truly inclusive, income distribution needs to be narrowed further. Based on the above analysis, the government must emphasize on the following policies in the Eleventh Malaysia Plan 2016–20 if it were to reduce income inequality further:

1. Seriously implement NEM's proposals for inclusiveness   The New Economic Model (NEM) launched in March 2010 proposes market-friendly affirmative action for the bottom 40 per cent of households by income, to be achieved through equitable, fair, and transparent processes for determining eligibility for government programmes, access to resources on the basis of need and merit, and sound institutional frameworks for more effective monitoring and implementation of programmes. This is in line with the policy suggestions made previously (see, for example, Ragayah 2008, 2009; Malaysia 1991, p. 33). However, a good plan alone is inadequate unless it is well-implemented. More than a year has passed since the introduction of the NEM, the ordinary public has yet to feel the changes. The government must have more political will to ensure that ordinary *rakyat* benefit from the programmes. Moreover, big cases of corruption still hog the limelight and needs to be tackled more seriously.

2. Reduce urban–rural, intra-ethnic, and regional gaps rather than ethnic disparities   Focus should be given to reducing urban–rural, intra-ethnic, and regional gaps rather than ethnic disparities as inequality between the ethnic groups has been declining over the years. At the same time, the large differences in mean incomes between the states and the regional disparity also mean that economic development in the laggard states have to be geared up.

3. Enhancing quality education for the low-income households Education is the sharpest tool for poverty reduction and upward social mobility. Generally, the government should emphasize on getting the right foundation for every child's education and this means strengthening the provision of early and basic education (Lee and Nagaraj 2012, p. 220). For the poor, there should also be more equal access to quality education. While talent and meritocracy are important, it is crucial to ensure this approach is not biased to educated urban parents who are able to provide their children with the right environment. Most scholarships are awarded to children of better-off parents because they are the ones with access to better facilities, more conducive environment, and tuition support. It is time that better-off parents take the financial responsibility of educating their children, if not fully at least partially, so as to release the funds for disadvantaged but deserving children, giving them opportunity to further their studies. Scholarships for overseas study should be awarded only to the best and brightest students who have been able to gain entry to world-class universities, and should be restricted to programmes that are either unavailable or in short supply in Malaysia. Other good students should stay at home to increase the talent pool in local universities and help Malaysia attain her ambition to be a regional education hub. The money thus saved could be used to fund promising students from rural areas who would otherwise not be able to continue their education.

4. *Giving back to society* Society must also play its role in redistribution. At the corporate level, corporate social responsibility should be enhanced. Efforts by non-governmental organizations, some of which are already doing good work, should be further encouraged. Many informal organizations, often at the individual level, have undertaken various ways to assist the poor, such as setting up orphanages to cater both for orphans as well as children of single parents or from broken homes, both to take care of their immediate needs as well as their education. All these should be strengthened.

5. *Increasing labour mobility and labour market competition as well as reducing rigidities in labour markets* Sharing information on job availabilities to reduce the costs of job search, as well as further easing of the regulations of setting up a new business, would result in competitive labour markets that make firms more efficient and conducive to better compensation practices. Regulations in hiring and firing workers should be reviewed. In addition, the government should intensify its efforts to encourage greater automation and mechanization of labour-intensive industries, to reduce the dependence on foreign unskilled labour. Employers must provide continuous training for workers and the latter must be willing to be retrained and become multi-skilled, in order to increase the productivity. Malaysian employers must be made to realize that the short-term strategy of using low-paid foreign workers as a captive labour force puts their long-term sustainability in question.

6. *Minimum wage*   As workers are paid below their productivity, the issue of how the minimum wage is to be implemented should be resolved as quickly as possible. Workers would also be motivated to be more productive with the higher incentive. Currently, the government has set up the National Wage Consultative Council to look into this matter. At the same time, employers must also provide workers with training and new skills while paying workers the appropriate incentives. At the same time, workers must also agree to undergo training as well as to multi-skill, so as to raise and then sustain their higher productivity.

7. *Increasing the retirement age*   Together with the NEM's concern that the Employees Provident Fund (EPF) only covers about half of the workforce (NEAC 2010, p. 170) is the inadequacy of the EPF, from both the amount and the management of fund withdrawn upon retirement. In 2007, only 0.45 per cent members have EPF savings exceeding RM500,000 while the average savings of active members aged 54 years was RM121, 163.53 (EPF 2007, pp. 100–1). The latter will surely be inadequate to support members' life after retirement of 15–20 years given the current life expectancy. While the government has been raising the retirement age, the private sector is still sticking to 55 years, which is early relative even to other ASEAN countries. While it has other implications, one way out of this (and at the same time retaining experienced workers) is to increase retirement age. In his 2012 Budget speech on 7 October 2011, Prime Minister Mohd. Najib Razak, who is also the Finance Minister, announced that the government will extend the mandatory retirement age of civil servants from 58 to 60 years old. However, for most of the private sector that accounts for almost 90 per cent of employment, the retirement age is still 55 years old and this sector is therefore encouraged to emulate the public sector.

8. *Levelling taxes*   Since most of the taxes have become less pro-gressive, the government should have the willpower to quickly implement the goods and services tax, which is claimed to be progressive. At the same time, a study should be carried out to explore the viability of introducing "levelling taxes", such as hereditary or wealth taxes.

Conclusions

Unequal income distribution is not conducive for promoting social cohesion and providing an income inequality has been brought down by the NEP, but it has fluctuated in the last twenty years and stubbornly remained at a level above acceptable in a country wanting to achieve a developed nation status. Several factors account for these movements in the trend: trade and globalization that resulted in high returns to the educated and skilled workers, together with labour market policies that tend to dampen wages of the unskilled workers are recipes for high inequality. This situation is spiced by the fact that there are constraints to internal migration that resulted in wide disparity in wages earned in different states and between urban and rural areas. While clusters and agglomeration effects enabled economies of scale to be exploited and thus encourage growth, they also tend to increase inequality. And state-government-party collusion that ends up in corruption and rentier behaviour just worsen the situation.

The Tenth Malaysia Plan 2011–15 (10MP Malaysia 2010, p. 364) targets the average annual growth rate over the five-year period to be 6 per cent per annum. Given the current and ongoing economic problems and slowdown in most of Malaysia's main export markets, this goal appears to be rather optimistic and may not be achievable. Assuming that the target growth rate is attainable, the strategies for accomplishing this growth tend to be inequality widening — driving growth by urban agglomerations, cluster- and corridor-based economic activities, and focusing on the National Key Economic Areas (NKEAs). While the 10MP provides for various programmes to assist the bottom 40 per cent of households, the strategies are not that much different from what have been recommended in the earlier Plans. To this extent, the outcomes are not expected to be really transformational. Further liberalization of selected sectors in the economy would also tend to enhance inequality. Moreover, one of the main explanations for the narrowing of inequality in the last several years is the improvements in the price of agriculture commodities as it lifted up the income of many rural households. Given the depressed outlook in most of the primary markets for these commodities, the demand for these commodities might not be expansionary and thus may not play its role in mitigating income inequality. On the other hand, two current developments might be able to improve income distribution. First is the negotiation on the minimum wage to be implemented, most probably by early next year. This would raise the income of many workers who have been paid less than their productivity and would blunt income distribution at the bottom. Second, the raising of the retirement age in the public sector hopefully will also influence the private sector to follow suit. If this happens, then workers would have longer time to accumulate more savings for their retirement, at the very least in the form of their Employees Provident Fund contribution and spend less time trying to survive on their savings. Whether the net outcome of these forces will widen or narrow inequality depends on which impacts are stronger. Currently, employers are rather resistant in doing away with cheap, unskilled foreign workers, and upgrading their capital and technological intensity, so as to enable workers to raise their productivity further. The net outcome on inequality depends on the strength of these forces and the ability of the government to implement the proposed policies in reducing inequality.

In order to improve income distribution, the government needs to emphasize on productivity through enhancing the quality education for the low-income households, improving labour mobility, labour market competition as well as reducing rigidities in labour markets, fixing the minimum wage so that workers would be paid their dues and feel motivated to increase productivity, improving inclusiveness (implement NEM's proposals for inclusiveness, reduce urban–rural, intra-ethnic, and regional gaps rather than ethnic disparities; giving back to society; and increasing the retirement age) as well as earnestly addressed corruption. However, the government must have the political will to implement these suggestions. History has shown that growth can cause income inequality to narrow or to widen, depending on structural factors as well as the policies implemented by the government of the day. Experience has also shown that a good plan may not necessarily be well-implemented. It is all up to the government of the day.

NOTE

1. Similar suggestions have been forwarded in Ragayah (2008, 2009, 2011 and 2012).

REFERENCES

Abdul Rahman Embong. "State-Society Relations in Malaysia: From Acquiescence to Contestations". Paper presented at the 3rd IKMAS Workshop, "Critical Transitions: Malaysia 50 Years and Beyond", Seremban, 7–9 October 2008.
Bourguignon F. "The Poverty-Growth-Inequality Triangle". Paper prepared for the Conference on Poverty Inequality and Growth. Agence Française de Développement/EU Development Network, Paris, 13 November 2003.
Economic Planning Unit (EPU). *Socio-Economic Statistics: Household Income and Poverty*, 2011. Available at <http://www.epu.gov.my/household-income-poverty> (accessed 5 August 2011).
Employees Provident Fund (EPF). *Annual Report 2007*. Kuala Lumpur: EPF, 2007.
Gill, Indermit and Homi Kharas. *An East Asian Renaissance: Ideas for Economic Growth*. The World Bank, 2007.
Gomez, E.T. *Politics in Business: UMNO's Corporate Investments*. Kuala Lumpur: FORUM, 1990.
———. *Political Business: Corporate Involvement of Malaysian Political Parties*. Townsville: Centre for East and Southeast Asian Studies, 1994.
Gomez, E.T. and Jomo K.S. *Malaysia's Political Economy: Politics, Patronage and Profits*. Cambridge: Cambridge University Press, 1997.
Ishak Shari. "Economic Growth and Income Inequality in Malaysia, 1971–1995". *Journal of the Asia Pacific Economy*, vol. 5, nos. 1 and 2 (2000): 112–24.
Lee Kiong Hock and Shyamala Nagaraj. "The Crisis in Education". In *Malaysia's Development Challenges: Graduating from the Middle*, edited by Hill, Hal, Tham Siew Yean and Ragayah Haji Mat Zin. Abingdon: Routledge Malaysian Studies Series, 2012.
Malaysia. *Migration Survey Report*. Malaysia: Department of Statistics, various years.
———. *Sixth Malaysia Plan 1991–1995*. Kuala Lumpur: National Printing Department, 1991.
———. *Tenth Malaysia Plan 2011–2015*. Kuala Lumpur: Percetakan Nasional Malaysia Berhad, 2010.
Morishita, A. "Politics and Timber in Malaysia". In *The Nippon Foundation: Asian Transformations in Action: The Work of the 2006/2007 API Fellows*, 2009. The Nippon Foundation, July 2009.

National Economic Advisory Council (NEAC). *New Economic Model for Malaysia: Part 1*. Putrajaya: Percetakan Nasional Malaysia Berhad, 2010.

Ragayah Haji Mat Zin. "Why Income Inequality Rises in Malaysia after 1990?" Paper presented at the 6th Convention of the East Asian Economic Association, Kitakyushu, Japan, 4–5 September 1998.

———. "The Impact of the Financial Crisis on Poverty and Inequality in Malaysia". In *Impact of the East Asian Financial Crisis Revisited*, edited by Shahid Khandker. The World Bank Institute and the Philippine Institute for Development Studies, 2002.

———. "Income Inequality in Malaysia". *Asian Economic Policy Review*, vol. 3, no. 1 (June 2008): 114–32.

———. *Growth with Equity: Reality and Aspiration*. Bangi: Universiti Kebangsaan Press, 2009.

———. "Sharing the Pie: Towards a More Equitable Malaysian Society". In *Malaysia at a Crossroads: Can We Make the Transition?*, edited by Abdul Rahman Embong and Tham Siew Yean. Bangi: University Kebangsaan Press, 2011.

———. "Poverty Eradication and Income Distribution". In *Malaysia's Development Challenges: Graduating from the Middle*, edited by Hal Hill, Tham Siew Yean and Ragayah Haji Mat Zin. Abingdon: Routledge Malaysian Studies Series, 2012.

Rasiah, R. and O. Zulkifly. "Economic Policy and Employment Growth in Malaysia". In *Employment and Development: Experiences of the OECD and Southeast Asian Economies*, edited by R. Rasiah and N. von Hofmann. Bonn: Friedrich-Ebert-Stiftung, 1998.

Razaman Ridzuan and Syed Ibrahim Mohd Jamaluddin. "Measuring Gross Domestic Product: Using Income Approach", 2009. Available at <http://www.statistics.gov.my/portal/download_journals/files/2009/Volume2/contents_Measuring_Gross_Domestic_Product.pdf> (accessed 12 December 2011).

Saravanamuttu, J. *Party Capitalism in Southeast Asia: Democracy's Bane?* Bangi: Institute of Malaysian and International Studies, Universiti Kebangsaan Malaysia, 2009.

Tham, S.Y. and C.S. Liew. "Foreign Labor in Malaysian Manufacturing: Enhancing Malaysian Competitiveness?" In *Globalisation, Culture and Inequalities: In Honor of the Late Ishak Shari*, edited by Abdul Rahman Embong. Bangi: Penerbit UKM, 2004.

———. "The Impact of Foreign Labor on Labor Productivity and Wages in Malaysian Manufacturing, 2000–2006". Paper presented at the World Bank and Institute of Policy Studies Conference (revised) on Cross-Border Labour Mobility and Development in the East Asia and Pacific Region, Singapore, 1–2 June 2010.

World Bank. "Malaysia Economic Monitor: Inclusive Growth", November 2010.

———. "Malaysia Economic Monitor: Brain Drain", April 2011.

Commentary 5

Transforming the Orang Asli Development Policy

Rusaslina Idrus

The term Orang Asli translates as "original people", and is an umbrella category that includes 18 ethnic subgroups of indigenous peoples in peninsular Malaysia. Comprising 0.5 per cent of the total Malaysian population, the population numbers 158,000 in 2008 (JHEOA 2008). The Department of Orang Asli Development (previously, Department of Orang Asli Affairs) is a national agency specifically assigned for the well-being of the community, yet more than half of the community continues to live below the poverty line (JHEOA 2008).

The Orang Asli groups traditionally practised swidden cultivation, as well as hunting and gathering. However, these days many more are sedentary farmers and grow cash crops such as oil palm and rubber. Some 85.7 per cent of Orang Asli live in rural areas, 11.3 per cent in urban areas and 3 per cent in small towns (Department of Statistics, Malaysia 2008). Only a small percentage of Orang Asli, such as the Batek in Taman Negara, are semi-nomadic and still pursue hunter-gathering. Nevertheless, the forest remains an important resource for the community and some 40 per cent live close to forest areas and are still dependent on the forest for their livelihood. Many Orang Asli can be described as agro-foresters, cultivating fruit trees and other useful forest plants such as rattan. The forest and their customary lands, however, is more than just a source of economic needs. It serves an important spiritual function in their lives and is an important part of their identity as indigenous peoples.

Government programmes targeted for the Orang Asli tend to focus on a discourse centred on "changing the mindsets" of the community (Rusaslina Idrus 2010). This is based on a false assumption that the Orang Asli are against development. The Orang Asli have repeatedly asserted that they are not anti-development rather they want development that they too can benefit rather than put them in harms way (Wan Zawawi 1996). In many cases, the Orang Asli are pushed out from their land to make way for development projects in the name of the greater good.

While Malaysia as a whole has experienced a significant reduction in poverty, from 52.4 per cent in 1970 to 3.8 per cent in 2009 (Ragayah 2010), the poverty rate of the Orang Asli community stands at 50 per cent of the population, while 33 per cent are categorized as hardcore poor (JHEOA 2008). The Orang Asli have limited access to amenities such as electricity and treated piped water. In year 2000, 46.7 per cent of Orang Asli households had no electricity while 55.5 per cent did not have treated piped water (Department of Statistics 2008). It is not surprising that the health of the Orang Asli is much poorer than that of the national population. The average life expectancy is 52 years for females and 54 years for males, a striking difference to the national average life expectancy of 72 years for females and 68 years for males (Nicholas 2003, p. 319). Infant mortality rate amongst the Orang Asli is reported to be 15.3 out of every 1,000 live births as compared to the national figure of 6.5 out of every 1,000 live births (Chun 2012). The problem of malnutrition among Orang children is prevalent and this is linked to the degradation of the living environment due to the destruction of surrounding natural resources (Khor and Zalilah 2008).

The level of education attainment is also low with a high dropout rate. Although the number of children going to school has increased over the years, a review of enrolment over the years indicates a high dropout rate between year six and form one. The annual dropout rate over the time period of 2000 to 2008 was between 30–40 per cent. Similarly, the dropout rate in secondary schools was between 40 and 50 per cent over the same 2000 to 2008 period. In 2008, 50 per cent of the students who started out in form one (in 2004) dropped out before reaching form five (Department of Statistics, Malaysia 2008). The repeated failure of government projects in addressing Orang Asli basic development needs, signals a need for a revamp of the development strategy for the community

One fundamental challenge faced by the Orang Asli is the lack of land security. Much of the Orang Asli's livelihood and way of life is connected to the land and forest. Many have argued that without addressing the fundamental issue of land ownership, government policies and projects aimed at providing development for the Orang Asli are doomed to failure. According to statistics from the Department of Orang Asli Affairs, only 14 per cent (19,714 hectares) of total Orang Asli land have been gazetted as Orang Asli reserves or areas, 30,850 hectares approved but yet to be gazetted, while 81,535 hectares are under application (JHEOA 2008). Much of the land that had been allocated to be gazetted was done so back in the 1970s. Many Orang Asli therefore are viewed as squatters on state land. At best, Orang Asli are tenants-at-will on government land. This means that whenever the government wants land for "development" projects, the Orang Asli are subject to eviction, often without proper consultation or compensation. There are many examples of Orang Asli villages dispossessed to make way for highways, dams, oil palm plantations and even golf courses. Often, they have to leave behind their farms and other sources of livelihood such as their community forests. As one Orang Asli elder relayed to me, "Without land, how are we to live?"

More recently, in 2010, there was a proposal to amend the Aboriginal Peoples Act with regards to the land policy and the focus on the department. This proposal to provide land titles to the Orang Asli included allotting between two and six acres of land per Orang Asli household. However, there is a catch. Not only will the land come from existing Orang Asli reserves and areas, but it also has to be developed for commercial agriculture, following the Rubber Industry Smallholders Development Authority (RISDA) and Federal Land Consolidation and Rehabilitation Authority (FELCRA) model. In this model, the existing Department of Orang Asli Affairs will be converted to a statutory body and be responsible for developing the land. The Orang Asli households are expected to work on this land and only get their land titles after the crops are mature. Even after getting the land titles, any transactions concerning the land will require permission from the Department of Orang Asli Affairs.

While Orang Asli leaders have long advocated for land titles for their community, this was far from what they had in mind. They point out that, first, the proposal was formulated without adequate consultation with the community. It was predetermined that the land would be developed for commercial agriculture, in disregard of the Orang Asli's needs and wants. Their existing crops, orchards and subsistence farms will be converted to market-dependent monoculture. The Orang Asli may also lose their communal forests, which are important sources of food, medicine and other resources. Small farmers who switch to monoculture — such as oil palm and rubber — take enormous risks, as they are subject to price fluctuations in the global market for those products.

Additionally, the area designated is reported to be less than half the total amount of land that is already acknowledged as Orang Asli land. It is uncertain what will happen to the rest of their customary land. Also according to the new policy, only current heads of households can apply for the land. Orang Asli leaders attest that this will exclude unmarried adults, single mothers and the entire next generation.

Moreover, this proposal disregards the Orang Asli's unique position as indigenous peoples with special ties to the land. The Malaysian courts, for example in the case of *Sagong Tasi and Ors* v. *State of Selangor and Ors 2002*, have acknowledged this distinct relationship and recognized the Orang Asli's customary rights to ancestral land. According to the United Nations Declaration for the Rights of Indigenous Peoples, to which Malaysia is a signatory, "[i]ndigenous peoples have the right to determine and develop priorities and strategies for the development or use of their lands or territories and other resources" and states have to "obtain their free and informed consent prior to the approval of any project affecting their lands or territories".

The Department of Orang Asli's response to the Orang Asli's objection is to insist that the policy is in the best interest of the community. The department continues to describe the community's objection as a rejection of development and as being instigated by outsiders. In March 2010 some 3,000 Orang Asli marched in Putrajaya to hand a memorandum to the Prime Minister expressing their unanimous objection to the new land policy. The Orang Asli since then have continued to protest against this new land policy, holding demonstrations in many states demanding for their land rights.

Government transformation programme for the Orang Asli needs to address the fundamental problem of land security for the community. Any initiative related to land and development for the Orang Asli has to be carried out with consultations with the community, indigenous leaders and experts. First and foremost, the right of the Orang Asli to self-determination, including pertaining to their land, needs to be acknowledged and respected.

REFERENCES

Chun, Michelle. "Health Ministry takes over Orang Asli Hospital". *Sun Daily*, 24 February 2012. Available at <http://www.thesundaily.my/news/304330>.

Department of Statistics, Malaysia. *Orang Asli in Peninsular Malaysia: Population and Housing Census of Malaysia 2000*, compiled by Norfariza Hanim Kasim. Monograph Series no. 3. Putrajaya: Department of Statistics, 2008.

Jabatan Hal Ehwal Orang Asli (JHEOA). *Data Maklumat Asas Jabatan Hal Ehwal Orang Asli*. Kuala Lumpur: Bahagian Perancangan dan Penyelidikan, JHEOA, 2008.

Khor Geok Lin and Zalilah Mohd Shariff. "The Ecology of Health and Nutrition of 'Orang Asli' (Indigenous People) Women and Children in Peninsular Malaysia". In *Health and Nutritional Problems of Indigenous Populations*, edited by Kaushik Bose. Delhi: KRE Publishers, 2008.

Nicholas, Colin. "The Orang Asli: First on the Land, Last in the Plan". *Kajian Malaysia*, vol. 21, nos. 1–2 (2003): 315–29.

Ragayah Haji Mat Zin. "Affirmative Action and Poverty Eradication". Paper presented at the Writer's Workshop on Malaysia's Affirmative Action Policy: Historical Review, Critique and Analysis, Institute of Southeast Asian Studies, Singapore, 6–7 December 2010.

Rusaslina Idrus. "From Wards to Citizens: Indigenous Rights and Citizenship in Malaysia". *Political and Legal Anthropology Review*, vol. 33, no. 1 (2010): 89–108.

Wan Zawawi Wan Ibrahim, ed. *Kami Bukan Anti Pembangunan: Bicara Orang Asli Menuju Wawasan 2020*. Persatuan Sains Social Malaysia, 1996.

17

MIGRANT WORKERS IN MALAYSIA
A Much Needed Labour Source

Theresa W. Devasahayam

Malaysia depends heavily on imported labour. As of 2010, migrant workers comprised around 16 per cent of the country's total labour force. The proportion of foreign workers in Malaysia's labour force has been growing steadily over recent decades. In 1990, foreign workers amounted to less than 250,000 while in 2007, their numbers soared to more than 2 million[1] (Asian Development Bank Institute 2012). In July 2008, 35 per cent of employers registered with the Ministry of Manpower employed migrant workers (International Organization for Migration 2010). The country's reliance on imported labour has been said to be a result of the global restructuring of production and its absorption into the global economy (Kaur 2004). Moreover, the country's dependence on foreign labour has been tied to its industries being labour intensive owing to the lack of technological innovation (Azizah 2001).

Migrant workers have been a much needed labour source critical to Malaysia's relatively strong economic growth in the last two decades. In 2010, Malaysia's economy grew by 7.2 per cent because of a recovery in exports and stronger domestic demand, in particular investment, in spite of the 2008 global economic crisis. Although the economic growth rate was moderate at 5.1 per cent in 2011, nonetheless, the economy expanded (Asian Development Bank 2011). In particular, strong growth has been recorded in the manufacturing and plantation sectors. While these sectors have boosted the country's economy, they have also been dominated mostly by foreign workers because of their cheap labour (Azizah 2001).

The employment of migrant workers in the country, however, has been a complex terrain. While on the one hand, the government has acknowledged the demand for these workers by Malaysian employers, resulting in its having to carefully and strategically regulate the import of labour, on the other, it has had to stem the reliance on imported labour by discouraging employers to hire migrant workers. The strong presence of migrant workers in the country has also led to a backlash from the public who blame migrant workers for the worsening security in the country. But the hard facts on being particularly a low-skilled or unskilled worker in Malaysia have been bleak. Amidst these complex issues, the Malaysian state has had to confront the humanitarian concerns of these migrant workers employed on its shores.

Migrant Workers: Who They are and What They Do

Labour migration in Malaysia is regulated by the Ministry of Home Affairs (International Organization for Migration 2010), while the Immigration Act of 2002 governs the inflow of migrant labour into the country. Malaysia's labour policies are largely directed at ensuring a "skills mix". As such, it distinguishes labour migrants according to two categories based on the level of skills — "workers" and "expatriates". High-skilled workers are categorized as *pegawai dagang* or *expatriates* and include professionals as well as those with technical and managerial skills, in contrast to low-skilled workers who are classified as *pekerja asing* or foreign contract workers (Azizah 2001). Correspondingly, each migrant worker group enters the country on a different employment pass: expatriates are granted the employment or work pass, while low-skilled workers are employed on a permit or contract worker pass or visit pass, as in the case of domestic workers.

Suffice it to say, around 93 per cent of Malaysia's labour migrants tend to be low- and semi-skilled (Asian Development Bank Institute 2012), engaging mostly in 3D (dirty, dangerous, and difficult) jobs shunned by the local population because of the low wages these jobs fetch. These migrants are employed on short-term contracts, suggesting that this group of foreign workers is barred from permanently putting down roots in Malaysia (Kaur 2007; Crinis 2005). Malaysian law also demands that they undergo health checks involving HIV and pregnancy testing and should a migrant (female) worker fail these tests, he or she would be immediately deported (Human Rights Watch 2011). Moreover, these workers are subjected to other labour laws which reinforce their temporary status as migrant workers; migrant workers employed in the domestic work sector, for example, are not permitted to bring their families along with them.

Crucially, entry policies also tend to delimit the numbers and profile of low-skilled and unskilled migrant workers in tandem with labour demands (Garcés-Mascareñas 2012). Initially in the 1980s, migrant workers were found only in the plantation and domestic work sectors; this has changed in the later decades which saw approval for migrant workers to enter the construction, manufacturing, and service industries (Garcés-Mascareñas 2012). The profile of migrant workers and the kinds of jobs they are slotted into are also differentiated along gender lines (Azizah 2001). For example, the plantation and construction sectors are dominated by male migrant workers, while the domestic work and services sectors absorb mostly female migrant workers. Increasingly, however, migrant women have been employed in the manufacturing sector such as the garment industry (Azizah 2001; Crinis 2005). Yet a significant difference in the reason for the import of male and female migrant workers separately has become evident. Male migrants are mainly recruited in response to the labour shortages, while female migrants are mostly imported to meet the domestic needs of increasing numbers of Malaysian women who desire for a career and, in turn, choose to transfer their domestic responsibilities to other women (Kaur 2008).

Although both male and female migrant workers in Malaysia come mainly from Asia, the bulk hail from neighbouring ASEAN (Association of Southeast Asian Nations) countries. Around 67 per cent of the migrant workers in Malaysia come from the region; the rest come from South Asian countries, such as India, Nepal, and Bangladesh.

While the Malaysian government has held to a diversified migration policy (Kaur 2004), generally there has been a fairly rigid correlation between occupational segregation and nationality in the low- and semi-skilled foreign labour force. For example, Indonesians work in the plantation and construction sectors together with Thai workers although their numbers are relatively small, while Bangladeshis are concentrated in the manufacturing sector (Azizah 2001). Among migrant women, Filipinas work as domestic helpers while much smaller numbers are employed in the manufacturing sector. In Sabah, however, Filipinos have also been found in agriculture, logging, and fisheries.

While the majority of labour migrants in Malaysia originate from South and other Southeast Asian countries, the largest proportion comes from Indonesia (International Organization for Migration 2010; Edwards 1999). According to the Malaysian Ministry of Human Resources, 50 per cent of the approximately two million migrant workers, employed in Malaysia in 2008, are from Indonesia, reflecting the scale of Indonesian labour migration to Malaysia (International Organization for Migration 2010; Edwards 1999), followed by Myanmar at 7 per cent, Vietnam at 4 per cent, and the Philippines, Thailand, and Cambodia, constituting the rest of the 5 per cent (Asian Development Bank Institute 2012). Since 1998, however, migrants from India and Nepal have been slowly rising (Kaur 2008). The scale of Indonesian migration to Malaysia can also be seen in the country's female migrant labour force and, in particular, its foreign domestic worker population of which more than 90 per cent come from Indonesia (Human Rights Watch 2004). However increasingly, migrant domestic workers in Malaysia come from other countries aside from Indonesia. For example, growing numbers of women from Cambodia have entered the domestic work sector. Estimated at around 40,000 to 50,000, their numbers have risen since 2009 because of Indonesia's pronouncement of a ban on its women taking on jobs in Malaysia as domestic workers. In response to this change in migration policy in Indonesia, recruitment agencies turned to Cambodia to fill this labour gap (Human Rights Watch 2011).

In contrast are the expatriates — the majority of whom come from India, Japan, the Philippines, and the United Kingdom (Azizah 2001). Unlike their low-skilled and unskilled counterparts, generally there are no limitations placed on skilled migrant workers in terms of the source countries from which they come. Mainly working for multinational corporations, these migrants are found mainly in the medical, computing, engineering, sports, and educational sectors. Like the low-skilled and unskilled migrant workers, however, they work on temporary contracts although they have the option of applying for citizenship provided their employers are willing to support their application (Kaur 2008). Moreover, they are barred from marrying Malaysian nationals.

It must be noted that while migrant workers provide for a much needed labour source in a fair number of employment sectors in Malaysia, policies on migrant workers have been largely fluid depending on the economic climate of the country. For example in times of economic slowdown, measures have been taken to reduce the number of foreign workers; in contrast in economic peak periods, it has been found that greater numbers are allowed to enter the country (Azizah 2001; Garcés-Mascareñas 2012). Yet it must be noted that the government has in the past increased the annual levy with the intent of weaning employers off their dependence on foreign workers (Azizah 2000; *Migration News* 2010*b*). Interestingly on several occasions, employers have been found to petition the government to allow them to employ migrant workers because of dire labour shortages in some sectors (*Migration News* 2011).

The Process of Recruitment for Work in Malaysia

Since the late 1970s during which Malaysia saw a significant influx of migrant workers, "the … state has alternated between tightening immigration controls and loosening them through bilateral agreements and amnesties" (Kaur 2008, p. 8). Unlike the migrant workers who fall in the high skilled category, low- and semi-skilled migrant workers are mostly recruited through private agencies. These agencies work under specific bilateral agreements or Memoranda of Understanding (MoUs) between Malaysia and the labour sending country, with the exception of domestic workers who are recruited under a system of sponsorship undertaken by a national citizen. Thus far, Malaysia has signed MoUs with several countries including Bangladesh, Cambodia, China, India, Indonesia, Kazakhstan, Laos, Myanmar, Nepal, Pakistan, the Philippines, Sri Lanka, Thailand, Turkmenistan, Uzbekistan, and Vietnam (Kanapathy 2004; *Migration News* 2011). These MoUs stipulate that migrants must have the ability to communicate in English or Bahasa Malaysia, must not have a criminal record, and would be repatriated to their country of origin, if they are found to flout Malaysian laws (Kanapathy 2004).

In principle, these MoUs also provide a governance structure for the recruitment and repatriation of migrant workers and therefore regulate the supply of migrant workers into the country (Kaur 2007). These MoUs have been critical for establishing the rules governing transnational labour migration by specifying the terms and conditions of workers and the roles of the two governments involved, as well as ensuring that workers return to their own countries upon completion of their employment contracts. In this case, employers undertake the responsibility of purchasing the workers' return tickets and facing heavy fines, if the workers are not immediately repatriated on completion of their contracts (Kaur 2007). Moreover, the MoUs establish guidelines on how migrant workers should be treated and protected while employed in Malaysia (Kaur 2007). These MOUs, however, are not set in stone but rather may be revised as the situation calls for by either the labour receiving or sending country.

Because the Malaysian government signs MoUs with different labour sending countries, the "agreement" it has established with one labour sending country may differ from another. For example in May 2011, the Malaysian government concluded an MoU with Indonesia with the aim of guaranteeing migrant domestic workers the right to retain their passports and have a weekly rest day. But these protections are yet to be extended to Cambodian domestic workers employed in the country (Human Rights Watch 2011).

Among employers, those desiring to hire migrant workers have to submit the necessary documentation should they want to recruit a migrant worker. However, employers have to demonstrate that they are not able to find workers from the local pool of citizens and permanent residents. Applications for all categories of migrant workers have to be submitted to the Ministry of Home Affairs except for applications for domestic workers for which employers have to approach the Immigration Department. For each category of migrant workers, employers are also expected to pay an annual levy which may range from RM410 to RM1,850 (Malaysian Investment Development Authority 2012). In sectors that face critical labour shortages, the levy tends to be much lower compared with other sectors "where the problem of excess labour demand has been perceived to be less serious" (Kanapathy 2004, p. 8, as cited in Kaur 2008, p. 12).

The Perils of Low-Skilled Workers

Because the bulk of foreign workers in Malaysia are concentrated in low-paid and low-status jobs, being vulnerable to labour abuses such as withholding of wages, and verbal and physical abuse in the destination economy are not uncommon. While in principle most migrant workers are protected under Malaysian labour laws, these laws do not apply to migrants employed as domestic workers since domestic work is not covered by the country's labour laws (International Organization for Migration 2010). For this reason, migrant domestic workers are especially at greater risk of facing labour abuses compared with other migrant groups. Furthermore, migrants employed in the domestic work sector are especially vulnerable because of the nature of their work which confines them to the household of their employers (International Labour Organization 2010). Moreover because they enter the host country at the sponsorship of their employers, this leaves them at the mercy of their sponsors who feel that they have full monopoly over their domestic workers' activities and movements (Kaur 2007).

The inability to be assured of their worker rights in the labour receiving country is also an issue. Although the Trade Union Act 1959, the Employment Act 1955, and the Industrial Relations Act 1967 do not bar migrant workers from becoming members of trade unions and engaging in trade union activities, in reality actual participation in these organizations has been difficult (International Organization for Migration 2010). For this reason, migrant workers tend to turn to their recruitment agencies should they need assistance, since these agents tend to be their first line of contact and possibly the only contact the worker has in the labour destination country. Instead of receiving help, however, it is not unheard of that migrant workers end up facing intimidation and find themselves being forced to return to the same abusive employer or even face abuse by the very recruitment agents whom they have turned to for help (Human Rights Watch 2011).

Because of pressure from the Indonesian government in the past, Malaysia has had to deal head-on with issues of exploitation and abuse related to especially women migrants working in the country. Both the countries have been struggling to develop an MoU governing the recruitment and employment of the estimated 300,000 Indonesian domestic helpers in Malaysia (*Migration News* 2010*a*). Because of the numerous labour abuses faced by women migrants in the domestic work sector, Indonesia suspended the deployment of its women to Malaysia wanting to enter the domestic sector in June 2009. It was this incident that sparked off the two countries to negotiate an agreement on several issues, including the rights of domestic helpers to have a day off each week and to keep their passports (*Migration News* 2011). From 1 December 2011, both countries have agreed to resume the deployment of Indonesian women into Malaysia (*Migration News* 2012). In any case, Malaysia's changing policy toward migrant women did not come about independently or as a result of their having become more sensitive to the plight of women migrants but because of external pressures, that is, from the Indonesian government.

Notwithstanding, abuses felt by this migrant group have also occurred in the labour sending country. Human Rights Watch (2011) has highlighted how some prospective migrant women from Cambodia entering the domestic work sector in Malaysia were found to be forcibly confined in training centres by recruitment agents for periods from three months up to six months before their departure abroad for work. In some cases, these women were found without adequate food, water, and medical care as well as denied contact with their own families. Furthermore, some women have also faced verbal, physical, and psychological abuse at the hands of recruitment agents. Moreover, should any woman attempt to escape from these training centres, they were found to have faced harsh treatment or threats for their actions.

That aside, prospective migrants are caught in a viscous cycle of desiring to secure work for which they have little choice but to depend on these recruitment agents because of the lack of social networks, and yet at the same time are aware that these agents tend to be exploitative since their aim is to reap the highest profit for themselves. Hence, their only recourse to finding work abroad is through these recruitment agencies to whom these migrants end up paying hefty fees to cover the cost of using the services of the agency, purchase a one way air ticket, process the necessary travel documents, and secure insurance and bank guarantees in both the labour sending and receiving countries. Among prospective migrant women, repaying these exorbitant recruitment and training fees, for which many would not have paid up fully on leaving their home countries because these women tend to come from poor families, is a huge concern. Usually these women end up foregoing the first six to seven months of their salary once they start to work in Malaysia. And should they encounter an abusive employer, these migrant workers are more likely not to leave their jobs.

This is not to say that there have not been positive experiences among migrant workers in Malaysia. Among many of them, the desire to stay on for work in Malaysia by having their contracts renewed is not uncommon. These workers usually report having been treated well by their employers and receiving their wages on time. The reality, however, for many migrant workers has been dismal since they face employment abuses either in the destination country or before arriving in Malaysia for work.

For those desiring for justice in the labour destination country, they often face a series of obstacles. For example, the Malaysian police are not interested in following up on these cases. But if they do and should a case make it up to the level of the courts, legal proceedings are extremely lengthy. For many women migrant workers, requiring a safe place to stay such as a shelter becomes imperative although not always easy to access. Moreover, waiting for significant periods of time becomes difficult for many migrant workers, especially since their families back home rely on the money they send home (Human Rights Watch 2011). Moreover, while labour sending countries, such as Cambodia, have already national policies in place to protect the rights of their citizens travelling abroad for work, implementing these policies have been met with numerous obstacles. For example, the Ministry of Labour of Cambodia does not have a proper procedure to implement the country's national policy on migration and to monitor compliance to this directive. For these reasons, most migrant workers in Malaysia who have suffered labour abuses are unable to seek redress either in Malaysia or their own sending countries.

Undocumented Migrant Workers: The Documented Facts

While Malaysia has a strong presence of migrant workers, the country has also become a hub for undocumented and illegal migrants. Estimates have it that there are around two million undocumented migrants in Malaysia (Allard 2011). These individuals may be employed in Malaysia in spite of violating immigration laws by not utilizing formal migration channels. Interestingly, it has been pointed out that migrant women have generally more possibilities of legal employment in Malaysia compared to men (Yamanaka and Piper 2006; Kaur 2007), which implies that men are more likely to use informal migration channels to secure employment. Among the reasons for avoiding legal channels of recruitment are the administrative costs entailed in securing employment (Garcés-Mascareñas 2012; Kaur 2004). Besides, quotas maintained for low- and semi-skilled migrant workers have made it difficult, if not impossible, for many to enter the country for employment through legal channels (Kaur 2004).

Undocumented workers usually take up jobs away from public scrutiny to avoid detection and apprehension such as domestic help, restaurant cooks, and construction and plantation work (Azizah 2001). In spite of the benefits that come with being legally employed in Malaysia such as receiving protection under Malaysia's labour laws, there is a persistently high proportion of undocumented migrant workers in Malaysia which has forced the government to police human traffickers, since it is this group of migrants that tend to be most susceptible to exploitation and mistreatment (Kaur 2004).

On the fate of such workers, some scholars have argued that their high numbers will continue as long as the formal recruitment process continues to be costly, cumbersome, time-consuming, and restrictive for both employers and workers (Azizah 1997). Others, however, have pointed out that "illegality has become synonymous to deportability" (Garcés-Mascareñas 2012, p. 192). In this case, deportability is seen as a way of ensuring "temporality" and "turn[ing] illegal immigrants into a flexible labour force that is 'importable' and 'exportable' at will" (Garcés-Mascareñas 2012, p. 193). This assertion has been verified by the fact that deportation campaigns in Malaysia occur mostly in times of economic crisis.

Because of the complex issues around undocumented and illegal workers and their rising numbers in the country to meet labour shortages, the regularization of migrants has been the preoccupation of the Malaysian government for a few decades already, although there have been changes in perceptions and policies directed at migrant workers in recent years. In the past decade or so, the government has led a number of "crackdowns" on illegal Indonesian workers in Malaysia. Specifically since 2002, Malaysia passed a law that introduced a range of new, harsher penalties for migrant workers and their employers (Hugo 2007). This was followed by another attempt in 2009 where the Malaysian government temporarily froze the recruit-ment of migrant workers because it felt that the problem of illegal migrant workers had spiralled to uncontrollable levels (*UCA News*, 18 May 2012). Unlike its neighbours in the region, the Malaysian government announced in July 2010 that it was considering a programme that would permit employers to employ illegal migrants already in the country to meet the country's labour shortage.

Having become concerned over the issue of human trafficking and the illegal deportment of migrant workers, the Malaysian government is currently undertaking a series of reforms to provide a more comprehensive migration framework to ensure the protection of migrant labour rights. In collaboration with several labour sending countries, the Malaysian Government intends to provide pre-departure training sessions for migrant workers before their arrival into Malaysia (International Organization for Migration 2010). It is also intending that the legislation and process governing labour migration be amended. Specifically, it is planned that the Workmen's Compensation Act 1952 be amended to cover migrant domestic workers, and for new provisions to be introduced in the Employment Act 1955 to protect the wages and work conditions of migrant women and to control the abuses felt by this group (International Organization for Migration 2010). Furthermore, the Malaysian government intends to strengthen the manpower capacity of government agencies responsible for the employment of migrant workers and to effectively enforce the law and improve statutory inspections in places of employment with a special focus on employers (International Organization for Migration 2010).

Conclusions

Although migrant workers have made a significant contribution to the Malaysian economy, in society at large this group of workers has been "demonised because of their increased visibility and the threat they are seen to pose to local jobs and morality" (Crinis 2005, p. 92). Criticisms levelled at migrant workers in recent years by the public have revolved mostly around the decline in security; in this regard, the country's rising crime rate has also been attributed to foreign workers (Healy 2000). In spite of the negative outcomes on the country's social stability and the local labour force, the continued demand for labour in some critical areas, such as the manufacturing, plantation, and domestic work sectors, has led to a "situation where foreign labour is needed but not wanted" (Crinis 2005, p. 93).

In fact in the last two decades, the manufacturing and agricultural sectors, both dominated by migrant workers, have only seen a growth. For example, while the annual growth rate of the agricultural sector was at 0.4 per cent in 1991–2001, this figure soared to an estimated 3.4 per cent in the period 2001–11 (World Bank 2013). In the manufacturing sector, although the average annual growth has dropped from 8.4 per cent in 1991–2001 to an estimated 4.0 per cent in 2001–11, this sector is more likely going to keep up its demand for foreign labour. But because the agricultural and manufacturing sectors comprise 11.9 per cent and 24.4 per cent of the country's Gross Domestic Product (GDP) respectively (World Bank 2013), we can expect that the numbers of migrant workers in these sectors not to decrease dramatically in the coming decade especially since these sectors have been found in recent years to contribute significantly to the country's economic growth. While foreign workers have been integral to the country's economic growth, some have argued that this trend has a negative effect in the economy since income inequalities will only grow (Edwards 1999).

But with the introduction of the minimum wage policy in 2012, we can expect that this would have a spill-over effect on the numbers of migrant workers employed in the country, since this would drive up the cost of hiring a migrant worker and therefore reduce their numbers. But while the Malaysian government acknowledges the importance of migrant labour towards the country's economic growth, the rationale for extending the minimum wage policy to migrant workers was also to reduce the country's dependence on foreign labour. According to Executive Director of the Malaysian Employers Federation (MEF), Mr Shamsuddin Bardan, the plan is to reduce the number of foreign workers in the country to 5 per cent of the total labour force by 2015 (Bernama Media, 8 May 2012). Hints on the government's plan to reduce the number of migrant workers from 2 million to 1.5 million surfaced much earlier on when it raised the levy employers had to fork out to hire migrant workers, with the exception of the agricultural sector (*Migration News* 2010b). Employers and migrant advocates, however, have been disgruntled at this government move, arguing that employers should not be penalized since the migrant workers they hire are hired in low-paid jobs and tend to stay with the same employer. Hence, while the numbers of foreign workers across the board might gradually decrease, particularly in response to the installation of the new minimum wage policy, this may not necessarily take immediate effect in the critical labour shortage sectors that contribute significantly to the country's GDP.

Overall, the trend towards hiring migrant workers to fill the country's labour shortages may continue in the coming decade or so although its numbers are more likely to plateau with the minimum wage policy. While it is understandable that the Malaysian state's migration strategies and policies are centred largely on economic growth, in an increasingly globalized world where labour needs may be met through human flows from abroad, the state cannot escape from international scrutiny in how it treats foreigners in its own land. Thus because of surmounting pressures against the Malaysian government by international and non-governmental organizations as well as labour sending countries, the Malaysian state cannot afford to ignore the rightful protections belonging to this group of workers. Given this situation, the Malaysian state is forced to take steps to improve the work conditions of migrant workers as long as there continues to be a demand for this group of workers.

NOTE

1. It must be noted that some sources have cited the figure to be around 3.6 million instead of 2 million with almost half of them undocumented workers (*Migration News* 2011). Should this figure be accurate, as much as a third of Malaysia's labour force constitutes migrant workers.

REFERENCES

Allard, Tom. "Malaysia Plans Amnesty for Illegal Migrants". *The Sydney Morning Herald*, 8 June 2011.

Asian Development Bank. "Fact Sheet", 31 December 2011. Available at <http://www.adbi.org/research-policy-brief/2011/11/28/4814.social.security.labor.migration.asean/growth.of.intraasean.labor.mobility> (accessed 19 March 2014).

Asian Development Bank Institute. "Growth of Intra-ASEAN Labor Mobility". Available at <http://www.adbi.org/research-policybrief/2011/11/28/4814.social.security.labor.migration.asean/growth.of.intraasean.labor.mobility/> (accessed 4 August 2012).

Azizah Kassim. "Illegal Alien Labour in Malaysia: Its Influx, Utilization, and Ramifications". *Indonesia and the Malay World*, vol. 25, no. 71 (1997): 50–81.

―――. "Indonesian Immigrant Settlements in Peninsular Malaysia". *Sojourn: Journal of Social Issues in Southeast Asia*, vol. 15, no. 1 (2000): 100–22.

―――. "Recent Trends in Migration Movements and Policies in Malaysia". In *International Migration in Asia: Trends and Policies*. Paris: OECD, 2001.

Bernama Media. "Malaysia Should Reduce Dependence on Foreign Workers, says MEF", 8 May 2010. Available at <http://my.news.yahoo.com/malaysia-reduce-dependence-foreign-workers-says-mef-130215213.html> (accessed 19 March 2014).

Crinis, Vicki. "The Devil You Know: Malaysian Perceptions of Foreign Workers". *Review of Indonesian and Malaysian Affairs*, vol. 39, no. 2 (2005): 91–111.

Edwards, Chris. "Skilled and Unskilled Foreign Labour in Malaysian Development — A Strategic Shift?". In *Technology, Competitiveness and the State: Malaysia's Industrial Technology Policies*, edited by K.S. Jomo and G. Felker. London: Routledge, 1999.

Garcés-Mascareñas, Blanca. *Labour Migration in Malaysia and Spain: Markets, Citizenship and Rights*. Amsterdam: Amsterdam University Press, 2012.

Healy, Lucy. "Gender 'Aliens' and National Imagery in Contemporary Malaysia". *Sojourn: Journal of Social Issues in Southeast Asia*, vol. 15, no. 2 (2000): 222–54.

Hugo, Graeme. "Indonesia's Labor Looks Abroad". Migration Information Source, Migration Policy Institute, 1 April 2007. Available at <http://www.migrationpolicy.org/article/indonesias-labor-looks-abroad> (accessed 19 March 2014).

Human Rights Watch. *Help Wanted: Abuses against Female Migrant Domestic Workers in Indonesia and Malaysia*, vol. 16, no. 9 (C) (July 2004): 1–109.

―――. *"They Deceived Us at Every Step": Abuse of Cambodian Domestic Workers Migrating to Malaysia*. New York: Human Rights Watch, 2011.

International Organization for Migration. *Labour Migration from Indonesia: An Overview of Indonesian Migration to Selected Destinations in Asia and the Middle East*. Jakarta, Indonesia: International Organization for Migration, 2010.

Kanapathy, Vijayakumari. "International Migration and Labour Market Developments in Asia: Economic Recovery, The Labour Market and Migrant Workers in Malaysia". Paper prepared for the 2004 Workshop on International Migration and Labour Markets in Asia, organized by the Japan Institute for Labour Policy and Training (JILPT), supported by the Government of Japan, Organisation for Economic Cooperation and Development (OECD) and the International Labour Office (ILO), 5–6 February 2004. Available at <http://www.jil.go.jp/foreign/event_r/event/documents/2004sopemi/2004sopemi_e_countryreport6.pdf> (accessed 19 March 2014).

Kaur, Amarjit. "Mobility, Labour Mobilisation and Border Controls: Indonesian Labour Migration to Malaysia since 1900". Paper presented at the 15th Biennial Conference of the Asian Studies Association of Australia, Canberra 29 June–2 July 2004. Available at <http://coombs.anu.edu.au/SpecialProj/ASAA/biennial-conference/2004/Kaur-A-ASAA2004.pdf> (accessed 10 May 2012).

———. "International Labour Migration in Southeast Asia: Governance of Migration and Women Domestic Workers". *Intersections: Gender, History and Culture in the Asian Context*, issue 15, 2007. Available at <http://intersections.anu.edu.au/issue15/kaur.htm> (accessed 10 May 2012).

———. "International Migration and Governance in Malaysia: Policy and Performance". *UNEAC Asia Papers*, no. 22 (2008). Available at <http://www.une.edu.au/data/assets/pdf_file/0004/22288/No22.pdf> (accessed 19 March 2014).

Malaysian Investment Development Authority (MIDA). "Invest in Malaysia". Available at <http://www.mida.gov.my/env3/index.php?page=employment-of-foreign-workers> (accessed 21 March 2014).

Migration News. "Southeast Asia". *Migration News*, vol. 17, no. 4 (October 2010*a*). Available at <http://migration.ucdavis.edu/mn/more.php?id=3642_0_3_0> (accessed 19 March 2014).

———. *Migration News*, vol. 17, no. 3 (July 2010*b*). Available at <http://migration.ucdavis.edu/mn/more.php?id=3623_0_3_0> (accessed 19 March 2014).

———. *Migration News*, vol. 18, no. 2 (April 2011). Available at <http://migration.ucdavis.edu/mn/more.php?id=3682_0_3_0> (accessed 19 March 2014).

———. *Migration News*, vol. 19, no. 1 (January 2012). Available at <http://migration.ucdavis.edu/mn/more.php?id=3738_0_3_0> (accessed 19 March 2014).

UCA News. "New Migrant Policy in Pipeline". Dhaka, Bangladesh, 18 May 2012. Available at <http://www.ucanews.com/news/new-migrant-policy-in-pipeline-/49877> (accessed 19 March 2014).

World Bank. "Malaysia at a Glance", 17 March 2013. Available at <http://devdata.worldbank.org/AAG/mys_aag.pdf> (accessed 20 March 2014).

Yamanaka, Keiko and Nicola Piper. "Feminized Migration in East and Southeast Asia: Policies, Actions and Empowerment". Occasional paper, United Nations Research Institute for Social Development, no. 11. Geneva: United Nations Research Institute for Social Development (UNRISD), 2006. Available at <http://www.casaasia.es/encuentromujeres/2011/files/feminized-migration-in%20-asia.pdf> (accessed 19 March 2014).

Commentary 6

Malaysian Women's Labour Force Participation

Sri Ranjini Mei Hua and Theresa W. Devasahayam

Malaysian women have made significant strides in the areas of education and health survival; however these have not translated into their improved contributions to the economy. There is a significantly larger percentage of women (36 per cent) compared to men (49 per cent) who have attained university enrollment. In fact, females are not discriminated against in Malaysia's education policy. The integration of women in the development process was introduced in the Sixth Malaysia Plan (1991–95), supporting the objectives of the National Vision Policy for Women launched in 1989, which aims for equitable access to opportunities for men and women. As it was generally recognized that education facilitates the pathway to a better quality of living, and employment opportunities of females, the enrollment of both males and females has risen rapidly. From 1990 to 2009, investment in higher education increased by more than five times in Malaysia (World Development Indicators 2009) as shown in Table 17.1. Since the 1990s, the enrollment rates of females have been equal to, or have exceeded, those of males at all education levels (UNDP 2004) as shown in Figure 17.1.

Malaysia took first ranking in terms of women's enrolment in primary, secondary and tertiary education, among the 136 countries covered in the Global Gender Gap Report 2013. In addition, women's healthy life expectancy outcomes have been relatively good as they have been found to live longer than men. According to the report, the number of years that women and men can expect to live in good health in Malaysia is 66 and 62 respectively. However, in terms of labour force activity, they still earn less and have limited economic opportunity compared to their male counterparts, a trend that persists globally (Korinek 2005; ILO 2007).

A significant finding in the Global Gender Gap Report 2013 was that among the ten countries of ASEAN, Malaysia had the lowest female labour force participation rate, with less than 50 per cent of

TABLE 17.1
Investment in Education

	Pre-primary		Primary		Secondary		Tertiary	
Economy	1990	2009	1990	2009	1990	2009	1990	2000
Brunei Darussalam	47.79	91.43	113.77	106.53	76.54	98.20	5.39	17.15
Cambodia	5.19	12.93	93.87	116.48	25.31	40.36	0.60	7.02
Indonesia	17.86	50.09	118.75	120.82	47.95	79.46	8.66	23.50
Lao PDR	7.26	22.00	100.74	111.84	23.72	43.86	1.13	13.37
Malaysia	33.52	70.83	92.44	94.64	56.04	68.71	7.26	36.46
Myanmar	2.24	6.64	95.25	115.82	20.25	53.11	5.14	10.74
Philippines	9.44	48.64	109.15	110.10	70.71	82.46	24.30	28.69
Thailand	41.84	92.45	100.10	91.05	29.06	77.03	16.12	45.03
Vietnam	30.51	40.72	103.34	104.11	35.50	66.90	2.83	9.68
Japan	48.37	88.79	99.34	102.29	96.05	101.02	29.07	58.62
United Kingdom	50.77	80.53	105.58	106.43	83.85	98.98	26.62	59.00
United States	59.75	57.81	104.97	98.25	92.19	93.57	71.71	85.93

Note: The final year for Vietnam is 2001.
Source: World Development Indicators (WDI), the World Bank.

FIGURE 17.1
Education Attainment for Malaysian Women, 2008
(%)

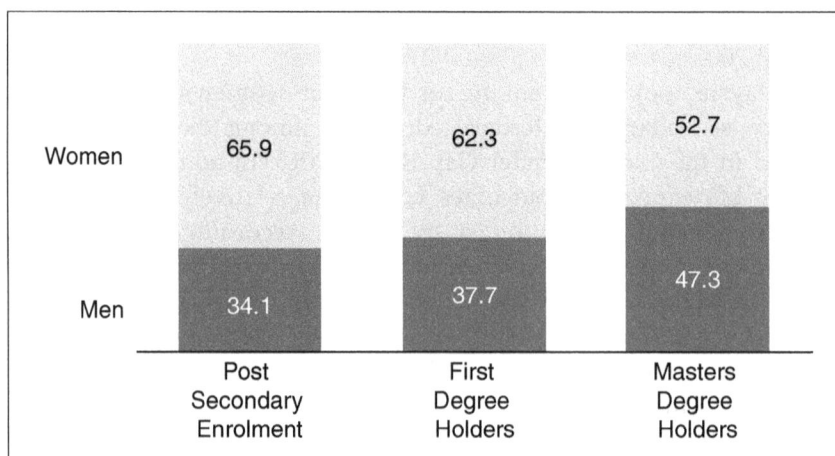

Source: Economic Planning Unit, Department of Statistics and International Labour Organization — Labour and Social Trends in ASEAN 2008.

women contributing to the economy. The gender gaps are prevalent in employment and education, particularly in the fields of science, technology, and engineering (Ahmad 1998). In order to enhance the economic contribution of women in Malaysia, the government plans to increase the female labour force participation rate from 46 per cent in 2013 to 55 per cent by 2015. Malaysia's female labour force participation rate of 46 per cent in 2013 was relatively low compared to its neighbouring countries such as Vietnam (78 per cent), Thailand (70 per cent), and Singapore (63 per cent). In terms of Malaysia's labour force participation rates of men and women, the percentage of women represented is 33 per cent less than men of whom almost 80 per cent are in the labour force. Since 1980, male labour force participation has consistently been over 80 per cent. The lower representation of women in employment occurs in spite of equal education opportunities accessible to both men and women. Interestingly, this trend of significantly lower representation of women in the workforce has also been observed in the two other predominantly Muslim countries in Southeast Asia — Indonesia (53 per cent) and Brunei Darussalam (58 per cent).

FIGURE 17.2
Labour Force Participation of Women in Malaysia Against Neighbouring Countries, 2008
(%)

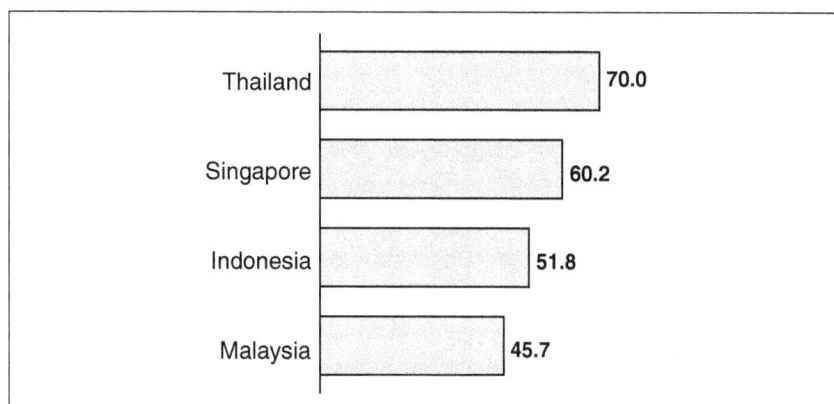

Source: Economic Planning Unit, Department of Statistics and International Labour Organization — Labour and Social Trends in ASEAN 2008.

Although women's participation in senior and highly-skilled positions has been increasing in Malaysia (in 2013, 26 per cent of women were in senior management positions), it was still the lowest recorded in ASEAN (Grant Thornton International Business Report 2013). Furthermore, these positions tended to be confined to the financial, human resources, and sales domains.

In the very top levels of management, however, the figures have not looked promising: only 7.8 per cent of women in Malaysia are represented on boards. However, the low representation of women on boards is consistent with the region: 6.4 per cent in Singapore, 8.1 per cent in China, and 8.6 per cent in Hong Kong. Yet, it is in stark contrast to women's representation on boards in the Philippines where the figure is significantly higher at about 30 per cent. There is an increasing body of evidence which suggests that companies with more women on their boards perform better in terms of higher sales return, greater return on investments, and equity (Joy, Carter, Wagner and Narayanan 2007), which provides sufficient justification to improve the gender balance on corporate boards.

The factors affecting women's employment are manifold and include, but are not limited to the following: ethnicity, religion, socio-economic status, socio-cultural norms and government policies (Lim 2001). In fact, the labour force participation of women has been clearly differentiated along ethnic lines. By and large conservative attitudes towards women's roles persist across the ethnic groups, suggesting that women's primary role is that of caregiver in the family. As society continues to assign the primary role of caregiver to women, combining work and family has not made it easy for women to engage in paid employment and women tend to leave their jobs upon marriage and having children (Kaur 2004). In the fourth Malaysian Population and Family Survey, almost 60 per cent of women who had worked before, stopped working because of inability to access the needed childcare services. Another study found that work-family conflict was positively correlated with the number and ages of dependent children (Huang, Hammer, Neal and Perrin 2004).

Malay women tend to face the strongest objections and restrictions from their husbands in terms of engagement in paid employment outside the home (Lim 1990). This trend is based in Islam where women's primary role is that of caretaker of the children. Consequently, it is the Malays (primarily Muslim) who hold the highest fertility rate in the country at 2.6, while the rates for Chinese (1.5) and Indians (1.7) have been below the replacement level. Moreover, affirmative action of the government policies, which favour the ethnic Malay majority, have also been significant in contributing to the relatively higher fertility among them compared to the Chinese and Indians (Jones 1990). Moreover, the shortage of childcare provision and eldercare support has been problematic for women such that they are discouraged from engagement in wage work. In fact, the state has provided tax incentives for employers to provide daycare centres for their employees' children but few employers have agreed to extend such assistance (UNDP 2004).

Competing demands of family and career continue to restrict women's work mobility and limit their participation in the labour force. However, the Malaysian government is committed towards harnessing the full potential of women in the labour force as it plans to increase their labour force participation rate from 46 per cent in 2013 to 55 per cent by 2015. In reducing the burden of caregiving among women, the government aims to increase the number of registered community-based nurseries and daycare centres under the Social Welfare Department or JKM (*Jabatan Kebajikan Masyarakat*) so as to enable women to balance with greater ease both family and work commitments, under the Tenth Malaysia Plan (2011–15). Moreover, flexible work arrangements are being promoted in the public and private sectors (Economic Planning Unit 2010). In the long term, in order to achieve a substantive change in the quantity and quality of women's labour force participation, there needs to be a change in employers' as well as family attitudes towards working women. The participation of women in the labour force is particularly important as Malaysia strives towards achieving a developed country status by 2020 in its latest Malaysia Plan.

NOTE

1. It must be noted that some sources have cited the figure to be around 3.6 million instead of 2 million with almost half of them undocumented workers (*Migration News* 2011). Should this figure be more accurate, as much as a third of Malaysia's labour force constitutes migrant workers.

REFERENCES

Ahmad, Aminah. "Women in Malaysia: Country Briefing Paper". Asian Development Bank, Manila, December 1998. Available at <http://www2. adb.org/documents/books/country_briefing_papers/women_in_malaysia/ women_malaysia.pdf> (accessed 23 March 2012).

Department of Statistics, Malaysia. "Population Distribution and Basic Demographic Characteristics", 2010. Available at <http://www.statistics.gov. my/portal/download_Population/files/census2010/Taburan_Pen_duduk_ dan_Ciri-ciri_Asas_Demografi.pdf> (accessed 10 February 2012).

Grant Thornton. "Women in senior management: setting the stage for growth". Available at <http://www.gti.org/files/ibr2013_wib_report_final.pdf> (accessed 26 March 2013).

Hausmann, Ricardo, D. Laura Tyson, and Saadia Zahidi. "Global Gender Gap Report 2011". Geneva, Switzerland: World Economic Forum, 2011D. Available at <http://www3.weforum.org/docs/WEF_GenderGap_Report_ 2011.pdf> (accessed 8 February 2012).

Huang Yueng-Hsiang, B. Hammer Leslie, B. Neal Margaret and A. Perrin Nancy. "The Relationship Between Work-To-Family Conflict and Family-To-Work Conflict: A Longitudinal Study". *Journal of Family and Economic Issues*, vol. 25, no. 1 (2004): 79–100.

ILO. "Equality at Work: Tackling the Challenges". ILC Report I(B), 96th Session (Geneva), 2007. Available at <http://www.ilo.org/public/portugue/ region/eurpro/lisbon/pdf/equality_07.pdf> (accessed 6 March 2012).

Jones, Gavin W. "Fertility Transition among Malay Populations of Southeast Asia: Puzzles of Interpretations". *Population and Development Review*, vol. 16, no. 3 (1990): 507–37.

Joy, Lois, Nancy M. Carter, Harvey M. Wagner, and Sriram Narayanan. "The Bottomline: Corporate Performance and Women's Representation on Boards". Catalyst, 2007. Available at <http://www.catalyst.org/file/139/ bottom%20line%202.pdf> (accessed 4 February 2012).

Kaur, Amarjit. *Costed Not Valued: Women Workers In Industrialising Asia*. New York: Palgrave Macmillan, 2004.

Korinek, Jane. "Trade and Gender: Issues and Interactions". OECD Trade Policy Working Paper, no. 24 (2005). Available at <http://www.oecd.org/ dataoecd/38/50/35770606.pdf> (accessed 6 March 2012).

Lim, Lin Lean. "The Impact of Islam on Female Status and Fertility in Malaysia". *Malaysian Journal of Economic Studies* XXVII, nos. 1 and 2 (1990): 1–25.

———. "Female Labour Force Participation". Gender Promotion Programme. Geneva, Switzerland: International Labour Office, 2001.

Mahari, Zarinah. "Demographic Transition in Malaysia: The Changing Roles of Women". Paper presented at the 15th Conference of Commonwealth Statisticians, New Delhi, India, 7–10 February 2011.

National Population and Family Development Board (NPFDB). *Fourth Malaysian Population and Family Survey* (MPFS-4), 2004.

OECD. "Policy Brief: Can Policies Boost Birth Rates?", 2007. Available at <http://www.oecd.org/dataoecd/6/57/39970765.pdf> (accessed 8 February 2012).

Department of Statistics, Malaysia. "Population Distribution and Basic Demographic Characteristics", 2010. Available at <http://www.statistics.gov.my/portal/download_Population/files/census2010/Taburan_Penduduk_dan_Ciri-ciri_Asas_Demografi.pdf> (accessed 10 February 2012).

Tey Nai Peng. "Social, Economic and Ethnic Fertility Differentials in Peninsular Malaysia". Paper presented at IUSSP Conference on Southeast Asia's Population in a Changing Asian Context, Bangkok, Thailand, 10–13 June 2002. Available at <http://www.iussp.org/Bangkok2002/S03Peng.pdf> (accessed 15 February 2012).

The Global Gender Gap Report 2013. World Economic Forum, 2013. Available at <http://www3.weforum.org/docs/WEF_GenderGap_Report_2013.pdf> (accessed 26 February 2014).

UNDP, Malaysia. *Achieving the Millennium Development Goals Successes and Challenges*. Full report, 2004. Available at <http://www.undp.org.my/uploads/mdg2.pdf> (accessed 15 February 2012).

World Development Indicators, the World Bank, 2009. Available at <http://www.scribd.com/WorldBankPublications/d/17512073-World-Development-Indicators-2009-> (accessed 22 March 2012).

18

GROWTH AND LIVEABILITY
The Case of Greater Kuala Lumpur, Malaysia

Tan Teck Hong and Phang Siew Nooi[1]

Introduction

Malaysia is a developing nation striving towards a developed status by the year 2020 as envisaged by the Malaysian government. Since the beginning of the twenty-first century, also known as the urban century, this country has managed to maintain a semblance of stability in economic growth, social development, and mainstream politics. In the past, Malaysia's development and growth was structured according to the availability of its natural resources and agricultural activities which were exploited for export earnings. Indeed, the country has been exceptionally endowed with vast quantities of oil and gas, and this source of revenue has contributed 40 per cent to the federal revenue (Bank Negara Malaysia 2011). It can be assumed that the continuous rise in cruel oil prices from US$37.00 a barrel in 1980 to above US$145.00 a barrel in 2008, has enabled the government to implement and fast track many high cost projects. These include the twin-towers in Kuala Lumpur, the new federal administrative centre in Putra Jaya, and a host of others. The subsequent consequences from these projects have increased economic activities in the urban conurbation, with the opening up of neighbouring lands for industrial sites and housing construction.

This paradigm shift in economic policy, from an economy that was dependent on agriculture to industry driven, has led to rapid industrialization and to the concentration of economic activities in a few urban areas. This is so as to take advantage of infrastructural facilities like ports, telecommunication, electricity, airports, and institutions of higher learning, which are already in place in these urban centres. This pattern of development has inevitably resulted in the rise of a service sector to cater to the needs of the industrial sector, thus compounding the concentration of population in the existing urban centres and towns such as Kuala Lumpur, Penang, Johore Baru, Ipoh, Klang, Petaling Jaya, and Kota Kinabalu. Ultimately, these towns and cities become attractive, simultaneously serving as the nerve centres of the nation, containing within them the "goods and services" required by everyone.

Urbanization Dilemma

Malaysia has been undergoing rather rapid urbanization and the proportion of urban population to total population especially in Peninsular Malaysia has increased at a rather fast pace. In Malaysia, the term "urban" was reclassified as the "gazetted area and their joining built-up areas with a combined population of 10,000 persons or more at the time of the census" (Department of Statistics 2000). Throughout the years from 1995 until today, this country has experienced a transformation from a rural to an urban setting, where the urbanization rate increased from 34.2 per cent (1980) to 62 per cent (2000), and to 71 per cent in 2010 (Department of Statistics 2010). This phenomenal rate will continue to set the pace for more urbanization, which will result in further growth in the major towns and cities as people gravitate to these urban centres which also tend to have a higher degree of economic development. For instance, Kuala Lumpur, which is the capital city of the nation, was fully urbanized, followed by Selangor (91.4 per cent) and Penang (90.8 per cent) in 2010. The

TABLE 18.1
Levels of Urbanization by States in Malaysia, 1980–2010

State	1980	1991	2000	2010
Johor	35.2	47.8	63.9	71.9
Kedah	14.4	32.5	38.7	64.6
Kelantan	28.1	33.5	33.5	42.4
Melaka	23.4	38.7	67.3	86.5
Negeri Sembilan	32.6	42	55	66.5
Pahang	26.1	30.4	42.1	50.5
Perak	32.2	53.6	59.5	69.7
Perlis	8.9	26.6	33.8	51.4
Pulau Pinang	47.5	75	79.5	90.8
Sabah	19.9	33.2	48.3	54
Sarawak	18	37.5	47.9	53.8
Selangor	34.2	75.2	88.3	91.4
Terengganu	42.9	44.5	49.4	59.1
Kuala Lumpur	100	100	100	100
Malaysia	34.2	50.7	62	71

Source: Department of Statistics of Malaysia, 2000, 2010.

degree of urbanization for each state in the country is reflected in Table 18.1.

Rapid urbanization is causing many problems. The problems associated with rapid urban include transportation and traffic woes, lack of housing resources among the low income group, and social crime. In the recent Economist Intelligence Unit (EIU) Liveability Index Survey, the capital of Malaysia, Kuala Lumpur was ranked 78th among the 140 cities survey. Similarly, a study by IBM ranked Kuala Lumpur below international best practices in areas such as city service, people, business, communications, transport, waste, and energy. Although Malaysia has gone through the industrial development process for the past thirty years, its liveability lags many other Asian countries.

It is estimated that over 75 per cent of the nation's population will be urban by 2020, up from 71 per cent in 2010. This high population growth in urban areas will be the fundamental obstacle in securing a better quality of life in the long term, as cities will continue to attract

FIGURE 18.1
The Relationship between Wealth of a City and Its Quality of Life

Trend line of countries' expected spending according to wealth, 2006

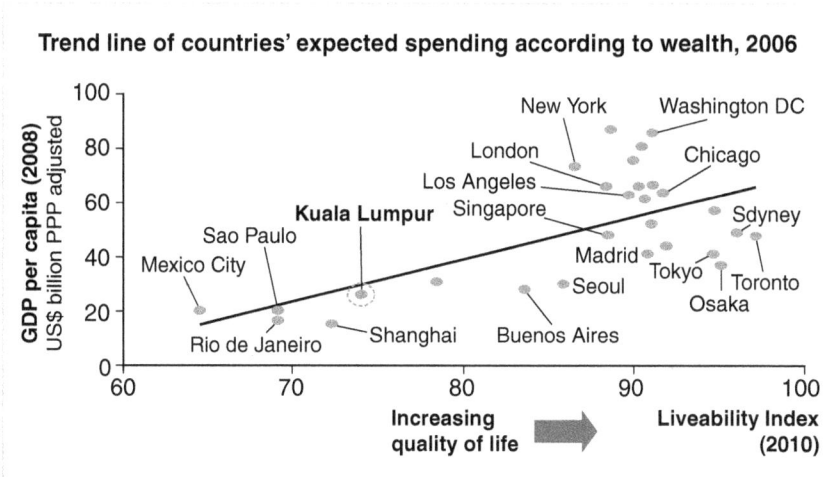

Source: Economic Planning Unit (2010).

in-migrants as it is often associated as the power houses of a nation. In real terms, there is a need to ensure that the nation's cities do not lose their "liveability", as there is a close link between the wealth of a city and its quality of life; i.e., the wealthier a city is, the higher is its quality of life index (see Figure 18.1).

Spiralling Decline in Quality of Life

The decline in quality of life is one of the major issues that arises out of poor management of country development. For a country to be liveable and sustainable, it is necessary to raise the quality of life index for the people. In order to create a place for sustainable and quality living, the Malaysian government needs to provide a high quality of living by curbing crimes to ensure personal safety and security, and improving the living environment with quality public infrastructure and facilities and housing opportunities. The government faces a great challenge of raising the Malaysian quality of life index as the people's essential social services ranging from the transport system and crime rate to provision of affordable housing are most stressed in urban areas, particularly in Greater Kuala Lumpur (GKL).

Greater Kuala Lumpur (Greater KL) is one of the National Key Economic Areas (NKEAs). It has a geographical focus that comprises ten local authorities consisting of City Hall and the town councils of Kajang, Selayang, Ampang Jaya, Subang Jaya, Shah Alam, Klang, Petaling Jaya, Putrajaya, and Sepang. Under the Economic Transformation Programme (ETP), the growth target of economic activities in Greater KL will increase total employment from 2.5 million in 2010 to 4.2 million by 2020. In order to fulfil employment demand, the population for Greater KL will have to increase from 6 to 10 million. As Greater KL's population will increase by more than 65 per cent over the next ten years, it is important to provide adequate housing with quality and harmonious living environment for the growing population. There are various issues that contribute to a city's liveability. Global surveys have demonstrated that cities perform well on liveability measures by providing for basic needs such as housing and safety, while also catering to the cultural and other demands of an increasingly diverse and cosmopolitan society.

Public Transport Infrastructure

In the urban areas including Kuala Lumpur and Johor Bahru, public transport remains a serious problem due to poor infrastructural coordination. With a large portion of the rural people migrating to urban areas and with rapid urbanization taking place, there is a great need to set in place an integrated, comprehensive, affordable, and efficient public transport system to facilitate travel within urban areas. There are various modes of public transportation in the country, such as the light rail transit system, buses, and taxis. However, they do not complement each other as far as traffic line and network are concerned. Malaysia invested heavily in the public transport infrastructure with three major rail systems completed in the Klang Valley in the mid-1990s. However, despite these developments, the ridership percentage dropped from 34 per cent in 1985 to 20 per cent in 1997, based on the study by the Japan International Co-operation Agency. In 2008, it fell down to between 10 per cent and 12 per cent, because the public transport system could not cope with the increase in the Klang Valley's population (Performance Management and Delivery Unit 2011). The main problems of the public transport system are high congestion during peak periods, unreliable service with cancellations and frequent delays, and poor access to public transport network. Furthermore, poor planning and enforcement are another contributing factor to the shortcoming of the public transport system in urban areas.

There was an intention to improve the city's transportation and traffic woes but the improvements were ad-hoc. The main problem with the public transport system is that Malaysia lacks a long term plan to project public transport needs far into the future so that the infrastructure can expand when needed. Because of the shortcoming of the public transport system in urban areas, residents are more likely to depend on private vehicles. For many years, the number of newly registered private vehicles has been increasing significantly in Malaysia, and this would in turn cause traffic congestion (see Table 18.2).

Traffic congestion in Malaysia stems from the high usage of private vehicles. The dependency on private vehicles has created road network bottlenecks in urban areas. Most urban dwellers prefer to use private vehicles because of the unreliable service with frequent delays, poor planning, and poor enforcement in the public transport network.

TABLE 18.2
New Passenger and Commercial Vehicles Registered in Malaysia, 1980–2010

Year	Passenger Cars	Commercial Vehicles	4 × 4 Vehicles	Total Vehicles
1980	80,420	16,842	–	97,262
1985	63,857	26,742	4,400	94,999
1990	106,454	51,420	7,987	165,861
1995	224,991	47,235	13,566	258,792
2000	282,103	33,732	27,338	343,173
2005	416,692	97,820	37,804	552,316
2006	366,738	90,471	33,559	490,768
2007	442,885	44,291	–	487,176
2008	497,459	50,656	–	584,115
2009	486,342	50,563	–	536,905
2010	543,592	61,562	–	605,156

Source: Malaysian Assurance Alliance (2011).

TABLE 18.3
General Road Accident Data in Malaysia, 2000–10

Years	Road Accidents	Road Deaths
2000	250,429	6,035
2001	265,175	5,849
2002	279,711	5,891
2003	298,653	6,286
2004	326,815	6,228
2005	328,264	6,200
2006	341,252	6,287
2007	363,319	6,282
2008	373,071	6,527
2009	397,330	6,745
2010	414,421	6,872

Source: Malaysian Institute of Road Safety Research (2011).

Because of the high volume of vehicles on the road, road safety is one of the major issues in urban transportation in Malaysia. As shown in Table 18.3, the rates of road accident and death have remained high since 2000.

Greater KL must first have a world class public transportation system in order to become one of the best liveable cities in the world. There is much to be done to meet the public transportation needs of urban dwellers. Recently, the government has taken a major step to make Greater KL a more liveable place by undertaking the MRT (My Rapid Transit) project. The multi-billion ringgit MRT (My Rapid Transit) system is an effort to ensure that the city is able to meet the increasing demands by its economic activities and growing population. The MRT system for Greater KL spans 141 kilometres with three major lines serving residents from a radius of 20 kilometres of the city centre (Performance Management and Delivery Unit 2010). At this point in time, the government can only afford to construct the first of the MRT's three lines. The first line, 51.3 km, is from Sungai Buloh to Kajang.

The project has understandably faced opposition from land owners who would be affected by tunnelling works for the underground section of the MRT Sungai Buloh-Kajang line. It is because only 70 per cent of the 51.3 km of the first line alignment runs on government land, while the rest is on private land. Unlike the experiences in Hong Kong and Singapore, the Malaysian government does not have specific laws that facilitate the development of the MRT project. Because of delays stemming from the land issue, the initial completion date has been postponed from 2016 to a year later.

Social Crimes

In a liveable city, personal security and safety issue should be made a top priority. However, the crime rate has become one of the main challenges to the Malaysian government. Malaysia has experienced a steady increase in the street crime index. As revealed in the 2010 Annual Report of Government Transformation Programme, there has been an increase in the street crime. Theft cases as measured by the Royal Malaysia Police have increased from 31,408 cases in 2006 to 42,014 cases in 2009. Furthermore, the overall crime index increased from 746 reported crimes per 100,000 population in 2006 to 767 in 2007 and 2008, respectively (see Table 18.4).

With crime dominating the headlines and becoming an alarming issue of every Malaysian cares for, public confidence has eroded with the people feeling unsafe in their neighbourhoods as snatch thefts, assaults, and rampant break-ins in urban areas make people a little

TABLE 18.4
Crime Rate in Malaysia

Years	Property Theft	Violent Crimes	Crime Index Per 100,000 Population
2006	31,408	165,372	746
2007	35,159	174,423	767
2008	37,817	173,828	767
2009	42,014	167,803	746

Source: Performance Management and Delivery Unit (2011).

more concerned about their personal security. All Malaysians concern whether they should be able to enjoy the right to live in a safe and secure environment, while enjoying a good quality of life without worrying about their safety.

Affordable Housing Provision

Subscribing to Maslow's theory of hierarchy of needs, shelter being a priority; the demand and supply for housing in the city becomes a primary challenge to the Malaysian government. Achieving equilibrium in this sector is highly unlikely given that land is a fixed asset and a depleting resource. This gives rise to inadequate supply of housing, especially for the low and medium income groups. Since urban land is scarce and expensive, this particular group will resort to setting up illegal settlements and as people continue to migrate to the cities without adequate shelter, they become squatters. Malaysia has suffered an acute housing shortage due to the ever-increasing need created by an urban migration and a growing population. The rapid rate of rural dwellers migration to urban centres has caused the growing demand for housing, particularly affordable low-income houses in many cities. The increase in urban growth was higher than the supply of affordable housing, which has resulted in a severe shortage in affordable housing as house builders are unable to produce housing at prices that are low enough for the most of urban migrants. The urban poor have responded to the shortage by the formation of extensive slum and squatter settlements. The existence of squatter settlements in many urban areas is evidence of the failure of the government's housing policy.

Under the Five-Year Malaysia Plans, the government is committed to the provision of housing but the planned targets have not been met, particularly in providing adequate housing to the lower income groups. As reported in Table 18.5, it is noticeable that the public sector has been giving low priority to the public low-cost housing programme in the country. Total housing needs for low-cost units during the 1986–2005 were estimated at 550,700 units, but only 57 per cent of this target was completed by the public sector.

A roof over one's head is one of a few necessities in life. Having a house has always been part of the Malaysian dream (Tan 2008). Although home owning is major goal for every Malaysian, this desirable goal is still difficult to obtain for some families. In recent times, however, it

TABLE 18.5
Housing Achievements (Low-Cost Housing) by Public Sector

Units	5th Malaysia Plan	6th Malaysia Plan	7th Malaysia Plan	8th Malaysia Plan
Targeted Units	120,900	126,800	95,000	208,000
Completed Units	74,332	46,497	78,228	113,235

Note: * Targeted units were not reported after Eighth Malaysia Plan.
Source: Malaysia (1986); Malaysia (1991); Malaysia (1996); Malaysia (2001); Malaysia (2006).

has been a stretch for the average Malaysian to afford a home. Prices of property in the hot areas of the Klang Valley rose by about 35 per cent in 2010 (Ministry of Finance's Valuation and Property Service Department 2011) and home price inflation appears to be spreading elsewhere in the country now. This is especially tough for younger households, whose wage increases have in no way kept pace with house price inflation over the past ten years. As a result, the housing domain of quality of life in urban areas is deteriorating.

Nowadays, providing decent and affordable housing in Greater KL to many urban migrants, who come from less developed parts of the country in search of jobs, appears to be a difficult task. House prices, particularly in urban areas, are generally not cheap because of the increased compliance and regulatory costs involved in the whole value chain of housing production. Additionally, the increase in labour costs, materials, land costs and upfront deposit, and capital contribution by house builders add on to production costs, which will be inevitably reflected in the house prices. As such, it is really a challenge for house builders to construct affordable houses of less than RM100,000 in urban centres of Malaysia. In Malaysia, the public sector holds an important social responsibility for fulfilling the needs of housing for those in the lower income group and government employees through the federal government, state government, and local council. The provision of houses for other Malaysians has been left to the private sector, but with prices of home skyrocketing and the price of land, the private sector has in recent years only concentrated on high-end homes. Even though there is a requirement for private housing developers to include affordable housing components in their projects, this is hardly adhered to these days. Also, the absence of large-scale townships makes it uneconomical to comply with this ruling because most of today's development projects are on much smaller plots of land.

The Malaysian government has launched many kinds of public low cost housing schemes for the past twenty years, but most of them have failed to provide an improved quality of life for their inhabitants (Tan 2012). In fact, many of the housing areas developed based on these schemes have turned into slums that are dishevelled and do not provide wholesome environment for families to live. Because of low price, many of these units are small at 650 square feet. The lack of space and privacy has resulted in children spending their time at corridors, on the landings of fire escape or at the car park bays provided. The price cap of public low cost housing units (less than RM42,000; US\$1 = RM3) has been a point of contention among house builders, as the current ceiling price of affordable housing is not able to cover the increased building costs over the years (Tan 2011*b*).

Coping with Urban Challenges

In order to cope with some of these urban challenges, the Malaysian government has implemented various measures. These measures do take into consideration the country's economy, development, and productivity. The government has to be pragmatic in its implementation in addressing vital issues of environment, politics, governance, as well as the ethnic composition of the population. Henceforth, urban management in the twenty-first century for Malaysia will increasingly take on an integrated approach, and will be much aligned to the Government Transformation Programme (GTP) that was launched in 2010. Some of the features of the GTP are indicative of the measures that the government will take to deal with the challenges of greater urbanization in Malaysia. Obviously the "People First, Performance Now" concept provides an overarching aim to which the whole nation is moving towards and provides the basis for future plans with regards to the development of the nation.

Cities are the powerhouses of economic growth and their sustainability lies within this overarching national objective, meaning, planning to meet the challenges in the urban areas needs to take into account the entirety of the growth and development of the nation. An overview of the features of the government and economic transformation programmes exemplify this concept. Some of the outstanding issues of the transformation programme that are relevant to deal with greater urbanization are reducing crime, improving urban transport, and improving housing affordability. Other significant area of contention where support for them will reduce the impact of urban challenge is good governance (accountability, transparency, equity, etc.).

Housing

In an effort to improve liveability by supplying quality affordable housing for Malaysians, the Prime Minister has recently announced My First Home Scheme in March 2011 and the scheme is targeted at young urban households earning RM3,000 or less to acquire homes costing from RM100,000 to RM220,000. This scheme also allows 100 per cent financing for first-time homebuyers aged between 25 and 34 years. To benefit more urban households, the government subsequently launched the 1 Malaysia People's Housing Scheme (PR1MA). This scheme, which is an addition to the My First Home Scheme, will see house units priced between RM220,000 and RM300,000 for first-time buyers with a household income of less than RM6,000 a month. A special corporation has been set up to facilitate the planning, development, registration, and delivery of the PR1MA houses to all eligible applicants. Under this programme, eligible buyers can apply for a unit of house between 800 to 1,400 square feet with three bedrooms and two bathrooms. The qualified buyers are eligible for a loan of up to 105 per cent from financial institutions with a 30-year payment scheme. The extra 5 per cent from the loan is meant to assist the buyers to cover the cost of insurance and legal aspects of the purchase. Both schemes are under the "Public Private Partnership" system.

With prices of house at an all time high in urban areas, it is certainly time to introduce a more progressive approach and embrace a social housing model that extends a helping hand to all needy Malaysians irrespective of race and religion. In order to ensure the success of the schemes, the schemes must be properly and sustainably implemented. There is a need for the government to build houses in the target area that come together with infrastructure and employment opportunities. Affordable housing should be built and equipped with proper amenities, as homebuyers find it more cost-effective to move into a well-connected neighbourhood (Tan 2011a). Following the experience of Housing Development Board (HDB) in Singapore, housing infrastructure and areas should be developed with the concept of communal activities. The rationale behind this would be to build a close and sustainable community where house buyers can find places within the area to work, shop, and go to school. As indicated earlier, many public housing developments have turned into slums that do not provide decent environment for families to thrive in. It is sensible that more decent housing facilities that provide an improved quality of life are provided to inhabitants, so that they will not end up without proper housing and add to the many social woes already plaguing Greater KL. It is important that this form of affordable housing under the scheme does not one day become the disenchantment of Greater KL. There are lessons to be learnt from affordable housing schemes in the past, as most of these housing areas have turned into slums. There should be well thought out and clearly defined master planning, as well-planned infrastructure will add value to the living environment and quality of life (Tan 2011c).

Government organizations and developers should explore ways to help ease the urban households' burden due to the rising construction cost and land prices in Greater KL. In order to provide greater opportunity for households to acquire homes costing from RM100,000 to RM300,000, there is a need for the federal government and the state government to work together with housing developers to build homes for them. The responsibility to build the houses should not only belong to the governments; it should be a joint initiative between governments and developers. Land matters in Malaysia falls under the jurisdiction of state governments; it is advisable the governments provide and allocate enough parcels of good government land for the projects while the developers provide their expertise. Furthermore, both federal and state governments should plan the logistics, locations, pricing, and implementation to ensure that there is action behind the words.

In order to prevent subsidized housing ending up in the hands of speculators who want to make profits from the property, the government should enact strict laws and regulations to ensure that this type of housing only benefits households who need genuine help for basic housing need. Households who are not eligible for My First Home and PR1MA housing schemes should not be allowed to access this type of housing. In addition, home buyers under the schemes are not allowed to sell their homes on the market for profit within the first few years. An exit system is required for households who return their subsidized housing to the government if they want to dispose off their first homes in the hope that other homebuyers in need can benefit from this scheme. These homes can only be repurchased by the government at a relatively low price.

Urban Transport

Traffic management has been a challenging problem. It cannot be addressed only by constructing more roads, bridges and underpasses. The MRT is not the only solution that will prevent Greater KL from choking up by 2020. What is very important is a reliable public transport network that enables all urban dwellers in Greater KL to move around from one end to another comfortably on public transport, whether by bus or MRT. Therefore, the government should take an integrated approach to traffic management and leverage advanced technologies and intelligent solutions. Through smarter solution, cities can infuse intelligence into their entire transportation system, therefore improving the road system for vehicles, increasing public transportation ridership and raising the quality of living.

It is an excellent initiative and it is hoped that the government will consider exploring the synergy of planning the housing and public transport projects together when it outlines the detailed MRT project, so that housing projects can be built around MRT stations. In the case of Hong Kong and Singapore, they have planned their housing projects and public transportation in such a way that despite the increase in population, mobility between city suburbs and centre remains unaffected.

Reducing Crime

The crime issue has dominated the Malaysian public's mind, especially the urban dwellers today, and the government has to respond. Being free from crime is necessary to improve the quality of life for city dwellers. It will be important to incorporate more street-safe and people-friendly measures. Therefore, the government, through its Ministry of Home Affairs has made reducing crime a National Key Result Area to arrest crime rates. As a result, several supportive initiatives have been introduced. These include implementing safe city programme, increasing patrols by police officers, as well as increasing availability and usage of mobile access devices to become the "eye and ears" of the Royal Malaysian Police (Performance Management and Delivery Unit 2011). Again, it is not enough that the government works at bringing about the change; it must be seen to be doing so.

Environment

The overall environment and quality of life of the people is not just about building skyscrapers and new structures which make up the hardware, but more importantly, it is about the intangible side of development. It is about the right time to undertake the green cause by having environmentally friendly and sustainable concepts and designs in the development plans to reduce the carbon footprint of the country. Nowadays, many neighbourhoods are actively making changes to become more sustainable, often aiming to promote development that is in line with the principles of economic, social, and environmental sustainability (Tan 2011c).

Achieving sustainability goes beyond merely greening the environment in the neighbourhood; it also incorporates efforts in designs and activities to reduce greenhouse gas emissions. It is important to retain a healthy balance between the built and un-built by retaining some parts of the natural environment as green lung and parks. Open space is important for residents to take a breather from the hustle and bustle of city life and to promote a happier and healthier city dweller. As pointed by Al-Hagla (2008), open spaces such as parks and garden play an important role in supporting sustainability objectives, as their primary function is for informal activities or relaxation and for social and community purposes.

There is also a crucial need to enhance the city's liveability in terms of culture and heritage. In this regard, it is imperative to ensure that historical buildings such as museums and art galleries should be properly maintained. It is because these buildings are part of integration in a cosmopolitan area. There must be an effort from the Malaysian government to ensure that the city's heritage can move with the times, since the socio-cultural environment is also among the fundamental criteria to nurture the city into a sustainable city.

Urban Governance

Due to the continuation of rapid growth, rising expectations of their populations and recent global political and economic events, the authorities responsible for urban planning are under increasing pressures to enhance present management of their towns and cities. Malaysians are demanding for better pubic services that commensurate with the nation's economic progress and perceived wealth. As a result, the federal, state, and local governments have within each of them the responsibility to formulate, facilitate, and provide the rules and regulations to ensure competency in good urban governance. The federal government has an important role to facilitate and update laws relevant to urban planning; for instance, the Town and Country Planning Act 1976 (Act 172) and amended version of 1995 (Act A933), Environmental Quality Act 1974, the Environmental Impact Assessment, Local Agenda 21 (LA 21) and the Housing Development (Control & Licensing) Act 1966 (Act 118) need to be carried out according to land use and environmental considerations. These Acts and regulations are to promote the development of urban centres with quality and equity between economic growth, social development, and environmental conservation.

It is essential that the federal government supports and enhances the capacity of local government and avoid the imposition of unnecessary financial and political burdens upon this level of government. Under the Local Government Act 1976 (Act 171), the local authority is the local planning authority when the State government adopts the Town and Country Planning Act 1976 (Act 172). In reality, very little planning and development control powers are vested in the local authorities. The federal government has no direct authority over the local authorities, with the exception of the Kuala Lumpur City Hall, Putrajaya, and Labuan. However, via the Ministry of Housing and Local Government, the local authorities are monitored and indirectly "directed". At the policy level, the National Council for Local Government (NCLG) plays a coordination role. Federal and state authorities are required to consult the NCLG to take its advice on proposed local government legislation in the Peninsular. It is important that for good urban governance, the responsibilities are clearly defined, understood and adhered to with support from the upper tier governments. Failure to do so may risks confusion of roles, conflict in policy objectives, and uncoordinated planning and execution of programmes.

Conclusions

Insofar as Malaysia is concerned, urbanization with its associated contemporary issues requires government intervention to seek new strategies to improve the quality of urban living and ensure that further urban growth will not plague the nation's efforts to achieve a standard of liveability commensurate with a developed country. Urban areas will be a permanent feature in this country, and will not go away, and within them lie the cities and towns which mirror the success and dynamism, or lack thereof, of a nation. The challenge in Malaysia is, therefore, the ability to balance some of these urban issues of economics, demography, infrastructure, and governance to ensure the nation's growth can be sustained. Indeed, human liveability in a city should become a necessity and not a choice.

The pressure of urbanization has made it increasingly necessary for urban planners to equip themselves, so that they can manage the city well and efficiently. Needless to say, politics in Malaysia is much entrenched in the system, but urban planners have to enhance their ability to cope with emerging issues of politics, finance, equity, corruption, and public awareness. Hence, capacity building is necessary for urban officials.

Another critical factor for the success in urban management hinges upon the commitment of the public to sustain government strategies and initiatives. Every individual should be encouraged to take responsibility for their urban environment and governance of their city. This encompasses the NGO, the private sector, and some international agencies. We should not lose the significance of the overarching ultimate objective and that is the desire for a better quality of life for all Malaysians.

There are social and living issues that need to be addressed as discussed earlier. The Government Transformation Programme (GTP) hopefully will bear the desired results to spearhead a more sustainable place, for not only the present population, but also to cater for the needs of generations to come. In our aspiration to become one of the liveable cities in the world, Greater KL must assume a major global and sub-global role for the benefit of all its communities.

NOTE

1. The authors would like to thank the Institute of Southeast Asian Studies and participants at the workshop for their support of this project and their comments on earlier drafts of this chapter.

REFERENCES

Al-Hagla, K. "Towards a Sustainable Neighbourhood: The Role of Open Spaces". *International Journal of Architectural Research*, vol. 2, no. 1 (2008): 162–77.

Annuar, A. "Bill to Set up PR1MA to be Tabled Soon". *The Sun Daily*, 5 July 2011. Available at <http://www.thesundaily.my/news/67914>.

Bank Negara Malaysia. "Monthly Statistical Bulletin January 2011". Kuala Lumpur: Government Printer, 2011.

Department of Statistics. "Malaysia Yearbook of Statistics 2000". Putrajaya: Government Printer, 2000.

———. "Population Distribution and Basic Demographic Characteristics". Putrajaya: Government Printer, 2011.

Economic Planning Unit. "Tenth Malaysia Plan, 2011–2015". Putrajaya: Percetaken Nasional Malaysia Berhad, 2010.

Malaysia. "Fifth Malaysia Plan, 1986–1990". Kuala Lumpur: Government Printer, 1986.

———. "Sixth Malaysia Plan, 1991–1995". Kuala Lumpur: Government Printer, 1991.

———. "Seventh Malaysia Plan, 1996–2000". Kuala Lumpur: Government Printer, 1996.

———. "Eight Malaysia Plan, 2001–2005". Kuala Lumpur: Government Printer, 2001.

———. "Ninth Malaysia Plan, 2001–2005". Kuala Lumpur: Government Printer, 2006.

Malaysian Assurance Alliance. "Summary of New Passenger and Commercial Vehicles Registered in Malaysia for the year 1980 to 2000", 2011. Available at <http://www.maa.or.my/info_summary.html>.

Malaysian Institute of Road Safety Research. "General Road Accident Data in Malaysia (1995–2010)", 2011. Available at <http://www.miros.gov.my/web/guest/road>.

Ministry of Finance's Valuation and Property Service Department. *Property Market Status Report Q4*. Putrajaya: Government Printer, 2010.

———. *Property Market Status Report Q1*. Putrajaya: Government Printer, 2011.

Performance Management and Delivery Unit. "Chapter 5: Greater Kuala Lumpur/Klang Valley". Putrajaya: Government Printer, 2010.

———. *Economic Transformation Programme Annual Report 2010*. Putrajaya: Government Printer, 2011.

Robbins, S.P. and M. Coulter. "Management". New Jersey: Pearson Prentice Hall, 2009.

Tan, T.H. "Determinants of Homeownership in Malaysia". *Habitat International*, vol. 30, no. 3 (2008): 385–414.

———. "Neighbourhood Preferences of House Buyers: The Case of Klang Valley, Malaysia". *International Journal of Housing Market and Analysis*, vol. 4, no. 1 (2011*a*): 58–59.

———. "Sustainability and Housing Provision in Malaysia". *Journal of Strategy Innovation and Sustainability*, vol. 7, no. 1 (2011*b*): 62–71.

———. "Measuring the Willingness to Pay for Houses in a Sustainable Neighbourhood". *The International Journal of Environmental, Cultural, Economic and Social Sustainability*, vol. 7 (2011*c*): 1–16.

———. "Housing Satisfaction in Medium- and High-Cost Housing: The Case of Greater Kuala Lumpur, Malaysia". *Habitat International*, vol. 36, no. 1 (2012): 108–16.

The Star. "Making Homes Affordable, Scheme to Assist First-Time Buyers to be Launched in July", 7 May 2011.

Thean, L.C. "How Liveable is KL?". *The Star*, 2 April 2011. Available at <http://biz.thestar.com.my/news/story.asp?file=/2011/4/2/business/8394133>.

INDEX

www.ingramcontent.com/pod-product-compliance
Lightning Source LLC
Chambersburg PA
CBHW072040020426
42334CB00017B/1335